BEHAVIOR MODIFICATION:
Contributions to Education

Edited by

SIDNEY W. BIJOU
The University of Arizona

ROBERTO RUIZ
Universidad Central de Venezuela

 LAWRENCE ERLBAUM ASSOCIATES, PUBLISHERS
1981   Hillsdale, New Jersey

Lawrence Erlbaum Associates, Inc., Publishers
365 Broadway
Hillsdale, New Jersey 07642

Library of Congress Cataloging in Publication Data

International Symposium on Behavior Modification,
    8th, Caracas, 1978.
    Contribution of behavior modification to education.

    Bibliography: p.
    Includes index.
1. Behavior modification—Congresses.   2. Handicapped
children—Education—Congresses.   3. Illiteracy—
Congresses.   I. Bijou, Sidney William, 1908–
II. Ruiz, Roberto.   III. Title. [DNLM: 1. Behavior
therapy—Congresses.   2. Education—Congresses.
W3 IN916AN 8th 1978c / WM 425 I61 1978c]
LB1061.I57 1978   370.15   80-27878
ISBN 0-89859-051-5

Printed in the United States of America

Contents

Preface

The papers in this volume are based on presentations at the Eighth Annual International Symposium on Behavior Modification held in Caracas, Venezuela, February 22–25, 1978. We say "based on presentations" because they are not verbatim accounts of the papers delivered but are extensive revisions prepared specifically for this publication.

The Symposium, sponsored by the Central University of Venezuela, focused on contributions of applied behavior analysis to many facets of education. Participants were invited selectively by the organizing committee so that the program would cover the range of levels of education from preschool to college and a variety of topics associated with educational problems.

Contributions related to programming early childhood education are offered by Etzel, LeBlanc, Schilmoeler, and Stella, and to the development of self-control in young children by Baer, Fowler, Rowbury, Stokes, and Holman. Behavioral techniques for teaching knowledge and skills to young handicapped children are evaluated by Bijou.

Going beyond early childhood, Sulzer-Azaroff discusses problems and trends in applying behavior principles to elementary classes, and Lovitt summarizes his research on curriculum development for mildly handicapped children with academic problems. Becker and Carnine review the extensive data on the national Follow Through research project involving socio-economic disadvantaged elementary-age children, emphasizing contributions of the Direct Instructional Model developed at the University of Oregon. Braukmann and his colleagues at the University of Kansas present recent research on young delinquents in an Achievement Place group home setting. The application of behavior principles to exceptional individuals is presented by Casalta, who describes his research on teaching reading to illiterate Venezuelan adults.

The papers by Keller, Sherman, and Sussman deal with problems, trends, and recent research in applying the personalized instruction method (PSI) in colleges and universities in the United States. Ribes describes the recently instituted behaviorally oriented psychology curriculum in effect at the professional school of the Autonomous National University of Mexico (Iztacala).

The final paper, by Ruiz and Chirinos, summarizes a panel discussion dealing with the problems and limitations of the application of behavior modification to education in Venezuela.

Unfortunately, a volume such as this is not a sufficiently adequate vehicle in which to describe the enthusiastic discussions that ensued during the Symposium and the many ways in which the presentations stimulated and promoted numerous, lively exchanges of reactions.

Sidney W. Bijou
Roberto Ruiz

APPLICATION OF BEHAVIOR ANALYSIS TO PRESCHOOL AND ELEMENTARY EDUCATION

1 Stimulus Control Procedures in the Education of Young Children

Barbara C. Etzel
Judith M. LeBlanc
Kathryn J. Schilmoeller
M. Elizabeth Stella
The University of Kansas

INTRODUCTION

For over three-quarters of a century, psychologists have been writing (e.g., James, 1890; Wundt, 1894); and, for over half a century, psychologists have been carrying out scientific experiments in an attempt to find answers to two questions: (1) *How* do children learn? and (2) *What* do they learn? Infrahuman animals as well as young children (both normal and retarded) have contributed to the pool of empirical data that has been gathered on topics such as discrimination learning, attention, and cognitive development.

As we reach the 1980s, much remains to be discovered about *how* and *what* children learn. Determining what a child has already learned is fairly easy if a person takes the time to find out. But, almost without exception, it is very difficult to tell an educator how to teach a child with procedures that guarantee learning will occur. This area of child psychology can be likened to the field of meteorology in that you can determine whether or not it *is* raining, but the prediction and control of that rain may be something scientists will not accomplish before the twenty-first century.

In spite of thousands of published studies and many theoretical positions, the field of human learning is almost an unexplored galaxy. This state of affairs is all the more troubling due to the large individual differences in the human species. Millions of children, for one reason or many, continue to demonstrate that our educational procedures do not communicate to them the knowledge that society has deemed important.

3

Two fields of descriptive psychology (individual differences and mental test-ing) have more than adequately demonstrated the tremendous variability between people on almost any dimension one can currently quantify. We say "more than adequately" because one would like to see as much time invested in how to reduce this variability through an enlightened technology of human learning rather than in the continued documentation of its variability. In addition, predic-tion and control of human learning cannot be accomplished entirely through the descriptive studies typical of the individual differences and mental testing fields because such research determines human diversity after the fact; that is, the behavior measured is some already learned response resulting from the or-ganism's own endowment and past learning history.

Learning can be viewed, on the other hand, as a transition in which the child moves from one "steady state" to another leading to a behavioral change. Sidman (1960) indicated that the most adequate scientific analysis of such a transition state can only be accomplished by studying the variables and processes that control behavior *during* these transitions. Thus learning must be studied while it is occurring—not after it has occurred.

Some scientists have studied children's learning *during* the acquisition pro-cess and thus have been able to relate the current variables in the learning situation to the organism's past history. However, traditional learning theorists have plotted data by averaging the individual curves of many subjects who served in problem-solving situations. The result is a typical learning curve in which the percentage of correct responses are plotted across trials, blocks of trials, or series of problems (Harlow, 1949). Such learning curves often obscure the individual differences of the children that the descriptive investigators have so vividly portrayed. It is here that the problem of developing a technology of human learning is overlooked for those children who did not learn the task at all or who learn very slowly. The averaging of individual learning curves of groups of children results in a visual configuration that is readily interpreted by most as though learning is a gradual process. Such curves no doubt had some influence on both Hull (1930) and Spence (1936) in their theoretical position of discrimina-tion learning regarding habit summation of the associative strengths of individual stimulus components involved in the discrimination.

The interpretation that learning is a gradual process has been challenged on several fronts. Touchette (1971) questioned that conclusion in his studies on the transfer of stimulus control. Glaser (1967), Hayes (1953), Sidman (1960), and Zeaman and House (1963) all argued that the averaging of a group of individual subjects' learning curves obscured individual performances. These observations contributed to the use of individual subject curves and the creation of two publi-cations (*Journal of the Experimental Analysis of Behavior* and *Journal of Applied Behavior Analysis*) that to this day analyze their results primarily through individual subject data. In addition, Zeaman and House (1963), Hayes (1953), and Kendler and Kendler (1959) proposed different methods for separating subjects into groups according to the amount of time it took a subject to reach a particular criterion of learning. For example, Hayes suggested plotting backward learning curves and dividing subjects into groups of fast and slow learners. His procedure for obtaining backward learning curves was applied to the data from a study by Covill and Etzel (1976) in which twenty 4- and 5-year-old children learned from both trial-and-error and errorless stimulus control procedures. Figure 1.1 shows that acquisition was rapid and occurred across two training sessions for 10 of these children. The other half of the children showed virtually chance performance for many sessions. In fact, some of the slow-solution children had to be given a series of cues after Session 10 to aid them in consistently responding to the correct stimulus. Although this study shows that these quick and slow children learned in very different ways with trial-and-error procedures, they were almost identical in their responses when the stimuli were manipulated using errorless stimulus control procedures so that errors were precluded. The apparent difference between the quick- and slow-solution subjects was in the use of efficient or inefficient (respectively) problem-solving patterns. An objective method of measuring these patterns from an analysis of stimuli chosen by the subject indicated that the slow-solution group did not systematically sample all

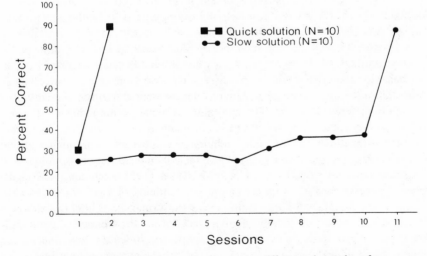

FIG. 1.1.   Backward learning curves demonstrate differences in number of sessions taken by slow- (circles) and quick- (squares) solution subjects to learn a match-to-sample task.

the possible solutions as did the quick group. Rather, the slow group selected one or maybe two possible solutions and continued to use only those solutions even though reinforcement (for correct responding) did not occur.

Ample evidence indicates that adding more trials (Hively, 1962) or repeating trials (Sidman & Stoddard, 1966) does not improve acquisition for some children. In fact, some evidence shows that these practices may result in poorer performance. On the other hand, a growing body of literature clearly suggests that careful arrangement of stimuli in the child's learning environment results in control of the stimulus–response relationships and learning occurs almost immediately.

In the 1960s in basic laboratory research on lower organisms, Terrace (1963) demonstrated that learning without differential reinforcement (no errors) produced more rapid acquisition and less "emotional" behavior. Subsequently other researchers, who were also convinced that discrimination learning did not have to entail errors, produced a dramatic series of studies with humans. They demonstrated that science was moving closer to the control and ultimate prediction of learning in normal and retarded children (Bijou, 1968; Moore & Goldiamond, 1964; Sidman & Stoddard, 1966). These scientists were the early advocates of the application of what has become generally known today in operant psychology as stimulus control procedures and, in particular, errorless stimulus control procedures.

Since that time, Bijou has been one of the most prolific writers on the topic. For example, his theoretical treatment of cognitive behavior, knowledge, and problem solving (Bijou, 1976, pp. 57–77) and his envisioning of the possible applications derived from his theoretical framework (Bijou, 1977) will, no doubt, change the direction of research on learning by many traditional educators and psychologists in years to come.

We have observed that the most critical difference in research strategy between traditional psychologists who study cognition and those who study cognitive behavior (theorist versus empiricist) is the degree of activity involved in manipulation of the independent variable. For example, traditional cognitivists may study different levels of IQ's and their relation to some behavior. Empiricists however would study how to train cognitive skills to a particular criterion and then to examine the functional relationship between the training and that behavior. Perhaps the difference is best seen in the two questions: (1) Will generalization occur (asked by a cognitivist)? and (2) How does one make generalization occur (asked by the empiricist)? Obviously the former is a fairly passive question and the latter, quite active (Stokes & Baer, 1977). Although both researchers may be equally involved in what is called *basic research,* it is the latter scientist, we suspect, that will move sooner toward a contribution to a technology of education.

Our concern here is for the education of young children—especially their cognitive skills that are generally spoken of as knowledge, thinking, or problem solving. We therefore restrict our remarks to those areas of the "active" type of empirical research that contribute most readily to a technology of cognitive education for young children.

In addition, we want to note that two points of orientation have dictated the content and comments of this review. The first is that the responsibility for a child's learning rests with the "arranger" of the conceptual environment; that is, the adult who wishes to "communicate" in some manner to a child must discover the most successful way in which to do this (Sidman & Stoddard, 1966). If a child does not emit behavior desired by the adult, then the problem lies with the manner in which the environment has been arranged—not with the child. This philosophy has at least one major advantage; it reduces blaming the child when procedures are not successful and increases searching by the adult for other ways to teach a child.

A second point of reference adopted for this review is that procedures or methods of teaching children are emphasized rather than theoretical explanations of causes of learning problems. This is not to say that speculation about the etiological factors involved in children's learning problems has no place. The important point is that, unlike the medical model (Ullmann & Krasner, 1965), knowing the cause of a learning problem does not help parents or teachers create an environment for successfully educating the child (LeBlanc, Etzel, & Domash, 1978).

Over the past 10 years, at the University of Kansas, Child Development Laboratory, we have concentrated much of our research on procedures that facilitate the development of cognitive skills and knowledge for the young child. This decade of research has resulted in the conclusion that three main areas of concern regarding the arrangment of the conceptual environment of a young child should be considered. These areas include (1) the child's preattending skills; (2) the degree of instructional control; and (3) the control the stimuli exert (attention) over appropriate conceptual behaviors. Consideration of these areas is essential for anyone arranging the cognitive environment of a young child.

PREATTENDING SKILLS

The first question that parents and teachers should ask about the conceptual training of a young child involves *preattending;* that is, do children demonstrate behavior that suggests that they can learn the task with minimal "prodding" to look at materials, listen to instructions, and sit quietly for a few minutes while the task is being taught? This does not necessarily involve a child's motivation to learn nor does it relate to task difficulty (i.e., can the child learn it?). Simply, the question is one of assessing whether or not the child engages in a variety of behaviors including posture, observing, or orienting responses that have a high probability of bringing the child closer to or in contact with the stimuli that will subsequently control responding.

Such behaviors have been discussed at the infrahuman level with such terms as *receptor-orienting acts* or *preparatory acts* (Spence, 1937, 1940). These are described as a series of behaviors that lead to the reception of appropriate stimuli on the animal's sensorium, such as the fixation of the head and eyes toward the critical stimuli. The animal has learned to look at one aspect of the stimulus environment rather than another because that preparatory response was followed by a final response in the chain that ends in reinforcement (Trabasso & Bower, 1968, p. 6).

In the educational environment, children lacking these preattending behaviors are often described as "flighty," "unsettled," "hyperactive," "distractable," "impulsive," "preoccupied," and "interested in their own whims" rather than what the parent or teacher wishes to teach. We have labeled these behaviors *preattending responses* because we arbitrarily reserved the term *attention* for the specific stimulus–response relationship that the parent or teacher is ultimately trying to teach. There is an old adage, "You can lead a horse to water but you can't make him drink." Preattending is similar to being led to water and attending would be consuming the water. Thus some children display behaviors that preclude our leading them to the educational water.

Our concern with preattending led us to carry out a study that (1) assessed the incidence of these behaviors in young children; and (2) developed training procedures to teach these behaviors to children found to be lacking them (Winslow & Etzel, 1972). This study found that most preschool children between the ages of 3 and 5 years were able, for example, to sit quietly, listen to a story, make comments about the story when asked, and look at pictures and point appropriately to objects.

Figure 1.2 shows the results of the preattending screening of 80 children between the ages of three and five. Of a fairly heterogeneous preschool population, 86% had a mean number of 4.4 inappropriate preattending responses during the session. In addition, 14% had a mean of 28.5 inappropriate preattending responses. The results of the screening session and the teachers' descriptions of children who needed training for preattending behaviors correlated perfectly. These children (the 14% of the larger population) became the experimental subjects for a training program.

In this study we wanted to know whether we had to manipulate the child's behavior or the child's environment to produce appropriate preattending responses in each child's repertoire. We had hoped there was something in the environment that we could alter, because that would be easier than the more time-consuming task of shaping each child's preattending responses. Thus we asked a series of questions about environmental manipulations by placing each child in a learning situation and observing each child's preattending responses as we altered the environment in some manner. Several months later we arrived at the following conclusions:

Means and Ranges of Total Inappropriate Preattending
Behaviors in First Screening Session

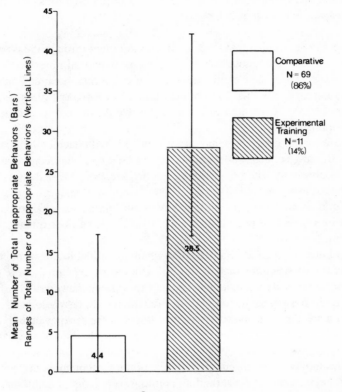

FIG. 1.2. Mean number of inappropriate preattending behaviors found in a heterogenous preschool population. Of the total population, 86% showed few inappropriate responses (open bar) and 14% showed many more inappropriate responses (striped bar).

1. Placing the children with inappropriate preattending responses in a very easy learning task—one that they can learn quite readily (or in some instances already know)—does not reduce inappropriate preattending responses or increase appropriate preattending responses.

2. Placing the children in a more difficult learning task tends to increase inappropriate preattending, but returning them to an easier task does not necessarily reduce inappropriate responses. Changing *some* aspect of the environment seemed to be more related to poor preattending than task difficulty per se.

3. Increasing the amount of consequences (reinforcers) that followed correct responses does not reduce inappropriate preattending behaviors or increase correct responses.

4. Using training programs that are errorless with most other children tends to result in more correct answers with these children, but they tend to have more errors than other children on the same programs. Such programs do not alter their inappropriate preattending behaviors.

We therefore decided that altering the environment through the type of materials presented or the amount of reinforcement given had no effect on any one child with respect to their continued use of inappropriate preattending responses in a learning task. We then went to our second strategy, that of shaping, one or more appropriate preattending responses that would replace a specific inappropriate response.

There were six different behaviors we trained, with each child receiving one or more training sequences depending on the type and number of inappropriate behaviors observed. The behaviors we trained were:

1. Children who chatted continuously about topics unrelated to the learning task during instruction were trained not to verbalize unless explicitly requested by the teacher.

2. Children who either did not point when instructed to do so, or, pointed at times other than when instructed, or to other areas of the stimuli were trained to point *only on command of the teacher* and to a particular area.

3. Children who responded with several fingers, their whole hand, elbow or banged repeatedly with their fists were trained to point by extending the index finger with the rest of the fingers and thumb curled back and the palm facing down.

4. Children who engaged in multiple points (often to many parts of the instructional materials) or just random pointing were taught to emit one point per request.

5. Children who looked at other stimuli in their environment (such as the teacher, the ceiling, their feet, or their hands) during the time the instructional material was being presented were taught to orient the head and upper body toward the stimulus materials when instruction was in progress.

6. Children who manipulated the materials with their hands while instructions were being given or who covered the materials with the hands or arms or who moved out of their chairs onto the floor, etc., were trained to keep their hands in their lap at all times during instruction except when explicitly requested to point.

Children were taught preattending skills during a simple learning task with the teacher first modeling the response and then physical and verbal prompts were faded as the child went through the learning sessions. In addition, an escalating reinforcement contingency was used (which has been referred to subsequently as a changing-criterion procedure, Hall & Fox, 1977). This required that the children engage in a larger number of appropriate preattending responses each session in order to earn their reinforcer for that day.

One other procedure was necessary to maintain appropriate preattending when the contingencies were shifted from these preattending skills to correct academic responses. A gradual shift in the ratio of reinforcers earned from appropriate preattending responses to correct task solution responses ultimately resulted in both types of behaviors being maintained. In addition the placement in the session of the contingency for appropriate preattending responses was moved slowly from the beginning of the training session to the end of the session before being completely eliminated.

Evidently no shortcut is available (unless one uses the questionable intervention of drug therapy such as ritalin) for changing a highly distractable child to a picture of quiet and serious concentration. Only direct behavioral intervention is effective. In addition, our research suggests that until such preattending responses are acquired, it is a waste of time to try to teach the cognitive skills necessary for the academic education of the child. Unfortunately, children are seldom taught these preattending responses by teachers or parents, both of whom tend to think that the child will outgrow the problem. However many adults exist in our society who are academic failures for this reason.

Psychologists are also not without blame. For years they have eliminated distractable subjects from their research populations with the footnote that X number of subjects were eliminated due to uncooperative behavior. Thus, our first area of concern, when arranging the conceptual environment of the young child, should be with appropriate preattending.

INSTRUCTIONAL CONTROL

A second area we researched in our laboratory is instructional control. This primarily involves the teachers' (or parents') behavior. Although educators for years have thought that the adult's behavior during the teaching process was very important, little has been documented as to what that person should be doing to be called a "good teacher." Although the most researched and most obvious good-teacher behavior is that of contingent feedback for correct responses, we decided to examine the quality and quantity of teacher's instructions because these behaviors are those required to start the operation of the learning process.

Miller and LeBlanc (1973, 1974) investigated the rate of acquisition of sight words and letter names under two different types of teacher instruction. In one procedure, the teacher gave several examples of how a word might be used when teaching the word. For example, a set of detailed instructions could be:

This is the word "dig."
You dig with a shovel.
You can dig in the ground, and you can dig in the sand.
It's fun to dig.
Point to dig and say, "dig."

In the other procedure, the teacher gives the minimal instructions:

> This is the word "dig."
> Point to dig and say, "dig."

Figure 1.3 shows the results from this investigation. Clearly the shorter set of instructions (the dotted bars) without the examples resulted in faster acquisition. The poorer performance of the children under the detailed instruction procedure was possibly due to the examples not being related to the final discrimination [being able to point to dig (S+)—not dog (S−)—when asked to find the word *dig*]; that is, digging with a shovel or digging a hole will not help the child associate the *i* with the word *dig*. Perhaps an instruction that pointed out the *i* in the word *dig* would be more relevant to the ultimate discrimination between dig and dog. This study is now in progress in our laboratories.

Massad and Etzel (1972) found that increasing the number of times the teacher had a child respond to a stimulus was important. In Fig. 1.4 the top graph shows that the mean number of errors in conditions of frequent child responses was clearly less than in the infrequent response procedure. The bottom graph shows that when teacher instructions and child responses were held constant (a control), increasing reinforcement in a learning session resulted in no differences between conditions. Child responding is clearly an important variable.

The pacing of instructions has also been found to be an important variable (Miller, Holmberg, & LeBlanc, 1971). For a child who finds teacher attention in

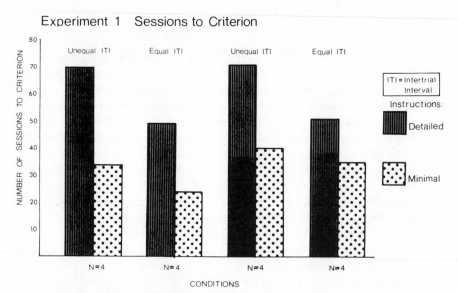

FIG. 1.3. Differences in sessions taken to learn sight words when instructions were detailed (solid bars) or minimal (dotted bars).

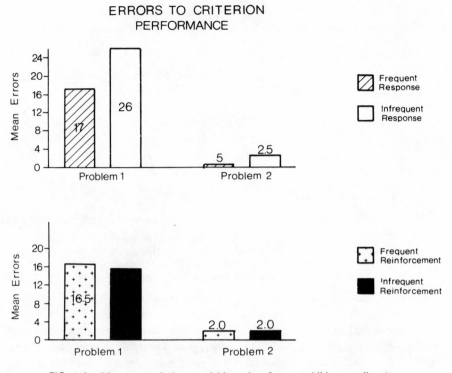

FIG. 1.4.   Mean errors during acquisition when frequent child responding (top graph, striped bar) was compared to infrequent responding (top graph, open bar). When frequent responding was required (bottom graph), frequent or infrequent teacher reinforcement did not differentially affect responding.

the form of instructions very reinforcing, then continuous instructions may not be too effective for altering a child's behavior because the child can often trap the teacher into longer and longer explanations (Fig. 1.5). To overcome this possibility the teacher gave a discrete set of instructions and moved away from the child's presence. Once the child carries out the instructions, in this case interacting with other children, the teacher's attention was then contingent upon the child playing with other children.

A similar type of trap has been observed in children who appear to have high error rates associated with their learning tasks. A study by Cunningham, Cooper, Plummer, and LeBlanc (1975) demonstrated that children often make errors during a problem-solving task if errors are followed by teacher instructions designed to correct the error (Fig. 1.6). Apparently the lowest number of incorrect responses (left graph) by a child occurred when no correction procedures were implemented during the first and last conditions (right graph). When correction of errors was eliminated, problem solving improved.

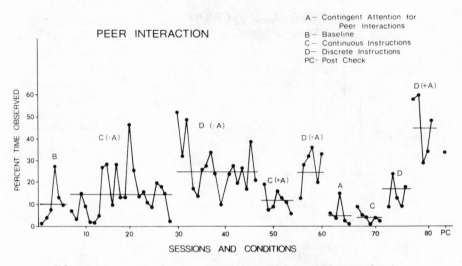

FIG. 1.5.   Percentage of time spent interacting with other children as a function of pace of instructions. Lengthy, continuous instructions (C) were compared to discrete instructions (D).

For some children, teacher instructions do not always operate as secondary reinforcers as the previous studies would suggest. Therefore, the analysis of the function of instructions for each individual child is important rather than simply studying teacher instructions in their own right. A study that emphasizes this point was carried out by Plummer, Baer, and LeBlanc (1977). Highly disruptive children in special learning environments are often controlled by such contingent

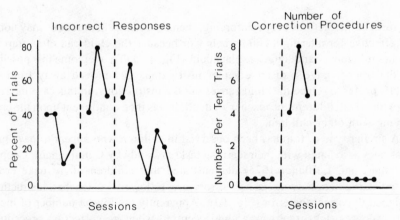

FIG. 1.6.   Effect of teacher instructions on child errors when teacher instructions were designed to correct errors. When number of teacher corrections (right graph) increased, number of incorrect responses by the child increased (right graph).

procedures as time-out or removal of materials. But, to the disappointment of some teachers, such procedures do not always result in more compliant behavior. Figure 1.7 shows the percentage of disruptive episodes a child emitted when a teacher gave instructions in an academic situation. A procedure called *paced instructions* was implemented and involved keeping the child in the learning situation with the teacher giving task-related instructions at a frequency of ap-

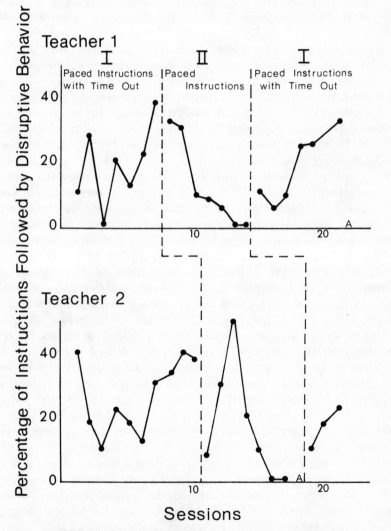

FIG. 1.7. Differential effect of paced instructions with and without time-out upon disruptive responses to teacher instructions. Paced instructions without time-out was effective in reducing disruptive behavior (Condition II).

proximately one instruction per 60 seconds until the child complied. Prior to the use of paced instructions, this child had not shown any decrease in disruptive behavior, even during time-out conditions. When both time-out and paced instructions were used (Condition I), the child continued to be disruptive. However, paced instructions without time-out reduced disruptives to zero (Condition II). The researchers suggest that some children might engage in disruptive behavior to obtain time-out from a learning situation. Consequently, when the contingencies are changed, the child must correctly respond in the learning situation in order ultimately to leave it. Thus, the disruptive behavior will decrease.

After Touchette (1971) reported a laboratory procedure called *delayed instruction,* several researchers utilized the essentially errorless technique to examine some applied aspects of children's learning. The technique is a powerful procedure that involves presenting training stimuli to which a criterion response has not been consistently acquired. At first, feedback that provides the correct answer occurs immediately after the stimulus presentation and before the child responds. Over time the teacher instructions are systematically delayed. Children who have not yet learned the correct response to the training stimuli simply wait until the teacher instructions are given—and then they respond correctly by imitation. However, across trials the delay between the presentation of stimulus materials and the instructions becomes a little longer. Ultimately children begin to respond to the training stimuli prior to the added instructions provided by the teacher. At this point the children are said to have learned the discrimination.

Two studies in our laboratory provide an applied version of this delayed instruction procedure to examine teacher instructions and child learning rates in an individual versus a group setting. The first measured receptive and productive responses during the training of a second language to preschool children (Radgowski, Allen, Schilmoeller, Ruggles, & LeBlanc, 1978). Figure 1.8 shows the average number of trials to a standard criterion of learning when subjects were trained in individual sessions and when they were trained in group sessions.

During *receptive* training, the preschool teacher spoke a foreign phrase and then engaged in a series of motor movements that portrayed the meaning of the verbal phrase. These teacher-produced motor movements were delayed longer and longer across trials. Children were said to have receptively learned the meaning of the verbal phrase when they engaged in the *correct* motor movement following the foreign phrase *before* the teacher made the motor movements. *Productive* training involved the teacher making a motor movement that was followed by the teacher giving the appropriate verbal foreign phrase. Children met criterion when they could verbalize the foreign phrase describing the teacher's motor movements before the teacher said the foreign phrase. This productive training of a French phrase to an English-speaking child is described in the following example. The teacher rolled a small ball across the table and then said in French "Roll the ball." If the child did not say "Roll the ball" in French

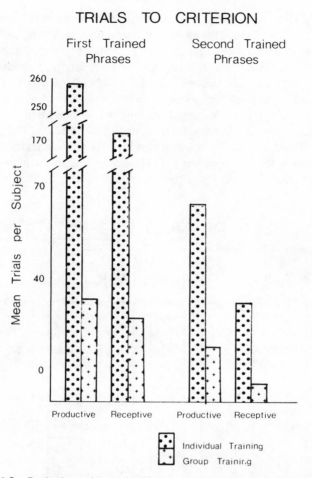

FIG. 1.8. Productive and receptive language is acquired more quickly when delayed cue instruction occurs in group (cross bars) rather than individual (dot bars) settings.

before the teacher, the child then verbally imitated the teacher. All children ultimately gave the correct verbal phrase to the teacher rolling the ball *before* the teacher said the phrase. Figure 1.8 shows children taught in a group setting, where they had both the opportunity to respond themselves and to observe other children responding (when it was not their turn), took fewer trials per child to reach the criterion for learning. Similar results were obtained by Sabbert, Holt, Nelson, Domash, and Etzel (1976) when they trained children to solve simple arithmetic problems with a variation of the delayed instruction procedure. Fifteen children were divided into five groups. The groups contained one, two, three, four, and five members each. The question examined was whether children could learn equally well in groups of varying sizes (from individual instruction to a group of five children) when the amount of instruction, materials, and number of trials presented remained constant across all groups. Figure 1.9 shows that the number of instructional card presentations for *each* group of children was 14. This meant that teacher instructions, materials, and child responses to the materials were exactly the same regardless of the size of the group. As the number of child members of the group increased, the number of opportunities for any *one* child to respond to a card decreased. For example, while S1 had 14 opportunities to respond, S9 had only 3. S9, however, could observe the other members of the group respond. In spite of the fewer individual opportunities each member of the larger groups had for responding, the percentage correct on the final criterion

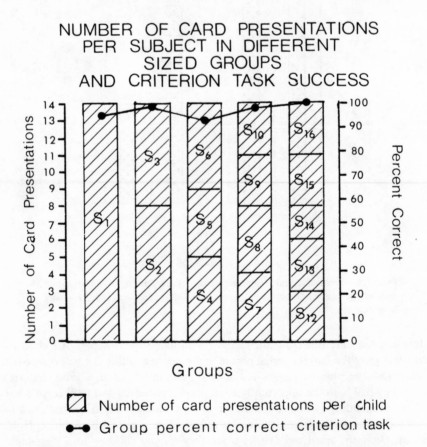

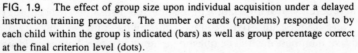

FIG. 1.9.   The effect of group size upon individual acquisition under a delayed instruction training procedure. The number of cards (problems) responded to by each child within the group is indicated (bars) as well as group percentage correct at the final criterion level (dots).

task was comparable for all groups (ranging from 94 to 100% correct). Because the delayed instruction procedure resulted in almost errorless responding during training, each child observed only correct answers being given by the other members when it was not their turn.

The results of these two studies suggest that, in a delayed instruction procedure, group training may be as efficient or even more efficient than individual training. This may be because fewer errors occur during training and the children also have opportunities to observe other children responding in the group. Although the group training did not increase the number of training trials, it should be noted that when the teacher was instructing the group, the children were all observing the child whose turn it was to respond. Those children who were not responding were also reinforced on occasion for watching the child who was responding. This emphasizes the importance of each child having the necessary preattending responses so that distractions do not occur.

STIMULUS CONTROL

The last area with which one must be concerned when arranging the conceptual environment of the young child is stimulus control (attention) of conceptual behaviors. Our experience in the laboratory has shown that many children are capable of learning quickly and with little or no *planned* intervention. These children appear to come into contact with stimuli, to respond to a trial-and-error format by very quickly acquiring the criterion response, and usually to generalize appropriately. Other children, often as many as 25% of the normal population, do not learn under trial-and-error conditions. A large group of preschool children ($N = 144$) were tested for an oddity abstraction (Etzel & Mintz, 1970). Of these children, 26% did not know what "point to a different one" meant (Fig. 1.10). We then proceeded to train these children by giving them feedback on a series of tests to see if they would learn the concept. The tests were all at criterion level, and the training was essentially trial and error. The graph in Fig. 1.10 shows the learning curve over the four tests. Of the group that did not demonstrate knowledge of the oddity concept, some profited from the trial-and-error training (learners). By the fourth learning task, all of these children were responding at 100% correct. Children who did not improve by the second trial-and-error experience were divided into two groups. The control group continued the trial-and-error experience, and the experimental group was given an errorless program training the oddity abstraction. The experimental group learned the abstraction and maintained criterion performance. The other half, for whom we did not intervene with a program, continued to make errors on trial-and-error training. Our experience with this errorless program on the oddity abstraction led us to an investigation of the various errorless stimulus control procedures that were available in the literature and an examination of their success.

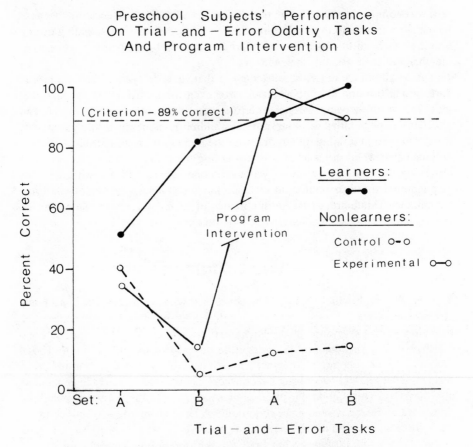

Preschool   Subjects'   Performance
On Trial - and - Error Oddity Tasks
And Program Intervention

FIG. 1.10.   Correct responding during testing on two similar oddity tasks. Learners (closed circles) reached criterion after trial-and-error training. Nonlearners
receiving programmed training (open dots, solid line) also learned, whereas nonlearners not receiving program training (open circles, dashed line) did not.

Following Terrace's (1963) work in which both fading and superimposition
were used to teach pigeons a red–green and a vertical–horizontal discrimination,
there was a series of studies that indicated promise in the application of these
procedures to humans. Landmark studies by Sidman and Stoddard (1966) and by
Bijou (1968) were published. These studies expanded the number of possible
errorless procedures that could be used with humans—especially with retarded
people.

Sidman and Stoddard (1966) described two procedures, which, in our laboratory, we differentiate with the labels *stimulus fading* and *stimulus shaping*. The
stimulus-fading procedure, successfully used in the Sidman and Stoddard study
to teach a circle-ellipse discrimination, started with an illuminated circle (S+)

and seven dark keys (S−). The middle key remained dark throughout the program, as seen in Fig. 1.11A. Slowly, across several trials, the yellow background color was increased (faded) in these other seven windows (B and C). At stage C the child would have to discriminate the S+ (illuminated key with a circle in it) from the S− (illuminated blank keys) on the basis of the circle—not just the background as in the A and B examples. To accomplish the final discrimination of choosing the circle (S+) over many ellipses (S−), Sidman and Stoddard slowly faded in the form of the ellipse on the already illuminated windows (D and E). The program resulted in errorless performance for most of their subjects at criterion level (F).

A second errorless procedure reported by Sidman and Stoddard is best described as a stimulus-shaping rather than as a stimulus-fading procedure. In fact Sidman and Stoddard used the term *stimulus shaping* and noted that it was analogous to response shaping; that is, the overall topography or configuration of the stimulus is changed. For example, in their successful reversal program, they were able to reverse this discrimination from the circle being the S+ to the ellipse

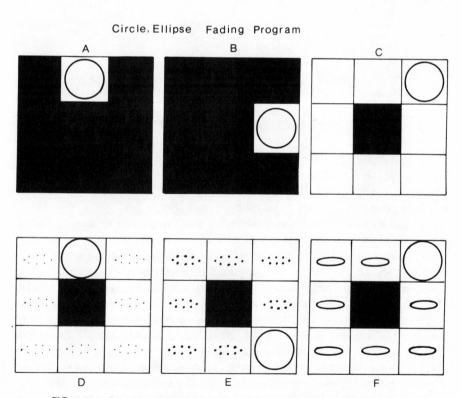

Circle, Ellipse Fading Program

FIG. 1.11.   Representative steps in the errorless training of a circle–ellipse discrimination using stimulus-fading procedures (Sidman & Stoddard, 1966).

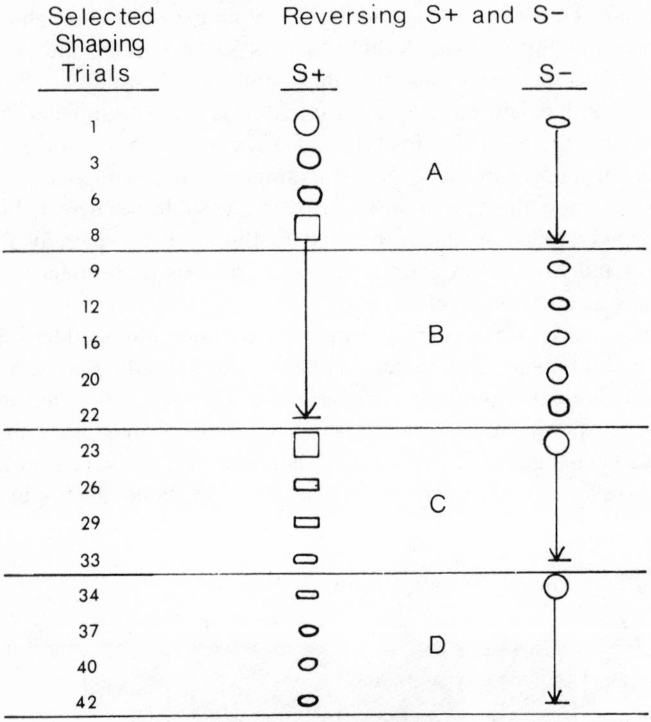

FIG. 1.12.   Selected trials illustrating a stimulus-shaping procedure used to reverse a circle–ellipse discrimination (Sidman & Stoddard, 1966).

as the S+ (Fig. 1.12). They did this by slowly shaping the circle to a square (the left column, stage A). Then the ellipse was shaped to a circle (right column, stage B). The last shaping was carried out on the square that changed slowly to a flat rectangle (stage C) and then to an ellipse (stage D).

Bijou (1968) also used a stimulus-shaping procedure when he taught retarded children a left–right discrimination. Figure 1.13 shows an example of how one of the S− stimuli was slowly shaped from a "square C" (lower left illustration) to the mirror image (S−) of the sample stimulus (lower right illustration).

Bijou's procedure and Sidman and Stoddard's reversal program were similar in that the actual *configuration* of the stimulus was changed. We have found that it is helpful to make a distinction between *fading* and *shaping* because it calls attention to two very different procedures. A simple comparison of stimulus shaping and stimulus fading is seen in Fig. 1.14. As you see, fading does not alter the overall configuration or topography. In fading, an exaggeration of some physical dimension of a stimulus would be made so that correct responding immediately occurs. Then this dimension is slowly faded out. This involves a gradual shifting of stimulus control from this dominant stimulus dimension to a

Sample Stimulus   Correct Match (S+)

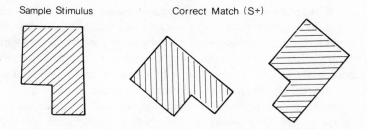

Selected Samples of S– Shaping to Mirror Image of "Flag"

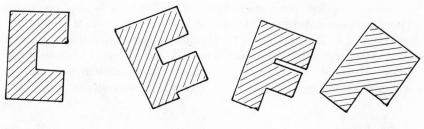

"Square C"

Intervening Steps

Mirror Image
of Flag

FIG. 1.13. Examples of steps in a stimulus-shaping program used to train a left–right discrimination (Bijou, 1968).

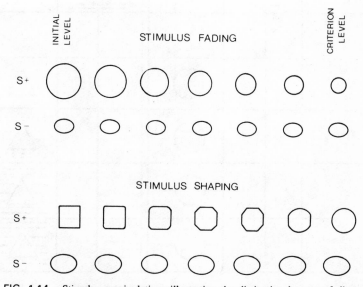

INITIAL LEVEL   STIMULUS FADING   CRITERION LEVEL

S+

S–

STIMULUS SHAPING

S+

S–

FIG. 1.14. Stimulus manipulations illustrating the distinction between fading and shaping as different procedures for gradual stimulus manipulation.

final criterion dimension. Thus, it would be appropriate to say that a large circle was *faded* to the criterion-sized circle because its circular topography was *not* altered in the process. Stimulus *shaping* on the other hand involves a change in the topography of the whole stimulus complex so that the stimulus first presented to the subject in the training program bears little resemblance to the final stimulus complex. Thus, the square could be changed to a circle in shaping.

Making a distinction between *stimulus shaping* and *stimulus fading* rather than using the generic term *fading* to cover both procedures that use graduated stimulus change has important consequences for researchers. It has been our observation that many of the studies subsequent to the Sidman and Stoddard (1966) and Bijou (1968) publications have used fading (not shaping) procedures and many have not had outstanding success in achieving errorless training.

For example, Gollin and Savoy (1968) taught children two different discriminations and then tested them on a conditional task that was made up of the stimuli from both of the previous two tasks. Two groups of children were used—a trial-and-error group and a fading group. Figure 1.15 illustrates the *fading* pro-

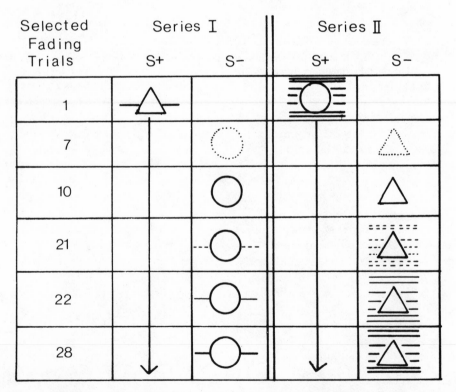

FIG. 1.15.   Selected fading trials used to train conditional discriminations (Gollin & Savoy, 1968).

cess in the two different discriminations across selected trials. For example in Series I the criterion discrimination on trial 28 was between a triangle and a circle, both of which had a single line in the background. The procedure involved presenting the child with the S+ stimulus first (the triangle with single line). The other window was black. During approximately the first half of the training trials the form of a circle (S−) was faded in. During the last half of the trials the single bar background of the circle was slowly added. Series II for the fading group was trained in a similar manner. Because the circle with the multiple bars was the S+ *this* time, the triangle was faded in first and then ultimately the multiple bars. The *trial-and-error* group simply learned Series I with repeated presentations of stimuli at the criterion level (noted as trial 28). They then learned Series II also with the stimuli at criterion level. Both groups were then tested on the conditional task that had the criterion stimuli from both Series I and II randomly intermixed. The fading group had quite a few errors during acquisition and it is questionable that it should be referred to as a near-errorless procedure. However, it was clear that the trial-and-error group did significantly better on the *conditional* test.

Several reasons may explain why the fading group did not perform better on the conditional test. But the most *important* reason is that the *intensity* of the stimuli was the main manipulation. Yet intensity is not the basis upon which the *final* discrimination is made. If a child were using intensity of the S− to discriminate it from the S+, there would be no need to observe circles, triangles, or their backgrounds. However, when intensity becomes equal for both stimuli on the final trial, the child would *not know* the solution because the basis of their strategy (intensity differences) would no longer be present. When an experimenter has used a cue that is *not related* to the final discrimination to achieve errorless responding during acquisition, we have found that most children will be *unsuccessful* when tested at the end of training to see if they have, in fact, learned the discrimination. Bijou[1] and Schilmoeller and Etzel (1977) have referred to this practice as the use of a *noncriterion-related* cue.

Considering Gollin and Savoy's problems with the fading procedure and believing those problems stemmed from the use of noncriterion-related cues (using an intensity cue to teach a discrimination not based on intensity), a study using the Gollin and Savoy stimuli was conducted in our laboratory (Schilmoeller, Schilmoeller, Etzel, & LeBlanc, in press) that used stimulus-shaping procedures. Figure 1.16 shows the shaping steps involved in Series I for both the S+ and S− stimuli. For example, for the first 15 trials, the tree on the hill (lower half) is held at the level as seen in the first picture of the S+ stimuli, while the S− (the apple with a worm through it), illustrated in the upper half, is slowly shaped to the criterion level of circle with single-stripe background. Then on trial 16 the S+ (tree and hill) is slowly shaped to the triangle with the single stripe.

---

[1]The authors are indebted to Sidney W. Bijou for his suggestions concerning the labels "criterion- and noncriterion-related" cues.

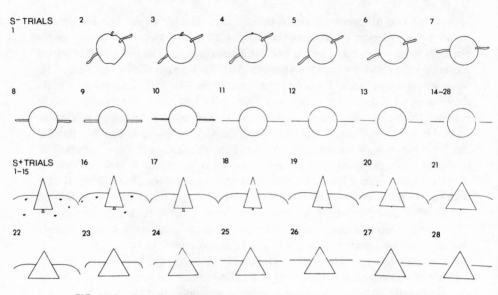

FIG. 1.16.   Stimulus shaping used in a revised training program of Series I of the Gollin and Savoy (1968) conditional discrimination. S− and then S+ were shaped from familiar to abstract stimuli.

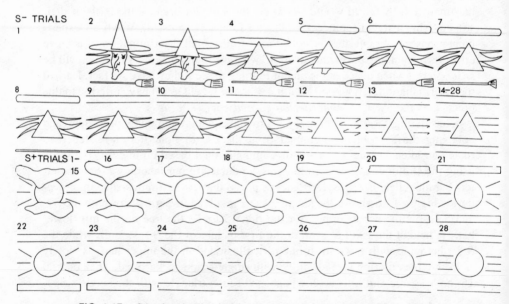

FIG. 1.17.   Stimulus shaping used in a revised training program of Series II of the Gollin and Savoy (1968) conditional discrimination. S− and then S+ were shaped from familiar to abstract stimuli.

Figure 1.17 shows the stimuli for Series II. The same procedure was followed in that the S− was shaped first (the old straggly haired witch and the broom) while the S+ (the sun and clouds) remained at the initial entry level. Then during the last half of the program the sun and clouds were shaped to the circle with the multiple-stripe background. When the conditional discrimination was presented, in which both sets of stimuli were intermingled at the criterion level, the child would be responding to the shaped stimuli that earlier were the tree on the hill and the clouds and sun. This program was arranged so that it *shaped* the criterion-related cues. Further, these cues, the form *and* the background, were integrated into one comprehensive stimulus so that background was not separated from the form. Thus *both* were part of the total stimulus complex and were more likely to be used continuously across all training trials by the children in making the discrimination. The results of this study showed the shaping group was clearly more successful on the conditional test than either the fading or trial-and-error subjects (Fig. 1.18).

A slightly different approach to fading was taken by Schwartz, Firestone, and Terry (1971) in a study designed to compare what they labeled extrinsic and intrinsic fading (Fig. 1.19). They also used a trial-and-error group for comparison purposes. The problem to be solved by the children was to choose the symmetrical shape consistently in a symmetrical–assymetrical pair of stimuli when many different forms were presented in symmetrical and asymmetrical pairs. In extrinsic fading the S+ (symmetrical shape) started as an outlined figure and then over trials both S+ and S− were of equal colored intensity. The intrinsic method of fading was designed to call attention to the dividing line between the two equal sides of the symmetrical form by coloring in one-half of

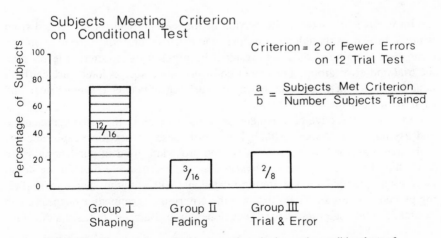

FIG. 1.18. The percentage of subjects meeting criterion on the conditional test of the Gollin and Savoy task following training using shaping, fading, or trial-and-error procedures.

S−   S+

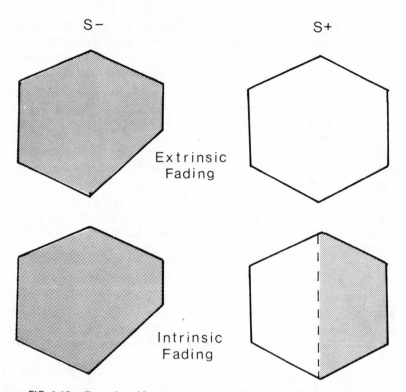

Extrinsic
Fading

Intrinsic
Fading

FIG. 1.19.   Examples of S+ (symmetrical) and S− (asymmetrical) stimuli at the beginning of training using extrinsic and intrinsic fading (stimuli designed by K. Schilmoeller based upon specifications by Schwartz, Firestone, & Terry, 1971).

the form. Over trials the white portion of the symmetrical form changed from white to brown. Although both intrinsic and extrinsic procedures resulted in few errors during training, they both resulted in more errors at criterion levels than the trial-and-error group. The use of color or even a split colored surface (both noncriterion related) did not teach the difference between symmetrical and asymmetrical shapes.

Several studies have been conducted in our laboratory that used symmetrical and asymmetrical shapes. Although none of these studies have replicated the Schwartz, Firestone, and Terry study, the procedure used in our laboratory to teach this discrimination was *stimulus shaping* because we thought we could more easily manipulate the criterion-related cue with stimulus shaping with fading procedures. Figure 1.20 illustrates the criterion discrimination shapes (noted as trial 25) that one program used (developed by F. Barrera[2]) to teach a discrimi-

---

[2]This program was developed by F. Barrera and K. J. Schilmoeller as part of a graduate class project in Human Development 930—Seminar in the Conceptual Development of Preschool Children: Errorless Stimulus Control Procedures—taught jointly by B. C. Etzel and M. E. Stella.

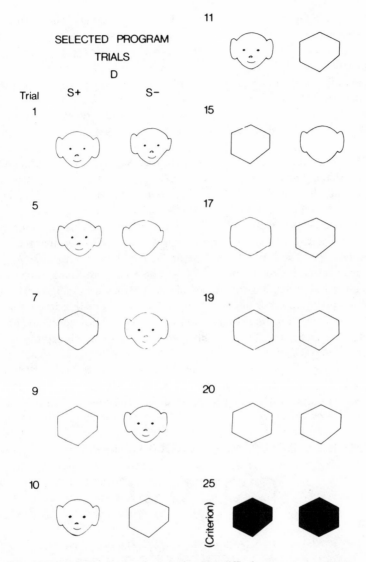

FIG. 1.20.   Use of stimulus shaping to train a difficult symmetry–asymmetry discrimination. The S− (figure with one small ear) was shaped to criterion level, followed by S+ (equal-sized ears) shaping.

nation between the symmetrical and asymmetrical forms. When analyzing these two stimuli we decided that the element most easily identified in the asymmetrical shape (the S−) that could be used to discriminate it from the S+ might be the *short* and *long* vertical sides as compared to the *equal vertical sides* of the symmetrical shape. Figure 1.20 shows the beginning forms that were used to reflect our analysis. A person with two large but equal-sized ears and one with a small ear and a large ear was used (trial 1). Figure 1.20 also shows further steps in the shaping procedure (trials 1–10) where the person with the one small ear is beginning to resemble the asymmetrical stimulus. Later the symmetrical face is also shaped (trials 11–20). Our experience with this program has been that we can teach the symmetrical–asymmetrical abstraction fairly errorlessly if the child can *enter* the program and respond differentially to the equal-eared, big–little-eared faces. If that discrimination is *not* in the child's repertoire, then another program is designed that teaches the children to respond to these small differences.

McCleave and Baer (in Baer, 1970) offered support for our contention that stimulus shaping may, in some situations, be more successful than stimulus fading if the element shaped is criterion related. When teaching a child to discriminate a backward C from the usual C, they initially used a size cue and then a thickness cue on the backward C. When these cues were faded to the criterion size or the criterion thickness, errors occurred. This indicated that the child had not learned the discrimination based on the direction of the opening of the backward C as compared to the usual C's. The procedure found to be successful was one involving shaping an initial oval into a backward C (Fig. 1.21). The left side was slowly closed to the size comparable to the opening in the regular C's (see selected program steps). Thus, stimulus shaping allowed the experimenters to manipulate *that part* of the stimulus where the ultimate discrimination would most likely be made.

Occasionally, shaping and fading are used within a program so that different stimuli can be associated with different procedures. A study by Schilmoeller and Etzel (1977) employed shaping to achieve the criterion-level discrimination of

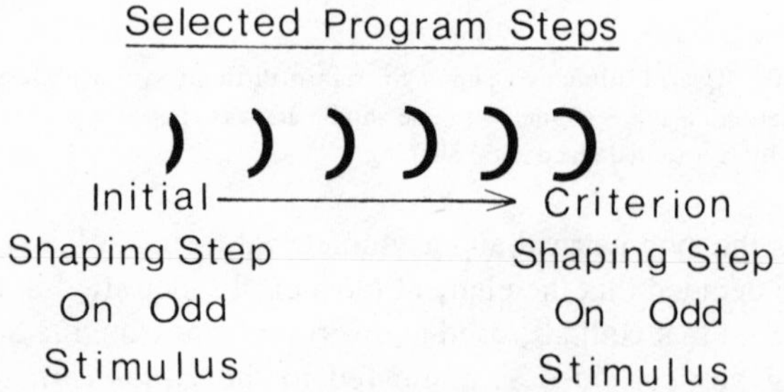

Criterion Level Oddity Task

C ƆC C C C

Selected Program Steps

))))) Ɔ

Initial ⟶ Criterion
Shaping Step   Shaping Step
On Odd   On   Odd
Stimulus   Stimulus

FIG. 1.21.   Stimulus shaping used to train an oddity discrimination (Baer, 1970).

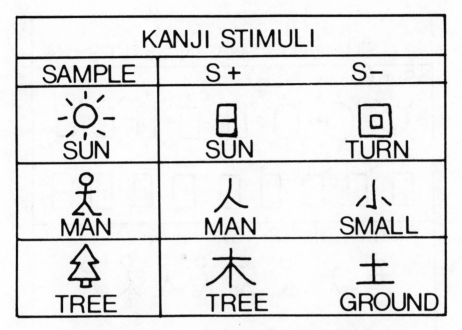

FIG. 1.22. Sample stimuli used in a match-to-sample task (left column) are shown with their correct criterion-level match (center column) and distractor stimulus (right column).

three Japanese characters that initially appeared in the form of a sun, a man, and a tree (Fig. 1.22). The S− stimuli were chosen because they looked very similar to the S+ stimuli, thus making the task fairly difficult. The stimulus-shaping steps for each of the three S+ stimuli are summarized in Fig. 1.23.

Stimulus shaping is probably dependent on how successful the experimenter is at manipulating *only that element* in the stimulus complex upon which the discrimination is based. For example if *HAT* were to be discriminated from *HOT* and *HUT,* it would be important to emphasize the *A* in a shaping program teaching HAT (developed by Parr, Stella, & Etzel, and reported in LeBlanc et al., 1978). Figure 1.24 shows selected shaping steps where the *A* in HAT was designed to have more control over the response HAT than the *H* or *T.* Likewise the *G* in LOG may more likely serve to control the response than the *L* or *O.* Evidence of what element controls a response could only be determined, however, by empirical study.

Stimulus shaping has on occasion been used with stimulus elements that were *added* to (superimposed on) a stimulus complex rather than shaped within the stimulus complex. Schreibman (1975) reported that the procedure that faded in the intensity of the S− stick figure arms resulted in a higher proportion of errors among deviant children when intensity could no longer be used as the basis of

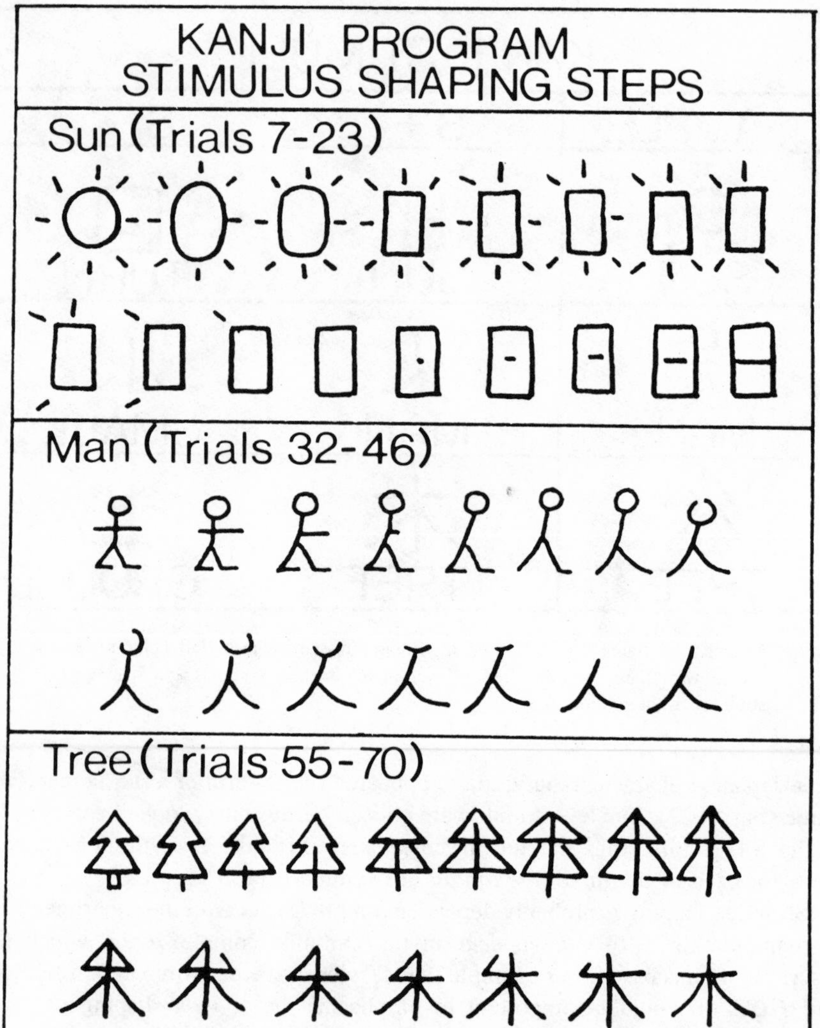

KANJI PROGRAM
STIMULUS SHAPING STEPS

Sun (Trials 7-23)

Man (Trials 32-46)

Tree (Trials 55-70)

FIG. 1.23.   Shaping steps used to transfer control of responding from the initial level (first stimulus of each series) to the final criterion level (last stimulus of each series).

discrimination. For Schreibman's stick figures the critical element for a criterion discrimination would be based on the direction (up versus down) of the right arms of the two stick figures (Fig. 1.25, note under stage 3). When programming this discrimination (using a superimposition and shaping procedure) for a retarded child we decided to use stimuli extended from the critical arm of the two stick figures that might be logically related to the position of the arm. As seen in Fig. 1.26 (selected trials) the dog was added to the S− stick figure with a leash

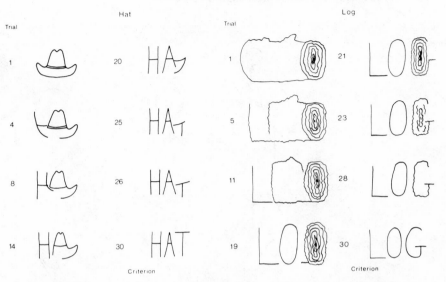

FIG. 1.24. Selected shaping steps used to train simple words. Control of responding is transferred from the picture to the word across trials.

Within–Stimulus Prompting Procedure

Stage One :   Fade in S–

S+   S–

Five Steps

Stage Two :   Fade Out Size

Five Steps

Stage Three :   Fade in Redundant Components

Five Steps

FIG. 1.25. Programming a discrimination by fading the critical element (within-stimulus prompt) used as the basis for discrimination at criterion level (Schreibman, 1975).

FIG. 1.26.   Selected trials of a program using superimposition and shaping procedures to program an up–down (arm) discrimination.

connecting the hand and the dog's collar. For the S+ stick figure a balloon was extended into the air connected to the hand by a string. As the program developed, the balloon left the hand and disappeared into the air (illustrations 2 and 3 in Fig. 1.26). Further in the program the dog dug a hole and disappeared from sight (illustrations 4 and 5). The final trials (illustration 6 in Fig. 1.25) had the arms on the stick figures shaped to an angle similar to the criterion level. This program was successful in teaching the up–down discrimination through the superimposition and shaping of the critically related cue.

Slow learners and mentally retarded children appear to be very slow to observe, or often do not observe, the relevant cue in a learning situation (Covill & Etzel, 1976; Zeaman & House, 1963). It stands to reason that *any procedure* that allows stimuli in the child's conceptual environment to control the child's responding more quickly and with fewer errors would be welcome into the technology of education. We suggest that *stimulus shaping* is a fruitful procedure that should be added to an ever increasing list of errorless stimulus control procedures such as fading, superimposition and fading, superimposition and shaping, and delayed instruction.

SUMMARY

For those children who appear to have problems or difficulty in their conceptual development, regardless of the cause, an intervention into one or more of the areas identified as preattending behaviors, instructional control, and stimulus control is suggested. These three developing technologies go beyond motivational procedures and have been shown also to require intervention when the manipulation of reinforcement procedures alone does not result in learning. Research in these three areas will help educators find new strategies for the difficult-to-teach child. Success in developing these technologies will advance education into the twenty-first century.

ACKNOWLEDGMENTS

This research was partially supported by grants to the Department of Human Development by the National Institute of Child Health and Human Development (#HD-02528) through the Bureau of Child Research at the University of Kansas and by Kansas Research Institute for the Early Childhood Education for the Handicapped (USOE #300-77-0308). Fellowship support of the fourth author was received from a training grant (#HD-00247) to the Department of Human Development at the University of Kansas and of the third author from a training grant (#HD-07066) to the Bureau of Child Research at the University of Kansas. Both grants were awarded by the National Institute of Child Health and Human Development.

REFERENCES

Baer, D. M. An age-irrelevant concept of development. *Merrill-Palmer Quarterly of Behavior & Development*, 1970, *16*, 238–245.
Bijou, S. W. Studies in the experimental development of left–right concepts in retarded children using fading techniques. In N. R. Ellis (Ed.), *International review of research in mental retardation*. New York: Academic Press, 1968.
Bijou, S. W. *Child development: The basic stage of early childhood*. Englewood Cliffs, N.J.: Prentice-Hall, Inc., 1976.

Bijou, S. W. Practical implications of an interactional model of child development. *Exceptional Children*, 1977, *44*, 6–14.

Covill, J. L., & Etzel, B. C. Effects of errorless learning on problem solving skills. In symposium, *Stimulus control: Contributions to the analyses of learning*, presented at the 84th Annual Convention of the American Psychological Association, Washington, D.C., September 1976.

Cunningham, P. J., Cooper, A. Y., Plummer, S., & LeBlanc, J. M. *Correction procedure effects upon an already acquired discrimination.* Presented at the 83rd Annual Convention of the American Psychological Association, Chicago, Ill., September 1975.

Etzel, B. C., & Mintz, M. S. *Stimulus control procedures to preclude or greatly decrease errors during the acquisition of the oddity abstraction with three- and four-year-old children.* Paper presented at the meeting of the American Psychological Association, Miami Beach, 1970.

Glaser, R. Some implications of previous work on learning and individual differences. In R. M. Gagne (Ed.), *Learning and individual differences.* Columbus, Ohio: Merrill Books, Inc., 1967.

Gollin, E. S., & Savoy, P. Fading procedures and conditional discrimination in children. *Journal of the Experimental Analysis of Behavior*, 1968, *11*, 443–451.

Hall, R. V., & Fox, R. G. Changing-criterion designs: An alternate applied behavior analysis procedure. In B. C. Etzel, J. M. LeBlanc, & D. M. Baer (Eds.), *New developments in behavioral research: Theory, method, and application.* Hillsdale, N.J.: Lawrence Erlbaum Associates, 1977.

Harlow, H. F. The formation of learning sets. *Psychological Review*, 1949, *56*, 51–65.

Hayes, K. J. The backward curve: A method for the study of learning. *Psychological Review*, 1953, *60*, 269–275.

Hively, W. Programming stimuli in matching to sample. *Journal of the Experimental Analysis of Behavior*, 1962, *5*, 279–298.

Hull, C. L. Simple trial-and-error learning: A study in psychological theory. *Psychological Review*, 1930, *37*, 241–256.

James, W. *The principles of psychology* (Vol. II). New York: Holt, 1890.

Kendler, T. S., & Kendler, H. H. Reversal and nonreversal shifts in kindergarten children. *Journal of Experimental Psychology*, 1959, *58*, 56–60.

LeBlanc, J. M., Etzel, B. C., & Domash, M. A. A functional curriculum for early intervention. In K. E. Allen, V. A. Holm, & R. L. Schiefelbusch (Eds.), *Early intervention—A team approach.* Baltimore: University Park Press, 1978.

Massad, V. I., & Etzel, B. C. Acquisition of phonetic sounds by preschool children: 1. Effects of response and reinforcement frequency; 2. Effects of tactile differences in discriminative stimuli. In G. Semb (Ed.), *Behavior Analysis and Education* (Vol. 3). The University of Kansas Support and Development Center for Follow Through, Department of Human Development, 1972.

Miller, R. M., Holmberg, M. C., & LeBlanc, J. M. *Experimental analysis of contingent teacher attention and continuous and discrete teacher primes.* Paper presented at the Biennial meeting of the Society for Research in Child Development, Minneapolis, Minn., April 1971.

Miller, R. M., & LeBlanc, J. M. *Experimental analysis of the effects of detailed and minimal instructions upon the acquisition of pre-academic skills.* Paper presented at the 81st Annual Convention of the American Psychological Association, Montreal, Canada, August 1973.

Miller, R. M., & LeBlanc, J. M. *Experimental analysis of detailed and minimal instructions and their effect on acquisition of a word recognition task.* Paper presented at the 82nd Annual Convention of the American Psychological Association, New Orleans, La., August 1974.

Moore, R., & Goldiamond, I. Errorless establishment of visual discrimination using fading procedures. *Journal of the Experimental Analysis of Behavior*, 1964, *7*, 269–272.

Plummer, S., Baer, D. M., & LeBlanc, J. M. Functional considerations in the use of time out and an effective alternative. *Journal of Applied Behavior Analysis*, 1977, *10*, 689–705.

Radgowski, T. A., Allen, K. E., Schilmoeller, G. L., Ruggles, T. R., & LeBlanc, J. M. *Delayed presentation of feedback in preschool group foreign language training.* Paper presented at the American Psychological Association Annual Convention, Toronto, 1978.

Sabbert, J. K., Holt, W. J., Nelson, A. L., Domash, M., & Etzel, B. C. A functional analyses of teaching different sizes of groups. In symposium, *Stimulus control: Contributions to the analyses of learning,* presented at the 84th Annual convention of the American Psychological Association, Washington, D. C., September 1976.

Schilmoeller, G. L., Schilmoeller, K. J., Etzel, B. C., & LeBlanc, J. M. Conditional discrimination after errorless and trial-and-error training. *Journal of the Experimental Analysis of Behavior,* in press.

Schilmoeller, K. J., & Etzel, B. C. An experimental analysis of criterion-related and noncriterion-related cues in "errorless" stimulus control procedures. In B. C. Etzel, J. M. LeBlanc, & D. M. Baer (Eds.), *New developments in behavior research: Theory, method, and application.* Hillsdale, N.J.: Lawrence Erlbaum Associates, 1977.

Schreibman, L. Effects of within-stimulus and extra-stimulus prompting on discrimination learning in autistic children. *Journal of Applied Behavior Analysis,* 1975, *8,* 91–112.

Schwartz, S. H., Firestone, I. J., & Terry, S. Fading techniques and concept learning in children. *Psychonomic Science,* 1971, *25,* 83–84.

Sidman, M. *Tactics of scientific research: Evaluating experimental data in psychology.* New York: Basic Books, Inc., 1960.

Sidman, M., & Stoddard, L. T. Programming perception and learning for retarded children. In N. R. Ellis (Ed.), *International review of research in mental retardation* (Vol. II). New York: Academic Press, 1966.

Spence, K. W. The nature of discrimination learning in animals. *Psychological Review,* 1936, *43,* 427–449.

Spence, K. W. The differential response in animals to stimuli within a single dimension. *Psychological Review,* 1937, *44,* 430–444.

Spence, K. W. Continuous versus non-continuous interpretations of discrimination learning. *Psychological Review,* 1940, *47,* 271–288.

Stokes, T. F., & Baer, D. M. An implicit technology of generalization. *Journal of Applied Behavior Analysis,* 1977, *10,* 349–367.

Terrace, H. S. Discrimination learning with and without "errors." *Journal of the Experimental Analysis of Behavior,* 1963, *6,* 1–27.

Touchette, P. E. Transfer of stimulus control: Measuring the moment of transfer. *Journal of the Experimental Analysis of Behavior,* 1971, *15,* 347–354.

Trabasso, T., & Bower, G. H. *Attention in learning: Theory and research.* New York: John Wiley & Sons, 1968.

Ullmann, L. D., & Krasner, L. (Eds.) *Case studies in behavior modification.* New York: Holt, Rinehart and Winston, Inc., 1965.

Winslow, M. K., & Etzel, B. C. *Assessment of preattending behavior: Procedural comparison and acquisition training.* Paper presented at the meeting of the American Psychological Association, Honolulu, 1972.

Wundt, W. *Logik: Eine Untersuchung der prinzipien der Erkenntnis* (Vol. II). Stuttgart: Ferdinand Enke, 1894.

Zeaman, D., & House, B. J. The role of attention in retardate discrimination learning. In N. R. Ellis (Ed.), *Handbook of mental deficiency: Psychological theory and research.* New York: McGraw Hill, 1963.

2 Uses of Self-Control Techniques in Programming Generalization

Donald M. Baer
The University of Kansas

Trevor F. Stokes
The University of W. Virginia

Jacqueline Holman
The Australian National University, Canberra

Susan A. Fowler
Trudilee G. Rowbury
The University of Kansas

INTRODUCTION

As the discipline of behavior analysis becomes more complete and more powerful, its occasional inadequacies become correspondingly more apparent. One of the most important of these is that behavior changes do not always generalize to the responses, settings, and times that they are meant to. "Meant to" is sometimes the operative term. It is not always possible to make all the behavior changes that are necessary to the solution of some problem—so a few behaviors are changed that exemplify the total class that requires change, in the hope that the remainder will emerge. In the same way, it is not always possible to change behavior in every setting in which it needs to be changed—so it is changed in a few settings that should exemplify all relevant settings, again in the hope that generalization will occur. And, finally, it is rarely possible to maintain a behavior change directly indefinitely into the future—and so it is made here and now, in the hope that its desirability will make it endure later.

Recently, it has been recognized that hoping is too often not enough. Consequently, the question is asked whether a certain amount of extra effort, invested wisely, might not accomplish the generalization that cannot always be hoped into existence. And, indeed, a survey of the literature of this field shows that the outline of a technology of generalization already exists in current practice (Stokes & Baer, 1977). That technology is largely implicit in current techniques, rarely recognized as a technology or as a target for technological research, and is

39

largely uncodified. Nevertheless, a beginning is emerging just now, from which may very well grow a formidable, diverse, and effective set of generalization–facilitation techniques. These techniques, if they are to accomplish the necessity that exists for them, must represent less effort than directly accomplishing every necessary behavior change, in every setting desired, thereafter maintaining them for the remainder of the client's life; that is, they must be possible to apply when and where therapists and teachers can work.

In the variety of techniques already suggested by the early improvisations and accidental discoveries of the field, one particular class has strong logical appeal but almost unknown empirical characteristics. That is the group of techniques often called *self-control*. Self-control is the most obvious, most attractive answer to the pragmatic question, What behavior-change agent can go with the subject to every necessary setting, at all times, to prompt and reinforce every desirable form of the desired behavior? No one but the *subject's* own self can possibly meet that specification—and the subject's own self *always* meets that specification. With that answer in hand, it is inevitable that we should then ask how to teach the subject to become not only a case of behavior change but also an agent of the generalization and maintenance of that behavior change.

Inevitably, the approach must be to give the subject a *response*, one that is not the behavior change itself but is a behavior that can extend and maintain the behavior change. *We* produce, extend, and maintain behavior change by prompting and reinforcing it; then perhaps we can accomplish its generalization by teaching our subjects to prompt and reinforce their own behavior changes, in all their necessary forms, settings, and times.

The logical appeal of this approach inheres almost entirely in the physical presence of our subjects at all the times and places that we need a generalization agent. The appeal diminishes sharply when we realize that merely having a potential generalization agent present at all the necessary times and places is still no guarantee that the agent will *behave* like a generalization agent at all those times and places. Giving a subject self-control responses designed to accomplish the generalization of some critical behavior change does not ensure that those self-control responses will indeed be used. They are, after all, just responses: They too need generalization and maintenance, just as does the behavior change that they are meant to generalize and maintain. Setting up one behavior to accomplish the generalization of another behavior may succeed—but it may also represent a problem in guaranteeing the generalization of two responses, where before we had only the problem of guaranteeing the generalization of one!

Still, it may be true that some responses do generalize and maintain better than others, and even if we do not know why this should be so, we still might take advantage of the fact that it is so (if it is) and use those responses experimentally to see if perhaps they will serve as needed. In effect, we must make some shrewd guesses about what those responses might be that have such excellent generalization characteristics, occurring in all settings and indefinitely into the future; then we must choose from that set a subset that could accomplish the prompting or generalization of the behavior changes that we wish to have generalized; and then we must make some experimental analyses of whether they work, when they work, how long they work, and how to make them work better, if they show some promise for our purposes.

What follows is a report of two experiments of just that sort. Each represents an attempt to teach subjects not only a behavior change but also another response that might contribute to the generalization of that behavior change. The first study teaches the children a self-monitoring response that could serve to prompt or reinforce their performance of an academic work habit in settings and times apart from when the children's teacher can maintain that work habit. The second study teaches the children not to prompt or reinforce their own academic practice behavior themselves but to recruit some other people who may be counted on to be present to do that for them. In each case, each child has been taught two classes of behavior: one that was the target of a behavior-change program (practicing recently taught academic skills) and one that may be used by the child to accomplish the generalization or maintenance of that behavior change.

STUDY I

A major goal for applied behavior analysts is to devise efficient procedures that promote maximal generalization at minimal cost: Self-mediated generalization procedures may fit these specifications and are begging for research (Kurtz & Neisworth, 1976). A promising direction may lie in teaching the self-management of academic productivity (the target response) rather than disruption (a supposed interfering response). The promise of these procedures is still implicit, but their potential simplicity favors experimental examinations.

The purposes of the current study thus were twofold: (1) to examine whether teaching a self-monitoring procedure in a laboratory setting would increase independent on-task behavior in a classroom setting; and (2) to analyze the durability of such training effects.

Method

Subjects and Setting

The subjects were six children, four boys and two girls, ranging in age (at the onset of the study) from 3 years, 10 months to 7 years. Three of the children were normal preschoolers whose transition to public school was not expected to be problematic. The other three had been referred as behavior problems and were co-enrolled in both remedial and regular settings. The remedial classroom provided training in relevant problem areas.

Throughout this study, training sessions were held 4 days per week in an experimental room close to the preschool classrooms; probes for generalization were held in the preschool classrooms themselves. Two children belonged to the same classroom and were probed concurrently; all other subjects were probed individually.

General Procedures

During the major part of this study, each child was asked daily to work with the experimenter in a small laboratory room. There, the experimenter introduced the child to the academic work to be done and to a self-monitoring device, a small bracelet with movable beads that the child would use to count work units completed. During certain experimental phases of the study, this bracelet was given to the child to use later in the day in the generalization setting (the classroom). Subjects were always thanked for coming to the small laboratory room to work with the experimenter, but no tangible rewards were dispensed. Later in the day, each subject was asked to complete similar work in the classroom by the regular classroom teacher, during the usual academic period, sometimes with and sometimes without the bracelet, according to the experimental design.

Observation Procedures and Behavior Definitions

During the experimental sessions, an observer in the classroom using a stopwatch and clipboard recorded child behaviors daily in continuous 10-second intervals for a period of 5 minutes.

Child Behaviors

Data were collected on three main child behaviors.

On-Task.   The child was to be seated in a chair with the four chair legs on the floor, have both feet on the floor (or ankles crossed with one foot on the floor), and be oriented toward the teacher if instructions were being given or toward the task if instructions had been completed. The child was to be engaging in task materials in compliance with teacher instructions. To be scored on-task, the child had to work for the entire 10 seconds. Examples included listening to teacher instructions, writing on assignment sheets, and self-recording (i.e., moving a bead on the bracelet to counting a page completed).

Off-Task.   The subject, having been instructed to be on-task, was not interacting with the task materials and/or was not physically oriented toward the task or the instructing teacher. Off-task responses were scored in precedence over on-task, in that any occurrence of them within the 10-second period was scored as off-task. Examples included reclining on desk, staring around the room, and playing inappropriately with the materials (e.g., repetitious flicking of the pages).

Disruptive.   This included any inappropriate physical or verbal disruption, as well as any peer-disturbing contact such as grabbing or pushing. It also included any nontask-related verbalizations, talking out, any vocal or manually produced sounds, or being out of seat without teacher permission. Disruptive responses were scored in precedence over *both* off-task and on-task. Examples included snatching another child's materials, placing feet on the desk, animal noises, whistling, rocking in chair, or gross motor scribbling.

The observer also noted the number of pages completed and (during treatment conditions) self-recording (i.e., each bead the child moved on the leather bracelet). Number and percentage correct of all attempted writing and math problems also were scored (at a later time) by the observer.

Teacher Attention.   In order to know whether teacher attention was held steady during all experimental phases of the study, all forms of instruction and praise were scored by the observer. These categories included prompts to self-control, be on-task, and praise, which could be either task- or nontask-related.

In the training setting (the laboratory), only the subject, the experimenter, and the observers were present; in the generalization setting (the classroom), the teacher was requested not to interact with a target child during the observation period unless safety was endangered or the disruptions were intolerable. Otherwise the data were taken under the usual operating conditions of the classroom during its academic work time. As many as eight peers could be working near the subject, and the teacher was free to attend to all other children.

Reliability Procedures

Occurrence and nonoccurrence reliability were assessed on each behavior for each child under all conditions of the study (i.e., approximately once every six sessions). Additionally, occurrence reliability was calculated for each teacher/experimenter behavior and for the subject's self-recording accuracy and permanent work products.

Design

A multiple-baseline design across subjects was used to demonstrate the effectiveness of the self-monitoring manipulation during the main part of the study (Experiment 1); a reversal design was implemented during the follow-up phases to examine whether or not the treatment effect maintained (Experiments 2 and 3).

Experiment 1

Baseline

During baseline (in both the training and generalization settings), each subject was presented with a workbook containing writing-practice items and math problems and was instructed, "Work as hard as you can, by yourself, while I do my work. I'll tell you when to stop.'' The teacher then engaged in some activity and did not attend to the subject until 5 minutes had passed. At the end of this observation period, some randomly chosen correct work items were selected, and the child was praised for accurate performance on them and for working alone.

Treatment

During treatment, each child was given the small leather bracelet containing wire strands with movable beads. The child was instructed to self-monitor academic productivity by moving a bead each time a page of work was completed. Two beads were of a different color than the rest, the first bead and the criterion bead. The ordinal position of the criterion bead was determined by the child's baseline production rate and was identified as the child's goal (e.g., by saying "Try to make it to the white bead"). (The position of the criterion bead was shifted as productivity increased.)

During self-monitoring conditions, in the laboratory only, the child was praised for each page finished (e.g., "Good for you, John! You worked the *whole* page and you remembered to push a bead."). In the generalization setting (the classroom), the only change from the baseline conditions was to allow the child to wear the bracelet during the work period. Usually no teacher attention was given to the target child until the observation period had elapsed. The child was then praised by the teacher (as in baseline) for working alone, for some randomly chosen correct items, and for reaching (or almost reaching) the criterion bead.

Experiments 2 and 3

Durability

Two months after the conclusion of training, maintenance data were collected approximately twice weekly for 3 months on three subjects who were still available (Experiment 2).

Following a two-month break (between semesters vacation), data were collected for another 3 months for two of those three subjects (Experiment 3). All follow-up information was collected under the same conditions that had characterized the prior generalization classroom data, except that now no daily training sessions occurred.

Results from Experiment 1

Child Behaviors in the Generalization Setting

Social Behaviors.   The results of Experiment 1 are presented in Fig. 2.1, which demonstrates a clear increase in on-task percentages between baseline and training conditions. On the average, both normal and deviant children improved in on-task responding by over 55% of their baseline levels.

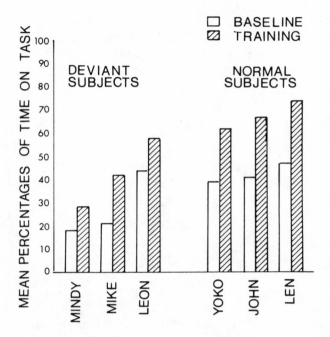

FIG. 2.1.   Mean percentages of time on-task for normal and deviant subjects under baseline (plain bar) and treatment (shaded bar) conditions in the generalization setting.

The effectiveness of the training program for the normal subjects, presented in Fig. 2.2, was shown by the immediate increase in on-task percentages (left-hand column) for each subject when training was begun. In addition, two subjects (John and Yoko) showed clear stabilization at high levels. The right-hand column shows the corollary division of off-task and disruptive behaviors: Improvements in on-task were associated with decreases in off-task behavior.

Similar information for the deviant children is presented in Fig. 2.3. Here, although an improved mean on-task percentage was still clear, the daily variability was greater. Additionally, the increments in on-task for each of these subjects were more clearly associated with decrements in disruptive responding.

Results from Experiment 2

Child Behaviors in the Generalization Setting

Social Behaviors.   Maintenance data for three subjects (two normal and one deviant) are presented in Fig. 2.4. Two of the subjects (John and Leon) showed durable benefits of training when the bracelet was present. A deterioration in on-task percentages and increases in off-task and disruptive responding occurred when the bracelet was withdrawn. The third subject, Len, reverted almost to his

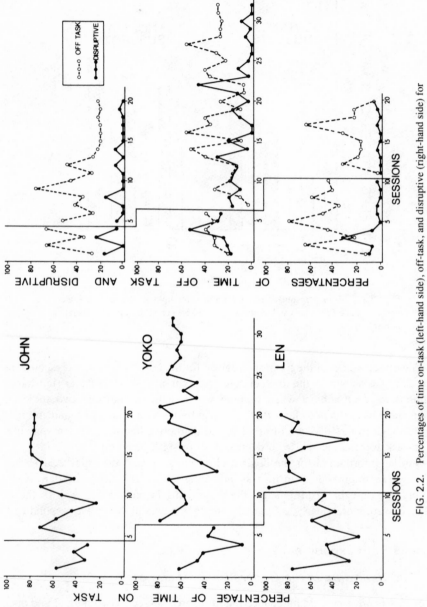

FIG. 2.2. Percentages of time on-task (left-hand side), off-task, and disruptive (right-hand side) for three normal subjects during baseline and treatment conditions in the generalization setting.

46

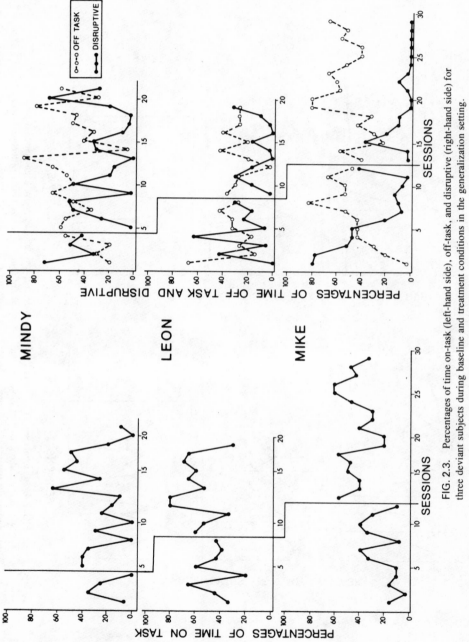

FIG. 2.3. Percentages of time on-task (left-hand side), off-task, and disruptive (right-hand side) for three deviant subjects during baseline and treatment conditions in the generalization setting.

47

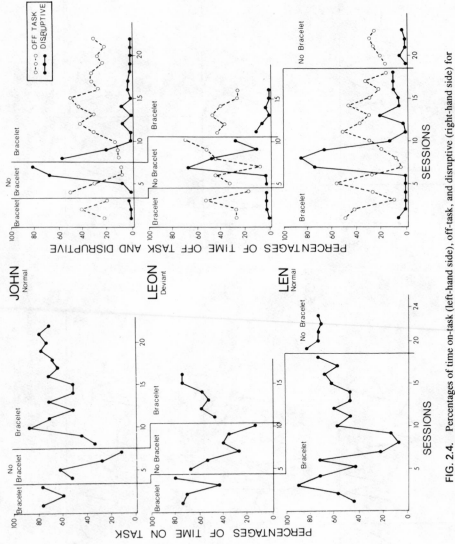

FIG. 2.4. Percentages of time on-task (left-hand side), off-task, and disruptive (right-hand side) for two normal and one deviant subject(s) during 5 months of follow-up under bracelet (treatment) and no-bracelet (reversal) conditions in the generalization setting.

48

baseline performance, even though using his bracelet. When the bracelet was no longer supplied, Len's on-task percentage stabilized at a slightly improved level.

Results from Experiment 3

Child Behaviors in the Generalization Setting

Social Behaviors.   Figure 2.5 presents a reanalysis of the data already shown in Fig. 2.4 for John and Len (to Session 19) plus an additional 3 months of follow-up data. The data in this graph now represent only those days on which both subjects were present. John and Len were the only two experimental subjects to come from the same classroom, and therefore their generalization probes were conducted concurrently.

Figure 2.5 clearly shows John to have been under experimental control: During the self-monitoring (bracelet) conditions he maintained higher and more stable levels of on-task behavior than during the reversal (no-bracelet) conditions. Len's performance prior to Session 19 was highly variable but showed a brief stable period of high on-task during the first no-bracelet condition.

Systematically replicating the self-monitoring and no-bracelet conditions for Len, in the absence of his peer John, did not again produce the clear and high stabilization of on-task behavior noted earlier. However, reanalysis of these data

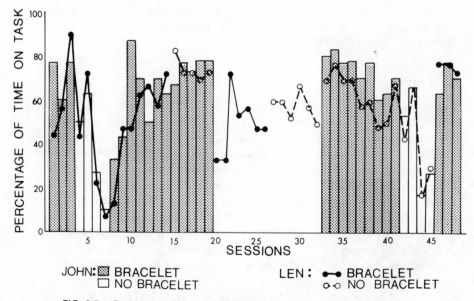

FIG. 2.5.   Percentages of time on-task for two normal subjects during 10 months of follow-up under bracelet (treatment, shaded bar or solid line) and no-bracelet (reversal, open bar or dotted line) conditions in the generalization setting.

to include only those data points when both subjects were present revealed clearly that, during the first reversal period for John, Len's on-task behavior showed a declining trend similar to John's. During the final series of follow-up phases (Sessions 33–48), John was again recruited into the experimental setting. The pattern seen earlier for John was repeated: high stable performance in the self-monitoring (bracelet) phases; decrement in on-task during the (no-bracelet) reversal. Additionally, although Len's on-task rate was variable during John's self-monitoring phases, his pattern closely matched John's, particularly during the reversal period. In the final condition of the study, both subjects were self-monitoring and both achieved high levels of on-task behavior. Thus, it appeared that John was under the control of his experimental bracelet and that Len was under the control of John.

Self-Recording Accuracy.   Throughout the course of all three experiments, self-recording accuracy, by both normal and deviant children, typically was 90% or better. Errors resulted generally from underestimates rather than overestimates of productivity.

Teacher Behaviors in the Generalization Setting.   Teacher attention in the generalization-probe sessions did not systematically vary among baseline, treatment, or reversal conditions in any of the three experiments.

Reliability.   Mean occurrence and nonoccurrence reliabilities of child social, academic, and self-recording behaviors in the generalization setting was 95% or better. Reliability of recording teacher behaviors was always 100%.

Discussion

The results of Experiment 1 indicated clearly that a fairly simple procedure (self-monitoring of academic task completions trained in a laboratory setting) facilitated increased on-task and decreased off-task and disruptive responding for both normal and deviant children. Mean shifts in on-task behavior ranged from 20 to 100% of baseline levels, with an average gain of more than 55%. Of prime importance was the finding that generalization from the training laboratory to the classroom setting occurred without elaborate reprogramming in the latter setting. Perhaps this transfer to the untrained setting was mediated primarily by the discriminative properties of the bracelet, which served to remind the subjects (1) to work; (2) to complete a certain amount of work; (3) to measure ongoing progress; and (4) to seek reinforcement from the teacher for having done so. Spontaneous child comments to the teacher (following task completions) suggest that the child was proud of the job finished (e.g., "Hey! I worked hard. I made it to the red bead."). Interestingly, teacher praise, which was programmed (during self-monitoring phases) to include references to the bracelet, varied widely from teacher to teacher and from day to day. On those rare occasions when a teacher forgot to refer to the bracelet, it was common for a child to prompt a comment; for example (pointing to the bracelet), "Look! I made it to here." The bracelet then provided a dual cuing or mediational function: It could cue the child to work and the teacher to praise, or it could cue the child first to work and then to elicit teacher praise. By monitoring academic rather than social behaviors, the bracelet may have minimized dependence on teacher presence during task completion (Marholin, Steinman, McInnis, & Heads, 1975).

This study systematically replicated earlier research showing that control of academic responding can lead to improvement in social behaviors (Ayllon & Roberts, 1974). The data also support research showing general improvements in a wide variety of self-managed behaviors (Lovitt, 1973). Typically, however, such programs have been introduced directly into the classroom structure by the teacher, following the programming of elaborate token systems for the whole class (Drabman, Spitalnik, & O'Leary, 1973; Glynn, 1970). When the opportunity to run a total classroom on behavior modification principles is lacking, the procedures presented in Experiment 1 may prove useful. For example, children who are labeled as behavior problems or emotionally disturbed often are placed in remedial classrooms to *supplement* their regular school experiences. The object of such special training settings usually is to improve both academic and social behaviors so that the children may be "mainstreamed" back into the regular public-school system. However, problems generally emerge when such mainstreaming is attempted, for generalization to the untrained setting seems rare (Turkewitz, O'Leary, & Ironsmith, 1975). Procedures implemented in the current study (which never utilized backup reinforcers) might provide a useful transition medium by facilitating generalization to the second setting without extensively altering that setting.

Two points may be noted here: (1) The improved performance of the subjects in the generalization probes following training was not a function of increased teacher attention, for the data demonstrate no systematic shift in teacher behaviors. (2) Because the experimenter/trainer did not act as an observer for four of the six children, whose results were much like the other two, it is unlikely that any of the results are confounded by a biased-observer effect.

The procedure worked extremely well for the normal children and less clearly for the deviant population. Despite this reservation, there was an overall increase in on-task behavior for the deviant children, promoting two out of the three subjects into the range of the normal (self-monitoring) children. Further, it should be noted that to some extent the generalization probes might have been perceived by the deviant children as punishing or at least discriminated as a period of "no teacher attention." Random spotchecks of the target children during academic periods (which were not generalization probes) suggested that teacher attention in the classrooms typically was fairly high. By contrast, the probes represented a very lean schedule. Thus, it is likely that higher and more stable rates of on-task behavior might have occurred for the deviant children if some teacher attention had been allowed during the probes (or if it had been reduced in the surrounding academic periods).

The general accuracy and honesty of self-recording displayed by subjects during the generalization probes is particularly noteworthy, because no contingency was ever placed directly on honest counting. Typically, the children were 90% accurate or better, and errors tended to be underestimates rather than inflations of their productivity. This confirms the informal assessment of other researchers that children usually do not cheat when engaging in self-evaluation (Drabman et al., 1973; Glynn, Thomas, & Shee, 1973). It is interesting to note that changes in behavior do not necessarily depend on complete accuracy of self-monitoring (Herbert & Baer, 1972).

Too little attention has been paid to the issue of durability and maintenance of effects achieved by successful behavioral interventions (Keeley, Shemburg, & Carbonell, 1976; Wildman & Wildman, 1975). Concern with the issue of durability, or generalization over time, is not new, and the need to research this area has often been urged (Baer, Wolf, & Risley, 1968; Gelfand & Hartmann, 1968; O'Dell, 1974). Despite such urging, the maintenance of interventions has remained a neglected research problem, and attempts to collect follow-up information typically have relied on relatively unreliable data such as telephone contacts. Experiments 2 and 3 in the current study were directed primarily toward this problem: the measurement and analysis of the treatment package following cessation of training.

The results of Experiment 2 are particularly encouraging, for it is apparent that its procedures successfully maintained improved on-task behavior in two of the three subjects still available (one deviant, one normal). Further, these effects were in evidence 2 months after treatment had been concluded; and for an ongoing period of 3 months (i.e., 5 months following the conclusion of training) self-monitoring effectively controlled behavior. Only the third subject, Len, had reverted to his baseline level of performance, even though retaining his bracelet. However, reanalysis of Experiment-2 data to include only data points when both subjects were present revealed clearly that Len's on-task behavior reliably showed trends similar to John's.

To examine whether Len's behavior was largely determined by his peer's, John was again recruited into the experimental setting. The pattern seen earlier for John was repeated: high stable performance in the self-monitoring phases and decrement in on-task during the reversal. (Thus, follow-up data were extended for 10 months beyond cessation of John's training.) Although Len's on-task rate was variable during John's self-monitoring phases, his pattern closely matched his peer's, particularly during the reversal period. Thus, it appeared that John was under the control of the experimental manipulation and Len was under the control of John.

The importance of such peer control and influence often has been noted (Bixenstine, DeCorte, & Bixenstine, 1976; Wahler, 1967) and in cases like this they are thoroughly valuable. It is not clear which variables were responsible for this control. It is not possible to specify whether modeling, reinforcing, or cuing components were the critical elements responsible for John's control of Len's behavior. Researchers interested in pursuing this question will need to code the extent of all social interactions as well as those behaviors assessed within the current study. Such pursuit should provide interesting and worthwhile information.

In summary, these results indicated that a fairly simple procedure—self-monitoring of academic task completions—increased on-task and decreased off-task and disruptive responding of both normal and deviant children. Of prime importance was the finding that generalization from the training laboratory to a classroom occurred without elaborate reprogramming in the classroom. In addition, a formal experimental analysis of follow-up data showed that these effects were durable in two of the three subjects available for up to a year following the commencement of training.

STUDY II

In this study, preschoolers were taught to increase positive teacher–child interaction concerning the quality of their academic work. After training in one setting, the children were reinforced for displaying improved independent work skills in a generalization setting with other teachers. The children were also taught to prompt or to cue positive teacher comments regarding their work quality and output. These skills may be especially important to young children who find themselves bereft of attention in classrooms, perhaps because they are labeled deviant or perhaps because they do not represent a problem to their teachers. Deviant children might benefit particularly from these special procedures because their ''deviant'' label often follows them through their schooldays and so it might be advantageous for these children to have skills in their repertoires that could be used, if required, to modify interaction with their teachers in a positive way.

Subjects and Setting

The children involved in this experiment were normal preschoolers attending morning classes at an experimental preschool at the University of Kansas. Paul, Betty, and Steve were 5 years old; Greg was 4 years old. The parents gave prior permission to involve the children in this study.

Two teachers were involved in this study as probers for generalization of skills taught by the trainer/experimenter. Mary (27 years old) was a trained teacher with 5 years experience in preschool and grade schools. Jane (21 years old) was a senior with 2 years experience in preschool teaching. Neither had been trained in behavior modification procedures. The probers remained naive concerning specific experimental procedures until the completion of the experiment.

The experimental setting was a small 7 by 5 foot (2.1 by 1.5 meter) tutoring room adjacent to the children's regular classrooms. The room contained a small table and two chairs. Experimental sessions with the trainer/experimenter were conducted in this room. This setting also served as the generalization setting on different days with the teacher/probers.

Behaviors

Social Interaction.   Observers scored student–teacher/prober interactions from behind a oneway mirror. *Cues* and *praise* were scored according to a 10-second interval recording procedure. Cues were defined as statements by the child to the trainer or prober inviting favorable comments or positive evaluations of the child's work or general behavior (e.g., "Look how much I've done" and "Is this right?"). Trainer or prober praise was defined as verbal encouragement, positive evaluative comments, and statements of approval of the child's general behavior or work (e.g., "That's very good" and "You're working well").

Assessment of the reliability of recording each child's behavior was conducted during each experimental condition. During reliability checks, two independent observers simultaneously scored the experimental sessions. Later comparison of agreements and disagreements about the occurrence of cues and praise showed 89% (24/27) observer agreement about cues, and 94% (47/50) about praise.

Academic Production.   During experimental sessions, each child worked on paper-and-pencil writing tasks that involved practice in tracing straight and curved lines and letters. These materials were taken from the pretest of the Behavior Analysis Handwriting Primer (Stonger, Weis, Brigham, Breunig, & Krompotich, 1974). Items were scored as correct if the lines had been traced completely and with deviations not greater than $1/16$ inch (1.6 millimeter) from a perfect line. Both the number of items attempted and the number correct were counted.

For each child during each experimental condition a comparison was made of the total items scored as attempted and correct by independent observers. Percentages of interobserver agreement were 100% (1095/1095) for items attempted and 92% (720/784) for items correct.

General Procedure and Design

One adult and one child were present during each experimental session. Each child was brought from the classroom to the tutoring room by the trainer or by one of the probers. The child was then asked to go over the lines on each page and go on to the next page after the completion of any page. Interaction was scored for 10 minutes.

Experimental sessions conducted by the trainer were interspersed unsystematically among generalization sessions conducted by the two probers. These generalization sessions allowed an assessment of spontaneous generalization of the work and cuing skills taught by the trainer. Training sessions ceased within 3 days after the institution of generalization-programming procedures. Thus, later in the experiment, only the probers alternated in conducting the experimental sessions.

Experimental control of the generalization-programming procedures was demonstrated in multiple-baseline designs. The generalization-programming procedures were introduced with each subject after different numbers of baseline sessions with the probers.

Training

During training, each child was taught the dimensions of good work. The trainer asked each child to practice good lines by staying close to the dashed lines on the writing pages, to erase and correct errors, and to work consistently and quietly. The trainer offered feedback and praise concerning the child's performance. In addition to this training, each child was taught, through instructions, role playing, feedback, and praise, to prompt or to cue the trainer for positive evaluations when their work had been of a high quality; that is, they were taught a number of different cues such as "Have I worked well?", "Have I been working carefully?", "How is this work?", "Look how careful I've been," and "How is this?". In this way, a chain of responding was taught: Do good work; then evaluate the quality of that work; and, when the quality was good, cue the trainer to evaluate that work. For example, the children were taught that good work often meant finishing a page without many mistakes (i.e., working carefully for a period of time).

Generalization

Generalization sessions were conducted in the same tutoring room as the training but on other days and with the teacher/probers (Mary and Jane). The 10-minute generalization sessions with these two probers were not as structured as the training sessions. The probers were asked by the trainer to instruct the children to work at their work sheets, but the probers were not told how to conduct the session. Because they were experienced teachers, it was assumed that they already had a certain teaching style, and the experimenter did not intervene or give feedback to the probers about their performance.

The intervention in the generalization sessions consisted of the trainer instructing each child to do the same with probers as they had been doing with the training (i.e., work carefully, evaluate their work quality, and ask the prober a few times about the quality of that work but do not ask too often). Initially, these instructions were given during training sessions. After training ceased, the instructions were given at the end of the preschool day when the trainer saw the children in their classroom. Some time after the generalization session had been completed, the children were contacted in their regular preschool classrooms by the trainer. They were asked if they had done careful work and if they had asked the prober about that work. If in fact they had followed the trainer's instructions and also reported that they had done so, they earned a small toy.

Results and Discussion

Figure 2.6 shows each child's cues to probers during the interspersed generalization sessions. During the baseline condition, spontaneous generalization from the training sessions occurred only in Steve's case. After the generali-

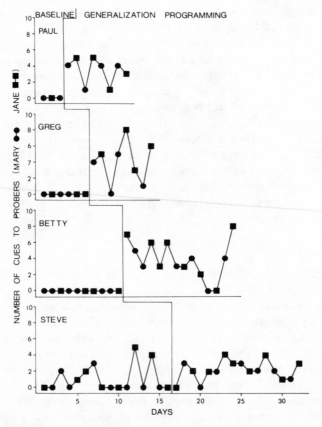

FIG. 2.6.   Number of cues given to probers during generalization sessions. One prober is represented by square points; the other prober, by round points. These generalization–probe sessions began after the trainer began training sessions; thus, the baseline period in this figure is a spontaneous generalization condition to be compared with the subsequent rate of cues given to probers during programmed generalization.

zation-programming intervention, however, each child increased in the number of cues presented to each prober.

Even though Steve's behavior changes were the least dramatic and probably were accounted for in large part by data projections from baseline trends, nevertheless they were the most impressive in their consistency and level. Such a low rate may be desired in that a potential problem with teaching these skills is that a child might cue a teacher too often, thereby becoming a "pest," a counterproductive outcome. Thus, such training should establish optimal rates of cuing (i.e., rates high enough to be consistently successful but low enough so that the child will work relatively independently and therefore not be considered a nuisance). A rate of two-to-four cues per session was sought; this rate of cuing was chosen after consultation with a number of preschool teachers.

Figure 2.7 shows the mean number of cues given and cued praises received

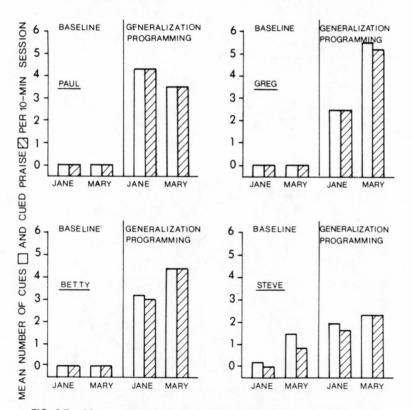

FIG. 2.7.   Mean number of cues given to and cued praise received from each prober during each experimental condition. Open bars indicate the mean number of children's cues to probers; shaded bars show the mean number of the prober's praises following cues.

with each prober during each experimental condition. This figure shows that the children increased their cues to each prober during the generalization programming condition. In addition, it shows that cues were very successful in evoking praise (i.e., praise occurring within 20 seconds of a cue). Approximately 90% of the cues were followed by praise.

Figure 2.8 shows each child's academic production during the generalization sessions. After the generalization-programming procedures were instituted, the number of correct work items and the percentage of correct work items increased and stabilized at a higher level for all children. In general, the children averaged

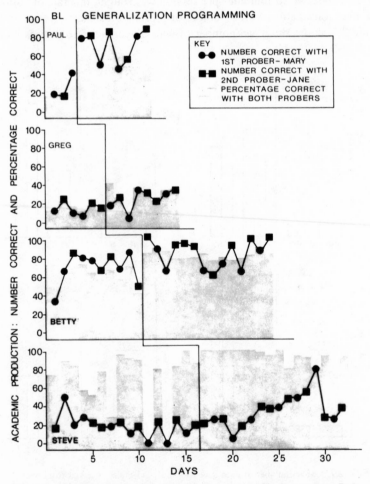

FIG. 2.8.   Children's academic production during generalization sessions. Bars represent the percentage of items correct of those attempted; lines superimposed on the bars represent the number of items correct.

34 items correct (47% of items attempted) during baseline and 55 items correct (72% of items attempted) during the intervention.

There was also a higher rate of teacher praise during the generalization-programming condition, but this may have been a function of the probers' recognition of increased accuracy of work output. Therefore, an analysis of schedules of praise for items correct and items attempted was made. Schedules were calculated by dividing the total number of items attempted or correct in each condition by the total number of praises in that condition. This analysis, shown in Table 2.1, reveals that the children had modified the probers' behavior, even after allowing for their increased work output. These data together with the data on cued praises are most significant, for they establish that the children were able to contact, recruit, and cultivate a dormant but readily available natural community of increased reinforcement. It could be expected, then, that the increased rate of praise evoked might maintain the children's improved performance, and the children's cuing might maintain the praise as a function of the reciprocal interaction (Baltes & Reese, 1977). Perhaps the trainer then could remove all experimental manipulations and the behavior changes might be maintained, a generalization across time.

In summary, preschool children were taught to make judgments concerning the quality of their own work. In addition, they were taught a relatively sophisti-

TABLE 2.1
(Experiment 1)
Variable ratio schedules
of praise from probers for
items attempted and items
correct, for each subject, for
baseline and generalization-
programming conditions.

		Attempted	*Correct*
PAUL	BL	VR 70	VR 20
	GEN	VR 21	VR 14
GREG	BL	VR 111	VR 18
	GEN	VR 18	VR 6
BETTY	BL	VR 103	VR 64
	GEN	VR 15	VR 16
STEVE	BL	VR 32	VR 13
	GEN	VR 13	VR 12
MEAN	BL	VR 79	VR 30
	GEN	VR 17	VR 12

cated skill of drawing their teachers' attention to the quality of that work. Furthermore, when those skills did not generalize spontaneously to relevant classroom situations, generalized responding was programmed by use of contingent delayed consequences dispensed by the trainer. When these generalized behavior changes were programmed, the children then were able to contact a sometimes dormant but readily available natural community of praise (Baer & Wolf, 1970) and were able then to recruit and cultivate an increase in their rates of cued praise and schedules of praise. Thus, if the introduction to this natural community of presumed reinforcement had been effective and the child displayed a repertoire of skills appropriate in quality, diversity, rate, and distribution, the presumed reinforcement community might then be expected to accomplish further improved performance and to maintain that improved performance. And, indeed, such increases were observed (but perhaps were due to the trainer). The trainer then might be able to fade and eventually withdraw all experimental support of the children's behaviors without detrimental effect. The examination of such an outcome is a high-priority question for future research. One final, and not insignificant, aspect of these techniques is a change in the usual locus of control in child behavior modification (i.e., the children became more active agents of their own behavior change rather than serving in contingencies applied by other powerful persons in their environment [Graubard, Rosenberg, & Miller, 1971]).

A final point is important at the end of this discussion. Generalization is a problem to be solved by an appropriate generalization technology. That technology is definitely possible and nearly exists already, and self-control techniques may prove to be an important part of it. But it probably is true that any generalization technology, no matter how good, always can be overcome by direct, nongeneralized contingencies. After all, the essence of behavior therapy and behavior modification is that we overcome generalization from some prior bad program conducted by someone else, earlier or elsewhere. We succeed often enough to suggest that we can always overcome generalized contingency effects with direct contingencies. Therefore, we certainly should proceed to develop the best generalization technology that we can and we should expect that it will be extremely valuable. However, it will not be totally dependable—and we should be glad of that, because otherwise we too often would find ourselves unable to overcome some of the bad generalizations brought to us for therapy, education, or modification.

REFERENCES

Ayllon, T., & Roberts, M. D. Eliminating discipline problems by strengthening academic performance. *Journal of Applied Behavior Analysis*, 1974, *7*, 71–76.

Baer, D. M., & Wolf, M. M. The entry into natural communities of reinforcement. In R. Ulrich, T. Stachnik, & J. Mabry (Eds.), *Control of human behavior: Volume II*. Glenview, Ill.: Scott, Foresman, 1970.

Baer, D. M., Wolf, M. M., & Risley, T. R. Some current dimensions of applied behavior analysis. *Journal of Applied Behavior Analysis,* 1968, *1,* 91–97.

Baltes, M. M., & Reese, H. W. Operant research in violation of the operant paradigm. In B. C. Etzel, J. M. LeBlanc, & D. M. Baer (Eds.), *New developments in behavioral research: Theory, method, and application. In honor of Sidney W. Bijou.* Hillsdale, N.J.: Lawrence Erlbaum Associates, 1977.

Bixenstine, V. E., DeCorte, M. S., & Bixenstine, B. A. Conformity to peer-sponsored misconduct at four grade levels. *Developmental Psychology,* 1976, *12,* 226–236.

Drabman, R. S., Spitalnik, R., & O'Leary, K. D. Teaching self-control to disruptive children. *Journal of Abnormal Psychology,* 1973, *81,* 10–16.

Gelfand, D. M., & Hartmann, D. P. Behavior therapy with children: A review and evaluation of research methodology. *Psychological Bulletin,* 1968, *69,* 204–215.

Glynn, E. L. Classroom applications of self-determined reinforcement. *Journal of Applied Behavior Analysis,* 1970, *3,* 123–132.

Glynn, E. L., Thomas, J. D., & Shee, S. M. Behavioral self-control of on-task behavior in an elementary classroom. *Journal of Applied Behavior Analysis,* 1973, *6,* 105–113.

Graubard, P. S., Rosenberg, H., & Miller, M. B. Student applications of behavior modification to teachers and environments or ecological approaches to social deviancy. In E. A. Ramp & B. L. Hopkins (Eds.), *A new direction for education: Behavior analysis.* Lawrence, Kan.: Support and Development Center for Follow Through, 1971.

Herbert, E. W., & Baer, D. M. Training parents as behavior modifiers: Self-recording of contingent attention. *Journal of Applied Behavior Analysis,* 1972, *5,* 139–149.

Keeley, S. M., Shemberg, K. M., & Carbonell, J. Operant clinical intervention: Behavior management or beyond? Where are the data? *Behavior Therapy,* 1976, *7,* 292–305.

Kurtz, P. D., & Neisworth, J. T. Self-control possibilities for exceptional children. *Exceptional Children,* January 1976, 212–217.

Lovitt, T. C. Self-management projects with children with behavioral disorders. *Journal of Learning Disabilities,* 1973, *6,* 15–28.

Marholin, II, D., Steinman, W. M., McInnis, E. T., & Heads, T. B. The effect of a teacher's presence on the classroom behavior of conduct-problem children. *Journal of Abnormal Child Psychology,* 1975, *3,* 11–25.

O'Dell, S. Training parents in behavior modification: A review. *Psychological Bulletin,* 1974, *81,* 418–433.

Stokes, T. F., & Baer, D. M. An implicit technology of generalization. *Journal of Applied Behavior Analysis,* 1977, *10,* 349–367.

Stonger, R., Weis, L., Brigham, T., Breunig, M., & Krompotich, N. Handwriting. In D. Jackson (Ed.), *Behavior analysis curriculum procedures for the behavior analysis classroom.* Lawrence, Kan.: University of Kansas Behavior Analysis Follow Through Project, 1974.

Turkewitz, H., O'Leary, K. D., & Ironsmith, M. Generalization and maintenance of appropriate behavior through self-control. *Journal of Consulting and Clinical Psychology,* 1975, *43,* 577–583.

Wahler, R. G. Child-child interactions in free field settings: Some experimental analyses. *Journal of Experimental Child Psychology,* 1967, *5,* 278–293.

Wildman, R. W., II, & Wildman, R. W. The generalization of behavior modification procedures: A review—with special emphasis on classroom applications. *Psychology in the Schools,* 1975, *12,* 432–448.

3

Issues and Trends in Behavior Modification in the Classroom

Beth Sulzer-Azaroff
University of Massachusetts, Amherst

INTRODUCTION

Since the widespread growth of the field of behavior modification in education began in the mid-sixties, its promise continues to be realized. As in mental health and many other areas of application, behavior modification has been effectively implemented to improve student conduct, teacher performance, academic quality and productivity, and various adaptive social and emotional behaviors. Behavior modification has been contributing toward making educational systems more effective and satisfying to students and school personnel.

In education, behavior modification has progressed through a series of stages and growing pains, just as the field has in other areas of application. Various issues have become manifest and trends have resulted. Many of these relate to the *zeitgeist* of the times: issues of humanism (Thoresen, 1973), issues of consumerism (Braukmann, Fixsen, Kirigin, Phillips, Phillips, & Wolf, 1975), and issues that relate to history and function have emerged. This chapter addresses itself to a sample cluster of such issues: what target behaviors to select; who the client is; and what sorts of contingencies to manage—individual versus group reinforcement and consumerism. It then considers various trends that have evolved as the field has attempted to come to grips with those issues.

The literature on behavior modification in classrooms has burgeoned exponentially. Consequently, it would not be feasible, within the confines of a short chapter, to survey the whole field adequately. Rather, examples of the issues and trends just cited are selected from the field and from the author's personal experience to serve as illustrative material.

SELECTING TARGET BEHAVIORS

The development of behavior modification in the classroom shares much in common with other areas of behavior modification application. Paralleling the development of behavior modification in the field of mental health (Ayllon, 1963), many early classroom studies were directed toward the reduction of 'noxious' behaviors. The elimination of disruptive (Madsen, Becker, & Thomas, 1968; Thomas, Becker, & Armstrong, 1968), unpermitted, out-of-seat (Englehardt, Sulzer, & Altekruse, 1971), and other behaviors that interfered with ongoing classroom routines were frequently targeted for change. It appeared that educators eagerly embraced procedures that would ease their difficulties in managing students who interfered with classroom learning. Illustrative are a series of classroom studies conducted by Sulzer and her students in the Carbondale, Illinois, area. In one case, a request for consultation derived from the staff of a curriculum research and development program. Two teachers who had in the past encountered only cooperative high-school students found themselves attempting to field test their newly developed curriculum materials in an elementary-school setting. Though apparently very popular with the students, they experienced serious difficulties as the youngsters roamed around the room, spoke without permission loudly enough to interfere with other students' work, and in general were making things unpleasant for the teachers. A few days' observation suggested that the teachers were giving the major portion of their attention to students when they were being disruptive. It was suggested that the teachers attend instead to students while they were engaged in nondisruptive behavior. Repeated measures were taken. A brief "reversal" back to withholding attention from desirable behaviors resulted in their reduction, providing convincing evidence that attention was indeed related to disruptive students' behavior.

One problem persisted, however, as a single student continued to disrupt. For example, he would climb on desks, make strange noises, and giggle foolishly. A closer look indicated that one teacher had begun to attend successfully to the nondisruptive behavior of all but this one student, continuing to attend to his disruption. Figure 3.1 illustrates this phenomen. You will note that from 4/2 through 4/5 the teacher appeared to be unable to sustain attending to the student following positive intervals and the student's disruptive behavior increased concurrently. On 4/17 a cuing system was instituted to inform the teacher that the student was working nicely and that attention should be delivered. The system apparently supported appropriately distributed attention, and the student's behavior improved. When cuing was removed at B, the teacher reduced his level of attending but still emphasized attention to positive behaviors. The student's behavior remained at an acceptable level.

Soon afterward, a number of other investigators in the region began to undertake similar programs. The study by Whitley and Sulzer (1970) essentially replicated that procedure, though an extensive follow-up period was added (see Fig.

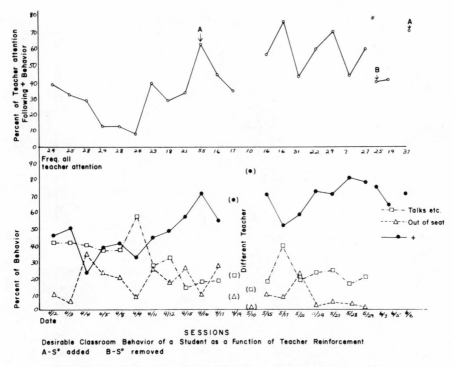

FIG. 3.1.   Desirable classroom behavior of a student as a function of teacher reinforcement. At point A, a cue was presented. Cuing continued until B.

3.2). It was found that as long as the major proportion of the teacher's attention was given to desirable behaviors (even if the overall frequency of attention declined), they would persist. The Englehardt et al. (1970) study replicated the procedure for out-of-seat behavior (see Fig. 3.3).

As that series of studies progressed, we began to question the value of selecting only noxious target behaviors. True, we could assume that all students would benefit. Offenders would no longer be subjected to frequent scolding and other aversive consequences, and classmates would be less often prevented from concentrating on their work. However, we felt that it would be more advisable to look more closely at those behaviors that are often specified as the goals of school curricula: academic performance and personal and social development. A shift toward promoting students' acquisition of positive, adaptive, constructive behaviors might even conceivably accomplish both purposes. (If the devil makes work for idle hands, probably the student engaged in accomplishing useful skills would stay on the side of the angels.) Apparently recognition of this point was shared by others. Winnett and Winkler (1972), taking issue with the social organization of classrooms that may tend to foster disruptive behavior and ques-

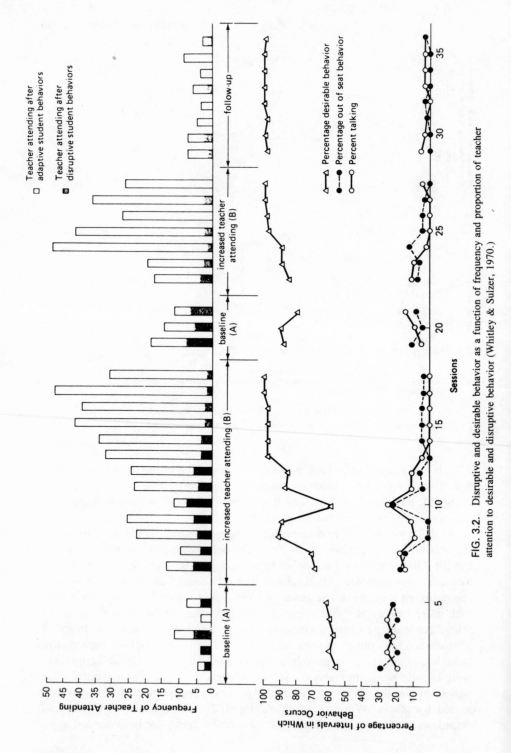

FIG. 3.2. Disruptive and desirable behavior as a function of frequency and proportion of teacher attention to desirable and disruptive behavior (Whitley & Sulzer, 1970.)

66

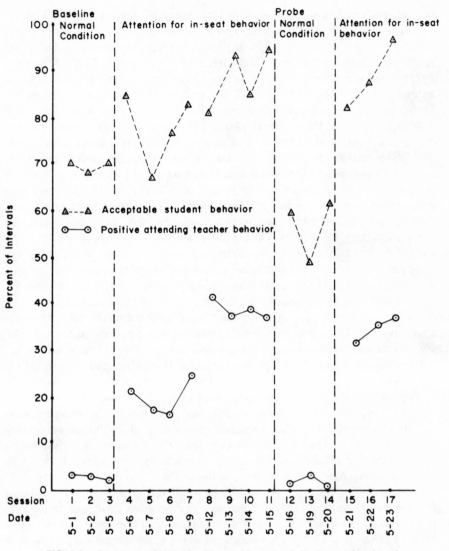

FIG. 3.3. Percentage of intervals of acceptable student behavior as a function of
teacher attending to attending behavior (Englehardt, Sulzer, & Alterkrause, 1970.)

tioning the arbitrary targeting of certain classes of behavior as inappropriate, also
suggested instead the targeting of skills such as productive social behaviors.

Literature by Birnbrauer, Wolf, Kidder, and Tague (1965), Brigham, &
Sherman (1968), and Buell, Stoddard, Harris, and Baer (1968), for example,
indicated that behavioral procedures could effectively promote classroom productivity, language development, and social skills. So we changed our focus.

Instead, such targets were selected as language skills for a youngster with seriously delayed functional speech (Wheeler & Sulzer, 1970) and academic performance such as reading, language, social studies, arithmetic, science, and spelling (Campbell & Sulzer, 1971; Sulzer et al., 1971; Sulzer, Hunt, & Loving, 1972). Later a number of behavioral procedures were combined to teach handwriting (Fauke, Burnett, Powers, & Sulzer-Azaroff, 1973). In each case we found, as did others in the field (Hamblin, Hathaway, & Wodarski, 1974; Salzberg, Wheeler, Devar, & Hopkins, 1971; and many more) that the immediate, consistent reinforcement of short academic tasks appropriate to the students' repertoires resulted in the students' effective acquisition of the skills.

In order to test whether or not misconduct would fall by the wayside when academic skill performance was increased, in Sulzer et al. (1971), data were collected on untreated conduct behaviors. These were derived from a list generated by the class members and included nonpermitted out-of-seat, shouting, hitting, and throwing objects. During one phase, points exchangeable for tangible and activity reinforcers were delivered for academic productivity. (Although if the student were engaged in misconduct at the time, point delivery was delayed until the student resumed acceptable behavior.) Figures 3.4, 3.5, 3.6, and 3.7 show that during that phase (C) academic productivity and accuracy rose and disruption decreased, although the proportion of teacher attention remained relatively constant. That effect was also demonstrated by Ayllon and Roberts (1974), who found that when academic performance was reinforced, there was an accompanying decrease in disruption. Similarly, Hay, Hay, and Nelson (1977) found a decrease in off-task behavior under those conditions.

Ferritor, Buckholdt, Hamblin, and Smith (1972) found that reducing disruptive behavior, however, did not necessarily lead to increased academic productivity (simultaneously noting that increased productivity alone did not necessarily reduce disruption). They did find, though, that reinforcement for a combination of nondisruptive behavior and academic productivity did produce both an increase in productivity and a decrease in disruption.

An alternative and very promising approach to the problem of classroom management is to identify those conditions that occasion disruption in the first place. Those conditions can then be managed and the problem behaviors avoided. The merit of this approach is receiving experimental support. Krantz and Risley (1977) have found that such ecological variables as scheduling and crowding were functionally related to disruption. On the basis of their studies, they recommended that academic work periods be preceded by quiet activities and that crowding be avoided to prevent disruption.

There are probably many other conditions that occasion either greater or lesser amounts of disruption. In Frankowsky and Sulzer-Azaroff (1978), we found, for example, that a group reinforcement contingency was accompanied by increased cooperation among group members. Other variables that may be important in this regard are assignment lengths, difficulty, and content; the nature of

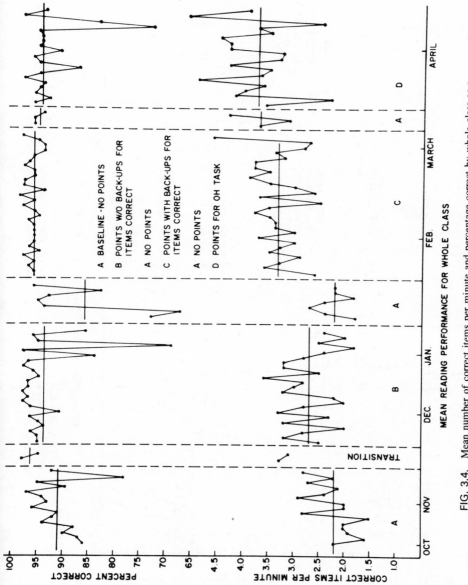

FIG. 3.4. Mean number of correct items per minute and percentage correct by whole class as a function of no points, points without any backup rewards for items correct, and points with backups for on-task regardless of correctness. Reading class. Horizontal lines indicate the mean for the phase (Sulzer, Hunt, Ashby, Koniarski, & Krams, 1971.)

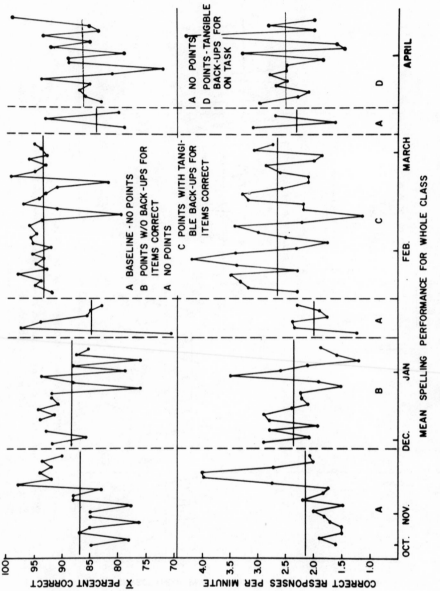

FIG. 3.5. Mean number of correct items per minute and percentage correct by whole class as a function of no points, points without any backup rewards for items correct, and points with backups for on-task regardless of correctness. Spelling class. Horizontal lines indicate the mean for the phase (Sulzer et al., 1971.)

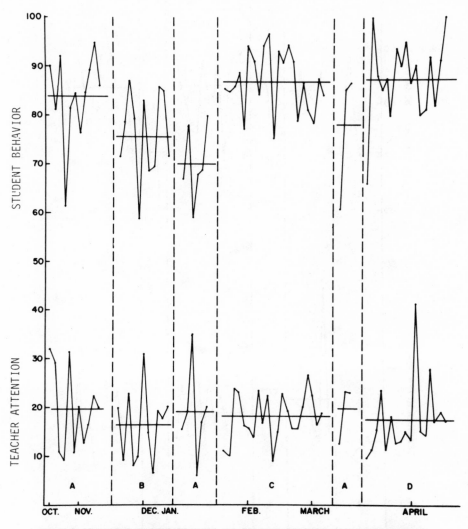

MEAN % DESIRABLE STUDENT BEHAVIOR AND POSITIVE TEACHER ATTENTION – READING

FIG. 3.6. Mean percentage of intervals in which students in class engaged in desirable behavior and percentage of intervals in which teacher attended to students. (Note the improvement in behavior during C and D, although teacher attending remained essentially unchanged.) Reading class (Sulzer et al., 1971.)

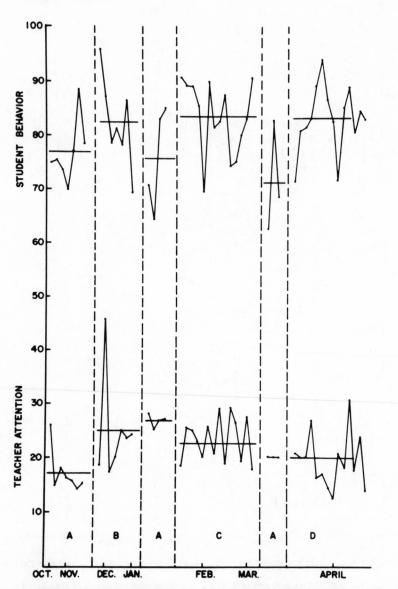

MEAN % DESIRABLE STUDENT BEHAVIOR AND POSITIVE TEACHER ATTENTION: SPELLING

FIG. 3.7. Mean percentage of intervals in which students in class engaged in desirable behavior and percentage of intervals in which teacher attended to students. (Note mean percentage of teacher attention was diminished during C and D, although student behavior improved.) Spelling class (Sulzer et al., 1971.)

instructions; public versus private instructions; physical conditions such as lighting, noise, and temperature.

Consequently, it appears that a few trends have emerged in the area of selecting target behaviors. First, there appears to be an increasing emphasis on the direct targeting of those behaviors that are of most critical concern in education: academic and those behaviors that lead to social and self-enhancement. Second, more efforts are beginning to be directed toward the prevention of problem behaviors through the identification and management of ecological conditions.

Now we turn to a second issue that has received widespread attention in the field: the specification of who is to be treated.

SPECIFYING THE CLIENT

Scanning the behavior modification literature in the field of mental health, one might note a gradual shift away from identifying the patient with deviant behavior as the *client* (e.g., studies presented in the early Ullman & Krasner books, 1965). The role of client began to be assumed by others in the environment, such as staff (Panyan, Boozer, & Morris, 1970), parents, (Budd, Green, & Baer, 1976), or members of the community (Hunt & Azrin, 1973). Similarly, in educational settings, changes in client specification are evolving in parallel form. One notes instances in which it is not the student per se who is the recipient of "treatment" but rather the instructional staff [e.g., teachers, (Cossairt, Hall, & Hopkins, 1973), tutors (Johnson & Bailey, 1974), proctors (e.g., Weaver & Miller, 1975), and even the physical environment (Krantz & Risley, 1977; Twardosz, Cataldo, & Risley, 1974).] This trend has been borne out in some of our own work as well.

In an attempt to assist a state institution for the retarded to emphasize training more heavily in preference to custodial care, the middle management supervisors (Thaw, Palmer, & Sulzer-Azaroff, 1977) served as the "clients." Those clients participated in an extensive training program designed to teach them not only behavior change but also training, supervisory, and organizational skills. This extensive training, replicated five times across essentially all the middle management personnel in the institution, appeared to promote increases in the frequency of ongoing training programs with residents. As with so many other training and treatment strategies, early behavior modification programs suspected and later verified that long-term maintenance would only occur under certain conditions: feedback (Panyan et al., 1970), feedback with goals (Sloat, Tharp, & Gallimore, 1977), intermittent reinforcement (Phillips, Phillips, Wolf, & Fixsen, 1973), follow-up consultation (Walker, Hops, & Johnson, 1975) among others. In several of our studies, we too found that focusing our attention on the broader social environment did tend to promote maintenance.

Recognizing the need to program maintenance following training of specific skills, in several instances, we turned to teachers (Holden & Sulzer, 1972; Souweine, Sulzer-Azaroff, & Fredrickson, 1977, parents (Hunt & Sulzer-Azaroff, 1974), and peer tutors (Schram & Sulzer-Azaroff, 1972). Each, in a sense, assumed the role of "client." In the first case, periodic telephone calls to teachers maintained their implementation of a perscriptive teaching program over many weeks (see Fig. 3.8). Similarly, in the Hunt and Sulzer-Azaroff (1974) study, when an attempt was made to teach severely handicapped children pre-writing skills in the classroom, it was apparent that additional home practice would be required. Parent assistance was obtained by sending home notes thanking them for their help.

The building principal is an individual whose presence is natural to the school setting. In Souweine et al. (1977) the building principal effectively "treated" the client-teachers by praising their use of management skills that they had recently acquired in an in-service training program (see Fig. 3.9).

The use of peers, who function as tutors, proctors, or change agents, has become more frequent (Solomon & Wahler, 1973). In several cases, we have directly trained peers to function in such capacities rather than providing training directly to the student. In one instance (Schram & Sulzer-Azaroff, unpublished paper), a "normal" high-achieving youngster was trained to teach picture names to an age-mate who had just begun to develop a functional vocabulary. Figure 3.10 indicates that the peer-tutor performed his job effectively. Similarly, in the personalized system of instruction (PSI) courses offered through the Mastery Learning Center at the University of Massachusetts, proctors are taught a variety of skills to be used in performing their quiz-scoring function. Figure 3.11 shows one example of how training in appropriate prompting strategies affects the proctor–student interaction (Johnson & Sulzer-Azaroff, 1977).

A broadened definition of who the client is must be considered if, as in the previous examples, instructional and training coverage are to be expanded and their effects maintained. When only students are the clients in a behavior modification program, the number of individuals served is limited by the time available to the behavior modifier. When, however, key individuals such as parents, teachers, professional and paraprofessional staff, peers, community groups, and even the physical environment become the subject of direct treatment (the "client"), those limitations are far less restrictive.

ANTECEDENTS VERSUS CONSEQUENCES

A survey of recent and current applications of behavior modification in education suggests that studies of the controlling properties of behavioral consequences have been very heavily emphasized. In many of the early studies in the field, the management of consequences has been the primary intervention strategy: in

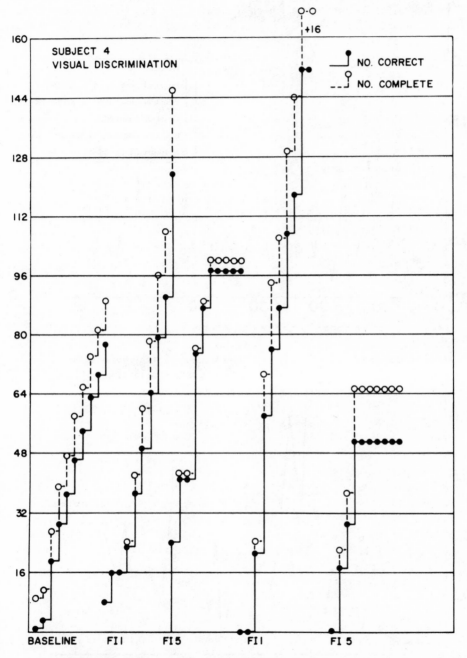

FIG. 3.8.   Cumulative number of visual discrimination items completed and cumulative number correct as a function of daily (F11) and weekly (F15) phone calls to teacher (Holden & Sulzer, 1972.)

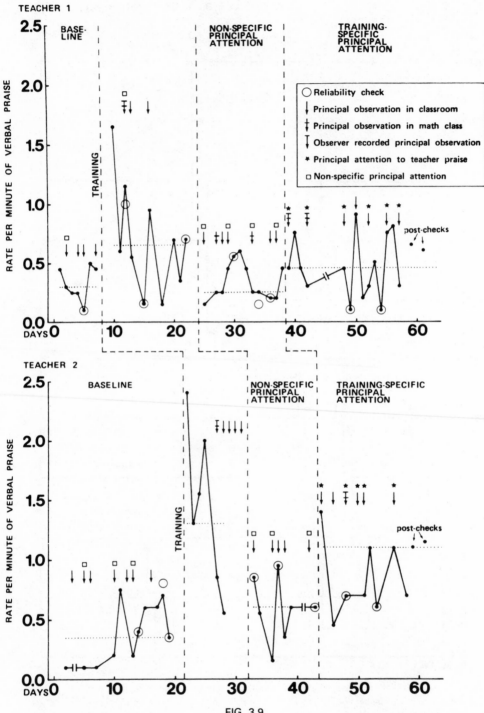

FIG. 3.9.

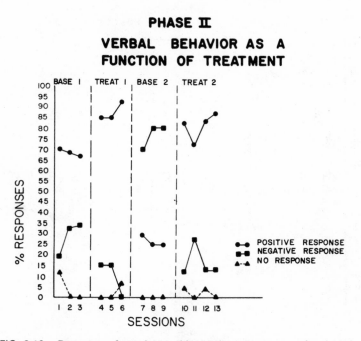

PHASE II

VERBAL BEHAVIOR AS A
FUNCTION OF TREATMENT

FIG. 3.10.   Percentage of negative, positive, and no response as a function of
food delivered by a "normal" age peer contingent upon correct verbal responses
by a child with delayed language (Schram & Sulzer-Azaroff, 1972.)

studies of the effect of teacher attention (Madsen et al., 1968; Thomas et al.,
1968; and others previously mentioned), tokens (Staats, Staats, Schutz, & Wolf,
1962; Wolf, Giles, & Hall, 1968), and food delivery (Wolf, Risley, & Mees,
1964). Reprimands (O'Leary, Kaufman, Kass, and Drabman, 1970), timeout
(Tyler & Brown, 1967), response cost (Iwata & Bailey, 1974), and other negative consequences also frequently have been applied to behaviors targeted for
reduction. In a sense, this very heavy emphasis on behavioral consequences is
surprising, because the roots of the practice of behavior modification in the
classroom initially stemmed from B. F. Skinner's work on programmed instruction.

Simultaneously teaching university students while working in the animal laboratory, Skinner and his colleagues had begun in the 1950s to experiment with the
application of principles of operant conditioning to the instructional process. A

FIG. 3.9.   (opposite) Rate per minute of teacher praise prior to workshop in use of
praise, following workshop (training), during an increased number of visits by the
principal, who commented on other than teacher's use of praise (nonspecific
principal attention) and when principal attention was contingent upon teacher's
use of praise (training specific principal attention) (Souweine, Sulzer-Azaroff, &
Fredrickson, 1977.)

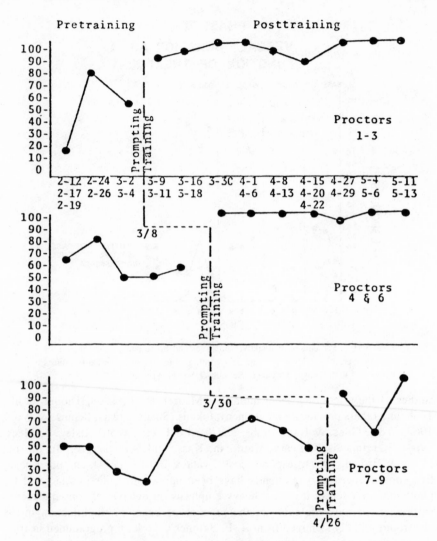

FIG. 3.11.   Mean percentage proctor noninformationally prompted quiz answers
that were initially omitted, unclear, or incorrect. Groups are plotted in multiple
baseline fashion as a function of prompting training (Johnson & Sulzer-Azaroff,
1978.)

number of papers on "programmed instruction," for example, *The Science of
Learning and the Art of Teaching* (Skinner, 1954), were published. Programmed
instruction incorporated the management of *both* antecedents and consequences
of behavior, according to guidelines that had been found to promote learning
effectively. Immediate feedback was used to reinforce each correct student response.

Antecedents were managed through the presentation of small bits of instructional stimuli and contained sufficient prompts to maximize the likelihood that the student would provide the correct answer. Prompts were faded until correct answers were apt to be forthcoming in the absence of any extraneous prompts or until they were under control of the *critical stimuli*.

An empirical approach to the development of programmed instruction was advocated, based on the assumption that "the student is always right." If errors were committed or recently acquired responses lost, it was assumed to be the fault of the program, not the student. Holland and Skinner's *The Analysis of Behavior* (1961) was developed according to the guideline that essentially all students who studied the text should respond correctly to almost every item. Many modifications of the materials were conducted until that goal was achieved.

The early to mid-sixties witnessed a flurry of research on programmed instruction. Investigated were such questions as the necessity for overt student responding (Stolorow & Walker, 1962) and other relevant variables (see, for example, Anderson, Faust, Roderick, Cunningham, & Andre, 1969). Many empirically based instructional programs were designed and much consideration given to antecedent stimuli. But many other programs were not submitted to such rigorous testing. Unfortunately, many of those untested programs failed to deliver the promise of superior instruction, so the publication wave of programmed instructional packages soon crested and began to ebb.

Filling the widening gap left by the waning of programmed instruction, another instructional technology, incorporating many of the same principles of behavior as programmed instruction, the personalized system of instruction (PSI) was advocated by Fred Keller (1968). This system is analagous in many ways to programmed instruction. However, the bits of information presented to students are usually selected from already available texts, supplemented by study questions. Usually, following the preparation of answers to a number of study questions, students take a quiz covering the concepts contained in the unit. Afterward, performance is reinforced via immediate feedback.

Research in PSI has tended to focus on such technical aspects as the use of study questions and/or objectives (though *not* necessarily the quality of questions or objectives), the inclusion of mastery criteria, the role of proctors, and incentives for student pacing. Not much emphasis, however, has been placed on methods for arranging the antecedent stimuli for dealing with higher-level instructional objectives (Hursh, 1976).

Some of the research conducted at the University of Massachusetts illustrates the emphasis on consequences and upon the technical operation of the system: Sulzer-Azaroff, Johnson, Dean, and Freyman (1977) studied methods for promoting accuracy of quiz scoring, whereas a series of studies by Johnson and Sulzer-Azaroff investigated various aspects of the proctoring component. For instance, one study examined how the learning of currently enrolled students would be affected by their serving as proctors (Johnson, Sulzer-Azaroff, & Maass, 1976). It was found that proctoring promoted higher final examination performance on related material.

Why behavioral antecedents have tended to be neglected in favor of consequences in the classroom management literature is difficult to explain. Perhaps the field was reacting against "traditional" education methods, with its emphasis on texts, lectures, rules, and instructions. Or perhaps it was a fascination with the operant conditioner's discovery of the critical necessary importance of consequential events. Maybe it was an outgrowth of some of the early behavior modification studies of seriously deviant child behavior: such as severe tantrums (Williams, 1959) or the extremely maladaptive behaviors of autistic children (Wolf et al., 1964). Perhaps studies such as Madsen et al.'s (1968) that showed that rules alone, in the absence of behavioral consequences, accomplished little, although many other researchers showed that the management of reinforcing or aversive consequences alone could accomplish a great deal. At any rate, there have been proportionally few studies in the behavior modification journals, on curriculum designed according to behavioral principles (although literally hundreds of behaviorally based curriculum items now exist) on the nature of instructions, conditions of modeling, and ecological variables.

However, perhaps as a function of a shift toward the targeting of more complex educational behaviors, such as academic, social, and self-enhancement skills, there seems to be a trend back toward the study of antecedent stimuli and their place as setting events. Wheeler & Wislocki (1977) noted the effect that the presence of an attendant had on peer conversation by retarded women. Trace, Cuvo, and Criswell (1977) designed and evaluated a program to teach coin equivalence to mentally retarded students. Gladstone and Spencer (1977) studied the effects of modeling on the use of praise by counselors working with the retarded. Risley and his colleagues have studied a number of ecological variables (Krantz & Risley, 1977).

A series of investigations conducted by Ellen P. Reese of Mt. Holyoke College and her students is also illustrative of this trend toward a heavier focus on antecedents in the antecedent–response–consequence contingency. The objective has been to identify procedures for teaching students with serious developmental delays to read. A recent study (Weidenman, Reese, & Sulzer-Azaroff, 1977) explored some of the factors that might affect the acquisition and transfer of reading skills through the fading-in of incorrect distractors. Figure 3.12 displays some of those results.

The data obtained suggest that a combination method of training using fading and nonfading (trial-and-error) procedure promotes better retention and transfer than either procedure alone.

Increasingly more attention is being given to the antecedent stimuli in PSI, particularly to designing instructional materials: study questions, objectives, and assignments that should promote higher-level performance. One example is a

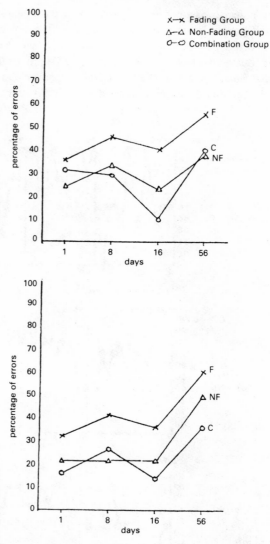

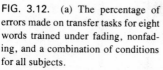

FIG. 3.12.   (a) The percentage of errors made on transfer tasks for eight words trained under fading, nonfading, and a combination of conditions for all subjects.

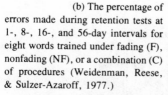

(b) The percentage of errors made during retention tests at 1-, 8-, 16-, and 56-day intervals for eight words trained under fading (F), nonfading (NF), or a combination (C) of procedures (Weidenman, Reese, & Sulzer-Azaroff, 1977.)

field activities manual designed by Sulzer-Azaroff, Brewer, & Ford (1978). The manual is designed to promote application, problem solving, and other higher-level skills as students develop their own sample instructional materials. *The PSI Guide* (Johnson, Chase, & Maass, 1977) and *Quizzes* (Maass & Sulzer-Azaroff, 1977) that accompany our recent text, *Applying Behavior Analysis Procedures with Children and Youth* (Sulzer-Azaroff & Mayer, 1977) are also designed with the intention of assisting students to be more able to apply their knowledge to the solution of novel problems. One has seen a similar focus on the antecedent-response–consequence combination in the management of classroom problem and nonacademic skill behaviors also. The antecedent stimuli, such as those involved in physical guidance, are faded and replaced by instructions in the graduated guidance (Foxx & Azrin, 1972) procedure. Thomas, Lukeris, Palmer, and Sulzer-Azaroff (1977) used graduated guidance to teach self-help skills to several young women in a residential facility for the retarded (See Fig. 8.13).

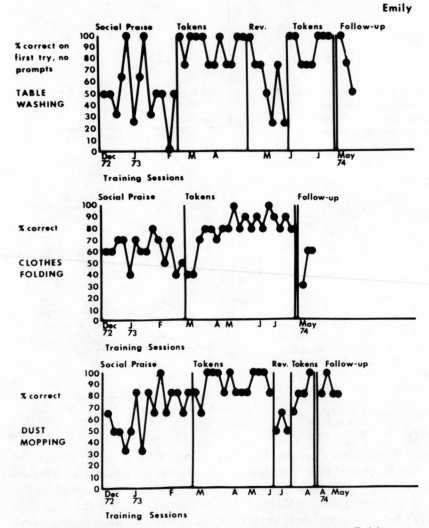

FIG. 3.13.   Percentage of correct units completed without any prompts. Training of skill was accomplished prior to December 1972. Data show the function of social praise or tokens exchangeable for edible and tangible backup rewards. Praise alone was the consequence during follow-up (Thomas et al., 1977.)

It is anticipated that as more complex instructional objectives are conceived, the reemphasis on combining antecedents, responses, and consequences should continue.

THE NATURE OF CONSEQUENCES

With such a heavy emphasis placed on the consequences of behavior, much attention has focused upon the specific nature of the consequential event to be delivered. Aside from the work on programmed and personalized instruction, early educational applications of behavior modification principles, as mentioned previously, involved students with severe deficits or maladaptive behaviors. Again, related to the laboratory research of the operant conditioners, food reinforcers (Lovaas, Freitag, Kinder, Rubenstein, Schaefer, & Simmons, 1966; Wolf et al., 1964) and aversive stimuli such as shock were used. Such contingencies were very effective with children with severe problems. However, as target behaviors have shifted toward the development of more adaptive academic and social and personal skills, and as student populations served have broader adaptive repertoires and are responsive to "conditioned" consequential events such as attention, praise, privileges, and preferred activities, more "natural" consequences are being utilized. Hopkins, Schutte, and Garton (1971) used contingent access to a playroom as a reinforcer for completion of assignments, whereas Campbell and Sulzer (1971) provided tokens for task accomplishment—to be exchanged for preferred activities and privileges natural to the school situation.

A concern expressed by some educators is that any use of arbitrary reinforcers as a consequence of behaviors that are "intrinsically reinforcing" (i.e., that are emitted at a high rate in the absence of any prominent reinforcement contingency) might actually do more harm than good (Green & Lepper, 1974). Students might become dependent on "extrinsic reinforcers," refusing to emit the behavior once those reinforcers are withdrawn. Though the question remains unresolved, one study conducted by Ramey and Sulzer-Azaroff (1977) showed that when performance of either an unpreferred *or* a preferred arithmetic assignment was reinforced with tokens exchangeable for small tangibles, the student selected to work on that type of assignment later in the day, though no reinforcer would be delivered at that time (see Fig. 3.14). Nevertheless, probably most behavior modifiers working in educational settings would not design a system for intrusively rewarding behaviors that are regularly emitted at high rates without programmed reinforcement.

In 1965, Skinner discussed *Why Teachers Fail* (Skinner, 1965). One of the points he made was that schools have become excessively punitive, and punishment results in various undesirable side effects. Azrin and Holz (1966) have also shown, in a series of laboratory studies, that punishment tends to promote aggression and withdrawal. Consequently, behavior modifiers working in educa-

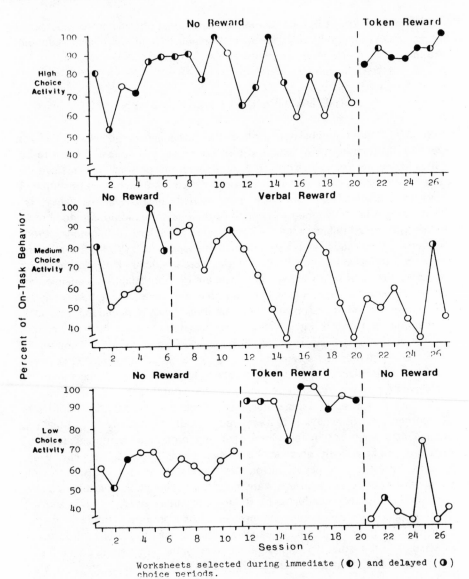

Worksheets selected during immediate (◑) and delayed (◐) choice periods.

FIG. 3.14.   Percentage of on-task behavior during high, medium, and low choice arithmetic activities. Circles darkened on the left side indicate that the particular activity was selected by the student for an additional work period immediately following the experimental session, in the presence of the experimenter but with no contingent praise or token rewards. Circles darkened on the right side indicate that the particular activity was selected by the student for an additional work period later on, in the classroom setting when the experimenter was not present nor were contingent rewards presented. It was only possible to select one activity during those two choice periods (Ramey & Sulzer-Azaroff, 1977.)

tional settings have tended to concentrate on positive rather than negative contingencies. As we have seen in the examples offered, school-related behaviors are reinforced more often than punished. Adaptive skills are reinforced with points, privileges and preferred activities. Minor maladaptive behaviors are often ignored, whereas adaptive alternative behaviors are reinforced, again usually positively. Occasionally, seriously disruptive behaviors are treated with response cost, timeout, (Burchard & Barerra, 1972), overcorrection, (Epstein, Doke, Sajwaj, Sorrell, & Rimmer, 1974; Besalel-Azrin, Azrin, & Armstrong, 1977) or punishment (Peterson and Peterson, 1977; Rusch, Close, Hops, & Agosta, 1976). However, almost always, some desirable alternative behaviors are simultaneously targeted for reinforcement. When Iwata and Bailey (1974) compared reinforcement and response cost effects on social and academic student behaviors, they found no differences. However, the reward condition led to more teacher approval comments, and the authors concluded that the positive approach was preferable. It is likely, however, that a combination of both positive and negative consequences, as Azrin and Holz (1966) found in the laboratory, best promotes the rapid reduction of the maladaptive response. Thus, positive contingencies probably will continue to be emphasized in educational applications of behavior modification.

REINFORCING THE BEHAVIOR OF INDIVIDUALS AND OF GROUPS

One trend that has characterized a segment of the research in classroom applications has been to arrange consequences contingent upon the behavior of a group of students. Although interventions are still often directed at individual students, particularly when their behavior is very atypical in comparison with their classmates, group contingency programs have flourished (Barrish, Saunders, & Wolf, 1969; Bushell, Wrobel, & Michaelis, 1968; Harris & Sherman, 1973; Hamblin et al., 1974; Switzer, Deal, & Bailey, 1977). Group contingencies are particularly appropriate to classrooms, because classes are composed of groups of students, and implementing a program with a group is natural and practical. Although in one instance (Axelrod, 1973) group contingencies have generated threats from fellow students, in most cases they are a powerful means for achieving change and no negative side effects are found (Switzer et al., 1977).

The positive results of group contingencies have been replicated in several of our recent studies (Elam & Sulzer, 1972; Frankowsky & Sulzer-Azaroff, 1978; Taylor & Sulzer, 1972; Ulman & Sulzer-Azaroff, 1975). In Ulman and Sulzer-Azaroff (1975) we found that group contingencies were not quite so effective as individual contingencies in promoting accuracy of arithmetic performance. However, the group contingencies resulted in higher percentages correct than no reinforcement (see Fig. 3.15). The Frankowsky and Sulzer-Azaroff

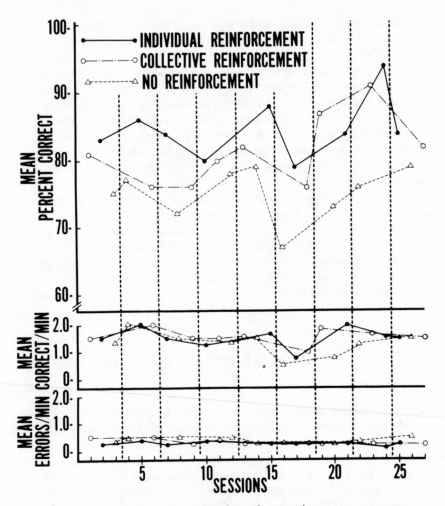

FIG. 3.15.   Mean percentage correct and rate of errors and correct responses per minute on arithmetic assignments by a group of institutionalized retarded students as a function of three conditions: Individual reinforcement (money earned by individuals for each item answered correctly), collective reinforcement (money earned by individuals pooled and distributed in equal amounts to all class members), and no reinforcement (no money earned). Type and difficulty of problems remained constant during sessions enclosed by adjacent dashed vertical lines (Ulman & Sulzer-Azaroff, 1975.)

study looked at collatoral side effects of a group contingency and found that the contingency was paired with more positive social interactions among the group members than when they worked on an individual contingency (see Fig. 3.16).

It appears that group contingencies will continue to be used and studied in classroom settings. Methods for promoting positive and reducing negative side effects should continue to be explored.

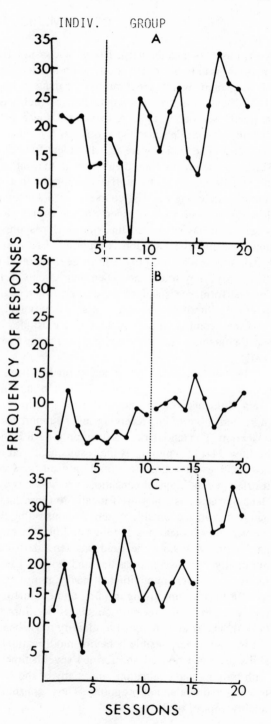

FIG. 3.16.   Mean frequency of positive verbal behaviors during individual and group task plus reward. During individual condition, students worked alone and earned tokens exchangeable for snacks and other backup rewards for themselves. During group condition, groups of two or three students worked on a group task and collected exchangeable tokens that were evenly divided among the group members (Frankowsky & Sulzer-Azaroff, 1978.)

CONSUMERISM

As in business and industry, issues of consumerism have begun to assume an important role in behavior modification in education. Consumerism has affected the manner in which programs are evaluated. For instance, Braukmann et al. (1975) have solicited the satisfaction of their clients and others directly and indirectly served by their Achievement Place program. Willner, Braukmann, Kirigin, Fixsen, Phillips, and Wolf (1977) used client satisfaction information to train staff. The clients were asked to identify staff behaviors that they preferred. The social behaviors were then taught to the staff and the clients rated the quality of interactions with the staff more highly than previously. In many college courses, including our PSI courses, it has become standard practice to ask students to evaluate various aspects of the course (Johnson et al., 1976). Informal observation has suggested that the more responsive we are to student suggestions, the more satisfaction is reported. Brownell, Colletti, Ersner-Hershfield, Hershfield, & Wilson (1977) have demonstrated the wisdom of such input. In their study, they found that when their clients were involved in the selection of their performance standards, they performed better than when standards were externally imposed. In order to assess any potential negative side effects of the "extrinsic reinforcement" system used in Ramey and Sulzer-Azaroff (1977), we asked students to rate their preference for the task so reinforced. (They liked it best!)

The consumer movement has probably been responsible for many of the educationally related legislative changes in the United States within the past few years. Students with special needs, and their parents, have been demanding and, more and more often, receiving legal support for their free, appropriate public education. The landmark, "Education for All Handicapped Children Act," Public Law 94-142, epitomizes the results achieved by such consumer efforts. The law includes provisions that imply a need for accountability, least aversive and restrictive conditions of education, and services by competent service providers. Behavior analysis lends itself ideally to those requirements, because by its very nature it is an accountable system demonstrating the functional relations between the variables it measures and the conditions managed. The foregoing discussion has emphasized how the field has tended to heavily rely upon positive and minimally intrusive approaches and how it has been responsive to consumer ratings. However, in addition, it has begun to attempt to improve the quality of its offerings by improving training and evaluation of its practitioners. An illustrative effort is one recently conducted by Sulzer-Azaroff, Thaw, and Thomas (1975). The study attempted to identify those behavioral competencies that were apt to lead to responsible behavior modification practice. The extensive list of skills has been revised and refined several times by various groups concerned with training and evaluation, and many of the skills are being incorporated into training and evaluation programs. Thus, consumerism has had its effect on the quality control of the field.

SUMMARY

The foregoing discussion has considered a sampling of issues and trends that have evolved as behavior modification of the classroom has developed as a field. We have seen the emergence of issues about selection of target behaviors, who should be considered the client to be served, how much emphasis should be placed on antecedent and how much on consequential contingencies, whether consequences should be negative or positive, whether they should be managed with individuals or groups, and what influence the consumerism movement may be having. A consideration of those issues by members of the field has led to a number of trends: toward the selection of more constructive target behaviors, toward a broader conception of the client role, toward a heavy emphasis on consequential contingencies and a reemerging emphasis on managed and nonpersonal ecological antecedents, toward a preference for positive rather than negative consequences, toward group contingency arrangements, and lastly toward an increasing responsiveness to the concerns of consumers. These trends support a conclusion that the field of behavior modification in the classroom is flexible and responsive, continually striving for a balance among effectiveness, efficiency, and an appreciation for human rights and humanistic values.

REFERENCES

Anderson, R. C., Faust, G. W., Roderick, M. C., Cunningham, D. J., & Andre, R. (Eds.), *Current Research on Instruction*. Englewood Cliffs, N.J.: Prentice-Hall, 1969.

Axelrod, S. Comparison of individual and group contingencies in two special classes. *Behavior Therapy*, 1973, *4*, 83-90.

Ayllon, T. Intensive treatment of psychotic behavior by stimulus satiation and food reinforcement. *Behavior Research & Therapy*, 1963, *1*, 53-61.

Ayllon, T., & Roberts, M. D. Eliminating discipline problems by strengthening academic performance. *Journal of Applied Behavior Analysis*, 1974, *7*, 73-81.

Azrin, N. H., & Holz, W. C. Punishment. In W. A. Honig (Ed.), *Operant Behavior: Areas of Research and Application*. New York: Appleton, 1966, 380-447.

Barrish, H. H., Saunders, M., & Wolf, M. M. Good behavior game: Effects of individual contingencies for group consequences on disruptive behavior in a classroom. *Journal of Applied Behavior Analysis*, 1969, *2*, 119-124.

Besalel-Azrin, V., Azrin, N. H., & Armstrong, P. M. The student oriented classroom: A method of improving student conduct and satisfaction. *Behavior Therapy*, 1977, *8*, 193-204.

Birnbrauer, J. S., Wolf, M. M., Kidder, J. D., & Tague, C. E. Classroom behavior of retarded pupils with token reinforcement. *Journal of Experimental Child Psychology*, 1965, *2*, 219-235.

Braukmann, C. J., Fixsen, D. L., Kirigin, K. A., Phillips, E. A., Phillips, E. L., & Wolf, M. M. Achievement place: The training and certification of teaching parents. In W. S. Wood (Ed.), *Issues in evaluating behavior modification*. Champaign, Ill.: Research Press, 1975, 131-152.

Brigham, T. A., & Sherman, J. A. An experimental analysis of verbal imitation in preschool children. *Journal of Applied Behavior Analysis*, 1968, *1*, 151-158.

Brownell, K. D., Colletti, G., Ersner-Hershfield, R., Hershfield, S. M., & Wilson, G. T. Self-control in school children: Stringency and leniency in self-determined and externally imposed performance standards. *Behavior Therapy*, 1977, *8*, 442-455.

Budd, K. S., Green, D. R., & Baer, D. M. An analysis of multiple misplaced parental social contingencies. *Journal of Applied Behavior Analysis,* 1976, *9,* 459–470.

Buell, J., Stoddard, P., Harris, F. R., & Baer, D. M. Collateral social development accompanying reinforcement of outdoor play in a preschool child. *Journal of Applied Behavior Analysis,* 1968, *1,* 167–173.

Burchard, J. D., & Barrera, F. An analysis of timeout and response cost in a programmed environment. *Journal of Applied Behavior Analysis,* 1972, *5,* 271–282.

Bushell, D., Jr., Wrobel, P. A., & Michaelis, M. L. Applying "group" contingencies to the classroom study behavior of preschool children. *Journal of Applied Behavior Analysis,* 1968, *1,* 55–61.

Campbell, A., & Sulzer, B. *Motivating educable mentally handicapped students towards reading and spelling achievement using naturally available reinforcers in the classroom setting.* Paper presented at the meeting of the American Educational Research Association, New York, 1971.

Cossairt, A., Hall, R. V., & Hopkins, B. L. The effects of experimenter's instructions, feedback, and praise on teacher praise and student attending behavior. *Journal of Applied Behavior Analysis,* 1973, *6,* 89–100.

Elam, D., & Sulzer-Azaroff, B. *Group versus individual reinforcement in modifying problem behaviors in a trainable, mentally handicapped classroom.* Unpublished paper, Southern Illinois University, Carbondale, Ill., 1972.

Englehardt, L., Sulzer, B., & Altekruse, M. The counselor as a consultant in eliminating out-of-seat behavior. *Elementary School Guidance & Counseling,* 1971, *5,* 196–204.

Epstein, L. H., Doke, L. A., Sajway, T. E., Sorrell, S., & Rimmer, B. Generality and side effects of overcorrection. *Journal of Applied Behavior Analysis,* 1974, *7,* 385–390.

Fauke, J., Burnett, J., Powers, M. A., & Sulzer-Azaroff, B. Improvement of handwriting and letter-recognition skills: A behavior modification procedure. *Journal of Learning Disabilities,* 1973, *6,* 25–29.

Ferritor, D. E., Buckholdt, D., Hamblin, R. L., & Smith, L. The non-effects of contingent reinforcement for attending behavior on work accomplished. *Journal of Applied Behavior Analysis,* 1972, *5,* 7–17.

Foxx, R. M., & Azrin, N. H. Restitution: A method of eliminating aggressive-disruptive behavior of retarded and brain-damaged patients. *Behaviour Research & Therapy,* 1972, 15–27.

Frankowsky, R. J., & Sulzer-Azaroff, B. Individual and group contingencies and collatoral social behaviors. *Behavior Therapy,* 1978, *9,* 313–327.

Gladstone, B. W., & Spencer, C. J. The effects of modeling on the contingent praise of mental retardation counselors. *Journal of Applied Behavior Analysis,* 1977, *10,* 75–84.

Green, D., & Lepper, M. R. Intrinsic motivation: How to turn play into work. *Psychology Today,* 1974, *8,* 49–54.

Hamblin, R. L., Hathaway, C., & Wodarski, J. Group contingencies, peer tutoring, and accelerating academic achievement. In R. Ulrich, T. Stacknik, & J. Mabry (Eds.), *Control of Human Behavior: Behavior modification in education,* Glenview, Ill.: Scott Foresman, 1974, 333–340.

Harris, V. W., & Sherman, J. A. Use and analysis of the "good behavior game" to reduce disruptive classroom behavior. *Journal of Applied Behavior Analysis,* 1973, *6,* 405–417.

Holden, B., & Sulzer-Azaroff, B. Schedules of follow-up and their effect upon the maintenance of a perscriptive teaching program. In G. Semb (Ed.), *Behavior Analysis in Education, 1972.* Lawrence, Kansas: University of Kansas, Follow-Through, Department of Human Development, 1972, 262–277.

Holland, J. G., & Skinner, B. F. *The analysis of behavior.* New York: McGraw Hill, 1961.

Hopkins, B. L., Schutte, R. C., & Garton, K. L. The effects of access to a playroom on the rate and quality of printing and writing on first- and second-grade students. *Journal of Applied Behavior Analysis,* 1971, *4,* 77–87.

Hunt, G. M., & Azrin, N. H. A community reinforcement approach to alcoholism. *Behaviour Research & Therapy,* 1973, *11,* 91–104.

Hunt, S., & Sulzer-Azaroff, B. *The effect of verbal and graphic feedback on parent consistence in running homework sessions with their children.* Paper presented at the meeting of the American Psychological Association, New Orleans, 1974.

Hursh, D. E. Personalized systems of instruction: What do the data indicate? *Journal of Personalized Instruction,* 1976, *1,* 91–105.

Iwata, B. A., & Bailey, J. S. Reward vs. cost token systems: An analysis of the effects on students and teachers. *Journal of Applied Behavior Analysis,* 1974, *7,* 567–576.

Johnson, K. R., Chase, P. N., & Maass, C. A. *Personalized system of instruction guide for Sulzer-Azaroff/Mayer's applying behavior analysis procedures with children and youth.* New York: Holt, Rinehart & Winston, 1977.

Johnson, K. R., & Sulzer-Azaroff, B. *An experimental analysis of proctor-prompting behavior in a personalized instruction course. Journal of Personalized Instruction,* 1978, *3,* 122–130.

Johnson, K. R., Sulzer-Azaroff, B., & Maass, C. A. The effects of internal proctoring upon examination performance in a personalized instruction course. *Journal of Personalized Instruction,* 1976, *1,* 113–117.

Johnson, M., & Bailey, J. S. Cross-age tutoring: Fifth graders as arithmetic tutors for kindergarten children. *Journal of Applied Behavior Analysis,* 1974, *7,* 223–232.

Keller, F. S. Goodbye teacher . . . *Journal of Applied Behavior Analysis,* 1968, *1,* 79–89.

Krantz, P. G., & Risley, T. R. Behavioral ecology in the classroom. In K. D. O'Leary & S. G. O'Leary (Eds.), *Classroom management.* New York: Pergamon Press, 1977, 349–366.

Lovaas, O. I., Freitag, G., Kinder, M. I., Rubenstein, B. D., Schaeffer, B., & Simmons, J. Q. Establishment of social reinforcers in two schizophrenic children on the basis of food. *Journal of Experimental Child Psychology,* 1966, *4,* 109–125.

Maass, C. A., & Sulzer-Azaroff, B. *Evaluating mastery of applying behavior analysis procedures with children and youth.* New York: Holt, Rinehart & Winston, 1977.

Madsen, C., Jr., Becker, W. C., & Thomas, D. R. Rules, praise and ignoring: Elements of elementary classroom control. *Journal of Applied Behavior Analysis,* 1968, *1,* 139–150.

O'Leary, K. D., Kaufman, K. F., Kass, R. E., & Drabman, R. S. The effects of loud and soft reprimands on the behavior of disruptive students. *Exceptional Children,* 1970, *37,* 145–155.

Panyan, M., Boozer, H., & Morris, N. Feedback to attendants as a reinforcer for applying operant techniques. *Journal of Applied Behavior Analysis,* 1970, *3,* 1–4.

Peterson, R. F., & Peterson, L. W. Hydropsychotherapy: Water as a punishing stimulus in the treatment of a problem parent-child relationship. In B. C. Etzel, J. M. LeBlanc, & D. M. Baer (Eds.), *New developments in behavioral research.* Hillsdale, N.J.: Lawrence Erlbaum Associates, 1977, 247–256.

Phillips, E. L., Phillips, E. A., Wolf, M. M., & Fixsen, D. L. Achievement place: Development of the elected manager system. *Journal of Applied Behavior Analysis,* 1973, *6,* 541–561.

Ramey, G., & Sulzer-Azaroff, B. *Effects of extrinsic rewards on the subsequent choice behavior of academically delayed children.* Paper presented at the meeting of the *American Educational Research Association,* New York, 1977.

Rusch, F., Close, D., Hops, H., & Agosta, J. Overcorrection: Generalization and maintenance. *Journal of Applied Behavior Analysis,* 1976, *9,* 498.

Salzberg, B. H., Wheeler, A. J., Devar, L. T., & Hopkins, B. L. The effect of intermittent feedback and intermittent contingent access to play on printing of kindergarten children. *Journal of Applied Behavior Analysis,* 1971, *4,* 163–171.

Schram, H., & Sulzer-Azaroff, B. *A "normal" peer as a language tutor for a language-delayed child.* Unpublished paper, Southern Illinois University, Carbondale, Ill., 1972.

Skinner, B. F. The science of learning and the art of teaching. *Harvard Educational Review,* 1954, *24,* 86–97.

Skinner, B. F. Why teachers fail. *The Saturday Review,* 1965.

Sloat, K. C. M., Tharp, R. G., & Gallimore, R. The incremental effectiveness of classroom-based teacher-training techniques. *Behavior Therapy,* 1977, *8,* 810–818.

Solomon, R. W., & Wahler, R. G. Peer reinforcement control of classroom problem behavior. *Journal of Applied Behavior Analysis*, 1973, *6*, 49–56.

Souweine, J., Sulzer-Azaroff, B., & Fredrickson, R. *Maintaining increased teacher praise through principal attention.* Paper presented at the meeting of the Association for Advancement of Behavior Therapy, Atlanta, 1977.

Staats, A., Staats, C. K., Schutz, R. E., & Wolf, M. M. The conditioning of reading responses utilizing "extrinsic" reinforcers. *Journal of the Experimental Analysis of Behavior*, 1962, *5*, 33–40.

Stolurow, L. M., & Walker, C. C. A comparison of overt and covert responses in programmed learning. *Journal of Educational Research*, 1962, *55*, 421–429.

Sulzer-Azaroff, B., Brewer, J., & Ford, L. *Making educational psychology work.* Santa Monica, Calif.: Goodyear Press (in press), 1978.

Sulzer, B., Hunt, S., Ashby, E., Koniarski, C., & Krams, M. Increasing rate and percentage correct in reading and spelling in a 5th-grade public school class of slow readers by means of a token system. In E. Ramp & B. L. Hopkins (Eds.), *A new direction for education.* Follow Through Program: University of Kansas, Lawrence, Kan., Department of Human Development, 1971, 5–28.

Sulzer-Azaroff, B., Hunt, S., & Loving, A. *Increasing rate and accuracy of academic performance through the application of naturally available reinforcers.* Paper presented at the meeting of the National Educational Research Association. Chicago, 1972.

Sulzer-Azaroff, B., Johnson, K., Dean, M., & Freyman, D. Experimental analysis of proctor quiz-scoring accuracy in PSI courses. *Journal of Personalized Instruction*, 1977, *2*, 143–149.

Sulzer-Azaroff, B., & Mayer, G. R. *Applying behavior analysis procedures with children and youth.* New York: Holt, Rinehart & Winston, 1977.

Sulzer-Azaroff, B., Thaw, J., & Thomas, C. Behavioral competencies for the evaluation of behavior modifiers. In W. S. Wood (Ed.), *Issues in evaluating behavior modification.* Champaign, Ill.: Research Press, 1975.

Switzer, E. B., Deal, T., & Bailey, J. S. The reduction of stealing in second-graders using a group contingency. *Journal of Applied Behavior Analysis*, 1977, *10*, 267–272.

Taylor, L. K., & Sulzer, B. *The effects of group and individual contingencies on resting behavior.* Unpublished paper, Southern Illinois University, Carbondale, Ill., 1972.

Thaw, J., Palmer, M. E., & Sulzer-Azaroff, B. *The middle managers and program development: A longitudinal approach to training institutional supervisory personnel.* Paper presented at the meeting of the American Association of Mental Deficiency, New Orleans, 1977.

Thomas, C. M., Lukeris, S. E., Palmer, M., & Sulzer-Azaroff, B. Teaching daily self-help skills for long-term maintenance. In B. C. Etzel, J. M. LeBlanc, & D. M. Baer (Eds.), *New developments in behavioral research.* Hillsdale, N.J.: Lawrence Erlbaum Assoc., 1977.

Thomas, D. R., Becker, W. C., & Armstrong, M. Production and elimination of disruptive classroom behavior by systematically varying teacher's behavior. *Journal of Applied Behavior Analysis*, 1968, *1*, 35–45.

Thoresen, C. E. Behavioral humanism. In C. E. Thoresen (Ed.), *Behavior modification in education: The seventy-second yearbook of the national society for the study of education.* Chicago: University of Chicago Press, 1973, 385–421.

Trace, M. W., Cuvo, A. J., & Criswell, J. L. Teaching coin equivalence to the mentally retarded. *Journal of Applied Behavior Analysis*, 1977, *10*, 85–92.

Twardosz, S., Cataldo, M. F., & Risley, T. R. Open environment design for infant and toddler day care. *Journal of Applied Behavior Analysis*, 1974, *7*, 529–546.

Tyler, V. O., & Brown, G. D. The use of swift, brief isolation as a group control device for institutionalized delinquents. *Behaviour Research & Therapy*, 1967, *5*, 1–9.

Ullman, L. P., & Krasner, L. (Eds.). Case studies in behavior modification. New York: Holt, Rinehart & Winston, 1965.

Ulman, J. D., & Sulzer-Azaroff, B. Multielement baseline design in educational research. In E. Ramp & G. Semb (Eds.), *Behavior analysis: Areas of research and application*. Englewood Cliffs, N.J.: Prentice Hall, 1975, 377–391.

Walker, H. M., Hops, H., & Johnson, S. M. Generalization and maintenance of classroom treatment effects. *Behavior Therapy*, 1975, *6*, 188–200.

Weaver, F. H., & Miller, L. K. The effects of a proctor training package on university students' proctoring behaviors in a personalized system of instruction setting. In J. M. Johnston (Ed.), *Behavior research and technology in higher education*. Springfield, Ill.: Charles C. Thomas, 1975.

Weidenman, L., Reese, E. P., & Sulzer-Azaroff, B. *The effects of fading, nonfading, and a combination of procedures on the training of word recognition in retarded individuals*. Paper presented at the meeting of the American Association of Mental Deficiency, Region X, Pittsfield, Mass., October 1977.

Wheeler, A. J., & Sulzer, B. Operant training and generalization of a verbal response form in a speech-deficient child. *Journal of Applied Behavior Analysis*, 1970, *3*, 139–147.

Wheeler, A. J., & Wislocki, E. B. Stimulus factors affecting peer conversation among institutionalized retarded women. *Journal of Applied Behavior Analysis*, 1977, *10*, 283–288.

Whitley, A. D., & Sulzer, B. Assisting a fourth-grade teacher to reduce a student's disruptive classroom behaviors through behavioral consulting. *The Personnel & Guidance Journal*, 1970, *48*, 836–841.

Williams, C. D. The elimination of tantrum behavior by an extinction procedure. *Journal of Abnormal and Social Psychology*, 1959, *59*, 269.

Willner, A. G., Braukmann, C. J., Kirigin, K. A., Fixsen, D. L., Phillips, E. L., & Wolf, M. M. The training and validation of youth-preferred social behaviors of child-care personnel. *Journal of Applied Behavior Analysis*, 1977, *10*, 219–230.

Winett, R. A., & Winkler, R. C. Current behavior modification in the classroom: Be still, be quiet, be docile. *Journal of Applied Behavior Analysis*, 1972, *5*, 499–504.

Wolf, M. M., Giles, D. K., & Hall, R. V. Experiments with token reinforcement in a remedial classroom. *Behaviour Research & Therapy*, 1968, *6*, 305–312.

Wolf, M. M., Risley, T. R., & Mees, H. L. Application of operant conditioning procedures to the behavior problems of an autistic child. *Behaviour Research & Therapy*, 1964, *1*, 305–312.

APPLICATION OF BEHAVIOR ANALYSIS TO EXCEPTIONAL CHILDREN AND ADULTS

4

Behavioral Teaching of Young Handicapped Children: Problems of Application and Implementation[1]

Sidney W. Bijou
The University of Arizona

INTRODUCTION

Teachers and administrators of handicapped young children first turned to behaviorally trained psychologists and educators for assistance in treating children with severe problems such as self-destructive behavior, hyperactivity, persistent tantrum behavior, destructive aggression, and extreme withdrawal. Because behavioral treatment programs are designed not only to reduce or eliminate problem behaviors but also to establish acceptable forms of behavior, special educators gradually became aware that behavior principles could also be applied to habilitate handicapped children (i.e., the principles could be used to teach body management, gross and fine motor coordination, self-care behavior, language skills, appropriate social behavior, and preacademic skills and knowledge). At present, there are, throughout the United States, numerous special classes that incorporate many features of behavioral teaching, even though they may not be committed to a total behavioral approach.

One such feature in evidence is the assessment of the skills and knowledge (competencies) by means of a developmental chart or a criterion referenced inventory (Glaser, 1971). This relatively new practice enables the teacher to actualize the long recognized dictum that good teaching begins "at the edge" of a child's competencies. In other words, the child's performance on a criterion referenced test provides the teacher with definite starting points for the teaching

[1]Based on papers presented at the VIII International Symposium on Behavior Modification, Caracas, Venezuela, February, 1978, and the Fourth Annual convention of the Association of Behavior Analysis, Chicago, Ill., May, 1978.

of skills and knowledge. The use of a criterion referenced inventory for curriculum planning also suggests to the teacher that her daily lesson plans are most effective when they are systematized and organized as interrelated goal-oriented teaching programs. In addition, the specificity of a criterion referenced inventory and its relationship to the activities of daily living remind the teacher that an educational goal is meaningful only when it is stated in observable terms.

A second behavioral feature that has crept into instructional practices is reinforcement. Reinforcing correct responses is viewed by too many teachers as *the main* characteristic of behavioral teaching, and for them a behavioral teacher is one who consistently provides contingent M and M's, sugar-coated cereal, or comments such as "That's good," or "Good work." Obviously this is an extremely limited concept of the behavioral approach.

The third behavioral feature that one now finds in teaching the young exceptional child is that the teacher is keeping records that monitor a child's performance on instructional program. This practice is a sharp contrast to keeping the kind of records that try to estimate whether a child is working above or below his intellectual capacity.

These three changes in teaching practices—assessment through criterion referenced tests, reinforcement, and monitoring progress on instructional programs—have brought about, slowly but surely, changes in the teacher's attitudes toward the learning potentiality of the handicapped child. The traditional practice of judging the learning potential of a child by his MA, IQ, or score on a "readiness" test has led to a pessimism on the teacher's part ("He doesn't have very much to work with, and there isn't much I can do about it."). Scores on intelligence, school achievement, and "readiness" tests indicate something about a child's past rate of learning and suggest his probable future rate of learning under the conditions of an *unchanged environment.* If, however, a special class provides a vastly improved academic environment, as it should, the child's future rate of learning cannot be adequately estimated from psychometric test scores. The best indicator of a child's learning rate in an enriched learning environment is most likely to be his performance on a sample instructional program which begins at his or her demonstrated level of competence and which uses meaningful contingencies. This "trying and seeing" method of estimating a child's learning rate usually reveals that a handicapped child can perform better than his psychometric test scores indicate and reiterates a well-known fact: The rate of learning a task (and it varies for different tasks) is related to the conditions of learning—those antecedent to a response, consequent to a response, and concurrent with a response—rather than to an intelligence or mental age test score.

The inclusion of behavioral techniques in the teaching of handicapped children and the accompanying positive changes in teacher's attitude toward the children's learning potential are significant advances, but they are minuscule compared to what they could be if more principles of behavior analysis were applied in their full and proper sense. Hence, much of current behavioral teaching provides the young handicapped child with a far less than optimum educational environment, mainly because behavioral principles are often partially, incompletely, and inappropriately applied.

Also contributing to the inadequacy of the educational environment is the limited development of educational tools such as workable formats for teacher, paraprofessional, and parent training.

This chapter discusses both problems of applications and of technological insufficiencies.

PROBLEMS ASSOCIATED WITH INCOMPLETE AND INAPPROPRIATE APPLICATIONS

Instances of incomplete and inappropriate application of behavioral principles to teaching are discussed in terms of (1) what a teacher does *antecedent* to a child's response, such as giving instructions, following a programmed sequence, and facilitating a correct response; and (2) what she does *consequent* to the response, such as reinforcing a correct response and disconfirming an incorrect response. This twofold categorization of events in teaching and learning is based on behavior analysis.

Antecedent Events

1. Giving Instructions to a Child.   In teaching a handicapped child, particularly a retarded child, instructions are usually repeated in a fixed format. For example, in training a child "to pay attention," the teacher might say, "Look at me," "Look at me," "Look at me," over and over. In training a child to dress, she might say, "Pull down your shirt," "Pull down your shirt," "Pull down your shirt," or, in teaching colors, she might ask "What color is this?" "What color is this?" "What color is this?".

The usual reason for not varying the instructions is the teacher's belief that a handicapped child requires lots of unambiguous repetition and even simple variations easily confuse him. This rationale is difficult to accept in light of current knowledge. In the first place, repetition of fixed instructions in itself does not necessarily improve learning an interactional sequence. Indeed, mere repetition may mitigate against learning if the instructions are not preceded by attending behavior, if setting factors such as fatigue strengthen behaviors incompatible with the correct response and if the correct response is not followed by meaningful (functional) reinforcers. In the second place, there is the danger that fixed format instructions may become boring to the child and thereby convert a reinforcing situation into an aversive situation which generates behaviors which are competitive with paying attention and with making the required response. And third, learning in relation to fixed instructions promotes rigidity and leaves little room for generalization; that is, responses tend not to occur when functionally equivalent instructions are given.

A more desirable practice is to vary the wording of instructions in a way that is natural to the situation. For example, in teaching attending behavior, the instructions might be "Look at me," "Look over here," "John, look this way," etc. The key word in the instructions, *look,* in this example, might occur in all the instructional statements and then be faded (gradually eliminated) to functionally equivalent words, such as "John, pay attention." It is also good practice gradually to replace complete instructional sentences with a single word ("John") or a gesture (pointing to the eyes).

The rate at which key words are faded and length of instructions are shortened should be determined by a child's responses. If a probe (trying a synonym for the key word or trying a form of short instruction) results in or decreases the promptness of responding or increases the error rate, the fading procedure should be stopped. If a probe does not produce these changes, the fading procedure should be continued. Teaching practices that follow such a procedure are described as being governed by *functional criteria,* or the reactions of the child.

A final note on instructions: If for some reason one were to insist upon using fixed instructions, he or she should prepare a second-order program that would systematically fade out the fixed instructions and fade in equivalent instructions of approximately the same or shorter lengths. Not to do so narrows the range of instructions to which a child will respond.

2. *Helping a Child Make a Correct Response.*   When a correct response is not immediately forthcoming or when incorrect responses persist, there is a tendency in teaching practice to repeat the instructions over and over again. The rationale for this practice is that a child will make the correct response eventually through self-effort, discovery, problemsolving, or the effects of differential contingencies for correct and incorrect responses. This may be so, but the procedure is generally ineffectual and runs the danger of making the teaching situation aversive. Furthermore, it may unwittingly encourage incorrect responses on the principle that similar environmental conditions produce similar responses, correct or incorrect. In order to help a child make a correct response, a teacher must alter the situation so that the correct response is more likely to occur.

For those inclined to help the child by altering the situation, their usual practice is to give a child assistance by providing the correct response, modeling, manual guidance, hints, cues, and suggestions and then to fade out that assistance either in an unsystematic way or according to the specific schedule outlined in a program manual. The first part of this procedure is basically sound. However, there is little justification for unsystematic fading procedures, and there is a serious question about fading support according to a schedule in a program manual because no set schedule is suitable without adaptation to a particular child.

In practice consistent with applied behavior analysis, the teacher gives a child the assistance to make the correct response and removes the assistance as soon as possible. The amount of help needed and the rate at which the help is eliminated should be gleaned from probes; that is, the teacher should try various forms and various degrees of assistance to determine just what the child needs to make the correct response. Once form and degree of needed assistance are established, she should probe to see how rapidly she can remove her assistance either without increasing the child's error rate or without decreasing the promptness of his responses.

3. Sequencing Curriculum Subjects. There is a tendency to teach curriculum subjects in the form of programs derived from commonsense task analysis. The programs are made on the basis of what a particular teacher and/or her aide think about what is required for a child to learn a task, and she then outlines the steps she thinks should be followed in teaching the task. She also arbitrarily decides on the number of correct responses that will constitute the criterion for the learning of each step. Teaching a subject on this basis consists of teaching one step until the child reaches the criterion of learning and then moving to the next one.

Sequencing subject matter in this way (''writing programs'') is popular because of the general belief that commonsense task analysis is the proper way to make an instructional program. Were this true, behavioral teaching would be a lot less demanding!

An instructional program based on commonsense task analysis rarely coincides with the way a particular child actually learns. Some of the steps may be too easy, some may be too short, and some may produce boredom or distractible behavior; other steps may be too difficult or too long and some may result in frustration, escape, or avoidance behaviors. In all instances learning is slowed down and undesirable behaviors are unwittingly generated.

Although the sequencing of curriculum subjects might well begin with a commonsense task analysis, this should be considered a first approximation, one that requires empirical ''validation'' or evaluation based on the performance of children for whom the program is intended. Such tryouts or dress rehearsals provide the children (the audience) an opportunity to criticize the programmer's efforts by the way they react and indicate, as in the theater, where the strengths and weaknesses are.

The empirically revised program (and it may be revised several times) should never be used ''raw.'' It, the ''barebones'' program, should be transformed into a tailor-made program which would take into account the language competence of the target child as well as the kinds of reinforcers which have been demonstrated to be meaningful (functional) for him. Sometimes this conversion is made by a program form which outlines the steps and the particular antecedent and consequent conditions which are functional for a child.

If a teacher prefers a published over a homemade program, she should review the program manual to see whether the program was validated against the performances of children similar to her pupils. If this information is lacking, the teacher should first test the program on a sample of her own children and revise it according to the results. She should then outline the antecedent and consequent conditions that should be used with the program in order to fit the program to a particular child.

Instructional programs, even the best, should be used *flexibly*. The teacher should continually probe to see how fast or slowly a child can move through a program. In other words, she should "jump back and forth" between completed and more advanced (or new) steps to determine whether it is necessary for the child to do all the steps in the program and whether it is necessary for him to fulfill all the criteria for each. This flexible procedure for teaching a program contrasts with the fixed procedure based on the average performances of handicapped children.

Consequent Events

1. Selecting Consequences for a Correct Response. In much of behavioral teaching the tendency is to use bits of food (e.g., sugar-coated cereal) and sips of a drink (e.g., orange juice) for the severely and profoundly retarded child and to praise (e.g., "Good," or "That's right") for the mildly retarded child. The rationale for the practice is that primary reinforcers are most effective for the essentially nonverbal, severely and profoundly retarded, and secondary reinforcers work better for the mildly retarded.

This prescription for selecting contingencies is not always effective because it fails to take into account the meaningfulness of a consequence for a particular child. It is true, that for *most* children food and drink are reinforcing, especially under conditions of mild food deprivation or when the specific "goodie" coincides with a child's appetite. But in a behavioral approach the contingency used should be meaningful (serve as a reinforcer) to *each* individual child or it will not strengthen learning. The teacher cannot assume that because a consequence, such as food, drink, or praise, serves as a reinforcer for most children, it will serve as a reinforcer for a particular child, whether he is severely and profoundly retarded, mildly retarded, or normal.

It is incumbent upon the teacher to determine when consequent stimuli are in fact reinforcing for a child (Bijou & Baer, 1978). Only when she has this information can she be confident that the contingency aspect of the total teaching process is in good order for each child.

In selecting a reinforcer one must consider and ask: How well does it fuse with the task? Suppose a teacher has made an inventory of demonstrated reinforcers for each of the children and has grouped them as follows: objects, activities, consumables, social interactions, and symbols of achievement. She could then select those that integrate easily and smoothly into each of the curriculum subjects that constitute the child's individualized program. Good reinforcers, from the point of view of teaching, should be meaningful and easy to manage and should not disrupt or interfere with the target performance. Accordingly, social reinforcers are preferable to edibles and drinkables, and natural (ecological) and intrinsic (learned) reinforcers are preferable to social reinforcers.

The preferred order of reinforcers deserves further comment. Good behavioral teaching aims to use a high saturation of natural and intrinsic reinforcers so that the child's learning becomes progressively and, finally, almost totally independent of the teacher. This goal of independence is achieved (1) by analyzing a child's behavior in relation to school subjects to discover which activities are *naturally* reinforcing for him (scissor cutting or pasting papers are possibilities) and which are *intrinsically* (learned) reinforcing (doing puzzles, reading simple stories, and carrying out simple directions are possibilities); (2) by utilizing these reinforcers in instructional programs whenever possible; and (3) by developing new intrinsic reinforcers by making the products of the child's activities reinforcing for him.

2. Varying the Frequencies of Positive Reinforcers.   There is a tendency to reinforce every correct response a child makes (continuous reinforcement). The usual rationale for reinforcing every correct response goes like this: (1) Continuous reinforcement, compared to some irregular schedule of reinforcement is easy for the teacher. (2) Continuous reinforcement lets the child know when he is right.

Reinforcing a child 100% of the time may be easier than reinforcing him, say, every other time or every third or fourth time, but the exclusive use of continuous reinforcement forecloses the possibility of teaching a child many highly desirable behaviors. On the other hand, reinforcing correct responses on some intermittent basis has been shown to (1) increase memory or enhance the maintenance of learned behavior; (2) encourage prolonged working on larger units of material without teacher assistance; (3) encourage persistence in work habits; and (4) promote independence in work and play activities (Vargas, 1977). There is little justification for not training children to acquire these attributes merely because the techniques for achieving them require some additional effort.

A second reason for using continuous reinforcement exclusively is the assumption that a child will not make progress unless he is informed about the correctness of each response. This is not true. Progress is maintained and is often accelerated when a reinforcer is given after a few or even after many correct responses. Intermittent reinforcement trains a child to respond to larger and larger units of material consisting of components held together by conditioned reinforcers in the sequence.

From what has been said, schedules of reinforcement should be an integral part of teaching and should be used along the following lines. In teaching a new subject, whether knowledge or skill, the teacher begins by reinforcing every correct response—a continuous schedule of reinforcement. After a given number of correct responses the teacher begins to probe, that is, to determine how much she can "thin" the reinforcement schedule without increasing errors or decreasing response promptness. So instead of reinforcing every correct response she gives reinforcement after every two successive correct responses. If this thinning does not adversely affect performance, she reinforces every third correct response, and so on. Probing is continued until a schedule is reached that maintains smooth performance with a minimum of reinforcers. At this point, reinforcements should be given flexibly. For example, if the teacher finds that reinforcement after four consecutive correct responses works, she can begin to reinforce on an *irregular basis,* for example, after two, six, four, three, or five correct responses, *centering on an average* of four correct responses. This variable ratio schedule of reinforcement has the double advantage of being easy for the teacher to follow and producing a steady performance on the part of the child.

It should be noted that the recommendation for decreasing the frequency of reinforcements to the point of stability in performance is based not on following a normative rule but by carefully observing the child's reactions to each probe. In this instance, as in many others, the child's reactions show the way to sensitive teaching practices.

3. Consequating Incorrect Responses.   The procedure for dealing with incorrect response varies widely but may be viewed as falling into five categories. The first is one in which there is no discernible consequence from the teacher or any other part of the environment. (Many tasks in and of themselves inform a child that a response is incorrect [e.g., misplacing pieces in a jigsaw puzzle].) Although this is a relatively harmless extinction procedure, it is not recommended because it is a slow and cumbersome way to weaken incorrect responses.

The second kind of consequence is a reprimand, such as, "You know better than that" or "You knew that word yesterday. How come you don't know it today?" Reprimands are not recommended. They are intended to suppress future occurrences of the incorrect response and are then, by definition, aversive. Because a teacher does not know, without making a test of functionality, whether a particular reprimand is in fact aversive for the child (it may be neutral or positively reinforcing), the intended consequence (suppression) will not necessarily be forthcoming. And even if it does, what has the child learned? Certainly not the correct response. Those children who do react aversively to reprimands may suppress the incorrect response in the future, but they may also develop undesirable side effects such as escaping from the teaching situation, the classroom, and eventually the school and surely a dislike of the "punisher."

The third kind of consequence for an incorrect response is simply an indication that the response is incorrect (e.g., "That's wrong."). This type of consequation is probably more effective than the first two but does not bring to bear the best conditions for replacing an incorrect response with a correct one.

The fourth is also an indication that the response is incorrect but it is followed by the correct response (e.g., "That's not right. The right answer is 6." or "That's almost right but it's upside down. This is the way you make a capital M."). This type of correctional procedure is more effective than the previous three. However, it would probably be even more so if it were followed by a question that would evoke the correct response, such as "Now, what's the right answer?" The correct response to this prompt should of course be reinforced. A caveat: The teacher should be sure that the child is attending to the material, such as the visual display of the arithmetic problem or the row of four colored blocks when he makes the correct response.

The fifth kind of consequence of an incorrect response is an indication that the response is incorrect, followed by a statement of the correct response and an "explanation" of why the correct response is correct. It is doubtful whether such an explanation further enhances the probability of a future correct response. The practice is based on the notion that learning is accelerated if the learner *knows* the reasons for a correct response. Perhaps some types of learning (e.g., complex problem solving) are improved by such a procedure, but it is questionable whether it is hopeful for the kinds of learning in a curriculum for young handicapped children.

PROBLEMS ASSOCIATED WITH LIMITED DEVELOPMENT OF EDUCATIONAL TOOLS

Problems in behavioral teaching stem not only from the incomplete application or the misapplication of behavioral principles but also from the limited development of educational tools for implementing classroom teaching. Urgently needed is a well-worked-out format for special teacher training, paraprofessional training, parent training, and procedures for helping a child make a transition to a new educational situation.

Format for Training

According to a behavioral point of view, formats for training teachers, paraprofessionals, or parents should be the same as that for the teaching of handicapped children. This is a derivative of the general proposition that all forms of human behavior in all settings may be analyzed in terms of behavior principles (Kazdin, 1975). The area of training, therefore, uses the same set of principles in teaching handicapped, normal, and gifted children, for treating or remediating problem behaviors and disorders, for parent training, for family and marriage counseling, for vocational training, for college teaching, for professional teaching, etc. All the training–teaching–treatment categories follow a common format: (1) setting goals in observable terms (with or without the aid of criterion referenced tests); (2) programming sequences to attain the goals; (3) implementation of the programs applying behavioral principles; (4) systematic and objective monitoring of performances; (5) modification of programs based on the data collected; (6) setting of advanced goals; etc. This formula will be applied here to the training of special teachers, paraprofessionals, and parents.

Special Teacher Training

The goals of a special teacher training program, gleaned from a rough task analysis, are twofold: (1) to provide knowledge of the approach so that the teacher can apply the principles thoroughly and creatively; and (2) to provide skills in teaching handicapped children, in training and supervising aides or paraprofessionals, and in working with parents and agency personnel.

In this curriculum, knowledge goals would be achieved through programs covering the behavioral point of view and its relationship to other viewpoints, the history and background of the approach, the underlying philosophy of science, the theory of human behavior and development (behavior analysis), single subject research methodology, the relationship between behavior analysis and applied behavior analysis, and the characteristics of a technology of special education and its relationship to elementary education.

These topics would be referred to as programs rather than courses and would be taught by personalized instruction or by the Keller method (Keller, 1968, 1974). This approach to college teaching consists of dividing a subject area into successive study units, each with a set of assignments. Using a study guide the student studies the first unit. When he believes that he has mastered the material of that unit, he reports to a study center to take a short essay examination covering the assignment. His answers are discussed with a proctor and if both the written and oral performance show mastery of the subject matter, he is permitted to proceed to the next unit; if they do not, he is asked to study the unit further and return for another examination. This procedure is repeated until the student completes the program. Proficiency is judged on the amount of material mastered; hence completion of the program would earn a student an *A* grade.

Goals for teaching skills would be attained through supervised clinical experience in a behavioral classroom for handicapped children. Training would consist of taking interactional histories, administering criterion referenced tests, writing programs, tailoring programs to individual children, managing contingencies in individual and group teaching situations, collecting and evaluating performance data, developing and managing programs for behavior problems, and staffing cases. Each phase of classroom training would be coordinated with the material covered in the knowledge programs.

Goals relating to skills in training and supervising paraprofessionals would be achieved through supervised exercises that require the student teacher to use clinical procedures to teach a group of aides the techniques of individualized instruction as they apply to one-to-one and small-group situations. The criterion of proficiency for the student teacher would be the satisfactory performances of the paraprofessionals she has trained in working with handicapped children, as indicated on a teaching checklist.

Goals for working with parents, teachers, and agency personnel would also be achieved through supervised exercises in which the student teacher participates in parent training programs and in teacher and agency personnel conferences concerned with helping a child make a transition to another class. Proficiency here would be based on observations as recorded on an interpersonal type of checklist.

Paraprofessional Training

Paraprofessional training would emphasize the development of teaching skills in relation to children and parents, with no attempt to cover courses in philosophy, theory, research, and technology, as in professional training. However, the format would be similar to the practicum part of teacher training in that it would consist of a short series of lectures or programs that would present an analysis of teaching in terms of antecedent conditions, behavior, consequences, and setting conditions. This didactic material would be followed by instruction in the use of criterion referenced tests and the various forms that are used in teaching curriculum subjects and in managing behavior problems. Experience in constructing and revising instructional programs, gathering and evaluating performance data, and teaching knowledge and skill subjects in individual and group situations would also be included. All this training would take place under the supervision of a trained behavioral teacher, and proficiency would be determined by observations of performance as recorded on a teaching checklist.

Parent Training

The objective of behavioral teaching is to help a child develop through the acquisition of new knowledge and skills that are functional in his daily life. The only way for this to occur in any significant degree is to combine an effective classroom teaching program with an effective parent training program. Hence, the primary objectives of parent training are to equip parents with the skills of the paraprofessional so that they can (1) strengthen and generalize all that the child learns in the classroom; (2) teach certain behaviors that are not included in the curriculum; and (3) cope with behavior problems. Parent training that accomplishes these goals prepares parents to deal more effectively not only with the child in the special preschool but also with their other children.

There are currently a number of different formats for parent training programs as an adjunct to preschool classes for young handicapped children. Some are modeled after the activities of social workers and tend to be loosely structured and ineffective, attempting, as they do, to deal with any and all personal family problems beyond the province of the school. Others use the visiting teacher format. These are also loosely structured and ineffective and are not remotely related to the teaching methods of the preschool. The more promising formats are some adaptation of the Portage Project (Shearer & Shearer, 1972), a home teaching program intended as a substitute for a special preschool. The aim is to train parents to teach their own handicapped child at home. However, training parents to complement and supplement the skills and knowledge their child is acquiring in the special class requires different strategies. But as of now a promising prototype for an adjunctive parent training program has not yet emerged from current efforts in research and development.

It should be mentioned in passing that when a well-thought-out and workable parent training format is finally available, there will remain the practical problem of getting parents to accept and follow through with the training program. Parents who are weighed down with personal and emotional problems and parents who see a conflict between such training and their racial and cultural beliefs and mores are not likely to be cooperative participants in the training program.

At times the problem of cooperation lies with parent surrogates. In families in which both parents or the single parent works full time, the child must spend after-school hours with a friend, relative, baby-sitter, or child-care facility. A parent surrogate, quite understandably, often lacks the essential motivation for training. How to overcome the practical problems of getting parent or surrogate-parent cooperation is still to be resolved.

Format for Transition to Subsequent Education

For a child in a special class to continue to make progress, it is essential that the teachers in his subsequent educational placements, whether another special class or a regular elementary class, are trained in behavioral techniques and individualized programmed instruction. Otherwise, a child leaving a behavioral class is not very likely to maintain and improve the skills and knowledge he achieved in that class.

If the child is to be enrolled in another special class, the present teacher can facilitate the transfer through conferences with the new teacher, the school principal, and the school psychologist. In general, the conferences would center on a discussion of the child's entering status based on teacher comments, the results of criterion and norm referenced tests, the procedure used for setting goals, the method of teaching, and the child's accomplishments in the preschool as measured by criterion and norm referenced tests. If the receiving special teacher follows a behavioral approach, the conferences would serve a briefing function and an occasion for comparing programs and teaching techniques. If she does not have a behavioral orientation, the meetings would be devoted to briefing the teacher on the child's achievements and to encouraging her to use individualized instruction for the child.

If the child is to be transferred to an elementary class, in accordance with recent mainstreaming policies, preparation for the transition is limited to the resources available. If the school has a policy of providing assistance in the form of resource teachers or aides, this personnel can be briefed on the child's progress and the methods used to achieve them. They can also be given suggestions (and materials) on how they or the regular classroom teacher can set up individualized programs for the child. If the elementary teacher does not have access to auxiliary resources, there is little she can do (considering the size of her class) to help the handicapped child continue to make progress without depriving the other children of time that is intended for all.

SUMMARY

Over the past decade the teaching practices of young handicapped children have incorporated many features derived from behavior analysis, among them criterion referenced tests for the evaluation of competencies, management of reinforcement contingencies, and systematic recording of performance on instructional programs (charting). These changes in teaching practices have brought about positive changes in teachers' attitudes toward the learning potential of handicapped children. Unfortunately, applications have too often been incomplete or inappropriate; hence the children are still deprived of the full benefits that applied behavior analysis has to offer.

A second factor retarding the development of an optimal learning environment is the lack of essential educational tools and, in particular, well-worked-out formats for teacher training, paraprofessional training, and parent training.

Many of the misapplications of behavioral principles have brought about a kind of rigidity and artificiality in children's learning. This undesirable consequence can be reduced or eliminated by checking teaching practices against modern applied behavior analysis, particularly that part concerned with the management of antecedent and consequent conditions. The resulting revised practices would be more sensitive to the personality characteristics of each child, would develop more flexibility in learning, and would stimulate other forms of behavior such as persistence and independence in work habits.

Formats for teacher, paraprofessional, and parent training can be improved through concerted action in practice and research. The key notion to be emphasized in both endeavors is that training formats for all three groups should be the same as that used in teaching young handicapped children, or any other group for that matter.

When we have applied more of our knowledge, have eliminated most of the misapplications of principles, and have the needed educational tools, we shall see that the young handicapped child has even greater potential than has heretofore been reported.

REFERENCES

Bijou, S. W., & Baer, D. M. *Behavior analysis of child development*. Englewood Cliffs, N.J.: Prentice-Hall, 1978.

Glaser, R. A criterion-referenced test. In W. J. Pophem (Ed.), *Criterion-referenced measurement: An introduction*. Englewood Cliffs, N.J.: Educational Technology Publications, 1971.

Kazdin, A. E. *Behavior modification in applied settings*. Homewood, Ill.: The Dorsey Press, 1975.

Keller, F. S. "Good-bye, teacher..." *Journal of Applied Behavior Analysis*, 1968, *1*, 79–90.

Keller, F. S. "Ten years of personalized instruction." *Teaching of Psychology*, 1974, *1*, 4–9.

Shearer, M. S., & Shearer, D. E. The Portage Project: A model for early childhood education. *Exceptional Children*, 1972, *38*, 210–217.

Vargas, J. S. *Behavioral psychology for teachers*. New York: Harper & Row, 1977.

5 Graphing Academic Performances of Mildly Handicapped Children

Thomas C. Lovitt
University of Washington

INTRODUCTION

This chapter is a presentation of the curriculum research my associates and I and other researchers have conducted with mildly handicapped children during the past several years using Applied Behavior Analysis (*ABA*) techniques. One purpose of this chapter is to show how these techniques may be implemented by classroom teachers. Another objective is to offer suggestions for future curriculum research using this same methodology.

Curriculum, as used in this chapter, refers to the many learning activities of children such as reading, mathematics, and spelling. Curriculum, as the term is used here, also includes the many teaching procedures that are selected to assist in the development of academic skills. Some of these procedures are modeling, feedback, and various reinforcement contingencies.

Following is an outline of this chapter. The first section is an explanation of the *ABA* methodology, presenting first a brief outline of the development of this method followed by a description of the basic components of the method.

In the second section is a description of several research studies. These studies are presented by subject matter area: reading, mathematics, spelling, and pupil management. In the third section there is a description of how teachers are currently using these techniques. In the final section some suggestions for future curriculum research are offered.

111

APPLIED BEHAVIOR ANALYSIS

A Brief History of Applied Behavior Analysis

Applied behavior analysis procedures, although used only recently in school situations, have a rich and substantial heritage. Skinner provided the substance of what is today known as *ABA*. One of his many contributions was his support of the belief that frequency of responding was the basic datum of science. Response frequency has become a key element of the *ABA* technology. Another contribution of Skinner's to today's technology is the notion of establishing functional relationships between independent and dependent variables. Perhaps his greatest gift to *ABA* was that he so dramatically proved that many behaviors are influenced by various reinforcement contingencies.

From that beginning of operant psychology, several branches of experimentation developed. Some researchers continued, as did Skinner, to use lower organisms as subjects. Others began to work with adults in institutions for the psychotic and retarded. Although many of these researchers contributed to what is now *ABA*, I would like merely to trace the development of *ABA* as it relates to children.

Some of the early work with children using operant procedures was basic or laboratory research. These studies were conducted in settings not natural to the child's environment, and the responses the children were required to emit were not normally in their repertories. The purpose for these studies was to learn about certain conceptual systems rather than about the ordinary behaviors of children.

One such study was the now classic Azrin and Lindsley (1956) research that examined the acquisition, extinction, and maintenance of a cooperative behavior. Baer and Sherman (1964) studied the generalized imitations of children. Bijou in 1958 studied the performance of children during extinction phases following various fixed-interval schedules. These laboratory studies with children accomplished what they set out to do: They demonstrated that many of the principles of operant psychology that applied to animals held true for children.

Encouraged by the successes of these laboratory findings, others began to use operant techniques with children in clinical settings. The classic study of this type was reported by Wolf, Risley, and Mees (1964). They investigated several behaviors of a young autistic boy in the clinic and the home. Lovaas (Lovaas, Freitag, Kinder, Rubenstein, Schaeffer, & Simmons, 1966; Lovaas, Freitag, Nelson, & Whalen, 1967) in several studies used operant procedures to change various behaviors of schizophrenic youngsters. There were several other studies of this type that used operant procedures to change—generally attenuate—the behaviors of children. They had in common the fact that they dealt with one child in a highly controlled situation.

Operant conditioners then became more venturesome and entered classrooms. Many research studies were conducted that demonstrated that these techniques were successful when used with a single individual or a small group of individuals within classrooms.

Perhaps the first study of this type was reported by the Zimmermans (1962). They used extinction and positive reinforcement procedures to increase the spelling abilities of one subject and attenuate the tantrums of another. Lloyd Homme and colleagues (Homme, deBaca, Devine, Steinhorst, & Rickert, 1963) demonstrated that the Premack principle was an effective strategy for controlling a wide range of nursery school behaviors.

The work of Harris, Wolf, and Baer (1964) and others at the Developmental Psychology Laboratory at the University of Washington is noteworthy for the extension of operant principles to group situations. They demonstrated in a series of studies how isolated play, crying, climbing, and other nursery school behaviors were amenable to the contingent praise of teachers.

Several other researchers demonstrated how these principles could be used in classrooms with one or more children to attenuate certain troublesome behaviors. O'Leary and his colleagues (O'Leary, Kaufman, Kass, & Drabman, 1970) did such work, as did Becker and his fellow workers (Becker, Madsen, Arnold, & Thomas, 1967). The favored targets of these researchers were talk-outs and out-of-seats.

Many of these researchers used the term *behavior modification* to describe their methodology. They had taken the vital features of operant conditioning—identification of an observable response, measurement of that response over a period of time, involvement of reinforcement contingencies to affect the frequency of that response—and adapted them in order to study classroom problems.

Along with this rash of studies that proved that operant or behavior modification techniques can effectively control troublesome behaviors of pupils, some researchers sought to demonstrate that these techniques were useful in changing the attending behaviors of pupils. Several investigators demonstrated that teacher praise was associated with pupil attending; that is, when teacher praise is arranged contingent on the attending of pupils, the amount of time they "pay attention" is increased. For example, Hall and his colleagues clearly demonstrated in several settings that teacher attention can alter the attending or studying behaviors of youngsters (Hall, Lund, & Jackson, 1968; Cossairt, Hall, & Hopkins, 1973).

Several researchers used *ABA* techniques to investigate various academic behaviors of children. One of the earliest attempts to obtain academic measures was the work conducted by Birnbrauer, Wolf, Kidder, and Tague (1965) at the Rainier School in Buckley, Washington. In their programmed learning classroom those investigators reported that measures in reading, writing, and arithmetic could be continuously obtained. Arthur Staats and his group conducted several studies that related to the effects of reinforcement contingencies on various reading behaviors (Staats & Butterfield, 1965; Staats, Finley, Minke, & Wolf, 1964; Staats, Staats, Schutz, & Wolf, 1962).

Perhaps the man who did most to stimulate the use of these procedures in academic settings was O. R. Lindsley. When he came to Kansas in 1965, his major objective was to adapt and extend the techniques of behavior modification in order to measure and change such skills as reading, writing, and arithmetic. He referred to his system as *precision teaching.*

One of the essentials of precision teaching is the movement cycle. According to Lindsley, every behavior, be it academic or social, should be defined as having a beginning and an end. Heretofore, behaviors were often counted on a sampling basis. Every *n* seconds an observation was taken. Another ingredient of his approach was frequency of responding. He maintained that behaviors should be measured and graphed in terms of movements per minute.

So it went from the operant conditioning work in the laboratories that was concerned with conceptual systems, to behavior modification that dealt with troublesome and attending behaviors in the classrooms, to precision teaching that emphasized the measurement of a wider range of classroom behaviors including academic skills.

Characteristics of Applied Behavior Analysis

Several applied behavior analysts, in attempts to explain the system, have identified various components. One of the most widely quoted explanations was a paper written by Baer, Wolf, and Risley (1968). They described *ABA* as being applied, behavioral, analytical, technological, and conceptually systematic.

In regard to *ABA* and curriculum research, I would like to characterize this system as comprising five ingredients: direct measurement, daily measurement, replicable teaching procedures, individual analysis, and experimental control.

Direct Measurement.   When *ABA* techniques are used, the behavior of concern is measured directly. If the researcher is concerned with the pupil's ability to add facts of the class, $2 + 2 = \square$, or to read words from a *Ginn* reader, those behaviors would be measured. When *ABA* techniques are employed, the same behavior that is scheduled for teaching is measured. This form of measurement is contrasted to more indirect methods that use such devices as normative tests that could measure behaviors not of immediate concern.

Daily Measurement.   A second important ingredient of *ABA* is that the behavior of concern is measured, if not daily, at least very often. If, for instance, the pinpointed behavior is the pupil's ability to add facts of the class $2 + 2 = \square$, he would be given the opportunity to perform that skill for several days during a baseline before a judgment is made. The reason for using several days' data is quite obvious; it could be that on one day the pupil performed very poorly, the next day better, and so forth. Many times in teaching and research the prepost test methodology is used. A test is given before and after a treatment. Judgments are then made based on the comparison of the two scores. Judgments or decisions derived from such limited data could be pernicious; the consequences for some children could be disastrous.

Replicable Teaching Procedures.   Another important feature of *ABA* is that, generally, the procedures used to generate the data in research efforts are adequately described. In most instances they are explained in enough detail that other interested researchers might replicate their studies. By contrast, other types of research sometimes explain general procedures rather casually. For example, one Brand X research study that used a phonics training program as an intervention simply said that "Daily phonics drills were conducted." It would be impossible for an interested teacher or researcher to replicate these investigations. In *ABA* research, if a phonics treatment were used, the reader would be informed not only about the amount of time used for instruction but also which phonics elements were stressed, how they were presented, what the nature of the pupils' responses were, and what type of feedback or reinforcement was provided.

Individual Analysis.   The very heart of *ABA* technology is that the data from individuals are presented. In fact, some have referred to this methodology as the single-subject method. In an *ABA* study, if data are obtained on five subjects, a graph of each subject's performance would generally be shown. In doing so, all the ideosyncratic behavioral patterns become obvious. An inspection of these graphs would likely reveal that although the general effects on all five might be the same, no two graphs of pupil performance were exactly alike.

Other research systems report the data of groups—experimental and control. Often a mean score is offered to explain the performance of a group. It might be that the average score represents the performance of no one. It could also be that if a treatment has been used and the group effect was positive, what in fact happened was that the effect was very significant for some, was ineffective for others, and had a slightly negative effect on others. But when the scores were averaged, the composite effect was positive.

Experimental Control.   In every research study, regardless of the methodology, the researcher is obligated, in one way or another, to prove that the effects on the dependent variable were attributed to the scheduled independent variable. He must establish a functional relationship.

The reason for such an effort is extremely important. For if researchers recommend that method C be used by all reading teachers because they found that it improved certain reading skills, they must be certain that variable C and nothing else caused the improvement.

In order to substantiate their claims, Brand X researchers often resort to statistical control. Their typical research method is to form control and experimental groups, give a pretest, provide a treatment for the experimental group and no treatment or a placebo for the control group, and then give a posttest at the end of treatment. The pretest and posttest data of the two groups are then statistically analyzed and the winner announced. The significance of the conquest depends on which probability level is achieved: .05, .01, .001.

By contrast, the applied behavior analyst would use experimental control to establish relationships between the independent and dependent variables. More specifically, he would use some form of replication.

The *ABA* design has been the favored form of replication. During the first phase no treatment is arranged. Then a treatment is scheduled throughout the next condition. In the recapitulation phase the treatment is removed. If the behavior changed in the second phase from the first condition and changed back to its original level in the return to the first phase, a reasonable case could be made that a functional relationship had been discovered. There are several other replication techniques available to the *ABA* researcher, such as the multiple baseline and crossover designs.

RESEARCH

In this section, research will be explained by subject matter area: reading, mathematics, spelling, and pupil management. Although the descriptions of these studies are quite brief, it is hoped that enough detail is presented so that interested teachers might apply some of the findings or techniques in their classes and curriculum researchers might replicate certain of the procedures.

Reading Research

Comparing Direct and Daily Measurement with Achievement Test Scores. Perhaps the most widely used technique for evaluating pupil progress is the achievement test. In many school systems an achievement test is given at the beginning and the end of the year. Achievement test scores pertain to such skills as reading, spelling, and arithmetic.

These scores are used for various purposes. Sometimes they are considered to document teacher competency. At other times they are used to make placement decisions: whether to assign students to special or regular classes, to high or low reading groups, or to one grade or another. At other times they are used for purposes of communication: to report pupil progress to teachers, administrators, or parents.

Earlier in this chapter I expressed some criticism about the use of achievement tests in education. The two important evaluative dimensions that are void when they are administered are direct and daily measurement. Often the achievement test measures a behavior that is indirectly related to the behavior of concern. And, inevitably, the achievement test provides an infrequent measure of performance, for generally they are given once or twice a year.

A few years ago we arranged a situation to compare the efficacy of using achievement tests and direct and daily measurement (Eaton & Lovitt, 1972). At the beginning and the end of the year we gave our pupils the *Metropolitan Achievement Test* (MAT) and the *Wide Range Achievement Test* (WRAT). Throughout the year we also obtained direct and daily data from the children in reading, writing, spelling, and arithmetic. At the end of the year we compared the reading subtest achievement test scores with the reading data obtained from direct and daily measurement. The findings are presented in Table 5.1. Several differences between the two measurement systems were evident. First it was discovered that the achievement tests did not agree among themselves. The fall tests disagreed more than one-half grade level for three of six children. The most discrepant scores were obtained by a pupil who received a 2.4 rating on one test and 4.4 on the other. The scores of the two tests in the spring disagreed four out of six times. The widest differences for a pupil on the two tests were 4.0 and 8.7.

In regard to placement, we compared the initial placement of pupils when direct and daily measurement procedures were used with their fall achievement test scores. Using the former placement method each child was required to read

TABLE 5.1
Achievement Test Scores and Placement According to
Direct and Daily Measurement (1970–1971)

| Child | Metropolitan Achievement Test | | Wide Range Achievement Test | | Direct and Daily Placement | | |
	Fall	Spring	Fall	Spring	Book	Fall	Spring
Paul L.	1.0 P²	2.7 E	2.7	2.5	Lippincott	—	2–2
					Palo Alto	Book 3	
					Bank Street*	Primer	2–2
Paul R.	2.6 E	4.0 I	2.5	2.5	Bank Street*	2–1	3–1
					Scott Foresman	2–1	4–1
John	1.1 P	4.0 E	KG 7	8.7	Lippincott*	Preprimer	2–1
					Palo Alto	—	Book 11
Fred	1.6 E	2.5 E	1.9	1.9	Merrill	—	Book 5
					Bank Street*	Primer	2–2
Jenni	2.4 E	6.8 I	4.4	4.8	Lippincott	3–1	Book 5
					Laidlaw	3–1	Book 5
					McMillan*	3–1	Book 5
Phil	None low enough	1.7 P	KG 5	1.9	Lippincott*	Preprimer	1–1
					Bank Street	—	1–1

P = Primary battery.
P² = Primary² battery.
E = elementary battery.
I = intermediate battery.
* = Reader used for oral reading instruction.

several days from a number of books representing different grade levels. We graphed correct and incorrect rate performances as they read from these texts. After several days we analyzed the data and selected the placement books for the children based on their relative performance. Three of the six direct and daily placements agreed within one-half grade level with an achievement test score. These agreements were all with the MAT.

A comparison of the book level in which they were reading at the end of the year with their spring achievement test scores revealed concurrence between an achievement test and actual placement four out of six times. These agreements were equal for the two achievement tests.

In regard to the data about pupil growth throughout the year, all the pupils gained when their MAT scores were considered: Their spring scores were all higher than their fall scores. According to the WRAT, however, there was no growth for two pupils and a deterioration for another. When direct and daily measurement was evaluated, all children improved. Furthermore, this improvement was indicated in three ways: Their correct rates increased from fall to spring, their incorrect rates went down, and they read from more difficult material in the spring than in the fall. Achievement tests provided only a grade-level difference score as a measure of improvement.

A final advantage of direct and daily measurement over achievement test measurement must be emphasized. When the former system is used, a teacher can see from one day to the next whether progress is being made. If the data indicate the child is not improving, a different teaching routine can be scheduled immediately. By contrast, if a teacher waits until spring to discover whether or not her teaching was effective, she would not have time to redesign her instruction if the pupil was failing. Figure 5.1 presents the oral reading data for a pupil throughout a school year.

Placing Pupils in Appropriate Books.   This study was conducted a few years ago with seven learning disabled youngsters at the Experimental Education Unit (EEU). The pupils were between the ages of 8 and 11. The purpose of the project was to place them at their instructional reading levels (Lovitt & Hansen, 1976a).

From our previous data we had observed that when children were placed in readers in which their correct rates were between 45 and 65 words per minute and their comprehension scores were no less than 50%, they were able to progress when only minimal instruction was provided. It was, therefore, the aim of this project to place the pupils in the highest reader in a series in which those conditions were met.

In order to do this, the teacher required them to read orally from eight different books representing grade levels of 1.5 to 6.0 in the *Lippincott* reading series. They were required to read 100-word selections from each book for five consecutive days. They were also required to answer comprehension questions. After each selection was read, the teacher asked six questions: two recall, two sequential, and two inferential. Recall questions pertained to facts in the story.

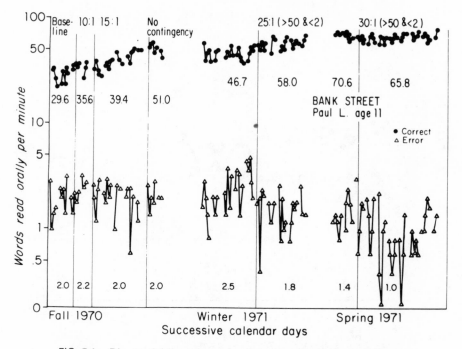

FIG. 5.1.   Direct and daily measurement of words read orally for Paul. Separations in the data points indicate absences, weekends, or vacations. The five vertical lines indicate different instructional procedures were in effect. The numerals below the correct and incorrect rate plots are correct and incorrect rate medians for each phase (Eaton & Lovitt, 1972.)

Sequential questions were about the temporal order of events. Inferential questions dealt with interpretation and synthesis. The correct and incorrect oral reading rates and the correct percentage score for answering the comprehension questions were graphed. The teacher studied these data to determine the appropriate reading level for each pupil.

The results for one boy are presented in Fig. 5.2. The top graph indicates Marty's correct and incorrect rates for oral reading in each of the texts; the lower graph shows his correct percentage for answering comprehension questions. His average comprehension scores ranged from 95.8% in the *Lippincott D* book (grade 1.5) to 50.0% in the *Lippincott I* text (grade 4). Although the first-grade material was generally easier for Marty to comprehend, his percentage scores fluctuated widely in each book: He achieved a 100% score in seven of eight books and a score below 50% in seven of eight books. When these data were analyzed, he was placed in the *Lippincott D* reader for instruction.

This placement technique was used with 14 boys at the EEU over a 2-year period. During the first year, five reading samples were obtained from each text. When these data were analyzed, we learned that three samples per text were

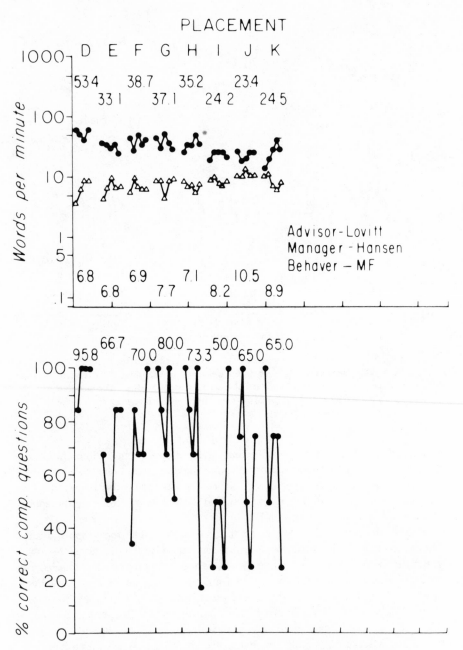

FIG. 5.2. *Lippincott* Books D through K. In the top graph the numerals above the data are correct rate medians for each book; the numerals below the data are the incorrect rate medians. The bottom graph shows the correct percentage of comprehension answers (Lovitt & Hansen, 1976.)

sufficient to predict an instructional reading level; therefore, the students during the second year were required to read only three samples.

The data of the other students were very similar to Marty's: Their correct rates and comprehension scores gradually declined and their incorrect reading rates rose as the grade level of the texts increased.

These data strengthen a belief held by many: When the difficulty of the material increases, the pupil's ability to read and comprehend gradually worsens. This decline, however, is more clearly noted for oral reading than for comprehension, at least for the type of comprehension that was monitored in this study.

Determining the Relationship Between Phonics Instruction and Oral Reading.   Perhaps no other aspect of reading instruction has generated more debate than the issue of phonics training. Some reading experts have stated categorically that pupils must have an extremely good phonics background before they begin formal reading instruction. They argue that unless the pupil has systematic part-word training, he will lack certain word-attack skills and will not become a proficient reader. Other reading experts do not agree that phonics skills transfer to other, more complex reading behaviors. They maintain that because the English language is so irregular, it is fruitless to teach phonics rules and generalizations.

As is the case with most controversies, extremists are rare in reference to the whole- part-word argument. Most teachers have taken moderate approaches on the matter. Nevertheless, the controversy persists.

The research described here was designed to bring data from an *ABA* approach to bear on this topic (Lovitt & Hurlbut, 1974). We sought to obtain data regarding two questions: (1) If the phonics skills of a pupil are improved, will his ability to read orally improve? (2) If his phonics skills improve, will concurrent gains be noted more in a phonics or nonphonics designed reader?

The pupil in this project was a 10-year-old boy. He had been described as dyslexic. Daily measures were obtained in seven areas: five in phonics skills and two in oral reading. The five phonics skills emphasized medial vowels, consonant blends, sound blending, translocation of letters, and digraph-diphthongs. In oral reading the pupil read from *Lippincott* and *Ginn* readers. The former reader was designed primarily on phonics principles; the latter, more on the whole-word method.

To assess the boy's performance in the phonics areas, five word sheets were constructed. The one for medial vowels contained a list of 20 three- or four-letter words; each contained a short medial vowel. The consonant list was made up of 20 words, each beginning with a different consonant blend. The sound blending list contained 20 consonant–vowel–consonant words. The translocation list was composed of 25 words that contained letter combinations that are potentially transposable (e.g., *flit* or *spot*). The digraph–diphthong sheet was made up of 26 sets of words. Each set featured a different combination (e.g., *ee* or *ay*).

A correct response for the medial vowel and consonant blend tasks was the accurate writing of only the vowel or the blend. A correct response for the sound blending, translocations, and digraph–diphthong tasks was the correct spelling of the entire word. A correct oral reading response was the correct pronunciation of a word. Errors consisted of omissions, substitutions, and additions.

Correct and incorrect rate scores were obtained in each of the seven tasks. To obtain these rates the teacher timed each performance (e.g., medial vowels) and counted the number of correct and incorrect responses. She then divided the number correct and the number incorrect by the time required to complete each task.

Two phases, a baseline and an intervention, comprised this project. During the baseline period the pupil was provided with feedback on his phonics performance. After he completed all the tasks, the teacher corrected his papers, pointed out the errors he had made, and told him the correct answers. No instruction was provided, however, as he read orally from the two books. As he read, if he erred on certain words, the teacher merely urged him to continue reading.

Throughout the next condition phonics instruction was scheduled. Prior to obtaining the seven measures, a 10-minute instructional period based on the Slingerland procedures was arranged. This approach emphasizes the notions of multisensory stimulation. Again, no instruction was focused on oral reading.

Three important findings came from this study: (1) when phonics skills were precisely defined and when instruction was directed toward them, those skills were improved; (2) when phonics skills improved, so did oral reading (correct rates increased, incorrect rates decreased); and (3) more improvement was noted as the pupil read from the phonics reader than from the nonphonics reader.

In regard to the last point, Fig. 5.3 is provided to illustrate the changes in oral reading rates across the two conditions for both readers. The data from the whole-word book are on the left portion of the figure and from the phonics book on the right. The vertical lines in both portions of the chart separate baseline and instructional phases.

Arranging Contingent Skipping and Drilling.   This study was based on the second investigation reported here and was conducted with seven intermediate-aged boys at the EEU. At the beginning of the study each student was assigned to the highest book in which his correct rate was between 45 and 65 words per minute, his incorrect rate was between 4 and 8 words per minute, and his comprehension score was above 50%.

Daily, each student read orally a selection of 500 words and answered several comprehension questions (Lovitt & Hansen, 1976b). Once again we used the *Lippincott* reading series. The students who read from the first- to third-grade readers were given 30 questions: 10 recall, 10 sequential, and 10 inferential. The students who read from the fourth- to sixth-grade books were given 20 questions: five recall, five sequential, five inferential, and five vocabulary. The pupils read the questions silently and wrote their answers. Short answers were required for

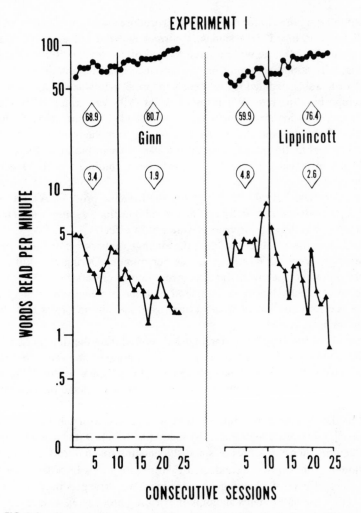

FIG. 5.3. Correct and incorrect rates throughout two phases as the boy read from *Ginn* and *Lippincott* texts. The numerals in the tear drops indicate correct and incorrect rate means (Lovitt & Hurlbut, 1974.)

the recall, sequential, and inferential questions. A multiple-choice format was used for the vocabulary questions.

An *ABA* design was used in this investigation. During the baseline condition the students received minimal feedback in respect to their efforts. This condition lasted for 7 days.

In the second condition, skipping and drilling were introduced. Each student was informed that he would be allowed to skip (not read) one-fourth of his text if on any day his oral reading and comprehension performances exceeded his average baseline scores by 25%.

If a pupil did not skip for 4 days, drill procedures were instituted. Three types of drill were arranged. If a student's correct rate did not exceed his average baseline rate by 25%, he was required to read orally several 100-word passages from his daily assignment until his performance met this criterion. The second type of drill was scheduled if a student's incorrect rate was not 25% lower than the average baseline rate. When this form of drill was arranged, he practiced phrases in which his error words were embedded. The third type of drill was employed if a student did not answer 25% more comprehension questions than he had during the baseline phase. When this drill was used, the student was required to redo his incorrect answers. These procedures continued each day until the student skipped.

During the last 2 weeks of the quarter the baseline procedures were reestablished. The students read orally and answered questions as they had before, but the skipping and drilling provisions were not in effect.

Throughout the baseline condition the average oral correct and incorrect rates for the group were 50.7 and 3.1 words per minute. During the skip and drill condition, the average correct and incorrect rates were 60.0 and 2.9 words per minute. When these data were compared with the baseline scores, it was noted that the correct rates for all students improved and the incorrect rates for four students improved.

Meanwhile, the average comprehension score during the first phase was 65.9 and 77.8% during the second condition. The comprehension scores of all pupils improved when the skipping and drilling procedures were scheduled. Throughout the second condition the pupils skipped 33 times, an average of 0.24 skips per day.

When the skip and drill intervention was removed in the third phase, the performances of the students generally maintained. In fact, the average oral reading and comprehension scores of some students improved during this condition.

Following this study we conducted two investigations in order to determine the relative effects of skipping and drilling. We arranged only the skipping provision with some students and only the drilling procedures with others. These data did not clearly indicate the relative effects of either component.

Figure 5.4 is included to show Marty's daily oral reading and comprehension scores. All three aspects of his performance were influenced by the skipping and drilling interventions.

Saying Facts About a Story. One of the problems with assessing reading comprehension by asking students questions about what they just read is that many of them can answer some of the questions without having read the passage. Although we have measured students' comprehension by asking them various types of questions, we have never been totally confident of this approach. We, therefore, designed a project to assess pupils' comprehension by requiring them to relate facts from the story.

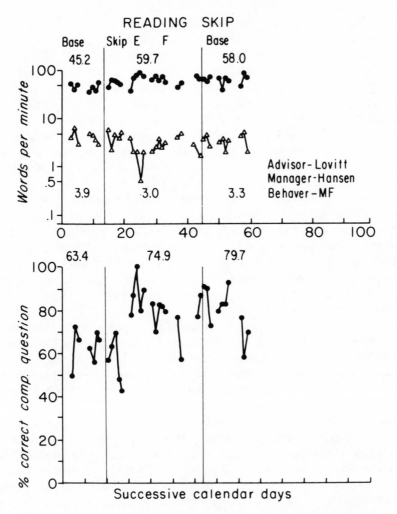

FIG. 5.4. The data in the top graph are the daily correct and incorrect rates throughout the three phases of the project. The numbers above and below the data are the medians for those conditions. The bottom graph shows the correct percentages for answering the comprehension questions (Lovitt & Hansen, 1976.)

Each day the students read silently a different story from the *Reading for Concepts* series. Every story was a factual account of some event or person and was about 150 words in length. The teacher timed the pupils' performance as they read.

When a student finished the story the teacher asked him to tell her about it. When he began to recite events, a timing watch began. Later, if the pupil hesitated for 5 seconds, the teacher asked him to continue. If he hesitated again, he was reminded again. When he hesitated for a third time, the session ended. At that time the timing watch was stopped.

Throughout his account of the story the teacher tallied each related fact as either correct or incorrect. Correct facts were any bits of valid information about the story. For example, each noun, action verb, adjective, or adverb was counted as a fact. Incorrect facts were any incorrect or creative statements. If the student repeated either a correct or incorrect fact, it was not counted.

Throughout the baseline phase the pupils received some feedback on their performances but were given no instruction. They were informed about their silent reading and say fact rates but were not coached on how to alter those rates.

During a second phase some instruction was scheduled. Several elements comprised this instruction. For one, the teacher demonstrated how to say facts. In order to do so she and the pupil read a story silently. This was a story from a different series than that used to obtain the daily measurement. When they finished reading, the teacher said facts about the story. While she did so, the pupil tallied the number of facts. (Prior to this the teacher had explained what constituted a fact.) When the teacher finished saying facts, she and the pupil reviewed some of her statements in order to assist the pupil further to understand the meaning of a fact.

Following this modeling procedure the teacher asked the pupil to read silently his assigned story and to keep in mind he would be asked to retell facts, as the teacher had, when he finished reading the story.

After the pupil said facts about the story, the second instructional technique was scheduled. The pupil now received feedback on his silent reading and retelling performances. He was told what his rates were that day and how they compared with those of previous days.

The third component of the instructional package was the scheduling of a reinforcement contingency. If on any day a pupil's correct rate for saying facts was higher than a trend line, he could select an event from a reinforcement menu. (The trend line accelerated at a rate of X1.25, i.e., 25% growth per week. It began at the midpoint of the correct rates in the baseline phase.) All these events had to do with leisure time (e.g., the pupil could talk with the classroom teacher for 5 minutes).

Following is a brief description of one girl's performance. In the first condition, when the instructional techniques were not scheduled, her correct rates for saying facts were about 6 per minute. During the second phase her median correct rate was 11.5 and the data were accelerating at 60% per week.

Mathematics Research

Using Modeling Procedures to Change Arithmetic Performance.   The instructional technique used in this study is perhaps the oldest and most widely used technique available—showing and telling someone how to do something.

Three studies comprised this experiment (Smith & Lovitt, 1975). *ABA* designs were used. In Studies 1 and 2 the intervention involved the demonstration of a problem, then leaving that sample as a model for the pupil to consult. In Study 3, components of that technique were investigated.

In Study 1 the pupils were assigned different types of problems. Some were presented problems like $470 - 249 = \square$; whereas others were assigned problems like $22 \times 13 = \square$ and $8 \times 0 = \square$. During the baseline phase the pupils received no instruction, feedback, or reinforcement. They worked for 2 minutes each day on the sheets.

Throughout the intervention condition the modeling technique was used. The pupils were shown how to do a problem of the assigned type and that model was left on their sheet. They could refer to it at any time. The data throughout this condition revealed that rapid acquisition occurred for all pupils. Throughout the intervention phase their scores were nearly all perfect. In the final condition, when the modeling intervention was removed, their scores, with few exceptions, remained high. Figure 5.5 shows the data for one pupil.

Throughout Study 2 the pupils were assigned different problems than those

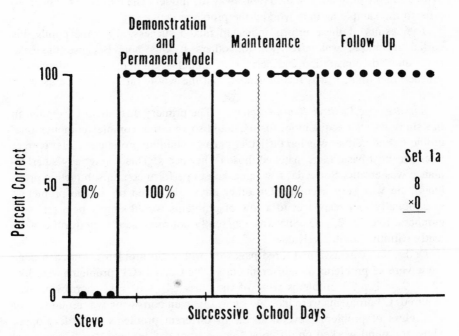

FIG. 5.5.   Percentage correct for the Set 1a problems for Study 1. Only successive data days are connected by lines. The curved line indicates a long school holiday (Smith & Lovitt, 1975.)

used in the first study. Again a baseline phase was scheduled. Their performances were generally zero throughout this period. Next, a feedback intervention was arranged. Following the completion of an assignment the teacher marked each pupil response as correct or incorrect. The corrected paper was handed back to the pupil. Because the students could not solve many of the problems, most of their responses were marked as errors. None of the pupils progressed during this condition, although the procedure was in effect for about 7 days.

In the third phase, the modeling technique used in Study 1 was scheduled. The results of that period were as impressive as those indicated in Study 1: Effects were immediate and lasting. When the intervention was withdrawn, the accuracy of the pupils continued to be good.

In Study 3, elements of the modeling intervention were used. Throughout this study different problems were again assigned. As in the other two projects, the pupils worked 2 minutes each day on the problems. In the first phase no teaching was scheduled. During the intervention phase the model alone was used for some of the pupils. The sample problem was placed on their work sheets, but they were not shown how to perform the problems. For other children only the demonstration was provided during the intervention period. The teacher showed them how to do a sample problem and then took away the model. The pupils were unable to refer to the sample as they worked the problems.

The results of these efforts indicated mixed success; for some pupils this partial technique was effective; for others it was not. Because the total technique—demonstration and permanent model—required about 2 minutes of instructional time, it was recommended that the whole intervention be used.

Withdrawing Positive Reinforcement.   The primary difficulty of the pupil in this study was not acquisition, for she could solve rather complex computational problems and neither was her difficulty one of obtaining proficiency. Her correct rates for most basic facts matched those of her peers. This young lady's performance was erratic. Some days, when asked to perform certain subtraction problems, she was very accurate. On other days, she erred on all the problems. Occasionally, her responses to a row of problems would simply be a series of numbers, like 21, 22, 23. She was apparently not motivated to perform consistently (Smith, Lovitt, & Kidder, 1972).

Daily, she was assigned three pages of arithmetic problems. On each page there were 25 problems of a different class. The Class 1 (C1) problems were like $18 - 9 = \square$. C2 problems were of the class $24 - 6 = \square$; borrowing was required. C3 problems were like $34 - 6 = \square$; again borrowing was required. For each class of problems several sheets of different problems were developed. Thus, the pupil worked on different figures from day to day.

A multiple-baseline design was used in the study. Throughout the baseline phase, which ran for 6 days, no instruction, feedback, or reinforcement was scheduled. When the pupil had responded to the problems on the three sheets, she submitted her papers to the teacher. No further interaction took place. Her performance during this period was variable. Her scores on two of the three sheets were high one day and low the next (see Fig. 5.6).

Throughout the second condition a withdrawal contingency went into effect; for each error she made on the C1 sheet, 1 minute of recess time was taken away.

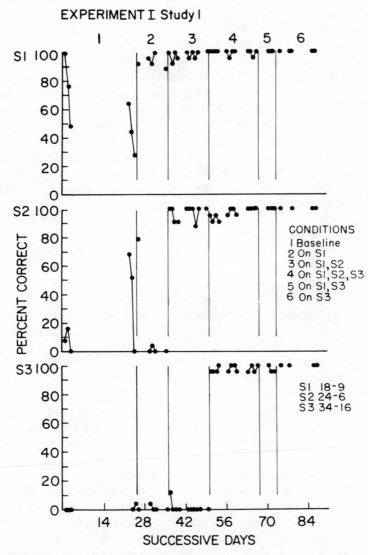

FIG. 5.6. Correct percentage scores for the three arithmetic sheets throughout the study (Smith, Lovitt, & Kidder, 1972.)

Those data revealed that her scores on C1 were high, but her scores on the other two sheets remained low.

During the next phase the same withdrawal contingency was associated with the C2 problems and the C1 items. In the next condition the contingency was arranged for all three sheets. Successively, as the contingency was arranged, the girl's performance improved.

During the next two conditions, the contingency was removed, first from the C2 sheet and then from C1. In the final phase the contingency was in effect for only the C3 sheet. As indicated in the figure, her accuracy on all the sheets remained high, even when the contingency was removed.

That the girl was sensitive to the withdrawal contingency was indicated by her response pattern in two ways. First, she reacted immediately. On each sheet, her performance improved greatly the day the contingency was scheduled. Second, this immediate accuracy was noted on only the contingency sheet; when the point removal technique was arranged for C1, only performance on that sheet improved, not on the other two.

It was somewhat encouraging when her accuracy continued to be high during the final two phases. When the contingency was removed from the C1 and C2 sheets, her performance did not collapse; apparently something was maintaining her behavior besides the withdrawal contingency.

Scheduling an Antecedent Event to Facilitate Subtraction.   The experiment described here was one of the initial *ABA* research efforts that investigated the effect of an event other than a reinforcement contingency (Lovitt & Curtiss, 1968). Three studies comprised the experiment; each used an *ABA* design. The pupil in the experiment was an 11-year-old boy.

Study 1 consisted of three conditions. Throughout the study the boy was required to perform 20 problems of the type $\square - 2 = 6$. In the baseline phase he received no teaching, feedback, or reinforcement. When he finished the problems, he was thanked and sent on to another academic activity.

During the second condition, he was required to verbalize each problem before he wrote the answer. He said, for instance, "Some number minus two equals six." He then wrote the answer. The teacher monitored his behavior during this phase and reminded him occasionally to verbalize each response. During a third phase, he was asked to refrain from verbalizing the problems and answers.

The data from this study indicated that his performance was far superior in the condition when verbalization was required than during the baseline phase when no verbalization was demanded. Further, his performance maintained, even improved, in the final condition when verbalization was no longer practiced.

Two other studies like the first were carried out. In the second, problems of the type $\square - 20 = 40$ were used. The problems in the third study were like $4 - 3 = 9 - \square$. Both of these studies were composed of three phases. During the first, no verbalization was required. The pupil verbalized each problem and answer

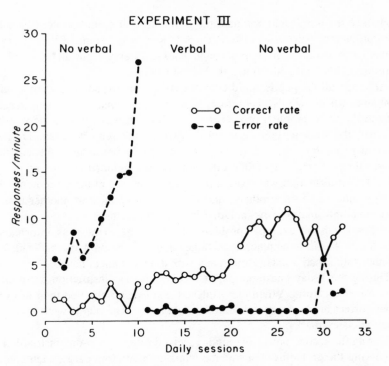

FIG. 5.7. Correct and incorrect rates for the pupil during the three experimental phases. The mathematics problems were of the type $4 - 3 = 9 - \square$. (Lovitt & Curtiss, 1968).

throughout phase 2; then in the final phase he no longer verbalized. Figure 5.7 shows the data in Experiment III.

The results of these studies were identical to those of Study 1. During the baseline phase his correct rate and accuracy were low and then much improved in the second phase. In the final condition the behavior of subtracting was maintained, in spite of the removal of the cue.

The experiment demonstrated that a technique that has been used for years by teachers and parents can be effective. Many teachers have encouraged their pupils to think before they make a response. More important, this experiment demonstrated the inclusiveness of *ABA* techniques. Clearly, all the teaching variables used by teachers for years—modeling, various aids, and mnemonic systems—can be evaluated within the *ABA* framework. These events can as easily be subjected to analysis as the many reinforcement variables that have for so long been monitored by this system.

Teaching Pupils to Solve Story Problems. Four pupils, three boys and a girl, were involved in this project. They were either 10 or 11 years old and attended a class for learning disabled students at the EEU.

Before the study began, the manager determined whether the students could pronounce the words and compute the problems that would be used later in the word problems. Thirty-two different words were used, some of them were *boy, mother, car, another, dogs, balls,* and *books.* Twenty-eight different add facts were used. They ranged from $2 + 2 = \square$ to $8 + 5 = \square$.

Although all the pupils could compute the problems, some of them could not pronounce all the words. Therefore, a brief instructional period was scheduled prior to the word problem project in order to teach the words to the pupils.

When the students could say all the words, the project began. During the baseline phase they were given two sheets of six problems each and told to answer them. Some extraneous information was included in nine of the problems. This information was written in the first sentence of three problems, in the middle sentence of three others, and in the final sentence of another three. No extraneous information was included in three problems.

Following is an example problem in which the extraneous information is included in the first sentence: "A father had 8 cats and a mother had 2 cats. Another father had 3 cats. How many cats did the fathers have?"

During this 8-day phase the pupils received neither instruction nor reinforcement for their efforts. When they finished, the teacher checked their answers as either correct or incorrect and returned the papers. The pupils were told to look over the check marks.

During the second phase the pupils received some one-to-one instruction prior to working the problems. For this the manager made four cards; each contained one of the problem types used in the study. Three of them included extraneous information in one of the three sentences, but the other contained no extraneous information.

Before the cards were shown to the pupils, the teacher informed them that occasionally some unnecessary information is included in word problems. Therefore, they must read the problems carefully in order to determine whether or not this is so. If a problem does contain unnecessary information, they should not use it as they calculate the answer.

Following this explanation the pupils were shown the cards one at a time. They were instructed to read the problem aloud and then determine whether there was unnecessary information in the problem and, if there were, to point it out. If they could do those steps correctly, they were asked to solve the problem. If they could not identify the extraneous information or in some other way were confused, they were given assistance. After they finally responded correctly to the four cards, they were given the 12 problems to solve just as they had during the baseline period. They were told to use the same approach for answering the problems they used when they solved the four example items.

The performances of all four children were better in the second than in the first phase. Verlinda's correct rates changed from $\div 1.2$ to X1.4; Brian's from X2.0 to X2.5; Jay's from X1.0 to X1.5; and Brent's from X1.5 to X3.2. The incorrect rate changes for the four youngsters were just as dramatic.

Spelling Research

Giving Free Time to Improve Spelling.   Perhaps the most significant feature of this investigation was the demonstration that leisure time could serve as an effective reinforcer for most of the members of a class (Lovitt, Guppy, & Blattner, 1969). In order to arrange leisure time as a contingent reinforcer the classroom was slightly modified.

The study took place in a regular fourth-grade class of 32 pupils. The project was conducted entirely by the classroom teacher who administered the spelling program, calculated and graphed the pupils' scores, and managed the contingency system.

An AB design was used. During the baseline phase the spelling program was administered in a rather traditional manner. On Monday the new words were introduced and the children read a story containing those words. On Wednesday a trial test was given. On Thursday they completed workbook exercises that pertained to the words and wrote each word several times. On Friday the final test was given. Each pupil's Friday score was graphed as a correct percentage score.

During the second phase of the study the pupils were presented the new list of words and given the same type of spelling assignments as before. During this phase the pupils were simply required to hand in their work; no specific time was scheduled for the completion of these activities as there had been in the first phase. A second difference between this condition and the former was that spelling tests were given four days a week rather than once.

During this phase the pupils were through with spelling for the week when they received a 100% score. If on Tuesday, the day of the first test, a pupil scored 100% and he had handed in the assignments, he was free during the time of the subsequent spelling tests to engage in a number of leisure time pursuits. He could read a comic book, work on a puzzle, draw pictures. A pupil continued taking the test until his score was perfect or through Friday.

Throughout the second phase the teacher recorded a pupil's score as 100% if he returned a perfect paper on Tuesday, Wednesday, Thursday, or Friday; otherwise, if he never achieved 100%, his Friday score was recorded. Furthermore, the teacher recorded on each pupil's graph a numeral that corresponded to the day the score was obtained (e.g., 1 = Tuesday, 2 = Wednesday).

As a result of being able to earn free time or to escape from spelling, the performances of most children improved. Twice as many 100% papers were recorded in the second condition as during the first. Many children obtained 100% scores in the second phase that had never before done so. Figure 5.8 shows the number of 100% scores in the two conditions.

This project, beyond the fact that a system to arrange free time in the classroom was devised, suggests a strategy for assisting teachers to gather data. Perhaps when they are requested to obtain data and graph the academic perfor-

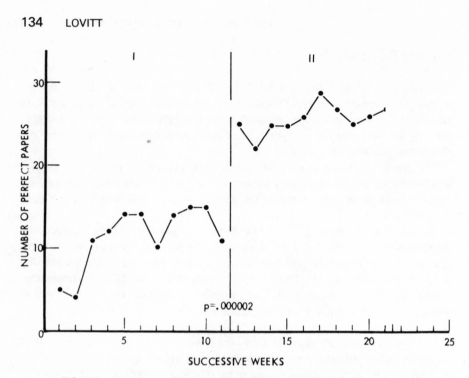

FIG. 5.8.   Number of 100% papers recorded each successive week throughout the two experimental conditions (Lovitt, Guppy, & Blattner, 1969.)

mances of pupils, spelling is the best place to begin. Two reasons might support such a statement. One, the procedures for instructing spelling are essentially the same from week to week. Furthermore, spelling performance is generally assessed at least once each week. Two, most teachers already record pupil performance in spelling. They indicate in their record books the weekly percentage scores of the pupils. It is a simple matter to convert these notations into percentage points on a graph.

Assessing and Modifying b–d Reversals.   There were seven students in this project: six boys who were either 9 or 10 years old and a girl who was 10.

The students were enrolled in a class for learning disabled students at the EEU. Their teacher reported that all the students often reversed the letters *b* and *d* when they wrote and when they read.

The initial purpose of the project was to determine the extent to which the children reversed the two letters. In order to determine this, the pupils were required to respond to a series of words by writing them (hear to write) and by reading them (see to say). Further, the pupils were required to identify the letters in final and initial positions.

A set of 40 words was developed. Five of them began with *b* and five with *d*.

Five ended with *b* and five with *d*. Five words began with *b* and ended with *b;* five others began with *b* and ended with *d;* five began with *d* and ended with *d;* and five began with *d* and ended with *b*.

All the words were common words and contained a short vowel. In each subset (e.g., those beginning with *b*) each word contained a different short vowel. This list was used to assess performance in both the see-to-say and hear-to-write channels.

On one day the pupil first read the words. As he did so, the manager wrote down the exact sounds he pronounced. Following, the manager read the words to him. He was asked to write down only the *b* or *d* sounds he heard, not the entire word. This order was reversed the next day.

During the baseline phase that ran for 5 days, the manager neither gave the students feedback regarding their performances nor instructed them about identifying the two letters. Their performances during this phase were very poor, particularly in respect to the see to say activity. The mean number of reversals of the children ranged from 15 to 31 in this period. Meanwhile, the mean number of reversals for the hear to write activity ranged from 3 to 38.

Throughout a second phase an instructional technique was scheduled. This phase ran from 4 to 9 days depending on the performance of the pupils. The criterion for ending the phase was that no more than two reversals could be made for two consecutive days. The technique focused on the see-to-say channels because most of the pupils had more difficulty with these modes than with the hear-to-write channels.

For the intervention the manager developed two sets of cards. There were six cards in each set. The letter *b* was on one card and *d* was on another. The words *bad, bab, dad,* and *dab* were on the other four cards. The letters on the first set were colored: *b* in red, *d* in blue, and *a* in black. The letters in the second set were all black.

The manager used the colored set first to rehearse the youngsters. He then used the black-and-white set. During the rehearsal period, which lasted about 5 minutes for each child, the youngsters were required to read the letters and words. They were given feedback and assistance during this training. Following this period, the youngsters were assessed on the 40 words in the two modes just as they were throughout the baseline period.

The performances of six children improved considerably in both modes during this second phase. Their mean range of reversals in the see-to-say activity was from 3 to 7. Not only did they improve in this activity, their performances in the hear-to-write channels improved even though they received no direct instruction for that activity. Their mean number of reversals in this mode ranged from 1 to 20.

Maintenance and generalization data were also obtained for these six pupils. Two weeks following the time a student reached criterion in the instructional period, he was again required to respond to the words. Shortly after that maintenance check the pupils were required to respond, by reading and writing, to a number of words that were longer than those used in the project. The maintenance and generalization scores were very good for the six pupils.

Throughout and following the project, the classroom teacher kept data in regard to the *b–d* reversals of the pupils while they read orally and wrote words during spelling and handwriting periods. She reported that although several reversals were noted during the beginning of the study, very few were observed during or following the treatment.

Pupil Management Research

Selecting either Math or Reading.   This study was designed to determine the effects of selecting either reading or mathematics on performance rates in those two activities (Lovitt, 1973). The project was conducted with two boys, one 8 and the other 12.

The first pupil was permitted to select whether to work on mathematics or reading for a 20-minute session each day. The mathematics material was from *Suppes* Book 2A; whereas Book 7 of the *Sullivan* materials was used for reading.

Following this period of pupil selection, two teacher-selected periods were scheduled. During the first of these, the pupil was required to continue for 40 minutes in the academic area he had chosen during the pupil-select period. In the next, which lasted for 60 minutes, the alternate academic material was scheduled.

The sequence of periods for the second pupil differed. In the first period, one of teacher selection, he was alternately programmed either mathematics or reading for 30 minutes each day. The mathematics assignment was from *Suppes* Book 3B and reading from the *Sullivan* Books 19 and 20.

In the second period, which also lasted 30 minutes, he was allowed to select either reading or mathematics. Finally, for the 30-minute third period, the boy was assigned the academic material alternate to that presented in the first period.

Three calculations were obtained each day, one each for mathematics and reading when the teacher selected the program and one for the pupil-select period. The results for the first pupil revealed that on 24 of 26 days his performance rate was greater when he selected the subject than his rate on the same program when it was chosen by the teacher. The performance of the second boy was similar: During 17 of 25 sessions his correct rate was greater when he selected than on the same material when it was scheduled by the teacher.

For these two boys it appeared that self-selection was a motivating variable. Being allowed to select, even between two relatively low-strength tasks (mathematics and reading), was for them a reinforcing event.

We have conducted a number of pupil-management projects during the past few years that focused on various management components. In some, the pupils graphed their own data; in others they specified their own performance objectives and designed their own daily schedules. Projects have been conducted wherein pupils timed their performances and counted and corrected their responses. In one project a pupil selected his own instructional technique.

Invariably, these projects showed that pupils were motivated when they were given a "piece of the action." This motivation was indicated by the fact that in the conditions where they were partially responsible for their behavior, their performances were generally better than when the teacher managed the entire situation.

Specifying Contingencies in Academic Areas.   This experiment was concerned with the comparative effects of teacher- or pupil-specified contingencies (Lovitt & Curtiss, 1969). The pupil in this experiment was a 12-year-old boy. The investigation consisted of three separate studies—two that manipulated the contingency manager and one that manipulated magnitude of reinforcement. In each study an *ABA* design was used.

Throughout these studies the boy received points for academic responses. In reading he was granted two points for each correctly read page. That ratio was 1:2. The ratios in the other academic areas varied. Points were redeemable for minutes of free time.

During Study 1, baseline data relevant to the pupil's academic response rates were obtained for 9 days. Each day a response rate figure was calculated that represented the boy's performance in all his subject matter areas. Throughout this period no attempt was made to explain to the student the response per point ratio in each academic area.

Following this baseline period, the next phase was instituted. It was the intent at this time to instruct the pupil about the relationship between correct answers and contingent points. Each day during this condition, the teacher explained the contingencies and placed a written copy of the ratios on the boy's desk. The contract was composed of nine agreements; each had a response per point ratio. For example, the pupil was granted two points for each page read and one point for 10 correctly answered problems. As he completed each academic assignment, he was shown how many responses had been made and was asked to calculate the number of points he had earned.

In the next condition, the copy of the response per point requirements was removed from the pupil's desk. He was now asked to specify his own payment for each of the nine areas. These new specifications were printed on a card that was attached to his desk. Throughout the last phase the teacher-imposed contingencies were again in effect.

During the next quarter Study 2 began. The procedures for this investigation were exactly like those in Study 1: Teacher contingencies were explained, written out, and attached to the student's desk in phases 1 and 3, while during phase 2 the pupil's contingencies were in effect. Figure 5.9 illustrates the data from Study 2.

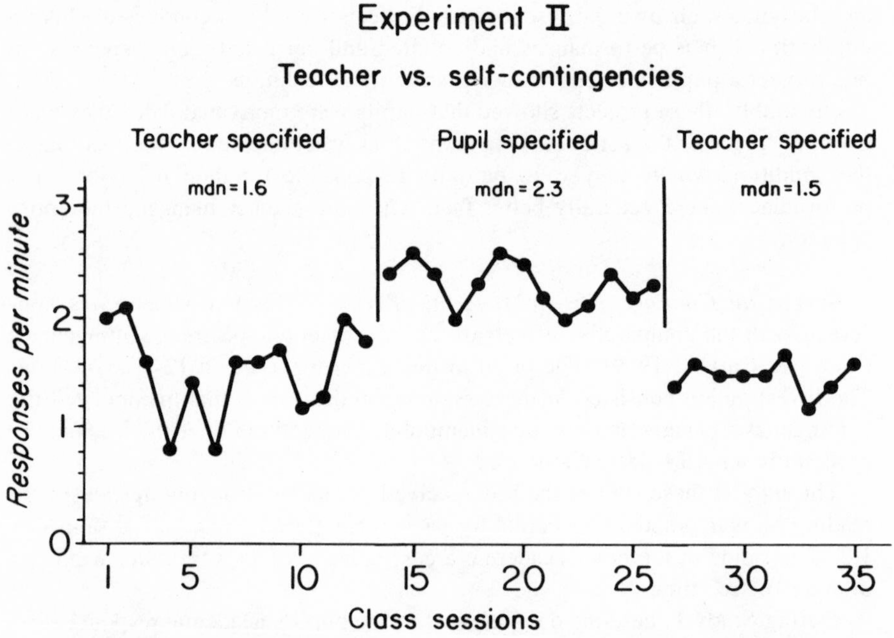

Experiment II

Teacher vs. self-contingencies

FIG. 5.9. Response rates throughout the three conditions of Experiment II (Lovitt & Curtiss, 1969.)

Following this replication study, Study 3 was conducted. Because during Study 2 the pupil altered all the teacher-imposed requirements to grant himself more points per response, it was necessary to determine whether being able to specify his own contingencies had effected the academic increase or whether this gain was due to the increased payoff. Study 3, therefore, consisted of three phases: (1) The teacher specified the response per point requirements she had placed in effect throughout Studies 1 and 2. (2) The teacher specified the requirements that the pupil had instituted during Study 2. (3) The teacher again specified her original requirements. The only difference between Studies 2 and 3 was that in Study 3 the teacher imposed the contingency requirements throughout, whereas in Study 2 the pupil set his own contingencies during phase 2.

The data from these experiments indicated that, for this boy, self-specified contingencies were associated with increased academic response rate. This was evidenced in Studies 1 and 2, because during the periods when the pupil arranged the contingencies, his median performance rate was higher than during the periods when the teacher imposed the contingencies. In addition, the data from Study 3 revealed that the response rate was due to the contingency manager and not to reinforcement magnitude, because his rates were about the same across all phases.

CURRENT PRACTICE AND FUTURE RESEARCH

In this section some remarks are included about the current use of *ABA* techniques in public-school situations. Also included are some comments about future research needs in this area.

Classroom Practice

It would certainly be misleading for one to say that great numbers of classroom teachers throughout the United States were using *ABA* techniques. Unfortunately, this is not true. The impact of this approach is indicated, for the most part, in special education classrooms.

There are, however, several teachers throughout the country who routinely use behavioral principles that emanated from that methodology as they interact with their pupils. They tend to reinforce good behaviors and ignore inappropriate behaviors. Moreover, there are other teachers who occasionally chart the frequencies of various inappropriate behaviors. There are other special education teachers who have established token economies.

In some parts of the country teachers have extended the use of *ABA* techniques. Some of them have kept data on several academic behaviors of their children. The precision teaching system, developed by O. R. Lindsley, has to a great extent been responsible for this.

Although there are pockets of teachers in several parts of the country who use precision teaching techniques, the following are the areas of greatest concentration: Seattle, Washington; Great Falls, Montana; Gainsville, Florida; Kansas City, Kansas; and Denver, Colorado.

In the Seattle area there are about 250 special education teachers who currently use precision teaching techniques. In those situations where data are kept, they are obtained for different purposes, some of which are more sophisticated than others.

One reason for some teachers obtaining data is for placement purposes. Earlier in this chapter a procedure for placing children in reading levels was described. When that method is used, children are assigned to various instructional levels on the basis of their performances, not because of their ages or grade levels. Several teachers have used procedures similar to those described for reading to place children at various levels in spelling and mathematics.

Another reason that some teachers have kept data on children is to monitor their progress. Many of them keep data in respect to children's performances in several academic areas: oral reading, comprehension, handwriting, mathematics. By charting performances over a period of time, teachers can discern at any point how their pupils are progressing or if, in fact, they are progressing at all.

Another reason for keeping data in respect to pupil performance is to be apprised of the effects of instructional techniques. If, for example, a teacher obtains data from a pupil during two different conditions as she works on mathematics problems, he can determine the effects of the different situations. Using such an evaluative strategy, teachers can learn quickly about the effects of their instructional practices.

Still another reason for gathering pupil performance data is for purposes of communication. Teachers can consult the performance charts of their pupils and thus communicate objectively with the pupils themselves, their parents, other teachers, or administrators.

Yet another reason for obtaining pupil data, and certainly the most sophisticated, is to provide assistance for making programming decisions. Some teachers rely on performance data to inform them about when to abandon one instructional technique in favor of another or to move from one type of material to other.

To indicate the extent to which a precision teaching data system may be incorporated in a classroom, Table 5.2 is included. In that table the subjects in

TABLE 5.2
Data System

School Olympic View   Teacher C. S.   Date 12/14/77

	Charts			Perform. Aims		Progress Lines		Phases		Looks		Communications					
Subjects	6c	%	0	Set	Met	Set	Used	Comp.	Anal.	M	A	M B	B M	A M	M A	M O	O M
Oral reading	20			13	11	12	1	10	10	100	60	42				1	
Say words	11			11	7	11	1	24	18	51	24	14				2	1
Say sounds	12			11	9	12	2	17	13	56	35	8				2	
English	11							55	4	47	41					1	
Lang. arts	1							2		2	1						
Soc. studies	11							16	12	32	23					1	
Write letters	1																
Write cursive	11			4	4	5	1	25	18	47	24	2	1			1	
Math: add	4			4	2	4	1	16	13	39	13					1	
Math: mult.	25			16	14	16	5	74	56	133	50	5				1	
Total	107																

which data are kept are listed. Alongside the subjects are descriptors about the various types of charts that relate to those subjects (6C = six cycle; % = percentage; O = other). Information is also included about the number of performance aims that were set and, of those, how many were met. Also shown is information about the number of progress lines that were set and used. Information about the number of completed and analyzed phases per subject is provided. Data regarding "looks" or inspections are also indicated (M = manager; A = advisor). Finally, data are included about the various types of communications in reference to each subject ($_B^M$ = manager to behaver; $_M^B$ = behaver to manager; $_M^A$ = advisor to manager; $_A^M$ = manager to advisor; $_O^M$ = manager to other; and $_M^O$ = other to manager).

As revealed by this table, this teacher keeps 107 charts, most of which are daily. Also indicated is that she uses the charts for decision making and communication purposes. Admittedly, this teacher is not representative of other special education teachers. She maintains more charts and makes better use of them than anyone I know. Her situation is described simply to indicate what is possible.

Future Research Needs

There are several curricular areas that should be investigated using *ABA* or precision teaching techniques. Certainly more research should be focused on the basic skills: reading, handwriting, spelling, and arithmetic. Although those areas have received some attention, further investigations should attempt to determine minimum competency levels for each subject to establish the best sequences of subskills within each subject.

The greatest curriculum research needs, however, are in the more complex subject areas. Only a few *ABA* investigations have dealt with reading comprehension, creative writing, complex language processes, music, art, or social studies. Indeed, one of the most frequent criticisms of the *ABA* system is that the approach is adequate for only the most basic behaviors.

There is also a need for *ABA* to consider other research organizations if their goal is to disseminate their findings to public schools and other applied situations. The current approach of *ABA* is to conduct research in either a laboratory school or a carefully selected public-school classroom. When their research was completed, it was written up and submitted to a journal. According to many researchers they fulfilled their scientific obligation at that point and it was then up to classroom teachers to read, digest, and implement their procedures. The naivete of such a long-used strategy is frightening.

Although there must be several approaches to the matter of disseminating research, we have developed a process that we believe will improve greatly the relationships between teachers and researchers. In this system teachers from the public schools and the university are involved. The initial responsibility of the public-school teachers is to identify curricular needs. The initial responsibility of the teachers at the university is to arrange situations to develop materials or procedures to respond to those needs. When materials or procedures have been developed at the university and successfully used in that location, they are transmitted to the public schools. If they are not successful in those locations, they are brought back to the university and further research is arranged. If they are successful, they are transported to other public-school situations.

Research models such as this should increase positive interactions between researchers and teachers. Accordingly, research will play a more prominent role in designing the features of classrooms and, following, children will be better served.

REFERENCES

Azrin, N. H., & Lindsley, O. R. The reinforcement of cooperation between children. *Journal of Abnormal and Social Psychology*, 1956, *52*, 100–102.

Baer, D. M., & Sherman, J. A. Reinforcement control of generalized imitation. *Journal of Experimental Child Psychology*, 1964, *1*, 37–49.

Baer, D. M., Wolf, M. M., & Risley, T. R. Some current dimensions of applied behavior analysis. *Journal of Applied Behavior Analysis*, 1968, *1*, 91–97.

Becker, W. C., Madsen, C. H., Jr., Arnold, C., & Thomas, D. R. The contingent use of teacher attention and praise in reducing classroom behavior problems. *Journal of Special Education*, 1967, *1*, 287–307.

Bijou, S. W. Operant extinction after fixed-interval schedules with young children. *Journal of the Experimental Analysis of Behavior*, 1958, *1*, 25–29.

Birnbrauer, J. S., Wolf, M. M., Kidder, J. D., & Tague, C. E. Classroom behavior of retarded pupils with token reinforcement. *Journal of Experimental Child Psychology*, 1965, *2*, 219–235.

Cossairt, A., Hall, R. V., & Hopkins, B. L. The effects of experimenter's instructions, feedback, and praise on teacher praise and student attending behavior. *Journal of Applied Behavior Analysis*, 1973, *6*, 89–100.

Eaton, M., & Lovitt, T. C. Achievement tests vs. direct and daily measurement. In G. Semb (Ed.), *Behavior analysis and education—1972*. Lawrence, Kan.: University of Kansas Press, 1972, 78–87.

Hall, R. V., Lund, D., & Jackson, D. Effects of teacher attention on study behavior. *Journal of Applied Behavior Analysis*, 1968, *1*, 1–12.

Harris, F. R., Wolf, M. M., & Baer, D. M. Effects of adult social reinforcement on child behavior. *Young Children*, 1964, *20*, 8–17.

Homme, L. E., deBaca, P. C., Devine, J. V., Steinhorst, R., & Rickert, E. J. Use of the Premack principle in controlling the behavior of nursery school children. *Journal of the Experimental Analysis of Behavior*, 1963, *6*, 544.

Lovaas, O. I., Freitag, G., Kinder, M. L., Rubenstein, B. D., Schaeffer, B., & Simmons, J. Q. Establishment of social reinforcers in two schizophrenic children on the basis of food. *Journal of Experimental Child Psychology*, 1966, *4*, 109–125.

Lovaas, O. I., Freitag, L., Nelson, K., & Whalen, C. The establishment of imitation and its use for the establishment of complex behavior in schizophrenic children. *Behaviour Research and Therapy*, 1967, *5*, 171–181.

Lovitt, T. C. Self-management projects with children with behavioral disabilities. *Journal of Learning Disabilities*, 1973, *6*, 138–150.

Lovitt, T. C., & Curtiss, K. A. Effects of manipulating an antecedent event on mathematics response rate. *Journal of Applied Behavior Analysis,* 1968, *1,* 329-333.

Lovitt, T. C., Guppy, T. C., & Blattner, J. E. The use of a free-time contingency with fourth graders to increase spelling accuracy. *Behaviour Research and Therapy,* 1969, *7,* 151-156.

Lovitt, T. C., & Hansen, C. L. Round one—placing the child in the right reader. *Journal of Learning Disabilities,* 1976, *6,* 347-353. (a)

Lovitt, T. C., & Hansen, C. L. The use of contingent skipping and drilling to improve oral reading and comprehension. *Journal of Learning Disabilities,* 1976, *9,* 481-487. (b)

Lovitt, T. C., & Hurlbut, M. Using behavior-analysis techniques to assess the relationship between phonics instruction and oral reading. *Journal of Special Education,* 1974, *8,* 57-72.

O'Leary, K. D., Kaufman, K. F., Kass, R. E., & Drabman, R. S. The effects of loud and soft reprimands on the behavior of disruptive students. *Exceptional Children,* 1970, *37,* 145-155.

Smith, D. D., & Lovitt, T. C. The use of modeling techniques to influence the acquisition of computational arithmetic skills in learning disabled children. In E. Ramp and G. Semb (Eds.), *Behavior analysis: Areas of research and application.* Englewood Cliffs, N.J.: Prentice-Hall, 1975, 283-308.

Smith, D. D., Lovitt, T. C., & Kidder, J. D. Using reinforcement contingencies and teaching aids to teach subtraction skills to learning disabled pupils. In G. Semb (Ed.), *Behavior analysis and education—1972.* Lawrence, Kan.: University of Kansas Press, 1972, 342-360.

Staats, A. W., & Butterfield, W. H. Treatment of nonreading in a culturally deprived juvenile delinquent: An application of reinforcement principles. *Child Development,* 1965, *4,* 925-942.

Staats, A. W., Finley, J. R., Minke, K. A., & Wolf, M. M. Reinforcement variables in the control of unit reading responses. *Journal of the Experimental Analysis of Behavior,* 1964, *7,* 139-149.

Staats, A. W., Staats, C. K., Schutz, R. E., & Wolf, M. M. The conditioning of textual responses using "extrinsic" reinforcers. *Journal of the Experimental Analysis of Behavior,* 1962, *5,* 33-40.

Wolf, M. M., Risley, T. R., & Mees, H. L. Application of operant conditioning procedures to the behaviour problems of an autistic child. *Behaviour Research & Therapy,* 1964, *1,* 305-312.

Zimmerman, E. H., & Zimmerman, J. The alteration of behavior in a special classroom situation. *Journal of the Experimental Analysis of Behavior,* 1962, *5,* 59-60.

6

Direct Instruction: A Behavior Theory Model for Comprehensive Educational Intervention with the Disadvantaged

Wesley C. Becker
Douglas W. Carnine
University of Oregon

INTRODUCTION

During the past decade a variety of approaches to teaching children from economically disadvantaged homes have been studied within a planned-variation quasi-experiment called *Follow Through*. Follow Through was given its name because it was viewed as a program that would follow through on the educational efforts initiated in Head Start for preschool children. Although initially planned as a service program like Head Start, a restriction in funds led to a shift in focus from service to "finding out what works" (Egbert, 1973). The project was administered by the U.S. Office of Education with funds from the Office of Economic Opportunity.

In Follow Through the developers of a variety of promising programs for teaching the disadvantaged in the primary grades (K–3) were invited to propose model programs. The models were to have an educational program at the core but would also include comprehensive services and maximum involvement of the communities being served. School districts and model sponsors were brought together at a "show-and-tell" meeting held in Kansas City in February, 1968, and through subsequent negotiations became aligned with one another. Follow Through eventually came to serve 75,000 low-income children annually, from 170 communities, under the guidance of 20 model sponsors. Several of the models had their theoretical base in behavior theory—especially the University of Kansas Behavior Analysis Model and the University of Oregon Direct Instruction Model. A national evaluation compared the performance of 13 model sponsors in the "Cohort II Study" and 16 model sponsors in the "Cohort III Study."[1]

---

[1]Cohort II children entered kindergarten or first grade in the fall of 1970; Cohort III children entered the program in the fall of 1971.

Clearly, the most effective model in comparison to control groups and in comparison to national norms was the Direct Instruction Model. In this chapter we examine the Follow Through outcome data for nine major sponsors, discuss the procedures used by the Direct Instruction Model to achieve its results, and attempt to place the findings within the context of current research on effective teaching behavior, programming strategies, and classroom operations.

THE FOLLOW THROUGH EVALUATION

The basic data for the National Evaluation were collected by Stanford Research Institute and analyzed by Abt Associates Inc. following a design adopted by Garry McDaniels for the U.S. Office of Education with guidance from the Huron Institute and a panel of educational experts. Considerable controversy exists about this evaluation. Questions have been raised about the fairness of the measures, the adequacy of the samples, the appropriateness of various analyses, and the kinds of conclusions that have been drawn. The major report of the evaluation was published by Abt Associates Inc. in April 1977 (the Abt IV Report). When coupled with an earlier report (Abt Associates Inc., 1976, the Abt III Report), these reports present the major data base and analyses in the National Evaluation of Follow Through.

Because of concerns by some in education that the Abt reports would not be fair to some educational models focusing on cognitive and affective outcomes, the Ford Foundation commissioned a group under the direction of Ernest House (House, Glass, McLean, & Walker, 1977) to examine the Abt IV Report and to present an independent appraisal and interpretation of the data. In presenting the findings we will attempt to keep the reader informed of how other analyses or interpretations might influence the data and the conclusions. A more detailed discussion on the evaluation of Follow Through and the nature of the Direct Instruction Model is in preparation (Engelmann & Becker, in preparation).

Design

The design treated each site (school district) implementing a model and its comparison group as the basic unit for analysis. The design also permitted aggregation of effects within models across sites to study model effects. Although the Abt reports present data on 16 sponsors, we restrict this presentation to the nine major model sponsors who are responsible for 51 out of 62 sites in the Cohort II Study and 60 out of 77 sites in the Cohort III Study. Major sponsors were evaluated in four to eight sites with kindergartens and worked in as many as 20 school districts. Some minor sponsors had but a single site. A smaller sample of first-grade starting sites was also included where available. In most cases the children were tested at entry and each spring thereafter until third grade was completed. The Cohort II analytic sample included 4205 Follow Through children and 2901 comparison children on whom there were complete data. The Cohort III analytic sample included 5050 Follow Through children and 3584 comparison children.

One problem with the design was that more often than not the comparison groups were the children left over after the most disadvantaged (economically) were selected for Follow Through (FT). Because of this, socioeconomic-related and entry-score covariates were used to adjust outcomes for initial differences that tended to favor Non-Follow Through (NFT). Under these conditions, covariance analysis will tend to underestimate by an unknown amount the FT versus NFT differences at the end of third grade (Campbell & Erlebacher, 1970).

Another problem with the design is that no provision was made for evaluating adequacy of model implementation for the sites used in the National Evaluation. Thus, there is a problem in differentiating adequacy of model from adequacy of its implementation. *The results clearly confound the two, and conclusions should retain this caution.*[2] Social–political problems also enter into analysis. For example, in Grand Rapids, Michigan, a change of program directors in 1971 led to the site failing to continue implementation of the Direct Instruction Model. In the middle of the 1972 school years, after struggling to get the site to follow model procedures, we withdrew as sponsor. An attempt to reestablish the model in 1973 failed. Grand Rapids continued to be funded and continued in the National Evaluation as a Direct Instruction site, even though neither of these actions was justified in terms of the Follow Through agreements. Grand Rapids represents 2 of the 16 data points for our model. On most measures they perform more than a year below our other kindergarten-entering sites.

Tests

The test battery included measures of basic academic skills, cognitive-conceptual skills, and measures relating to affect or self-image. The four measures of Basic Skills are from the Elementary Level, Form F, of the Metropolitan Achievement Test (MAT) (1970): Word Knowledge, Spelling, Language (usage), and Math Computation. The Cognitive–Conceptual Skills include MAT Reading, MAT Math Concepts, MAT Math Problem Solving, and Raven's Col-

---

[2]Two studies of implementation were commissioned. One was carried out by Stanford Research Institute under the direction of Jane Stallings (Stallings, 1975) and used classroom observations with a sample of classrooms in first and third grade for seven sponsors. The results tended to show that classroom operations were discriminable between sponsors and that different models were in fact in operation. However, adequacy of implementation was not assessed nor were the observations necessarily focused on the groups in the National Evaluation. Nero & Associates (1976) studied implementation processes and communalities of problems across sponsors through sponsor interviews and site visitations. This report serves to highlight the implementation issue but does nothing to alleviate the problem of adequacy of implementation.

oured Progressive Matrices (1956). The Affective Measures include the Coopersmith Self-Esteem Inventory (1967), and the Intellectual Achievement Responsibility Scale (IARS+ and IARS−) (Crandall, Katkowsky & Crandall, 1965). The Coopersmith was designed to assess children's feelings about themselves, the way they think other people feel about them, and feelings about school. The IARS measures the extent to which children attribute their success (+) or failures (−) to themselves or to outside forces.[3,4]

The Children Served

The Direct Instruction Model has provided services to students from low-income homes in 20 communities. Our communities included a cross section of "poor" America—rural and inner-city blacks, rural whites, Mexican Americans in Texas, Spanish Americans in New Mexico, native Americans in South Dakota and North Carolina, and a variety of ethnically mixed communities. Approximately 8000 low-income students were in the program at one time. More than 27,000 names have entered our computer file. Other sponsors have usually served a similar range of communities.

The Model Sponsors

Before presenting the data, we need to introduce the nine sponsors who provided the bulk of the Follow Through data. Although the names of their projects (TEEM, EDC, Responsive Education, etc.) may not be familiar to the reader, the philosophy espoused by each probably is.

1. Responsive Education Model (Far West Laboratory for Educational R and D).   This model, based on the work of Glenn Nimnicht, is highly "eclectic." Techniques include those used by O. K. Moore (the "talking typewriter"), Maria Montessori, and Martin Deutsch. The Follow Through Resource Guide (Nero & Associates, 1976) provides this description:

---

[3]The reliabilities (internal consistency) of the MAT scores computed by Abt Associates for Follow Through children are comparable to those published by the test developer. They range from .88 to .97, with Total Reading and Total Math falling at the upper end of this range. Internal consistency coefficients for the other measures as reported by Abt Associates (1977) are .80 for the Coopersmith, .85 for the Raven's, .59 for IARS+, and .65 for IARS−. The IARS measures are too low in reliability to be useful for individual judgments but could be useful for group comparisons.

[4]The House et al. report (1977) attacks all the measures listed above except the MAT as unreliable and invalid. Although we would agree that the self-report measures of affective outcome must be treated with caution, it is unlikely that they would be questioned if the proponents of affective outcomes had done well on them. Furthermore, the House report argues that because six of the models showed FT above NFT and seven the reverse, a finding consistent with their measuring chance effects, the affective measures are questionable. However, this argument fails to deal with the fact that *a few models across their sites produce the positive effects.* The effects are not random *by site* as their argument would have to predict [p. 30]. On the other hand, we must agree with their argument that the Raven's is not a measure of academically related skills and that it is inappropriate as a measure of cognitive-academic outcomes.

The Responsive Education program is based on the belief that in order to build a viable pluralistic society the educational process must strengthen educational experiences which respond to the uniqueness of learners as individuals and group members. For this reason, a basic tenet of the program recognizes and encourages parental and community involvement in the educational system [p. 90]. The learning environment . . . is made up of a number of learning centers; each center focuses on different concepts or tasks. The child's individual interest determines the child's choice of learning centers [p. 91].

Perhaps the statement that best summarizes the learning assumptions of the Responsive Education model is: " . . . in order to learn, a child needs a sense of personal worth and an environment in which materials and activities stimulate and respond to the child's interests. Given that essential self-esteem and that learning environment, the acquisition of academic skills will follow [Abt Associates, 1976, p. A-79].

2. Tucson Early Education Model (TEEM)—University of Arizona. The approach was first used with Spanish-speaking children by Marie Hughes (1971). Similar to the language-experience approach espoused by Sylvia Ashton Warner (1963), the TEEM program hinges on language development. TEEM, like the Responsive Education program, works from the child's interests. "Teaching elaborates on and explores what is already salient for the children—their environment and their current interests [Maccoby & Zellner, 1970, pp. 15–16]." The assumption is: "If language is made useful and if language and the written word surround the child, he will easily learn. Instruction takes place in learning by doing. A teacher who is making ice cream with a small group of children is teaching how to sequence, new words, new concepts, and new technical and social skills. She is also developing the children's attitudes toward learning [p. 16]."

3. Open Education (EDC)—Education Development Center. The program, modeled after the British Infant School revolution, is designed to promote the child's responsibility for his own learning. "There is a rich environment of materials for children to explore. They are encouraged to initiate activities, be self-directing, and become intensely involved in their interests. . . . The time schedule is flexible, permitting children to learn according to their individual rhythms of engagement and disengagement [Maccoby & Zellner, 1970, p. 6]."

The initial sponsor, David Armington, believes that learning will take place if the stage is set and the psychodynamic aspects of the environment are controlled. "It is believed that skills like reading and writing develop more surely if they are not treated as academic exercises but are taught in rich environments that stimulate the children's imagination and thought and foster their desire to communicate [Maccoby & Zellner, 1970, p. 7]."

4. Cognitively Oriented Curriculum—High/Score Educational Research Foundation. David Weikart's Follow Through program elaborates on the Piagetian theme. "The focus is on the development of children's ability to reason [Abt Associates, 1976, p. 211]." The program "focuses on the underlying cognitive processes that enable the child to acquire and organize knowledge of the world. It provides for the challenging of emerging abilities, builds on the child's interests, talents and long-term goals and applies these emerging abilities to concepts and skills in a wide range of subject and activity areas [Nero & Associates, 1976, p. 151]." The children schedule their own activities, develop a plan, indicate what materials will be used, whom the child will be working with, where the work will be taking place, and the general strategy of attack.

5. Florida Parent Education Model—University of Florida. The Parent Education model does not focus primarily on a school-based program. The model is based on the work by Gordon (1969) demonstrating that measurable, stable, and relatively long-lasting gains were achieved by working through the parents of disadvantaged youngsters and educating these parents in "developmentally beneficial" ways of interacting with their children. The model focuses on motivating parents to be the primary educators of their children.

Although not prescribing classroom curricula or organization, the sponsor provides for parent educators who spend part of their time in the classroom and serve as the link between school and home. These educators instruct parents in the presentation of different activities. "The aim is to create tasks that are soundly based on Piagetian educational philosophy. Lessons are designed to give a child meaningful experiences with a balance between the cognitive, affective and psychomotor skill areas of the child's life [Nero & Associates, 1976, p. 279]."

6. Bank Street College Model—Bank Street College of Education. Bank Street College of Education has long been an advocate of the early childhood education philosophy espoused by Head Start and middle-class traditional nursery schools.

The program is basically eclectic, incorporating strands of philosophy from Dewey, Piaget, and Freud. The program goals for children

> may be described in terms of the kind of people the children could become: confident, inventive, responsive, productive human beings. "Confident" people have ego strength which enables them to believe in themselves and to trust others. "Inventive" people have the capacity to probe, to reason, to organize their thinking processes, to solve problems, and to meet life creatively. "Responsive" people are sensitive to the rights and feelings of others and are free to express the joy, beauty and drama of life. "Productive" people have basic knowledge and skills as well as a deep comprehension of the meaning, value and function of their experiences [Nero & Associates, 1976, p. 4].

The program begins with "language experience" approach to reading. The classroom contains many options for "learning" experiences: "blocks, games and counting materials, tables for painting, quiet areas with rugs and comfortable chairs for reading or other individual work" A wide variety of activities is stressed. "One such example is a four page paper describing how language and mathematics experiences, dramatic play, social studies, and science questions can evolve from the study of foods and cooking activities in the classroom [Nero & Associates, 1976, pp. 7–8]."

The sponsors just described, with the exception of Parent Education, have obvious similarities. The words about *individualization,* concern for the global *whole person,* the assumption that the learning will be lasting if it is *child-initiated* or chosen, the idiom of the *open classroom,* the use of *subjectively based* theories (Piaget, Freud, Dewey), and the heavy use of *value-laden words* such as *individuality, creativity,* and *experience* all are familiar themes in popular methods textbooks. But planned variation in Follow Through also included sponsors whose programs were derived from a more objective or scientific base—principles of reinforcement and strategies of sequencing instructional material. These programs are the sometimes feared and frequently misunderstood cousins of B. F. Skinner's work. They seek to structure instructional sequences and use reinforcers in attempting directly to *cause* desired outcomes. Although the representation of the "behaviorists" in Follow Through was not so great as that of "cognitivists" and the "psychodynamically oriented," the representation was probably consistent with the relative popularity of the behavioral approach to teaching in 1967.

7. Behavior Analysis Model—University of Kansas. The University of Kansas has a rich history of documenting the effectiveness of behavioral techniques with problem children, young children, and low performers. Among the demonstrations that have come from the University of Kansas is an after-school skill-reinforcement program that achieved astonishing performance gains in the arithmetic and reading performance of disadvantaged black children in Kansas City, Kansas, who were initially several years behind their age-mates in academic performance (Wolf, Giles, & Hall, 1968).

The Behavior Analysis model, initially under the direction of Donald Bushell, "believes in a systematic and precise use of positive reinforcement [Nero & Associates, 1976, p. 314]." Its primary objective is not expressed in global or societal terms but in the children's mastery of reading, arithmetic, handwriting, and spelling skills. Acquisition of academic and social skills are reinforced with praise and tokens that can be traded for desired activities during "exchange" periods.

The program assumes that teaching is a technology and that child behavior follows scientific laws that can be used in constructing that technology. The most salient principle (from an educational standpoint) is that behaviors that are reinforced are repeated, whereas those that are punished or not reinforced tend to weaken. Other behavior principles guide procedures for sequencing instructional materials and continuously taking data on the children's performance.

8. Direct Instruction Model—University of Oregon.   This model developed from Becker's work on the use of reinforcement to change problem behaviors in the classroom and from Engelmann's work in the Bereiter–Engelmann (1966) preschool program—a program that has achieved perhaps the most dramatic performance gains of any school-based preschool program (Engelmann, 1968). Some of the disadvantaged children who completed their kindergarten year in the preschool could read on the third-grade level and could perform on the fourth-grade level in arithmetic. According to the Nero descriptions of Follow Through sponsors, the Direct Instruction model:

> is based on the assumption that every child can achieve well in school if he or she receives adequate instruction; conversely, pupil failure is a direct result of instructional failure. Disadvantaged children lag behind in developing relevant skills, particularly language concepts used in the school. For classroom success in these skills, their learning rate must be accelerated to reach the achievement levels of non-disadvantaged children [Nero & Associates, 1976, p. 348].

The approach does not come from exactly the same lineage as the Behavior Analysis model, but there certainly are connections. Both are scientific (objective) in approach; both assume that the use of positive reinforcement will aide in the instruction of specific skills. And both are concerned with a sequential, carefully constructed curriculum. The Direct Instruction Model uses the DISTAR® programs in Language, Reading, and Arithmetic as the central core of its programs. These programs have been developed by Engelmann, Carnine, and others associated with the Direct Instruction approach. Maccoby and Zellner observe that "Engelmann and Becker reason that it is not necessary to make a special effort to raise the self-esteem of the children; they believe that high self-esteem will be a by-product of competence (1970, p. 9)."

9. Southwest Educational Development Laboratory (SEDL).   Eight of the nine major Follow Through sponsors have been introduced. The remaining one does not fit neatly into a particular "camp." This sponsor is curricularly oriented; however, it differs from the other sponsors in that a majority of the sites served by this sponsor have a high percentage of non-English-speaking children (Spanish, French). The primary focus of the SEDL program is on language development. A bilingual approach is used where appropriate. The assumption is made that the child will demonstrate "an increased capacity to learn English and develop literacy in two languages if instruction is given in the native language [Nero & Associates, 1976, p. 210]." The reading program is based on a sequential presentation of oral subject matter followed by the same subject matter in written form. The programmed materials used by SEDL have been developed in both English and Spanish models.

In a sense, two major educational philosophies are represented in Follow Through: those concerned with principles of *natural growth* processes and those concerned with rules or principles for *changing behavior* in desired ways. Those from the first line concern themselves primarily with issues that supposedly relate to long-lasting effects of particular experiences. Those from the second line are most concerned with the immediate, and measurable. Although the first group discusses internal processes, the second deals with objective aspects of learned behavior. Although the first group stresses "process" and depreciates the value of content, the second group emphasizes the importance of specific content and specific behaviors.

Not only do the nine sponsors represent two major philosophical differences in instruction—they comprise an amazing array of specific differences. One extreme is represented by the traditional classroom program in the University of Florida Parent Education program, which makes no attempt to modify the school curriculum. The other extreme is represented by an almost complete replacement of the traditional sequence and assumptions in "open classrooms." Closer to the back-to-basics movement but not with the stick in one hand and the McGuffy reader in the other are the behavioral approaches that specifically express the idea that they are designed to produce student achievement in the more traditional skills, like reading, language, and arithmetic. However, all sponsors assert that their programs will teach these skills.

Basic Analyses

The major findings of the Abt Report are given in a series of tables, one for each sponsor, as illustrated in Table 6.1. For each variable, a covariance adjusted comparison was made with a *local* comparison group and with a *pooled* national comparison group. When FT exceeded NFT by at least one-fourth standard deviation on a given variable *and* when the difference was statistically significant, this was considered an educationally significant outcome and a plus (+) was placed in the table. When NFT exceeded FT by the same criteria, this was considered to be a significant negative outcome and a minus (−) was placed in the table. When the results were in between these limits, the difference was considered null and the table left blank. At the third-grade level, the one-fourth standard deviation criterion corresponds to about 2 months difference in grade-norm terms.[5]

---

[5]In the entering-kindergarten streams, 25% of the differences called null were educationally significant but not statistically significant, probably because of attrition effects on sample size. Only 5% were statistically significant but not educationally significant (Abt Associates, 1977, p. 132). The House et al. report (1977) argues that use of this dual criterion leads to a potential confounding of model effects with sample size. Because of the possible confounding, the House group reanalyzed the Cohort III-K, III-First, and II-First data using as a measure of effects the covariance adjusted difference between FT and NFT effects divided by the standard deviation of the outcome measure. The House report (1977, p. 42) shows a correlation of .31 between the square root of sample size and

TABLE 6.1
Summary of Effects
for Direct Instruction Sites

Domain	Outcome Measure	New York, NY III (Pooled)	New York, NY III (Local)	Grand Rapids, MI II (Pooled)	Grand Rapids, MI II (Local)	Grand Rapids, MI III (Pooled)	Grand Rapids, MI III (Local)	W. Iron Co., MI III (Pooled)	W. Iron Co., MI III (Local)	Flint, MI III (Pooled)	Flint, MI III (Local)	Providence, RI II (Pooled)	Providence, RI II (Local)	E. St. Louis, IL III (Pooled)	E. St. Louis, IL III (Local)	Racine, WI II (Pooled)	Racine, WI II (Local)	Dayton, OH III (Pooled)	Dayton, OH III (Local)	Tupelo, MS III (Pooled)	Tupelo, MS III (Local)	Tupelo, MS II (Pooled)	Tupelo, MS II (Local)	Williamsburg Co., SC III (Pooled)	Williamsburg Co., SC III (Local)	E. St. Louis, IL II (Pooled)	E. St. Louis, IL II (Local)	E. St. Louis, IL II (Pooled)	E. St. Louis, IL II (Local)
BASIC SKILLS	Word Knowledge	☐ ☐ + +	+ +		+					⊞ + +	+ +			⊞☐ + +		+ ☐ + +								+ + + +	+ + + +	+ + +	+ + +	+	+ +
	Spelling																												
	Language																												
	Math Computations																												
COGNITIVE CONCEPTUAL SKILLS	Raven's	+ +	⊞⊞	+ +	+	⊞ -	☐			⊞ + +	+ +	+ + +	+ +	⊞ + +		+ + + +								+ + + +	+ + + +	+ + + +	+ + +	+ +	+ +
	Reading																												
	Math Concepts																												
	Math Problem Solving																												
AFFECTIVE MEASURES	Coopersmith	- ☐	+	+	+	+ -		+		-		+		+				+	+	-				-					
	IARS (-)	☐ + +	+																										
	IARS (+)	+ +	+	+ + + +	+	-		+ +	+ +	-	+	+ + +	+ + +	⊞ + + +	+ + +	+ + + +	+ + + +	+ + +	+	+ + +	+ + +	+ +	+ +	+ + + +	+ + + +	+ + +	+ + +	+ + +	+ + +
	Total Reading																												
	Total Math																												
	Language: Part A																												
	Language: Part B																												

Site FT Sample*

	New York III	Grand Rapids II	Grand Rapids III	W. Iron Co. III	Flint III	Providence II	E. St. Louis III	Racine II	Dayton III	Tupelo III	Tupelo II	Williamsburg III	E. St. Louis II	E. St. Louis II
	18	10	41	12	3	17	25	18	21	43	41	45	60	43
	7	10	41	0	9	10	14	2	5	13	20	33	50	15
	18	6	36	6	6	20	27	21	23	45	38	38	53	31
	11		77	12	17		22			30	25	42	30	15

NATIONAL NORMS*

Outcome Measures	MAT Sample
Reading	20%
Math	12%
Spelling	22%
Language**	14%

Legend:
☐ Preschool Adjustment changes effect
⊡ Untrustworthy effect
+ FT-favoring effect
- NFT-favoring effect
blank Null effect

Notes:
* In terms of percentage of children performing one or more years below grade level.
No national norms comparisons were made for Cohort II-K children on the Language subtest.

Table 6.1 displays the Abt findings for each Direct Instruction site in the National Evaluation. The kindergarten-entering sites are shown first, followed by the first-grade-entering sites. At the bottom of the table, the percentage of students 1 year or more below grade level on major MAT measures is given. In the draft version of this table, median grade equivalents were given for each site. We use the medians from the draft report to summarize the level of performance for each model.

Grayouts.   The shaded areas in the tables are termed *grayouts.* Effects were grayed out for one of two reasons. First, a whole column was grayed out when the percentage of children attending preschool differed for FT and NFT by more than 50%. Second, a specific effect was grayed out when the covariance adjustment changed a site mean by more than one-half standard deviation. The Abt report calls the grayed out effects "untrustworthy." We believe that this is an inappropriate conclusion when a plus (+) FT effect is found under conditions where the operating biases favor a minus (−) effect (or vice versa). For example, the nature of the correlations between preschool attendance and outcome measures favor NFT. Under such conditions, plus (+) FT findings are actually *conservative estimates* of real outcomes. This is the case for each of our sites grayed out in Table 6.1. Furthermore, the magnitude of the actual "preschool effect" is so small (the highest correlation is −.09) that elimination of data for this reason is questionable.[6]

---

rank order on model effectiveness. Direct Instruction was right in the middle on the sample-size measure, thus showing no special benefit of this "confounding." Their analysis still left Direct Instruction in first place. However, the analysis inappropriately discards the Cohort II-K data and the preschool adjustments for the Cohort III-K data and confounds K-entering and first-entering effects with sponsor effects. A sponsor has 4 years to produce results in a K-entering site and only 3 years in a first-entering site. Of the 13 sponsors compared in their reanalysis, 5 had no first-starting sites, and 2 had 11 of the 24 first-starting sites used in their reanalysis. These criticisms leave the House reanalysis weaker than the Abt analysis they were trying to improve. In fact, a careful reading of the House report will reveal a clearly biased attitude aimed at showing that the "good guys" (those supporting the popular cognitive and affectively oriented ideologies) did not, in fact, lose.

[6]The grayout because of preschool differences eliminates effects as follows:

	Kind of Effect			
	+	O	−	Total
Direct instruction (less Grand Rapids)	21	22	2	45
(Grand Rapids)	1	13	1	15
Eight other major sponsors	16	262	127	405

In percentages, the preschool based grayouts eliminate 47% positive outcomes and 4% negative outcomes for Direct Instruction (excluding Grand Rapids), while the same procedure eliminates 4% positive outcomes and 31% negative outcomes for the other major sponsors. Two models, Cognitive

TABLE 6.2
Tabulation of Relation of Outcome Effects and the Direction of
Covariance Adjustments for Grayouts Based on Magnitude of Adjustment

Direct Instruction				Eight Other Major Sponsors			
Effect	Adjustment (Positive)	Adjustment (Negative)	Totals	Effect	Adjustment (Positive)	Adjustment (Negative)	Totals
+	35	1	36	+	32	3	35
0	28	1	29	0	96	29	125
−	10	3	13	−	45	24	69
Totals	73	5	78	Totals	173	56	229

The elimination of all outcomes where the covariance adjustment exceeds one-half standard deviation on the outcome measure can also be questioned. As Campbell and Erlebacher (1970) point out (and the Abt Report acknowledges), the effect of a covariance adjustment for the group initially lower on the covariates is to underestimate the correction. "This bias is due to error and uniqueness in the covariate, i.e., variance not shared by the dependent variable [p. 199]."

The appendices to the Abt IV Report show the direction and magnitude of the adjustment for each variable. In Table 6.2, we have shown the relation between direction of adjustment (positive, negative) and outcome effect (+, 0, −). Where an adjustment is positive (FT is initially lower than NFT on covariates), the built-in bias should favor minus (−) outcomes for FT. Where an adjustment is negative (NFT initially higher than FT), the built-in bias should favor plus (+) outcomes for FT. The arrows in Table 6.2 show the direction of the expected bias. The heavy outline boxes cover effects operating against the direction of the covariance adjustment bias. The data in Table 6.2 clearly show that for the Direct Instruction outcomes this grayout rule is inappropriate. A more conservative procedure would not gray out the effects in the heavy outlined boxes and would indicate that the remaining grayed results (on the average) *underestimate* true FT effects rather than being called "untrustworthy." The general effect of applying this grayout rule is to attenuate real differences between model sponsors. In the analyses to be presented, the effects of these alternative decision rules will be shown.

Curriculum and Responsive Education, especially benefit by this inappropriate elimination of data. Responsive Education has 51 negatives and 1 positive eliminated (24% of *all* their outcomes), while Cognitive Curriculum has 41 negatives and 5 positives eliminated (the negatives are 34% of *all* their outcomes). In other words, the effects of this questionable procedure for eliminating data is to greatly attenuate the differences between successful and unsuccessful models.

FT versus NFT Comparisons by Model

To summarize model effects, the authors of the Abt Report counted the number of pluses for a given group of measures (such as basic skills), subtracted the number of minuses, and divided by the number of comparisons. Both *local* and *pooled* comparisons were included. Sites were counted if the number of grayed-out effects was 50% or less, but only the non-grayed-out effects were counted. Engelmann and Becker (in preparation) independently adopted a similar index which they gave the name Index of Significant Outcomes (ISO). It was basically the index developed by Abt multiplied by 1000 to eliminate decimal points.[7] For a given group of effects, if a sponsor is more positive than negative, the ISO is positive. If the average effect is more negative than positive, the ISO is negative. The ISOs permit a relative comparison of programs and of skill areas within programs.

In the tables that follow we present the ISO values for sponsors on Basic, Cognitive, and Affective Measures as given by these three rule systems:

1. *Abt IV rules:* (a) Eliminate the site if more than 50% of effects are grayed out; (b) count only non-grayed-out effects; (c) count both local and pooled comparisons.

2. *Use all data:* Count all pluses and minuses in tables to compute ISOs.

3. *Selectively keep grayouts:* (a) Keep all data grayed out for the preschool difference; (b) keep those pluses and minuses where the effect is in the opposite direction to the expected bias (Table 6.2, heavy outline boxes); (c) eliminate site if more than 50% of effects are still grayed out; (d) count only non-grayed-out effects with (a) and (b) treated as non-grayed out.

Additionally, we show the effects for Direct Instruction with and without the inclusion of Grand Rapids. The Cognitive Measures are graphed without the questionable Raven's Coloured Progressive Matrices.

Basic Skills

Figure 6.1 and Table 6.3 show the results for the various analyses of relative outcomes. As is apparent from Fig. 6.1, Direct Instruction is the only model to

---

[7]In another publication (Becker & Engelmann, in press) we have published data summaries using ISOs which differ from those presented here in that they included all data grayed out by Abt Associates, and used the following rule for counting pluses and minuses: Only one of the analyses (local or pooled) had to be plus (or minus) to count the effect plus (or minus) as long as the other was not minus (or plus). In the two cases where one analysis was plus and one was minus, the effect was counted zero. The effect of this approach was to increase the magnitude of the negative outcomes for some sponsors, but the basic relations among sponsors on the ISOs was nearly the same. The Responsive Education model improved the most using the present analytic rules.

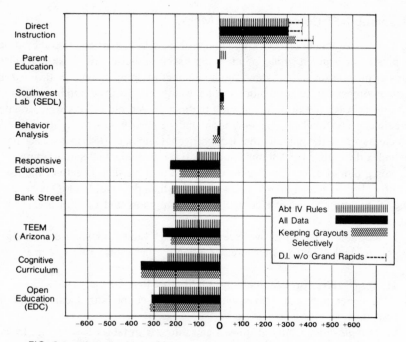

FIG. 6.1.   ISO's for Basics Measures (Word Knowledge, Spelling, Language, Math, Computation).

show substantial positive effects. Parent Education, Behavior Analysis, and SEDL show an average effect near zero, and all other models show substantial negative effects (performances below the level of their comparison groups after the statistical adjustments for initial inequalities). Using the Abt IV rules, the ISOs range from +309 for Direct Instruction to −274 for Open Education (EDC). The All Data analysis shows a similar result for Direct Instruction as the Abt IV analysis but *lowers* the ISOs for four of the five models with negative effects. The Selective Keeping of Grayouts analysis improves the ISO for Direct Instruction (+339) and gives middle-ground values to models with largely negative outcomes. When Grand Rapids is eliminated from the Direct Instruction Model data, the ISOs range from +366 to +419 for the various analyses, a substantial improvement.

Table 6.3 gives a breakdown of the Basic Skills ISOs by variable using the All Data analysis. This breakdown shows that the positive ISOs for Direct Instruction were largely achieved through highly successful relative outcomes for MAT Language (+656) and MAT Math Computation (+562). Without Grand Rapids, these ISOs are +786 and +643, respectively. No model program produced a positive outcome on Spelling. Direct Instruction ranked second on Word Knowledge, third on Spelling, and first on Language and Math Computation.

TABLE 6.3
ISOs for Basic Skill Measures Using the All Data Analysis

	No. Sites	Word Knowledge		Spelling		Language		Math Computation	
		ISO	Rank	ISO	Rank	ISO	Rank	ISO	Rank
Direct Instruction[a]	16	+065	2	−065	3	+656	1	+562	1
Southwest Lab	8	−250	5.5	000	1	+250	2	+062	3
Parent Education	12	+125	1	−042	2	−167	5	+042	4
Behavior Analysis	13	−038	3	−269	4	−115	4	+385	2
Bank Street	12	−208	4	−500	8.5	000	3	−125	7
TEEM (Arizona)	15	−367	7	−500	8.5	−200	7	+033	5
Responsive Education	16	−250	5.5	−406	7	−188	6	−062	6
Open Education (EDC)	10	−300	6	−400	6	−250	8	−300	9
Cognitive Curriculum	9	−389	8	−333	5	−500	9	−222	8
[a] Direct Instruction (less Grand Rapids)	14	+071		−035		+786		+643	

Cognitive–Conceptual Skills

Figure 6.2 and Table 6.4 present the results for Cognitive–Conceptual Skills. Many expected the Direct Instruction Model to do well on Basic Skills but not on Cognitive–Conceptual Skills. The data show this assumption to be incorrect. The Direct Instruction Model ranks first on Reading (comprehension), first on Math Concepts, and first on Math Problem Solving. The model does not perform particularly well on the Raven's (with relative comparisons), but neither does anyone else. More positive than negative results for Cognitive Measures are found for only one other model, Southwest Labs' Language Development Approach (SEDL.) Substantially negative average ISOs are found for TEEM (−160), Behavior Analysis (−190), Open Education (−236), and Cognitive Curriculum (−249). Those programs whose espoused goals were to improve cognitive–conceptual skills were apparently unsuccessful. The relatively poor performance of Behavior Analysis on Cognitive Measures in comparison to Basic Skills merits attention. It suggests that the systematic use of reinforcement procedures may not be enough in overcoming the current inability of schools to teach language competencies to students from economically disadvantaged homes.

In evaluating the capabilities of models to produce meaningful educational outcomes in the cognitive area, we believe the analyses without the Raven's and without Grand Rapids most clearly show what the Direct Instruction model can do. ISOs of from +375 to +544 suggest that even with some implementation problems the model can be substantially effective in a wide variety of circum-

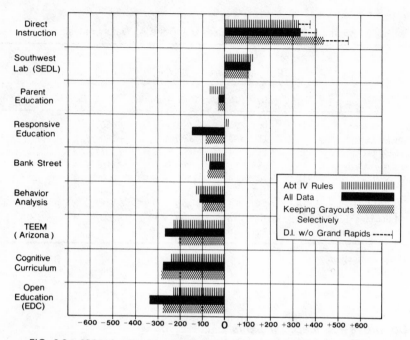

FIG. 6.2.   ISO's for Cognitive Measures (Reading Comprehension, Math Concepts, Math Problem Solving).

TABLE 6.4
ISOs for Cognitive Skill Subclasses Using All Data

	No. Sites	Reading		Math Concepts		Math Problem Solving		Raven's Progressive Matrices	
		ISO	Rank	ISO	Rank	ISO	Rank	ISO	Rank
Direct Instruction[a]	16	+219	1	+312	1	+479	1	−200	7
Southwest Lab	8	+062	2	+250	2	+062	2	−062	4
Parent Education	12	000	4	−083	4	000	3	+042	2
Responsive Education	16	−094	5	−188	6	−156	6	−094	5
Bank Street	12	+042	3	−167	5	−083	4	−042	3
TEEM (Arizona)	15	−300	8	−333	8	−167	7	+067	1
Behavior Analysis	13	−154	6	−077	3	−115	5	−385	9
Open Education (EDC)	10	−400	9	−300	7	−300	9	−100	6
Cognitive Curriculum	9	−222	7	−389	9	−222	8	−222	8
[a] Direct Instruction (less Grand Rapids)	14	+214		+429		+571		−179	

stances. The findings in the area of mathematical reasoning are especially impressive.

Affective Measures

Figure 6.3 and Table 6.5 present the ISOs for the Affective Measures. In the Abt IV Report these findings are discussed as follows [Abt IV-B, 1977, p. 73]:

> To some observers the performance of FT children in Direct Instruction sites on the affective measures is an unexpected result. The Direct Instruction model does not explicitly emphasize affective outcomes of instruction but the sponsor has asserted that they will be the consequence of effective teaching. Critics of the model have predicted that the emphasis of the model on tightly controlled instruction might discourage children from freely expressing themselves and thus inhibit the development of self-esteem and other affective skills. In fact, this is not the case.

The findings again show the Direct Instruction Model to rank first on the Affective Measures. The different approaches to data analysis make little difference on these measures. It is interesting that the other major sponsor focusing on the use of positive reinforcement (Behavior Analysis) ranks second on these measures.

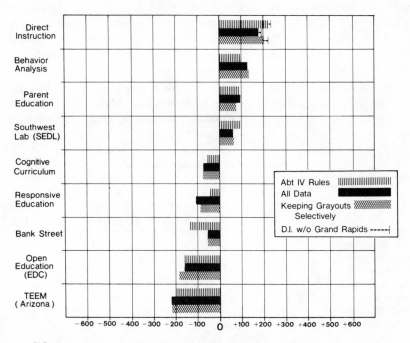

FIG. 6.3.   ISO's for Affective Measures (Coopersmith Self-Esteem. Intellectual Achievement Responsibility Scale).

TABLE 6.5
ISOs for Affective Subclasses Using All Data

	No. Sites	Coopersmith Self Esteem		IARS−		IARS+	
		ISO	Rank	ISO	Rank	ISO	Rank
Direct Instruction[a]	16	+156	3	+188	2	+188	1
Behavior Analysis	13	+231	1	+231	1	−077	5
Parent Education	12	+042	4.5	+125	3	+125	2
Southwest Lab	8	+188	2	000	4	000	3
Cognitive Curriculum	9	−056	8	−111	5	−056	4
Responsive Education	16	−031	7	−188	7	−094	7
Bank Street	12	+042	4.5	−125	6	−083	6
Open Education (EDC)	10	000	6	−250	9	−250	8
TEEM (Arizona)	15	−167	9	−233	8	−267	9
[a]Direct Instruction (less Grand Rapids)	14	+179		+179		+214	

Table 6.6 gives the rankings for Basic, Cognitive, and Affective Measures using ISOs based on the average of the three analytic methods. There is a clear correlation between positive academic outcomes and positive affective outcomes. The table also shows a substantial correlation between Basic and Cognitive Measures, which we believe should be expected. The major deviations in rankings are the relatively poor performance of Behavior Analysis on Cognitive Measures noted earlier, and the better ranking (although still negative ISOs) for Weikart's Cognitive Curriculum on the Affective Measures.

In summary, these control-group comparisons clearly show the Direct Instruction Model to be effective in comparison to traditional programs (the comparison

TABLE 6.6
Ranks for Average ISOs by Area

	Basic Skills	Cognitive Measures (less Ravens)	Affective Measures	Average Rank
Direct Instruction	1	1	1	1
Southwest Lab	2	2	4	2
Parent Education	3	3	3	3
Behavior Analysis	4	6	2	4
Bank Street	5	4	7	5
Responsive Education	7	5	6	6
TEEM (Arizona)	6	7	9	7.5
Cognitive Curriculum	9	8	5	7.5
Open Education (EDC)	8	9	8	9

groups) and in comparison to the other model approaches to compensatory education having the same resources available. The consistency of these findings cannot easily be attributed to accident or fancy. When normative levels of performance are examined, this conclusion becomes even stronger.

Normative Performance

The Abt III and IV Reports provide median grade-equivalent scores by site and by sponsor for four MAT measures: Total Reading, Total Math, Spelling, and Language. The means for these data by model (converted to percentiles) are presented in Tables 6.7 through 6.10. The tables display percentiles on a one-fourth standard deviation scale. With this display differences between sponsors of one-quarter standard deviation or more are easily detected and a norm reference is provided. The 20th percentile, which represents the average expectation for disadvantaged children without special help, was chosen for a baseline in drawing the graphs in Tables 6.7 to 6.10.[8]

The Direct Instruction Model is clearly highest in normative performance and is close to or at national norms on all measures. These data include Grand Rapids. Without Grand Rapids the percentiles are 43 for Total Reading, 56 for Total Math, 54 for Spelling, and 56 for Language. Because models are ordered by average ISO rank (Table 6.6), a comparison of statistical and normative performance is readily made. The Direct Instruction program remains first in each case. SEDL and Parent Education models show the greatest drop in standing in going from ISOs to normative comparisons.

Only four sponsors have reading programs that are making some headway toward average performance by the end of third grade (Direct Instruction, Behavior Analysis, Bank Street College, and Responsive Education). In Math, Direct Instruction is at least one-half standard deviation ahead of all the others. In Spelling, the Behavior Analysis program is the only program other than Direct Instruction approaching national norms. In Language (usage, punctuation, and sentence types) the Direct Instruction program is three-fourths of a standard deviation ahead of all other programs.

The normative performance data add much to the interpretation of the statistical comparisons. The Direct Instruction program is apparently able to make

---

[8]A U.S. Office of Education report (1976) substantiates this approach: "Analyses of all test scores showed that the typical student who received compensatory assistance in reading was at the 20th percentile for grade 2 and the 22nd percentile for grades 4 and 6 [p. 88]." Moreover, in a footnote to page 88 this additional information is given: "In conjunction with the Emergency School Aid Act evaluation, children in grades 3, 4, and 5 of a nationally representative sample of minority isolated schools (50% or more non-white) performed at the 23rd, 18th and 19th percentiles, respectively, on reading achievement in the Spring 1973; similar results were obtained for mathematics achievement [Ozenne, D. G., et al., 1974]." The educational requirement for Title I eligibility (1 year or more below grade level) is the 20th percentile for Metropolitan Total Reading.

TABLE 6.7
M.A.T. Total Reading

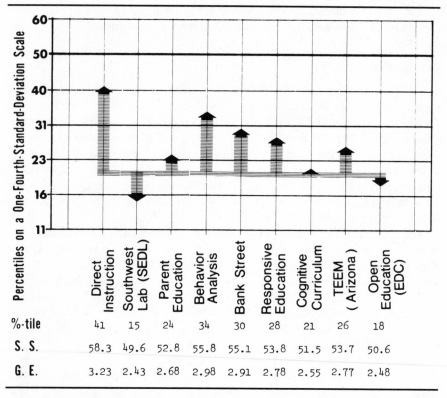

%-tile	41	15	24	34	30	28	21	26	18
S. S.	58.3	49.6	52.8	55.8	55.1	53.8	51.5	53.7	50.6
G. E.	3.23	2.43	2.68	2.98	2.91	2.78	2.55	2.77	2.48

Note: Grade equivalent for 50th percentile is 3.5.

effective use of teaching time in most areas of skill development so as to show a superior outcome nearly across the board.

Site Variability

A major conclusion in the Abt IV Report (1977) is this: "But the main lesson of site variability is that the models are not powerful enough to countervail unmeasured site-specific determinants of outcomes. Any model can 'fail' by having a group perform lower on a test than it would have without Follow Through (Vol. IVA, p. 140)." With respect to the Direct Instruction Model, this statement fails to recognize that we did not serve as sponsors for Grand Rapids for nearly 2 years for the Cohort II children and for 3 years for the Cohort III children. But the Abt Report also errs in the logical basis of its conclusion. The conclusion about variability is based on control-group comparisons. The sponsor did not select the

TABLE 6.8
M.A.T. Total Math

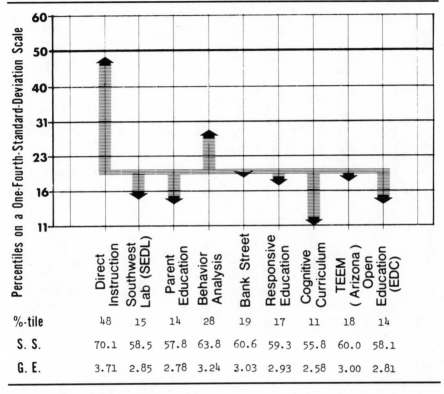

	Direct Instruction	Southwest Lab (SEDL)	Parent Education	Behavior Analysis	Bank Street	Responsive Education	Cognitive Curriculum	TEEM (Arizona)	Open Education (EDC)
%-tile	48	15	14	28	19	17	11	18	14
S. S.	70.1	58.5	57.8	63.8	60.6	59.3	55.8	60.0	58.1
G. E.	3.71	2.85	2.78	3.24	3.03	2.93	2.58	3.00	2.81

Note: Grade equivalent for 50th percentile is 3.75.

control groups nor monitor any special programs they might have (and many did have special programs through other Federal and local funds). In some of our sites, our model performs at or near grade level for specific measures and yet a minus (−) occurs in the summary table. This kind of variability should not be attributed to a model weakness. If all disadvantaged groups performed at grade level, there would be no need for Follow Through. The question of implementation variability is more appropriately explored with norm-referenced measures of "absolute performance" rather than indices of significance. Table 6.11 shows the median-grade equivalents on the MAT (from Abt III and Abt IV appendices) for the Direct Instruction Model's K-starting sites.

Without Grand Rapids, the norm data for Math, Spelling, and Language show that most of the variability is *above the grade norm*. In Reading this is not the case, but the range below grade norm is only .4 of a grade level. As we have argued elsewhere and discuss later in this paper, MAT Reading at the Elementary

TABLE 6.9
M.A.T. Spelling

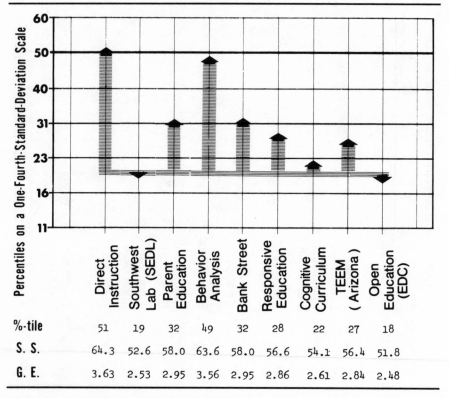

%-tile	51	19	32	49	32	28	22	27	18
S. S.	64.3	52.6	58.0	63.6	58.0	56.6	54.1	56.4	51.8
G. E.	3.63	2.53	2.95	3.56	2.95	2.86	2.61	2.84	2.48

Note: Grade equivalent for 50th percentile is 3.6.

Test level is heavily dependent on middle class home language inputs rather than what is taught in schools (Becker, 1977) and consequently, the reading skills are more difficult to impact than math and spelling. The point is that, except for reading, the variability indicates that school means for economically disadvantaged children are near or above the national norm. Variability of this type is hardly a problem.

SPONSOR-COLLECTED DATA

Detailed findings from the sponsor-collected data are presented in Technical Reports No. 76-1 and No. 78-1 (Becker & Engelmann, 1976; 1978b). In the space alloted here we can only summarize some of the highlights.

TABLE 6.10
M.A.T. Language

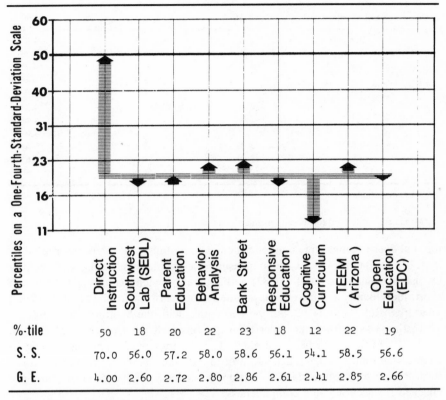

%-tile	50	18	20	22	23	18	12	22	19
S. S.	70.0	56.0	57.2	58.0	58.6	56.1	54.1	58.5	56.6
G. E.	4.00	2.60	2.72	2.80	2.86	2.61	2.41	2.85	2.66

Note: Grade equivalent for 50th percentile is 4.0.

Tests

We have attempted to test every child in the Direct Instruction program from 1969 to 1973 at entry and each spring thereafter through third grade. Financial cutbacks led us to omit second-grade testing one year. From 1969 until 1971, all children were tested with the Wide Range Achievement Test (WRAT) and the Slosson Intelligence Test (SIT). The SIT was used to measure general language competence. Beginning in 1972, the Metropolitan Achievement Test (MAT) was used at the end of first, second, and third grades. In sites where Stanford Research Institute was testing for the National Evaluation, copies of their data were provided to us. The MAT subtests and their reliabilities have already been mentioned. The WRAT has measures for Reading, Arithmetic, and Spelling. The Reading test is a reliable (.91–.92) measure of decoding skills (word read-

TABLE 6.11
Median-Grade MAT Equivalents for Direct Instruction Model Sites

	Total Reading	Total Math	Spelling	Language
	3.7	4.2	4.3	4.8
Norm (3.5) → 3.5		4.0	4.3	4.8*
	3.4	4.0	3.9	4.7*
	3.4	3.9	3.9	4.6*
	3.3	3.9	3.7	4.5
	3.2	3.8	Norm (3.6) →	4.2*
	3.1	3.8	3.4	4.1
	3.1	Norm (3.75) →	3.4	Norm (4.0) → 4.0
	(2.8)	3.7	3.4	(2.8)*
	(2.8)	(3.0)	(3.0)	(2.6)
		(2.8)	(3.0)	

( ) Grand Rapids.
Norm = 50th percentile.
*Means are substituted for missing medians.

ing) but does not measure comprehension. The Arithmetic test has lower reliability (.70–.80) but provides a rough measure of computational skills. The Spelling test has reasonable reliability (.83) and apparent content validity. The SIT is a short, individually administered test aimed at measuring what the Stanford–Binet measures. Reliability is .92 and the correlation with the Stanford–Binet .93.

Testing was carried out under the supervision of the University of Oregon field staff by local teachers and aides. Careful training for and monitoring of testing was followed using detailed procedural manuals modeled after the Stanford Research Institute data collection procedures. All data were carefully checked for accuracy and completeness.

The Data Base

We have data on 5922 kindergarten-entering children and 5565 first-entering children in our main analysis. Students are included in this analysis if they meet the OEO poverty guideline (low income), if they started the program at its earliest grade level, and if tests are available at more than one point in time. The data include students who may have left the program before completing it.[9] The N at prekindergarten and post-third grade are lower than maximum N's because not all cohorts were tested at entry and because students move.

---

[9]This data base provides a maximum sample size for measurement of program impact. To check for biases in outcome because of changes in students over grades (attrition), we have also analyzed year-to-year gains on the *same* students and full-term pretest to posttest gains (K–3 or 1–3) on the *same* students. These analyses do not materially change any conclusions except to make the actual gains about two-tenths of a grade level higher than those reported here. When the excluded non-low-income children are added to the analysis (20% of our children), there is another slight increment in the level of performance. Children who enter the program late perform a year lower on the average. This would be expected if the program is important.

Norm-Referenced Gains

Table 6.12 shows the sponsor-collected norm-referenced data on low-income children from our 13 kindergarten sites for six entry years (cohorts). The MAT results from this broader sample of sites and entry years are nearly identical to those found in the National Evaluation. The WRAT results in Arithmetic and Spelling confirm those from the MAT. In all cases but MAT Reading, our students are performing at the national average. On WRAT Reading, the Direct Instruction students perform at the 82nd percentile, a full standard deviation

TABLE 6.12
Norm-Referenced Gains on the Wide Range (Pre-K to Post-3) and
Post-3 Performance on the Metropolitan for K-Starting, Low Income,
E-B Model Follow Through Students.

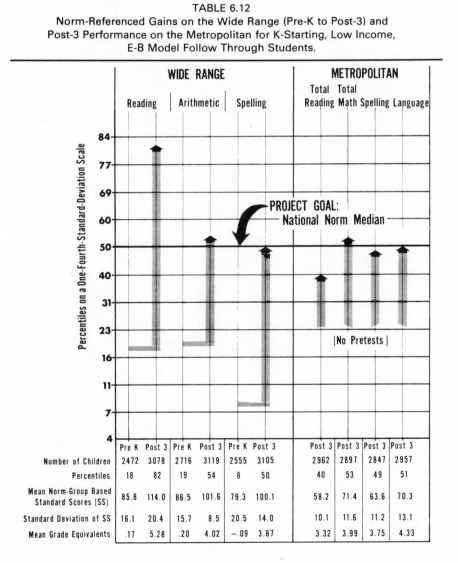

| | WIDE RANGE | | | METROPOLITAN | | | |
	Reading	Arithmetic	Spelling	Total Reading	Total Math	Spelling	Language
	Pre K · Post 3	Pre K · Post 3	Pre K · Post 3	Post 3	Post 3	Post 3	Post 3
Number of Children	2472 · 3078	2716 · 3119	2555 · 3105	2962	2897	2847	2957
Percentiles	18 · 82	19 · 54	8 · 50	40	53	49	51
Mean Norm-Group Based Standard Scores (SS)	85.8 · 114.0	86.5 · 101.6	79.3 · 100.1	58.2	71.4	63.6	70.3
Standard Deviation of SS	16.1 · 20.4	15.7 · 8.5	20.5 · 14.0	10.1	11.6	11.2	13.1
Mean Grade Equivalents	.17 · 5.28	.20 · 4.02	−.09 · 3.87	3.32	3.99	3.75	4.33

above the national norm. WRAT Reading measures decoding skills, and MAT Reading measures comprehension skills. This difference in performance levels is to be expected, given the tasks to be taught and the children being taught (see Becker, 1977, for the analysis).

Other Findings

Sponsor-collected data also support these conclusions:

1. There is a measurable and educationally significant benefit present at the end of third grade for beginning Direct Instruction in kindergarten.

2. Significant gains in IQ, which are largely maintained through third grade, are found.

3. Follow-up studies at fifth and sixth grade show significantly better performance by Direct Instruction Follow Through children than by comparison groups. These findings exist in spite of evidence that the schools did not systematically build on the skills the children had at the end of third grade and in spite of losses on normative measures between third and fifth or sixth grades.

4. Studies of low IQ students (under 80) show the program is clearly effective with students who have a higher probability of failure.

Summary

The various data analyses comparing different approaches to teaching the disadvantaged show rather overwhelmingly that the Direct Instruction model was more effective in terms of basic academic goals and affective outcomes. The Behavior Analysis Model also showed some successful outcomes. The Behavior Analysis Model was especially effective on Math Computation and Affective Measures in terms of ISOs and on Reading and Spelling in terms of normative performance levels. The Parent Education and SEDL programs were the only others to show a few positive outcomes. The reader should keep in mind that some of the poor outcomes may not be model program effects but due to implementation problems. Until this issue is faced squarely in the design of evaluation studies, conclusions about what works will have to continue to be qualified.

Given these outcomes, it is of interest to examine more carefully the Direct Instruction Model.

THE DIRECT INSTRUCTION MODEL

Major Features of the Model

Two major rules govern the selection of features in the model. The first rule might be termed *beat the clock* or *teach more in less time*. The second rule is *control the details of what happens*.

1. *To teach more in less time:*

• The model uses a teacher and two aides at levels 1 and 2 and a teacher and one aide after that. The aides are trained to teach and function fully as teachers and thus increase the amount of teacher–student interaction time.

• The daily activities are structured to reduce "wasted time" and to increase academic engaged time.

• Programs are designed to focus on teaching the general case where possible, so that through teaching a subset the whole set is learned. For example, by teaching 40 sounds and skills for hooking them together and saying them fast, we can teach a generalized decoding skill that is relevant to one-half of the more common English words. The programs are provided explicitly to the teacher. The teacher does not have to spend time trying to design them.

• Appropriate training is provided to ensure that efficient teaching procedures are utilized.

2. *To control the details of what happens:*

• Daily lesson scripts are provided that tell the teacher exactly what to say and do and even when and how to use praise.

• Training is provided so that the staff knows how to execute the details of the program.

• Student progress and teacher progress are monitored through the use of criterion-referenced "continuous progress tests" on the children each 2 weeks and biweekly reports of the number of lessons taught.

• Supervisors (one for each 8 to 12 classrooms) are trained to spend 75% of their time actually in classrooms working with teachers and aides.

• Training and monitoring procedures are explicitly detailed in manuals.

These components of the model were not all there at the beginning. To be sure, Engelmann began with the idea of control of teacher presentations and control of task sequences through the use of scripts, and he had formally contracted with Science Research Associates (SRA) for such programs prior to Follow Through. But only one program was actually in published form (and that a prepublication especially for Follow Through); the rest were outlines. The currently available programs are mostly third-generation derivatives. Similarly, the manuals for training teachers have been revised four times over the past 9 years. Each revision involves less exhortation and rhetoric and an increase in guided practice using the "model, lead, and test" format that is used with the children. The more teacher training became systematized, the more it became another application of the direct instruction methodology. At this point, we have separate "Program Implementation Manuals" available for teachers, supervisors, administrators, and parent workers (Oregon Follow Through Project, 1977). Each of the four manuals spells out the overall structuring, the detailed procedures, and tools for filling particular roles in the model.

The Academic Objectives

It is important to summarize briefly the academic goals of the nine DISTAR programs because they are what the model is all about—basic competencies. Those who are familiar with the Metropolitan Achievement Tests and the results discussed earlier will readily understand that we are not talking about a small set of ''rote'' responses to stimuli but the concepts. operations, and problem-solving sequences that are *intelligent behavior*.

In DISTAR Reading I and II, the focus is first on decoding skills and then comprehension. Decoding progressively involves learning to read individual sounds; to blend them into words; to read regular words, common irregular words (*is, said, was*), irregular word families (*hop-hope, bit-bite, rat-rate, hopping-hoping,* etc.); and to apply these word reading skills to passage reading. Comprehension is initially concerned with literal comprehension, following instruction, and remembering what was read (statement repetition). In Reading III, the children are taught to read for new information and to use that information. . Most of the Reading III stories have a science base to them to make available rules that can be used to solve problems in astronomy, muscle function, or measurement. After Day 60, most students are reading and doing workbook assignments on their own rather than working in groups. The student completing Reading III should be prepared to use upper-level textbooks to learn as long as the *new vocabulary and concepts* in those texts are taught in some way.

DISTAR Arithmetic I first teaches basic addition and subtraction operations and their related story–problem forms through a problem-solving approach. Then, number facts are memorized to speed up the process and to set the stage for more elaborate problems. In Arithmetic II, the students are introduced to multiplication and fractions. Addition and subtraction are extended and a variety of measurement concepts involving time, money, length, and weight are taught. The students are also taught how to derive unknown facts from known facts and how to work more complex story problems. In Arithmetic III, the students are taught algebra, factoring, and division, and the traditional operations are extended.

DISTAR Language I and II teach object names, object classes, object properties, and relational terms. The children are taught to make complete statements and to describe the world around them. The program focus on comprehension and language production. The students are taught logical processes such as conditionality, causality, multiple attributes, definitions, deductions, synonyms, and opposites. They are also taught how to ask questions in order to find out about something. Language III expands the logical use of language and teaches basic grammatical rules. Many activities in Reading and Language are also geared to writing and spelling skills. (Rather than reference these nine programs and their earlier versions, we refer the reader to the SRA catalogs).

Teaching Techniques

The techniques used in implementing a direct instruction program vary according to the skill level of the students. For example, initial decoding instruction involves small group teaching with the teacher signaling for unison responses. Later, the amount of small-group instruction decreases and independent activities and entire class teaching occurs more often. Also, oral responding with unison responses is less common in later grades. Other techniques such as monitoring, diagnosing, correcting, and reinforcing are important in all grades; however, they are used in different ways at different times. For example, diagnosing student skill deficits during early decoding instruction relies on students' oral reading responses; during later comprehension teaching, a diagnosis is often based on an analysis of students' answers to worksheet exercises. Another example involves feedback. For young children, feedback should be immediate; for older children, it is delayed. In general, the primary-grade teacher must be proficient in a variety of presentation techniques needed to maintain student participation in rapid question–answer exchanges. In contrast, intermediate-grade teachers must be more skilled in managing students working independently.

Scripted Presentations

Direct Instruction teachers learn to follow lesson scripts carefully. The use of detailed lesson scripts has been criticized because it presumably restricts and inhibits teacher initiative. In considering this possible limitation, the reader should evaluate some very important virtues afforded by the use of scripts. We are concerned with designing *disseminable* procedures for improving instruction. Scripts permit the use of *explicitly pretested* examples and sequences. The teacher knows that if the student has the prerequisite skills, the teaching sequence will work. The teacher does not have to spend time trying out various possible illustrations, choosing appropriate language, and analyzing possible teaching sequences. The scripts also make explicit the teacher behaviors required to follow them. Thus, the training requirements for a given program can be formalized in detail and executed. Next, note that a supervisor of a scripted program can walk into any room and within a few seconds be explicitly oriented to what should be going on and thus evaluate the situation and provide appropriate help. Finally, because the teaching sequence is standardized, it is easier to monitor the progress of the children with program-based tests. *Scripts are the production line of Henry Ford applied to education.* They make possible what Leon Lessinger (1976) has termed "the missing link in education," namely *quality control.* Although scripted presentations are not necessary or even desirable in all areas or levels of education, they most certainly can serve an important role when dealing with competencies that all children should have. They may also play an important role in teacher training (Clark, Gage, Marx, Peterson, Stayrook, & Winne, 1976).

Small Groups

Small groups have many advantages. They are more efficient than one-on-one instruction and provide for more adult direction, prompts, reinforcement, correction, and individualization than found in large-group instruction. They also permit an emphasis on oral communication, which is frequently a problem for children from non-English-speaking and economically disadvantaged backgrounds. Finally, small groups provide a setting where repetitious practice on important building blocks can be made fun and where other students can be used as models. By working with groups of 5 to 10 students at a time, 30 minutes of instruction in each subject area can be provided every day.

The research on small-group instruction generally shows positive benefits. Venezky and Shiloah (1972) reported performance on language tasks was superior for students responding individually in a small-group setting than for students receiving one-to-one instruction. Working with retarded children on language skills, Biberdorf and Pear (1977) reported that group instruction was more efficient in terms of material learned per unit time than individual instruction. Fink and Carnine (1977) and Fink and Sandall (1979) reported similar results. In contrast, a single study (Jenkins, Mayhall, Peschka, & Jenkins, 1974) reported that tutorials in remedial reading were more effective than instruction in small groups.

Unison Responding

A goal of direct instruction in small groups is a high student response rate. A high response rate, which is facilitated by unison or choral responding, provides for more active practice on each skill and gives the teacher frequent feedback on each student's progress.

Several studies point to the importance of frequent student responding. Durling and Schick (1976) reported that overt responding (vocalizing a concept) improved performance when compared to a nonvocalizing treatment. Abramson and Kagan (1975) found that subjects who overtly responded to questions while learning unfamiliar material out-performed students who merely read the material. Frase and Schwartz (1975) reported similar results. Effects of frequent feedback may interact with subject ability (and possibly task difficulty); that is, frequent responding and feedback may be more helpful for lower performers and with more complex tasks. Consistent with this, Tobias and Ingber (1976) reported that feedback yielded superior achievement primarily for students with low pretest scores. This finding is also consistent with that of Camp and Dahlem (1975), who reported that an anticipation method, that requires frequent responding, was superior to a study–test method for retarded children.

Signals

The scripts used in small-group teaching tell the teacher how and when to give signs for the group to respond together. For example, in sounding out a word, a finger is used to point to the letter being sounded out. The children say the sounds as long as the teacher touches it. The teacher moves his finger from sound to sound as they are to be said and lifts the finger away at the end of the word. This signaling procedure ensures that students blend the sounds, which minimizes word misidentification errors. The effective use of signals encourages all students to participate, not just higher-performing students, who, if allowed, will dominate. By pausing before signaling, the teacher provides instructionally naive students the extra second or two needed to come up with an answer.

A study conducted in a small group setting, with an ABAB design (Cowart, Carnine, & Becker, 1973) found that signaling was accompanied by more student attending and responding. When the teacher used signals, the children attended about 55% of the time and responded about 80% of the time. When the teacher did *not* use signals, the children attended about 35% of the time and responded 60% of the time. Slight improvements in test scores also accompanied the use of signals. The same study reported comparable signaling effects on attending and responding in an entire class teaching situation. For example, in one classroom the percentage of time attending averaged 53 and 54 during the two phases in which the teacher used signals and 41 and 20 during the two phases without signals. The responding percentages were 75 and 79 with signals and 67 and 47 without signals.

Pacing

Appropriate pacing contributes to student attentiveness and reduces errors. Students are usually more attentive to a lively, fast-paced presentation (as in Sesame Street) than to a draggy, slow one. Also, frequent responding, which results from rapid-fire teacher questions, often enhances student attentiveness and increases the amount of practice the students receive. However, quickly going from question to question does not mean that a teacher rushes students, requiring them to answer before they have had time to come up with an answer. For new or difficult tasks, the teacher pauses and gives the students extra time before giving a *do it* signal.

Rapid and slow rates of presenting beginning reading tasks were compared in an ABABAB design with the two lowest performing first graders from three classrooms serving as subjects (Carnine, 1976a). Off-task behavior was substantially lower and correct answers were higher during the fast-rate condition (5 seconds per task) than during the slow-rate condition (14 seconds per task). When the teacher asked approximately 12 questions per minute in the fast-rate condition, the students answered correctly about 80% of the time and were off-task only about 10% of the time. When the teacher asked about 5 questions per minute in the slow-rate conditions, the students answered correctly about 30% of the time and were off-task about 70% of the time. Massad and Etzel (1972) found that preschoolers learned sound–symbol relationships more rapidly and with fewer errors with frequent rather than infrequent responding. They also reported that response frequency influenced performance more than the various reinforcement schedules.

Corrections

Although correcting student errors is usually considered an important part of the instructional process, research on correcting errors is limited. The importance of correcting mistakes (as opposed to ignoring them) was investigated in a study conducted by Carnine (1977b). Preschool children were taught several sets of arithmetic facts: first without corrections, then with corrections, again without corrections, and finally with corrections. Accuracy on training questions averaged 55% higher during correction phases than during no-correction phases; posttest accuracy averaged 48% higher during the correction phases. In addition to providing corrective feedback, students must also attend to the feedback if it is to be effective. Fink and Carnine (1975) reported that student worksheet errors declined significantly when the students graphed their errors as compared with just being told the number of errors.

Research related to the modeling aspect of a correction indicates that telling adult subjects the answer after an error resulted in quicker learning than just telling the subject whether the answer was right or wrong (Bourne & Pendleton, 1958); but requiring the subject to say the answer following an error was more effective than just telling the subject the answer (Suppes & Ginsberg, 1962). Stromer (1975) reported that when corrections (modeling the correct answer following an error) and differential praise were introduced in tutorial situations, errors diminished. Although modeling the answer is usually appropriate for correcting mistakes on discrimination tasks, modeling the correct answer can be ineffective with errors that require the application of a multistep strategy. In these situations, the correction should prompt the student to apply the strategy.

A study by Carnine (1980a) investigated the importance of correcting word reading errors by prompting students to use the originally taught sounding-out strategy. Three groups of preschoolers were taught eight letter–sound correspondences and then given practice on the sounding-out strategy until they reached a 100% correct response criterion to a set of six words. After reaching criterion on the training words, the preschoolers received daily word-recognition practice, in which four new words were repeated three times. During baseline, the teacher used a whole-word correction procedure: The teacher identified the word and then asked the students to identify it. The intervention, a sounding-out correction procedure, was introduced with one group at a time according to a multiple-baseline design. In the sounding-out correction procedure, the students were required to sound out and then identify the word that was missed. Consistent improvement was noted in all three groups after the sounding-out correction was introduced, both in terms of correct training responses and correct responses to transfer words. The approximate changes in training performance on word identification were from 30 to 70% correct in group 1, 20 to 35% in group 2, and 15 to 25% in group 3. The smaller changes with each successive intervention suggest that the longer students receive a whole-word correction, the less effective is the introduction of the sounding-out correction. Other related research also suggests that correction on strategy tasks should prompt students to apply the strategy (Siegel, 1977; Siegler & Liebert, 1973).

Oftentimes errors can be anticipated and prevented. Fink (1976) investigated one such precorrection procedure with the two lowest performing first graders from four classrooms (mean IQs were 68 and 72) who consistently misidentified vowels when sounding out CVC (consonant–vowel–consonant) and CVCC words. The students received daily practice in identifying letter sounds and in sounding out words. In addition, they were precorrected in this way: Each student was instructed to identify the vowel *before* sounding out the word. An ABA design was used: no precorrection, precorrection, and no precorrection. The mean number of correct responses (out of six possible) changed from .71 to 3.75 and back to 1.20 for the first student and from .60 to 2.56 and back to .86 for the second student.

Praise

A number of studies have demonstrated that teacher attention is an effective tool in reducing children's inappropriate behavior within large-group instructional settings. Thomas, Becker, and Armstrong (1968) and Madsen et al. (1968) showed that frequent teacher attention in the form of praise was more effective than rules or teacher reprimands in increasing appropriate behavior. Similarly, Hall, Lund, and Jackson (1968) and Cossairt, Hall, and Hopkins (1973) demonstrated that teacher attention through verbal praise and physical contact increased children's study behaviors in a large group instructional setting. In addition, Cossairt et al. reported that higher rates of teacher praise coincided with higher rates of studying behavior.

Although the effects of positive teacher attention on appropriate classroom behaviors have been well established within large-group instructional settings, the effectiveness of the teacher attention variable within a small-group instructional setting has not received much attention. An exception is a study by Kryzanowski (1976). Four subjects in an ABAB design displayed clear increases in on-task behavior in a small group instructional setting as a function of increased verbal praise, with the average increase being 47%. The four subjects did exhibit a noticeable delay in reversing when baseline conditions were reinstated in Phase III, and none of the subjects reverted to baseline rates.

Although the study demonstrated that higher rates of verbal praise produce higher rates of on-task behavior within small group instructional settings, the question remains as to whether higher rates of on-task behavior is a necessary prerequisite to a child's learning. On-task behavior may increase a child's opportunity to respond appropriately to every task; however, it does not ensure that learning will be more efficient or complete. Siegel and Rosenshine (1973) reported that praise during DISTAR Language I small-group instruction was not a significant predictor of child achievement. Thus high rates of praise may only produce better behaved children and not necessarily smarter ones. Given the contradictory data concerning this question, further research is needed to investigate the effects of praise on learning in a small-group instructional setting.

Combined Effects

A final study investigated the combined effects of a set of direct instruction techniques. In a *high-implementation* condition, the teacher used praise, corrections, and rapid pacing, and in a *low-implementation* condition the teacher seldom corrected, used little praise, and presented tasks in a relatively slow manner (Carnine, 1981a). The subjects were preschoolers, who were taught reading in a small group setting. For assessing the strength of the combined variables, a design with almost daily reversals was followed: A B A B A B A B A B AAA BBB AAA BBBBB. Both on-task behavior and correct responding remained sensitive to the condition shifts throughout the experiment, with much larger changes occurring for on-task behavior than for academic behavior. The results suggest that this cluster of teacher presentation variables (praise, rapid pacing, and correcting) can strongly affect student performance across different educational programs. This study used the McGraw-Hill Sullivan Reading program, whereas the earlier cited research on isolated teacher presentation variables used DISTAR materials or experimenter designed materials.

Related Research on Teaching Practices

A number of largely correlational studies appear to be converging in support of the Direct Instruction approach to teaching basic skills, particularly with students from low socioeconomic backgrounds. These studies focus on student engaged time and on the ways in which the teacher structures and uses instructional time.

Academic Engaged Time

The Direct Instruction goal of teaching more in less time can be met by better utilization of the total school time available as well as by better teaching techniques. Better outcomes should be associated with *more available time* or more content covered in a given area and with *better student engagement* during that time (Rosenshine & Berliner, 1978). "More available time" is similar to Carroll's (1963) concept of "opportunity to learn." In a review of content covered studies, Rosenshine (1976) reports that in 15 of 16 studies significant positive relations were found between content covered and student achievement gain. In a review of studies of engaged time, Bloom (1976) reports that correlations with student gain were about .40 when the student was the unit of analysis and .52 when the class was the unit. Although these outcomes may seem obvious, it should be noted that they do not play a dominant role in current school planning practices.

Within Follow Through, data collected by Stallings and Kaskowitz (1974) show that only the Direct Instruction Model and the Behavior Analysis Model had more opportunity for engaged time in reading and math than the Non-Follow Through control groups. Rosenshine (1977) found substantial rank-order correlations between first- and third-grade outcomes and opportunity for engaged time for the major sponsors using the Stallings and Kaskowitz data (1974).

Using coded observations of "productive minutes" for samples of target students, McDonald (1975) found that engagement occurred about 70% of allotted time and that median productive minutes per day was under 30 for reading and under 25 for math in grades 2 and 5. These data suggest that there is much room for accelerating student progress on basic skills through increasing engaged time.

Direct Instruction

Rosenshine (1976) has used the term *direct instruction* (not capitalized) to summarize a converging set of studies relating teaching strategies to student outcomes. Rosenshine's *direct instruction* refers to teaching activities focused on academic matters where goals are clear to the students, time allocated for instruction is sufficient and continous, content covered is extensive, student performance is monitored, questions are at a low cognitive level and produce many correct responses, and feedback to students is immediate and academically oriented. The teacher controls the instructional goals, chooses material appropriate for the student's level, and paces the teaching. Interaction is structured but lively and fun, not authoritarian.

The studies covered in Rosenshine's (1976, 1977) reviews include classroom observation studies by Soar (1973) and by Stallings and Kaskowitz (1974) using Follow Through classrooms for a variety of major sponsors; studies by Brophy and Evertson (1974) from the Texas Teacher Effectiveness Study; studies by Good (Good & Grouws, 1975; Good & Beckerman, 1978; Good, Grouws, & Beckerman, in press); studies from the Far West Lab (Gall, Ward, Berliner, Cahen, Crown, Elashoff, Stanton, & Winne, 1975; Marliave, Fisher, Filby, & Dishaw, 1977; Tikunoff, Berliner, & Rist, 1975); and studies from the Stanford Center for Research and Development in Teaching (Clark et al., 1976).

Rosenshine (1977) summarizes the results as follows:

1. *Teacher direction.* With both lower- and middle-socioeconomic students, the most successful student gains are found where the teacher is a strong leader. The teacher approaches the task in a direct, businesslike manner without giving choices and organizes instruction around teacher-oriented questions.

2. *Student choice*. Where there is high student choice there is usually lower academic engaged time and lower achievement.

3. *Student groupings*. Primary grade students are consistently more engaged in learning when supervised by a teacher than when working independently. Teacher working one-on-one (with the rest of the class unsupervised) was usually related to poorer achievement. Larger groupings under teacher direction show better outcomes.

4. *Seatwork*. Activities requiring the students to work on their own, such as reading a book, doing workbook exercises, or writing a report, are called seatwork. McDonald (1975) and Good and Beckerman (1978) find this activity occurs from 42 to 62% of the time in elementary classrooms. The studies reviewed show that such unsupervised activities show less engaged time and are related to lower academic gains. (Better management and checkout procedures could conceivably change this outcome.)

5. *Verbal interaction*. Studies of teacher–student verbal interactions show the following:

a. *Little time is spent on discussion*. The time spent on discussion ranges from 5 to 30%.

b. *Factual questions and practice lead to better gains*. When the teacher focuses on questions that have a single answer, with many opportunities for student responses and adult feedback, student gains are better. Conversely, the use of "higher-order questions" (in the sense of Bloom's taxonomy) was not found to improve performance on tests containing higher level questions. The use of "convergent questioning with amplification and elaboration" and the use of "open questions with encouragement of expression" were found to be negatively related to achievement.

c. *Student initiated talk*. Student initiated questions were not significantly related to achievement. However, student initiated contacts during seatwork were positively associated with gains.

As a group, the studies reviewed by Rosenshine add significant support to the validity of the practices that characterized the Direct Instruction Model. It should be noted that these findings may be restricted to students from lower socioeconomic backgrounds in the primary grades. However, they may well have important implications for students from other backgrounds and grade levels as well. In our view, these studies have considerable implication for the future design of research comparing different educational programs and for a new generation of functional studies of classroom practices where *the dependent variable is mean and range of academic engaged time*. We return to this point in the section on implications.

Teacher Training

Teacher training has preservice, in-service, and classroom components. A 1- or 2-week preservice is held before the opening of school to familiarize teachers with various aspects of program implementation. During preservice, supervisors train teachers in the use of Direct Instruction materials, teacher presentation skills, reinforcement techniques, placement tests and grouping, and practice on key formats. In-service meetings are held regularly throughout the year and are usually held after school or during the late afternoon. The primary purpose of these meetings is to continue training on formats and on teacher presentation skills. Format practice is limited to formats that the teachers will soon use and that are difficult or involve new teaching skills. In-services are also held for working on specific problems. For example, if a new reinforcement system needs to be implemented, all teachers from a grade level may meet for training. The important goal is to provide relevant in-service for those teachers, grade levels, or classrooms that need training.

The actual effectiveness of preservice and in-service can be seen only through directly observing the teachers working with students, which is one of the responsibilities of the supervisor. By working directly with teachers and students, the supervisor can demonstrate many skills that cannot be role played in in-service settings. The supervisor sits next to the teacher, sometimes asking the teacher to try different techniques, demonstrating a task for the teacher, or calling on individual students to answer. The supervisor provides the teacher with the following kinds of information through direct demonstrations: how to test the children, how to pace the lesson, when to reinforce, etc.

Research on training teachers in Direct Instruction has been confined largely to reinforcement techniques (Horton, 1975; Rule, 1972; Saudargas, 1972; Thomas, 1971), corrections (Siegel, 1977), and signals and pacing (Carnine & Fink, 1978). Siegel's study is particularly interesting because it measured changes in teacher behavior and corresponding changes in student achievement. First, teachers were observed and rated as either high or low implementers. Half of each group were randomly assigned to receive training in how to use the Direct Instruction correction procedures. The training resulted in significantly improved correcting behavior; the low implementers after training corrected more appropriately than the high implementers who were not trained. Also, students of teachers who received training in corrections had significantly higher posttest scores than the students of the untrained teachers.

In the Carnine and Fink study (1978), one group of 13 teachers who had received intensive preservice and in-service training was used to collect data on pacing and signaling. These data were used as a *comparison standard* to evaluate the effects of training on pacing and signaling in a multiple baseline experimental study. Low implementation levels during baseline for three untrained teachers indicated that training was necessary. The training procedure included supervised practice, unsupervised practice, and self-critique. The results from the intervention indicated that training increased the level of signaling and rate of presentation well above the levels of the comparison standard. Observations made 1 week and again 4 weeks subsequent to the termination of training showed that performance levels achieved during training were maintained.

Programming Strategy

A final important feature of the Direct Instruction model is the programming strategy underlying the Distar programs. Program design involves specifying objectives, analyzing the objectives into teachable component groups, identifying preskills, selecting examples, and sequencing examples. *Teaching 2—Cognitive Learning and Instruction* (Becker, Engelmann & Thomas, 1975) discusses detailed approaches to the logical analysis of knowledge systems; general strategies for program design and sequencing of examples; and how operant principles are used in teaching concepts, operations, and problem-solving behaviors. A summary of the role of operant principles in programming to teach the general case is also found in Becker and Engelmann (1978b). In this section, a new structuring of programming strategies, taken from Engelmann and Carnine's book on programming (in preparation), is presented. This structuring focuses on *six shifting aspects of task design* and on *five types of task structures*.

Shifting Aspects of Task Design

1. The structure of most tasks in a direct instruction program shift according to fairly predictable patterns. The first shift is from *overtized* to *covertized* problem-solving strategies. In an overtized problem-solving strategy, the teacher makes explicit every step in the strategy, at first prompting the learner to perform on every step involved in solving a particular type of problem (a forward-chaining procedure). Initially the teacher requires the learner to follow the same steps in solving similar problems. Because an overt response is required at each step, the teacher can precisely pinpoint the *exact* skills in a strategy that are causing the learner trouble. Eventually the strategy is covertized, which means that the teacher no longer requires a response at each step. Responses at many steps may no longer be observable; possibly only the answer is overt. Covertization provides an essential link between teacher-directed and independent work.

2. A second shift is from *simplified contexts* that maximize the saliency of relevant features when a new discrimination is introduced to *complex contexts* characterized by applications in various settings that incorporate a wide range of irrelevant detail.

3. The third shift involves the *fading of prompts*. Early in instruction the teacher may use prompts (modified examples or special wording) to focus the learner's attention on relevant features. Later these prompts are faded.

4. The fourth shift is from *massed practice* on new skills to distributed practice (with gradually decreasing amount of practice) as the skill is incorporated in more complex applications. Early massed practice is designed to bring about mastery learning; the distributed practice aids retention.

5. The fifth shift concerns teacher *feedback*. Feedback is immediate in the beginning but is delayed as the learner becomes increasingly capable.

6. A final shift is from the *teacher* as a source of information to the *learner* as a source of information. As the learner's repertoire of skills increases, the

teacher serves less as a provider of new information and more as a guide as to how to use previously acquired information. The learner is called upon to determine how previously learned skills and information apply in various problem-solving situations.

These shifts can be illustrated in teaching the rule *when inflation grows faster than wages, purchasing power declines.* An overtized strategy could be applied to this item: "The rate of inflation for 1953 and 1954 was 3%. Wages grew 2% in 1953 and 4% in 1954. Tell me when purchasing power fell." In teaching the overtized strategy, the teacher presents these questions, "What's the rule that tells about purchasing power? . . . What's inflation in 1953? . . . How fast did wages increase in 1953? . . . Did purchasing power decline in 1953?" Covertization occurs when the student works the item without the teacher's questions.

The role of the teacher in guiding the learner to use previously acquired information is illustrated in the teaching procedure for the overtized strategy. The teacher asks a series of questions that directs the learner's use of previously learned information.

To teach the discrimination *purchasing power* in a simplified context, the teacher might say, "The purchasing power of $10 in 1940 went to $9.90 in 1941. Did the purchasing power of the money decline? In a more complex context, an item might be: "In the 1950s the average annual purchasing power of 50 million workers was 100 million dollars. In the 1960s the average annual purchasing power of 70 million workers was 140 billion (adjusted for inflation). Did the purchasing power of the workers fall between the 50s and 60s?"

A prompt question, "Is $9.90 less than $10?", could be added to the previous discrimination teaching exercise, which would change the item as follows: "The purchasing power of $10 in 1940 went to $9.90 in 1941. Is $9.90 less than $10? . . . So did the purchasing power of money decline between 1940 and 1941?" Fading would involve dropping the prompt question.

Massed practice might involve five items when the discrimination is introduced. Later distributed practice might consist of one item each week.

Immediate feedback would occur if the teacher gave feedback after every student response. In contrast, a worksheet on inflation, wages, and purchasing power returned a day after it was completed illustrates delayed feedback.

These shifts are designed to contribute to transfer, retention, and rapid learning. Initially the teacher shows students how to solve problems so that they can also solve new problems of the same type, which facilitates transfer and rapid learning. Initial teacher-centered instruction with discriminations presented in simplified contexts with massed examples, prompts, and immediate feedback minimizes student errors, which facilitates retention and rapid learning. With fewer errors, students learn new material more rapidly and remember it longer. The shift in teaching strategies and discriminations to independent exercises involving complex contexts with fewer practice examples, faded prompts, and delayed feedback almost defines transfer (to less structured settings) and is also essential for retention. These shifting components of task design are used to varying degrees with different types of tasks. We distinguish four specific types of tasks: basic discriminations (concepts), related learning discriminations, rules, and cognitive operations or problem-solving strategies.

1. Teaching Basic Discriminations

Basic discriminations must be taught with positive and negative examples. For example, teaching the discriminations *longer, not longer* or *blue, not blue* with rules or verbal explanations is impractical. Students who do not respond correctly to "Is the pencil longer than the pen?" are unlikely to benefit from this explanation: "Longer means greater extension in the horizontal dimension."

Design procedures for *basic discriminations* include *selecting and sequencing examples, specifying teacher instructions, and providing practice.* A principle central to the design of all tasks is *that the presentation should be consistent with only one interpretation.* If a presentation is consistent with several interpretations, students may learn an interpretation other than that intended by the teacher.

Selecting Examples. An application of this principle is illustrated in Fig. 6.4, which contains positive and negative examples of the discrimination *on*. The pair of examples from teaching set (a) illustrates the minimum difference between positive and negative examples of *on*. In set (a) the number of possible interpretations for *on* is minimized because of the small difference between the positive and negative examples. In contrast, the subsequent sets of examples [sets (b) through (e)] differ in terms of several features, which suggests additional interpretations. A student presented with set (e) examples might learn that *on* means a block, something not held in a hand, horizontally positioned objects, etc. None of these interpretations are possible from set (a). When Carnine (1981b) presented examples similar to those in Fig. 6.4 to different groups of

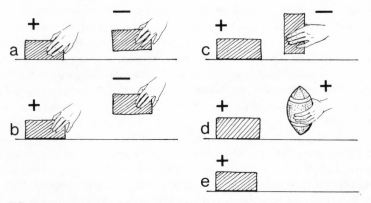

FIG. 6.4.   An example of the "only one" principle: positive and negative examples of discrimination of *on*.

preschoolers, he found a significant linear trend between the number of possible interpretations and errors on a transfer test. Preschoolers presented with set (a) examples responded correctly to 10.2 transfer items, whereas preschoolers presented with set (e) responded correctly to only 5.0 transfer items. In other words, the greater the number of possible interpretations that are consistent with a teaching demonstration, the greater the likelihood that some students will learn an interpretation other than the one intended by the teacher. Designing a presentation as in set (a) that is consistent with only one interpretation increases the *salience* of the intended relevant stimulus. "If a change in a particular stimulus results in a correlated change in a subject's behavior, we may say that this stimulus controls the subject's behavior. In any situation, it is obvious that some stimuli will gain control more rapidly than others, while yet other stimuli may apparently fail to gain control. We may categorize these differences as differences in salience [Mackintosh, 1977, p. 505]."

Ensuring that a presentation is consistent with only one interpretation requires selecting not only minimally different positive and negative examples (whenever possible) but also a range of positive examples. For example, if all positive examples of the preposition *on* involved a ball placed on the corners or on the front edge of a table, various misinterpretations would be possible. Carnine (1981b) found that students presented with a full range of positive examples of how to convert fractions into decimals performed higher on transfer tests (82% correct) than students who were presented with a restricted range of examples (4% correct). Similar results were found by Williams and Carnine (in press).

In a pilot study Carnine (1976b) found that a full-range of negative examples must also be included; otherwise inhibitory control might occur. One of three groups of students were presented a restricted range of negative examples (straight-sided geometric forms). When presented transfer items, these students made three times as many errors on non-straight-sided negatives as did students in the other two groups. These students seemingly learned the misinterpretation of identifying positive examples as "not negative" rather than identifying positives on the basis of presence of relevant features.

The preceding two studies suggest that a full range of positive *and* negative examples is needed to ensure appropriate "generalization." Another study (Carnine, 1976c) suggested the importance of presenting intended irrelevant characteristics in both positive and negative examples. Any feature that appears only in positive examples may be treated as relevant, whether the teacher "intends" for the feature to be relevant or not (Carnine, 1976c; Reynolds, 1962; Suchman & Trabasso, 1966b).

Miles, Mackintosh, and Westbrook (1970) demonstrated how to ensure that *only* the intended relevant feature (a tone) functioned as the relevant feature, whereas a second feature (a color) functioned as an irrelevant feature. The color was treated as irrelevant by having it appear as a characteristic of some positive examples and some negative examples. Only the tone was found in all positives and in no negatives (i.e., pecking was reinforced in the presence of the tone only). Test stimuli having the tone functioned more often as a discriminative stimulus than stimuli with the color. The results of this study and others (Warren, 1953) show that stimuli can be selected so that only relevant stimuli will control the target behavior. If various irrelevant characteristics are present in both positive and negative examples, no particular irrelevant characteristic will be correlated with reinforcement.

Sequencing Examples. Several procedures are relevant for sequencing examples. *First, minimally different different positive and negative examples of a discrimination* should be sequenced adjacent to each other and simultaneously rather than successively. Sequencing minimally different examples in this way increases the saliency of the discrimination's relevant features (Granzin & Carnine, 1977). Students taught conjunctive and exclusive disjunctive concepts with simultaneously presented minimally different positive and negative examples reached criterion in about half as many trials as students presented the same examples but successively and with multiple differences between adjacent examples. Similar results have been reported by Stolurow (1975); Tennyson, Steve, and Boutwell (1975); and Tennyson (1973).

A second sequencing procedure is that, whenever possible, positive and negative examples should be generated by changing a single stimulus (a dynamic presentation) rather than presenting a set of discrete stimuli, either simultaneously or successively (a static presentation). Carnine (1977b) reported faster acquisition and higher transfer scores for preschoolers who were taught the discriminations *diagonal* and *convex* with a dynamic rather than static presentation. In the dynamic treatment, examples of diagonal were generated by rotating a single line segment. In the static treatment, examples consisted of pairs of line segments drawn on cards. The differences in trials to criterion for the two treatments was 46.4 versus 10.6 for diagonal and 5.8 versus .05 for convex.

Carnine also (1980b) compared all three sequencing procedures just discussed. Preschoolers were taught a discrimination defined by leaf angle used by Trabasso (1963) in his study on various types of prompts. Preschoolers who received the dynamic presentation with minimum differences reached criterion in an average of 7.6 trials; preschoolers who received a static presentation with minimum differences took 12.8 trials; finally, preschoolers who received a static presentation with multiple differences required an average of 26.0 trials.

Although dynamic presentations and minimal differences are possible for many discriminations (prepositions, comparatives, and action verbs), in teaching students to label objects, dynamic presentations are not possible. The critical factor in teaching object names to young learners is selecting an adequate range of positive and negative examples so that the possibility of misinterpretations is minimized.

The direct instruction procedures discussed here for selecting and sequencing positive and negative examples are intended to result in presentations that are consistent with only one interpretation, which minimizes overshadowing. There can be no gainsaying the fundamental importance of overshadowing. The presence of a more salient or more valid stimulus is apparently able to interfere with the acquisition of control by less salient or less valid stimuli. . . . The occurrence of overshadowing implies . . . some interactions or competition between stimuli for control of behavior (Mackintosh, 1977, pp. 506–507).

Practice.   Because of individual learner differences, a specific number of examples will never be appropriate for teaching a discrimination to all students. A mastery learning approach in which examples are presented until the student reaches a specified performance standard probably results in higher retention scores than presenting the same number of examples to all students. Jeffrey and Samuels (1967) taught students a word-reading procedure using a fixed trials design; Carnine (1977c) taught students a similar procedure, but with a trials-to-criterion design. Subjects in the Carnine study identified about 92% of the transfer words correctly, whereas Jeffrey and Samuels' subjects identified only about 31% of the words correctly. Similarly, (Carnine, 1976b) students taught letter-sound correspondences with a trials-to-criterion design averaged 79% correct posttest identifications, whereas students who received 50 presentations of each letter averaged 28%. The stringency of a performance criterion also affects learner retention. Carlson and Minke (1975) reported higher scores for students who had to meet a 90% criterion than an 80% criterion and higher scores with an 80% criterion than a 60% criterion. Research on mastery learning has also been conducted by Houser and Trublood (1975) and Bloom (1976).

A mastery criterion should be set lower when the task involves labeling (the likelihood of reaching criterion through guessing is lower) or involves only a small set of discriminations (sampling all the concepts is possible in relatively few trials). A more rigorous criterion should be used for tasks that call for a *yes* or *no* answer (to prevent a learner from reaching criterion through guessing) and for tasks that sample a large set of concepts (to prevent a learner from reaching criterion on a task without responding to at least some examples of each concept in the set).

Although research cannot specify an optimal number of practice examples for every discrimination, studies do indicate that more examples than found in a single rational set facilitate transfer performance. (A rational set of examples illustrate a full range of relevant, negative, and irrelevant features). Klausmeier and Feldman (1975) reported that children who received a rule and three sets of rational examples correctly identified more transfer stimuli than did children who received a rule and a single set of rational examples. Repeating examples can also be beneficial, up to a point. Shore and Sechrest (1961) found that 9 examples presented twice resulted in higher transfer scores than 6 examples presented three times or than 18 different examples.

Teaching a Set of Discriminations. The discussion thus far has focused primarily on teaching a single discrimination. Additional procedures are needed for teaching a *set* of discriminations such as several letter-sound correspondences, prepositions, and sentence types. When teaching a set of discriminations, the discriminations should be introduced cumulatively [i.e., a discrimination is introduced and practiced until it is mastered (in the context of previously introduced discriminations) before a new discrimination is introduced]. Carnine (1976d) reported that preschoolers mastered six letter-sound correspondences in fewer trials when the letters were introduced cumulatively rather than simultaneously. Preschoolers in the cumulative group required an average of 178 trials, whereas the simultaneous group required 261 trials. Not only was the learning rate faster for the cumulative group, but retention was better: an average of 84% correct for the cumulative group on a posttest, in contrast to 66% for the simultaneous group. A similar study was conducted with addition facts rather than letter-sound correspondences (Carnine, 1978a). Preschoolers in the cumulative group required 197 trials on the average, whereas preschoolers in the simultaneous group required an average of 342 trials. Posttest differences were not significant. Another study on cumulative introduction (Fink & Brice, 1979) involved training moderately and severely handicapped preschoolers on a word-matching task. The cumulative group reached criterion in an average of 173 trials whereas a successive pairs treatment took 208 trials. Posttest differences were also significant: 90% versus 48%. Positive results from cumulative programming have also been reported by Cheyne (1966), Gruenenfelder and Borokowski (1975) and Ferster and Hammer (1966).

The *order* in which different discriminations from a set are introduced is also important. Concepts that are more *useful* to the learner or *easier* should be introduced earlier. For example, Carnine and Carnine (1978) found that decoding consonant–vowel–consonant (CVC) words is easier than decoding CVCC words, which in turn is easier than decoding CCVC words. (Mean correct responses to samples of each word type were 71%, 40%, and 22% respectively.) Introducing the easiest word type (CVC) first should minimize errors and thus increase teaching efficiency.

Another sequencing procedure is to separate discriminations (e.g., *b* and *d*) that are similar to each other either in sound or shape. That increased response similarity makes paired-associate learning more difficult is well documented (Feldman and Underwood, 1957; Higa, 1963; Underwood, Runquist, & Schulz, 1959). Carnine (1976d) reported that first graders made fewer errors (33% versus 52%) and that preschoolers reached criterion in fewer trials (178 versus 293) when similar letters (the letter-sound correspondences for *e* and *i*) were separated from each other in the order of introduction (*e c m u s i* versus *e i u c m s*).

In another study (Carnine, 1980c) the guideline of separating similar stimuli was investigated in a visual discrimination task. Preschoolers who received a similar–separated sequence reached criterion on a later letter matching task in significantly fewer trials than preschoolers in a similar–together treatment: a mean of 31 versus 69 trials. Moreover, Carnine (1977d) found that when a new member is added to a previously taught set that contains a similar member, the learner should not be required to label the new member in a discrimination task involving just those two members. Rather, the new member should be discriminated from less similar members, or initial discrimination training on the two similar members should call for yes/no rather than labeling responses. Students required to discriminate the two similar members by labeling them required 30 trials to reach criterion. Three other treatments that separated the similar members resulted in an average of about 15 trials each.

In addition to determining the order for introducing new discriminations, the instructional designer must also review earlier introduced discriminations. In most cases, reviewing every previously introduced discrimination in every session is too time-consuming. For example, a teacher cannot review 10 previously introduced prepositions before introducing the eleventh. As a consequence, teachers must select those few items for review that maximize retention. To do this, the teacher constructs a review set to include troublesome members (defined by high error rates), recently introduced members (those probably not yet mastered), members not recently reviewed, and finally members highly similar to the new member. These guidelines for selecting members for a review set are unnecessary if the discriminations are reviewed in other tasks. For example, a review set for comparatives such as *longer* is unnecessary if the learner encounters description tasks that involve comparatives: "Tell me which pencil is *longer*." However, review in some form is critical, either as part of a review set or as part of other tasks.

2. Teaching Related Discriminations

Discriminations that are systematically related to each other are usually introduced after basic discriminations. Two discriminations are systematically related if several examples of one discrimination can be transformed in a standard way into examples of the second discrimination. For example, the discriminations *singular nouns* and *plural nouns* are systematically related because the singular nouns *dog, hat,* and *elephant* can be transformed into plural nouns by following a standard procedure: adding *s* to produce *dogs, hats,* and *elephants.* Other illustrations of related discriminations include fractions and decimals ($^4/_{10}$ and .4); statements and command ("*The man did go to town,*" and "*Go to town*"); present and past tense (*The ball is rolling,* and *The ball was rolling*). The purpose of the related discrimination sequence is to increase the learning rate for the new related discrimination. For example, if students can write fractions but not decimals, the related discrimination sequence makes explicit the relationship between fractions and decimals. By building on the student's knowledge of fractions, the teacher can spend less time teaching the decimal notation.

The sequence for teaching a related discrimination is to begin with a review of several examples of the familiar discrimination (e.g., a review of statements precedes the introduction of commands). The teacher points to pictures of a person carrying out an action and says, "Make a statement about what you see." The learner responds. "The girl is washing her face." Next, a series of items for the new related discrimination is given. The teacher uses the same pictures but says, "Make a command about what you see." The learner responds, "Wash your face." The next step involves examples of the familiar and related discrimination removed from a simplified context (separate groups of commands and statements) to a more complex context (statement and command items are intermixed). Carnine (1977e) presented the same statement and command items to preschoolers who could generate statements but not commands. One treatment received all the statement items and then all the command items. The preschoolers in the related discrimination sequence made 67% more correct responses on a transfer test. In another study (Carnine & Stein, in press), preschoolers were taught 21 addition facts, either in a modified related discrimination sequence or in a random sequence. On the average, the preschoolers in the related discrimination sequence made over twice as many correct posttest responses. They also required more time to reach training criterion, but the difference was not significant.

3. Teaching Rules

Rules often describe a relationship between two discriminations. In the rule, *The hotter an object becomes, the more it expands,* the two key discriminations are *hotter* and *expands.* Rules are taught in three stages of decreasing structure: rule repetition, simple applications, and complex applications. For the rule, *The lower you eat on a food ladder, the more protein goes directly to you,* the learner first repeats the rule to ensure information retention. The simple applications follow the wording of the rule: "A pound of beans is lower on the food ladder than a pound of hamburger. Which food gives more protein directly to you?" The students indicate that beans would provide more direct protein. Complex applications do not use the words from the rule (e.g., the item would not state that beans are lower on the food ladder). The student must use the information in the application item to draw an inference about whether beans are lower on the food ladder and then draw a second inference that beans provide more direct protein than hamburgers. [If students are to perform on complex applications, they must have previously learned key concepts from the rule (e.g., food ladder)]. The teacher asks, "Which food gives more protein directly to you, peanuts or fried chicken?" The student answers, "Peanuts." The teacher asks, "How do you know?" and the learner answers, "Peanuts are lower on the food ladder." The last question tests whether the learner applied the rule in arriving at an answer. Carnine, Kameenui, and Ludlow (1978) used primary-grade students in comparing three rule-teaching treatments: (1) saying the rule and the key concept from the rule (the concept being "A food ladder has plants on the low step, little animals on the next step, and big animals on the high step"); (2) working application items relating to the key concept in addition to rule and concept saying; and (3) working rule application items in addition to concept application items and rule and concept saying. Only students in the third treatment responded correctly to transfer items at a level significantly higher than chance. The results suggest that merely saying a rule and even learning the key concept from a rule are not sufficient to ensure that students can apply a rule. Direct application exercises seem necessary to ensure successful applications.

Application exercises are also important for *definitions,* which can be viewed as simple rules that identify the relevant features for a single concept. Anderson and Kulhavy (1973) found that students who generated sentences incorporating a defined word scored higher on a transfer test than did students who repeated a definition three times. Although application examples are important in definition exercises, so is the definition itself. Klausmeier and Feldman (1975) reported that a definition and three sets of examples were more effective than a set of rational examples alone. Feldman, Merrill and Tennyson (1971), and Markle and Tiemann (1974) all found that a definition and set of examples were superior to just a set of examples.

In correcting mistakes on complex applications of either a rule or a definition, a model and test procedure is *not* adequate. Modeling does not make overt the strategy involved in coming up with the answer. Students are more likely to learn the strategy if it is demonstrated. For the rule involving the food ladder, a correction on a complex application would make explicit the comparison between peanuts and fried chicken ("Which food is lower on the food chain, fried chicken or peanuts?") and the subsequent inference about which provides more direct protein. ("So which food provides more protein directly to you?"). Note that the correction ends with the same question that the student originally missed. A correction should end with the student successfully answering the item that was initially missed.

4. Teaching Cognitive Operations

Thus far the discussion has surveyed direct instruction design procedures for teaching single discriminations, sets of discriminations, related discriminations, and rules. These types of tasks are the building blocks for teaching a cognitive operation, which is a sequence of steps used to solve any problem of a given type. Cognitive operations can be used to solve algebraic equations, calculate gas pressures, complete analogies, work long-division problems, etc. Initially, the steps of a cognitive operation must be made overt, both to show students the relevant steps and to provide a basis for teacher feedback as the students attempt to carry out each step.

The primary difficulty in designing cognitive operations is constructing the steps the students are to follow. The instructional designer first selects a problem appropriate for the operation (e.g., $9 - 2 = \Box$ in simple subtraction) and then generates a list of minimally different problems ($9 + 2 = \Box$, $9 - 3 = \Box$, $8 - 2 = \Box$, $9 - \Box = 2$). The minimally different problems alert the designer to the operation's range of application. The overt steps that make up an operation must allow the student to handle all the variations implied by the minimal differences. For example, the difference between $9 - 2$ and $9 + 2$ calls attention to the sign; the difference between $9 - 2$ and $9 - 3$ points out the importance of the second numeral. Constructing operations that take into account these minimally different problems sets the stage for transfer, enabling the student to use variations of the operation for working the minimally different problems.

After the minimally different problems have been listed, a teaching procedure is designed for each aspect of the problem identified by the minimal difference. In $9 - 2 = \Box$ and $9 - \Box = 2$, the difference relates to the placement of the unknown. Here is a teacher question that accounts for that aspect: "What are we going to figure out in this problem?" The question focuses the learner's attention on the unknown in both problems. "How many we end up with" is the answer for $9 - 2 = \Box$; "How many we minus" is the answer for $9 - \Box = 2$. Different strategies are signaled by different answers. In $9 - 2 = \Box$ the learner determines a number equal to $9 - 2$ by drawing counters for the second numeral and counting backward from the first numeral: "nine, eight, seven." In $9 - \Box = 2$ the learner determines the number subtracted by counting backward from nine to two (i.e., counting less on the side with the unknown until the sides are equal). After a teaching question (or set of questions) has been identified for each pair of minimally different problems, the separate procedures are combined to create the overtized cognitive operation.

The importance of identifying and teaching the critical aspects of a cognitive operation has been indicated in several studies by Carnine. In one study (Carnine, 1977c), a sounding-out operation in which students identified and blended the sounds represented by letters in simple words was compared with a whole-word treatment. Both treatments required about the same amount of time to reach criterion on the training words, but the group taught the operation correctly decoded an average of 92% of the transfer words, whereas the whole-word treatment resulted in an average of 28% correct responses. In a second study (Carnine, 1977f), performance of students taught an operation for beginning fraction skills was compared with the performance of students in a practice-only treatment. In an average performing classroom of first graders, transfer scores averaged 86% correct for the group taught the fraction operations and 48% for the practice group. For high-performing second graders, transfer scores favored the operation group 94% to 83%.

In Experiment 1 of a comprehension study (Carnine, Prill, & Armstrong, 1977, 1978), three educable mentally retarded students were taught an operation for working comprehension sequencing items (what happened first, second, etc.)

in a multiple-baseline design. They answered an average of 18% of the baseline items correctly and 96% of the intervention items correctly. This finding was partially replicated in Experiment 2 with economically disadvantaged Title I students (performance increased from 25% during baseline to 87% after training). In addition, these students were taught an operation for working literal comprehension items, which resulted in an increase in average performance from 57 to 96%.

In a fourth study (Kameenui, Carnine, & Maggs, 1980), three students were taught an operation for dealing with syntax complexity as it related to comprehension items. Passages with clauses and passive voice constructions accompanied by literal comprehension items were presented daily to the subjects. During baseline, the subjects worked the training items, received feedback, and then answered probe items. During intervention (a multiple-baseline design was used), a subject transformed complex structures into two simple sentences (the operation) and then worked the training items, received feedback, and answered problem items. Although baseline performance was somewhat variable, the intervention produced consistently high performance on the probes.

Various other researchers have also investigated the importance of teaching operations. Klausmeier and Meinke (1968) assigned subjects to one of three groups: minimal task directions, task directions plus a description of the structure of the stimulus materials, or task directions, structure information, and a conservative focusing operation that involves comparing minimally different examples. Half the subjects in each group also were told how to draw inferences. Subjects who had received the conservative focusing operation and been told how to draw inferences learned the concepts faster than subjects in other groups. In a similar study, Frederick and Klausmeier (1968) reported that subjects told to use a conservative focusing operation made fewer errors than subjects who received only feature information. The benefits of teaching operations have also been reported by Anastasiow, Sibley, Leonhardt, and Borich (1971); Egan and Greeno (1973); Francis (1975); Rosenthal and Carroll (1972); Rosenthal and Zimmerman (1972); Tennyson et al. (1975); Tennyson and Tennyson (1975); and Wittrock (1963). In contrast, findings by Gagné and Brown (1961) and Worthen (1968) were less favorable.

Constructing the steps that make up an overtized operation does not complete the designer's task, however. The range and structure of the examples to which the operation applies must also be considered. In an overtized operation for decoding words, the learner blends the most common sound for each letter to form a word. The range of applications becomes relevant through an analysis of minimally different words such as *dime* and *dim*. The sound for the letter *i* differs for the two words, which limits the application of the sounding-out operation. The operation does not work with *dime*, but the designer can increase the range or utility of the operation by prompting the difference between the *i*'s in the words *dime* and *dim* by placing a diacritical mark above the *i* in *dime:*

dīme. The diacritical mark prompts the learner that the value for *i* is different in *dime* than in *dim*.

The structure of examples is also important when it is an integral part of the cognitive operation (e.g., learning to construct the angle of reflection when the angle of incidence is given). The operation revolves around the rule *the angle of reflection equals the angle of incidence.* The structure of the example is critical because it is essential for overtizing the operation. An adequate structure for examples might consist of a wall with a mirror, a perpendicular line drawn on the floor from the mirror, and a calibration system for measuring the angle of incidence and thereby the angle of reflection (see Fig. 6.5). Several examples would be created using this structure. For each one, the teacher would place an object or light on a numbered position. The learner would determine the position relative to the center line and then identify the same position on the other side of the center line. By standing in that position the learner would see the object or light reflected in the mirror.

A specification of the cognitive operation and the range and structure of the examples as in the angle of incidence illustration above is the starting point from which the designer constructs a series of lessons for teaching the operation. These lessons for teaching a cognitive operation are sandwiched between two major instructional stages—teaching preskills and covertizing the operation. As indicated previously, covertization is the process of moving the learner from a highly structured, overtized operation to an unstructured, covertized context in which the learner carries out the steps without direction or assistance from the teacher. The operation is also covertized in the sense that the learner may carry out several of the steps without any observable responses.

Teaching Preskills.   Preskills consist of the basic discriminations, related discriminations, and rules that make up a cognitive operation. Preskills are taught through modules and clusters. A module is the simplest possible instructional unit—often involving a model and test or just a test. A cluster is a sequence of

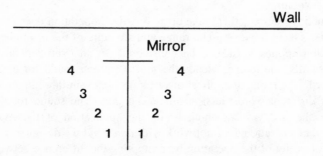

FIG. 6.5.   Example structure for angels of incidence and reflection.

modules. For example, a cognitive operation for simple subtraction includes this cluster: Teacher points to −2 and asks, "Read it." Student reads, "Minus 2." Teacher points to −2 and asks, "What do these symbols tell you to do?" Student responds, "Make two minuses." The teacher then instructs the student to make the minuses. This cluster is comprised of two modules in which the teacher says, "Read it," and "What do these symbols tell you to do?" The basic discriminations implied by the first module are identifying the symbols − and 2.

In preparing students to learn a cognitive operation, the designer first identifies the clusters that make up the operation and next identifies the modules that make up each cluster. The designer then constructs teaching procedures for the modules and clusters, selects examples for them, and finally sequences the modules and clusters along with their corresponding examples. This process of identifying, sequencing, and selecting examples for modules and clusters defines the preskill stage.

Various studies have investigated the role of preskill teaching. Gagné, Mayor, Garstens, and Paradise (1962) demonstrated that proficiency in skills from lower levels of a hierarchy predicted performance on more advanced skills. Gollin, Moody, and Schadler (1974) reported that preschoolers who were first taught to touch the smallest object made more correct responses when told to touch the *next* smallest object than preschoolers who were just taught to touch the next smallest object. Preskill teaching may also involve exposure to terminology that appears later in a difficult-to-understand passage (Royer & Cable, 1975). In a toilet training study by Mahoney, Van Wagenen, and Meyerson (1971), preskill teaching involved walking to the commode, lowering pants, and facing or sitting on the commode. In a study establishing the use of crutches by Horner (1971) preskill teaching was done through a five-step program for using parallel bars. The importance of teaching the clusters *before* introducing the entire operation was indicated in a study by Carnine (1980d). Primary-grade children who were pretaught the clusters that comprised a multiplication operation required less training time (a mean of 105 versus 137 minutes) and had higher transfer scores (an average of 81% versus 61% correct) than students who learned the clusters and the operation at the same time.

Although the Carnine study suggests the importance of teaching preskills before introducing the operation that incorporates them, the importance of a "logical sequence" for introducing skills has not been uniformly supported by other researchers. Neidermeyer, Brown, and Sulzen (1969) compared logical, scrambled, and reverse-order sequences; they reported no differences on posttest, but students in the logical sequence group made fewer errors during training and indicated that the program was more interesting. Danner (1976) found sentence recall and clustering of topics superior when passages were organized by topic. In contrast, a comprehensive study of sequencing methods (Kane, 1971) reported no posttest differences among seven different sequences for teaching fraction skills.

Covertizing Cognitive Operations.   The other major stage in teaching a cognitive operation is covertization, the process whereby the learner comes to solve applications with little teacher direction. Covertization begins after the learner consistently responds correctly when applying an overtized operation. Covertization can occur through any of three procedures: A *step is dropped* from the overtized operation, *several steps are replaced by a more inclusive instruction, or several steps are chained together so that the learner no longer responds after each step but rather produces a chain of responses following the chained steps.* For example, when the subtraction operation discussed earlier is covertized, the learner is no longer told to read the problem. Later the steps making the minuses, counting backward, and making the other side equal are replaced by a more inclusive instruction, "Work this problem." An example of covertization through *chaining* would be if the teacher said, "Read the problem, make the minuses, count backward for every minus, and write the answer. Raise your hand when you know the answer." In this chaining example the teacher provides more guidance than with an inclusive instruction. However, covertization is occurring because the student must remember the instructions and carry them out in the proper order.

Prompting and Fading.   Prompting and fading parallel the preskill and covertization stages. Prompts must be selected with care because they facilitate learning by intentionally introducing a misinterpretation. In the case of the diacritical mark in *dīme* mentioned earlier, the misinterpretation is that the long /i/ will always be signaled by the diacritical mark. This is not the case in conventionally printed material. For example, the word *hive* is not printed *hīve*. (Note that removing the diacritical mark necessitates modifying the decoding operation: a rule that a final *e* signals a long vowel sound.) Because of misinterpretations inherent in prompts, the designer should use them only when their advantages outweigh the difficulties that occur when they are removed. Second, the designer should leave in a prompt no longer necessary. Third, the designer must decide whether to drop a prompt abruptly or fade it in stages. Fading in stages is safe only when the prompted element remains in some form after fading (e.g., the errorless learning research). In correcting mistakes on faded applications, the preferable option is to *remind* the learner of the prompt rather than to reintroduce the prompt; however, if necessary, the prompt can be reintroduced.

Prompting often involves increasing feature saliency, thereby decreasing the number of trials required for subjects to reach criterion in discrimination tasks. Increased saliency results from greater physical differences between relevant and other features (Archer, 1962; Imai & Garner, 1965; Kamin, 1968; Trabasso & Bower, 1968) or from emphasizing a relevant feature by adding a marker or semiredundant cue (Gibson, 1969; Lumsdain, Sulzer, & Kopstein, 1969; Silver & Rollins, 1973; Trabasso & Bower, 1968; Trabasso, 1963). If an added marker is redundant with the relevant feature (present in only positive instances), learning will occur more rapidly but transfer is minimal (Anderson & Faust, 1967; Restle, 1959; Warren, 1953). If the added marker does not provide for competing solutions during training (the marker is present in both positive and negative instances), fewer trials are required to reach criterion and there is transfer to "harder" problems (Trabasso, 1963).

Although many applications of prompting and fading has been carried out using an errorless learning procedure (Sidman & Stoddard, 1967; Terrace, 1966; Touchette, 1969), several concerns and cautions remain. The problem of transfer of control during fading has been discussed by Touchette (1971, pp. 353–354).

> This approach (fading) allows, and may encourage, the subject to continue under the control of the gradually disappearing stimuli. Terrace (1966) noted that during repeated failures of a procedure to transfer stimulus control from brightness to line orientation, errors typically occurred only in the final few steps of fading. This observation, which has frequently been made but rarely reported, suggests that subjects continued under the control of the dimension that was being removed, rather than coming under the control of the desired dimension.

Other considerations involving prompts are: prompts with simple tasks may not facilitate acquisition for older subjects (Landau & Hagen, 1974); prompts are more effective when they directly relate to the relevant characteristic (Drotar, 1974; Lyczak, 1976; Trabasso, 1963); visual prompts may be more appropriate for young children than verbal groups (Silver & Rollins, 1973); visual prompts with structurally complex stimuli may retard acquisition and transfer (Carnine, 1976e).

IMPLICATIONS

Some Major Questions

The Follow Through comparisons carry a number of implications for education of the disadvantaged. The data permit tentative answers to a number of major issues in the field today.

Will Money Do the Job? Follow Through budgeted $700 to $800 per child for a comprehensive services program including parent involvement, health, nutrition, social and psychological services, and educational programs. Several sponsors have estimated that the educational program alone could be carried out for about $350 above basic school costs. A common outcry among educators on seeing the results for Direct Instruction and hearing of the costs is, "With $700 extra per child, we could get the job done with any program." The Abt IV Report provides a rather convincing demonstration that good will, people, material, Hawthorne motivation, health programs, dental programs, and hot lunch programs *do not cause* gains in achievement. All Follow Through sponsors had these program components, but most failed to do the job in basic instruction. Note also that Title I, which spends close to $300 per child for educational programs, has consistently failed to improve the academic performance of disadvantaged children since it was started in 1965 (McLaughlin, 1975).

Does Individualization Require Many Approaches?   The programs that tried hardest to teach different students in different ways (Arizona, EDC, Cognitive Curriculum, Responsive Education) failed. The popular belief that it is necessary to teach different students in different ways is clearly a fiction. The sequence of a teaching program is defined *by what is to be taught,* not whom. In the Direct Instruction Model, all children face the same sequences of skill development with the same teaching strategies. What is individualized is entry level, *when* corrections are used, reinforcement procedures, and number of practice trials to mastery (Bijou, 1977, p. 9).

Is Self-Directed Learning Best?   A principle underlying many of the Follow Through models is that meaningful learning can only occur through self-directed experiences. A common argument is this: "Teachers might teach some rote facts (soon to be forgotten), but higher cognitive learning must be self-directed." Beliefs of this sort are common to programs attributing their foundations to Piagetian theory as well as to a variety of child-centered approaches. It is our suspicion that these beliefs arise from observing children's interactions with the *physical environment,* as in Piaget's observations of his own children. The physical environment will teach by providing consequences. If the hand gets food to the mouth, a basis for reinforcement is present. If the foot misses the step, punishment is likely. Generalizing these observations of self-directed learning to verbal learning, however, is quite inappropriate. There is no way a child can learn the *arbitrary conventions* of a language system unless some person in that system provides directed and systematic teaching. Furthermore, there can be *no question* that concepts and problem-solving skills can be more effectively taught when sequences of critical examples are carefully programmed by a smart adult than through a child-directed process. False conceptions of learning processes are so prevalent among educators today that one has to believe that if schools are effective at all, it must be in spite of educators.

How Does One Teach Cognitive Skills?   It is apparent that those programs that focused on cognitive-process objectives dismally failed to achieve those objectives as measured by tests of reading comprehension, math problem solving, and math concepts. The only program clearly effective in this area, as measured by both ISOs and grade-norm data, was Direct Instruction. There is a clear implication that through careful analysis of what is to be taught and a careful application of programming and teaching technology, basic intellectual processes can be taught. The cognitively oriented programs had *objectives* only.

They lacked the analytic and programming skills necessary to build behavior toward those objectives.

Does Curriculum Make a Difference?   The Kansas Behavior Analysis Model and the Oregon Direct Instruction Model shared a foundation in behavioral principles. In fact, we trained our first group of teachers together at Lawrence in the summer of 1968. The models differed in choice of curricula. Engelmann designed new curricula for the Direct Instruction Model (DISTAR), whereas Bushell adopted available curricula (McGraw-Hill Sullivan Reading, Singer Math, SRA Reading Labs) except for a phonics preprogram modeled after the DISTAR phonic program and a writing program devised by the Kansas group. The mode of instruction also differed. The data presented earlier show that on ISO comparisons the Direct Instruction Model did better on all comparisons but especially on cognitive skills. On grade-norm data, the Kansas program was comparable to Direct Instruction on Spelling, was close on Total Reading, but fell behind on Math and Language. These differences suggest a superiority of the DISTAR programming strategies but may also be due to the additional verbal practice provided by the small-group method.

Future Research on Teaching

Our experiences in Follow Through and the current research on academic engaged time lead to these suggestions for future research on teaching processes: (1) There is a need to assess program implementation in field studies. (2) A *classroom-level measure* of academic engaged time offers promise as a dependent variable in research on the design of classroom procedures.

Assessment of Implementation.   The comparison of program effects in Follow Through is very likely confounded by differences in program implementation. This design oversight should not come as a surprise. We did not even have a notion of how to measure implementation of programs with different methods and goals 10 years ago. Now we see the possibility of using samples of classroom observations to assess student engaged time by content area and to assess teacher and aide performance in key activities. Teacher reports could be used to assess content covered by student (or group). Program-referenced tests could be used periodically to assess student error rates. Adequacy of training could be assessed by observers and by tests of teacher performance. Finally, administrative supports could be evaluated through the use of critical incidents, interviews, and analysis of monitoring and feedback systems. The cost of such assessments would be high but offer great promise in refining data interpretation. A preliminary step would be to determine the size of the sample of observations required to draw valid conclusions.

One might argue that a more appropriate method might be to compare alternative programs under more carefully controlled laboratory-type conditions. This approach might answer the question of which programs will do the job if well-controlled conditions could be found for long-term studies. However, it would not lead to specifications for installing and maintaining a program under field conditions. Field studies would still be needed to test and demonstrate such conditions. The systematic assessment of implementation processes is an important key to getting more information out of field research.

Classroom-Level Engaged Time as a Dependent Variable.   The logical and empirical linkages between engaged time and achievement gains suggest a new strategy for behavioral studies of principles for the design of classroom procedures. Rather than focusing on individual effects, engineering questions would center on conditions that increase the *mean* student engaged time and reduced low engagement. Classroom-level observation measures would be based on time samples of individual students following procedures like those developed by Marliave, et al. (1977) for use with an optical scan record form. Experiments might keep the instructional program constant but manipulate amount and type of teacher direction, group size, student response requirements, amount and type of feedback, behavior management methods, student choice of activities, student goal-setting, etc. One might also test the effects of various strategies on low-performing versus high-performing students. Studies to determine engaged-time requirements to achieve specified goals with various students could be undertaken. The end result would be an empirical basis for *classroom* planning, structure, and management that currently does not exist.

Redesign of Curricula

In the area of curricula redesign we see two major needs: (1) a need for programs that will permit the systematic teaching of vocabulary within schools; and (2) a need to apply behavioral technology for teaching cognitive process in more content area.

The Missing Building Block—Vocabulary.   In a recent *Harvard Educational Review,* Becker (1977) analyzed the Follow Through data for the Direct Instruction Model and related data and drew the conclusion that schools are currently designed for middle-class students whose parents are capable of teaching them the language. Schools fail systematically to teach a most important building block for intelligent behavior—namely, words and their referents. Some of the arguments for this conclusion and possible steps to be taken to redesign curricula are briefly summarized.

The relatively poorer performance on reading comprehension at the end of third grade, when the test moves to the "full adult vocabulary" reflected in fourth-grade textbooks, is interpreted to be largely a function of vocabulary deficiencies. Vocabulary instruction to an average-adult competency is a major task that involves at least 7800 basic words with twice as many meanings, another 16,000 related words, and about 1000 proper nouns. Basic words do not represent a teaching objective that can be accomplished by teaching some members of the set and getting ''generalization'' to the rest. It is what Becker has called a ''linear additive set'' (Becker et al., 1975) in which each member must be taught. Related words, on the other hand, can sometimes be taught as general cases by affixing basic words. We are currently attempting to identify and define a basic vocabulary which will make it easier to teach and which will make possible the development of various programs to teach language systematically where the home does not provide adequate instruction (Dixon & Becker, 1977). Our analysis has two major components. On the form side, we are attempting to identify a minimum set of morphographs contained in a basic and related vocabulary. Morphographs can be thought of roughly as roots and affixes. On the semantic side, we are attempting to identify a set of initial concepts (A) to be taught by demonstrations, which can then be used to define a larger set of words (B). Then A and B would be used to define a larger set, and so forth. The goal will be prescriptions for vocabulary growth by grade level based on an analysis of the language and instructional requirements, not just frequency in print. One can, for example, imagine a dictionary where higher-level words are always defined in terms of lower-level words. The system might also be used to control vocabulary usage in textbooks through computer analysis. Finally, the system could be used to develop systematic programs for the initial teaching of vocabulary and practice in its use.

Behaviorally Based Cognitive Programs. It is becoming more and more fashionable for psychologists to talk about a reconciliation of behavioral and cognitive psychology. To some degree this has already occurred in the clinical field. In *Teaching 2* (Becker et al., 1975) we have described the parallels in the conceptions of concepts and operations as viewed by Piaget and Engelmann. We foresee an integration of behavioral and cognitive views which retains the behaviorist's insistence on use of an objective language and which details the procedures for generating structures that will function as cognitive structures are said to function by the cognitive theorists. This integration will be hastened by the development of more extensive educational programs that systematically build ''cognitive structures'' through behavioral technology. The programming technology growing out of Engelmann's work is to task analysis as the moon rocket is to the Model T. A rapid acceleration in the development of effective curricula ought to occur in the coming decade.

Instituting Educational Change

We conclude with a brief discussion of some practical considerations in engineering changes in schools. The teacher–student interaction system (which is essential to getting better learning to occur) operates within a larger system (the classroom) which operates within a larger system (the school) which operates within a larger system (the district), and so forth. Power streams within these enlarging systems critically influence whether innovative changes will occur and be maintained.

According to the Rand Report (Berman & McLaughlin, 1975, p. 24), educational change agents in government make three fundamental assumptions:

1. The adoption by the schools of better technologies or treatments would lead to more effective educational practices.
2. The schools are motivated to search for better technologies. If they had reliable information that would make them aware of better practices, they would be willing to adopt them.
3. The schools lack money to experiment with innovations. By providing "seed money," federal funds would allow school districts to try out new practices and to continue them if they prove to be successful.

Berman and McLaughlin assert that each of these assumptions is myth. When new practices are adopted, they are usually so modified as to make them unrecognizable. When information on effective practices is available, it is not sought or acted upon. When federal funds are provided to encourage innovation, the funds are more likely used to finance local priorities or temporary programs that are dropped when the funds cease.

These conclusions are sobering, especially because the federal government's primary approach to solving educational problems is to "throw money at them." Both the Rand Report and an SRI Report evaluating the National Diffusion Network (Emrick, 1977) suggest conditions necessary to bringing about educational changes that are consistent with our own experiences. These include: (1) a congruence of goals (needs) between innovator and district; (2) strong local leadership in a person other than the school principal (who is usually "too busy"); and (3) local administrative support at a high level.

In our experience, the development of a congruence of goals and local commitment requires an *information exchange stage* and a *negotiation stage*. In the information exchange stage, district needs are specified and related to potential program benefits. Requirement for program implementation are specified and potential problems identified. Representatives of all potential stakeholders should be involved—teachers, principals, superintendents, school board members, parents, and program sponsors. In the negotiation stage, obligations of the district personnel to the program sponsor and obligations of the sponsor to the district are specified in detail. Staffing requirements, job descriptions, training requirements, monitoring, and testing requirements are all specified. A major objective of the negotiation stage is this: When a problem arises that could destroy the model or make it ineffective, the forces of power within the district are ready to resolve the issue in terms of what is best for the kids (usually the same as effective model implementation) rather than in terms of staff comfort.

Another objective is to establish administrative procedures that will anticipate problems and make clear to the staff where the priorities lie.

The potentials for changing society for the better will only be realized when change agents have a more complete understanding of the operation of the systems to be changed and develop effective strategies for entering into those systems. In the case of schools, a technology for improving instruction is one step, a technology for training staff is another, a technology for monitoring progress a third; but all of these will be useless without a technology for the maintenance of innovation within the ongoing system.

ACKNOWLEDGMENTS

Parts of this chapter are summarized from one of the author's books in preparation (Engelmann & Becker, in preparation) *Forward from Basics—The Case for Direct Instruction*. All rights are reserved by the authors.

The University of Oregon Follow Through Project was supported by funds from the U.S. Office of Education, Department of School Systems, Division of Compensatory Education, Follow Through Branch, under Grants OEG-070-4257 (286) and GOO-7507234.

The authors are indebted to their many co-workers in this endeavor, office staff, data staff, project managers, project directions, supervisors, teachers, aides, parents, and children who made this work possible.

REFERENCES

Abramson, T., & Kagan, E. Familiarization of content and differential response modes in programmed instruction. *Journal of Educational Psychology*, 1975, *67*, 83–88.

Abt Associates. *Education as experimentation: A planned variation model* (Vol. III). Cambridge, Mass.: Abt Associates, 1976.

Abt Associates. *Education as experimentation: A planned variation model* (Vol. IV). Cambridge, Mass.: Abt Associates, 1977.

Anastasiow, N. J., Sibley, S. A., Leonhardt, T. M., & Borich, G. D. A comparison of guided discovery, discovery, and didactic teaching of math to kindergarten poverty children. *American Educational Research Journal*, 1971, *7*, 493–510.

Anderson, R. C., & Faust, G. W. The effects of strong formal prompts in programmed instruction. *American Educational Research Journal*, 1967, *4*, 345–352.

Anderson, R. C., & Kulhavy, R. W. Learning concepts from definitions. *American Educational Research Journal*, 1973, *9*, 385–390.

Archer, A. E. Concept identification as a function of obviousness of relevant and irrelevant information. *Journal of Experimental Psychology*, 1962, *63*, 616–620.

Becker, W. C. Teaching reading and language to the disadvantaged—What we have learned from field research. *Harvard Education Review*, 1977, *47*, 518–543.

Becker, W. C., & Englemann, S. *Analysis of achievement data on six cohorts of low income children from 20 school districts in the University of Oregon Direct Instruction Follow Through*

Model. Follow Through Project (Tech. Rep. #76-1). Unpublished manuscript, University of Oregon, 1976.

Becker, W. C., & Engelmann, S. *Analysis of achievement data on six cohorts of low income children from 20 school districts in the University of Oregon Direct Instruction Follow Through Model*. Follow Through Project (Tech. Rep. #78-1). Unpublished manuscript, University of Oregon, 1978. (a)

Becker, W. C., & Engelmann, S. Systems for basic instruction: Theory and applications. In T. Brigham and C. Catania (Eds), *Handbook of applied behavior research*. New York: Irvington Press/Halsted Press, 1978. (b)

Becker, W. C., & Engelmann, S. The direct instruction model. In R. Rhine (Ed.), *Encouraging change in America's schools: A decade of experimentation*. New York: Academic Press, in press.

Becker, W. C., Engelmann, S., & Thomas, D. R. *Teaching 2—Cognitive learning and instruction*. Chicago: SRA, 1975.

Bereiter, C., & Engelmann, S. *Teaching disadvantaged children in the preschool*. Englewood Cliffs, N.J.: Prentice-Hall, 1966.

Berman, P., & McLaughlin, M. W. *Federal programs supporting educational change (Vol. IV). The findings in review*. Santa Monica, Calif.: Rand Corporation, 1975.

Biberdorf, J. R., & Pear, J. J. Two-to-one *versus* one-to-one student–teacher ratios in the operant verbal training of retarded children. *Journal of Applied Behavioral Analysis*, 1977, *10*, 506.

Bijou, S. W. Practical implementations of an interactional model of child development. *Exceptional Children*, 1977, *44*, 6–14.

Bloom, B. S. *Human characteristics and school learning*. New York: McGraw-Hill, 1976.

Bourne, L. E., Jr., & Pendleton, R. B. Concept identification as a function of completeness and probability of information feedback. *Journal of Experimental Psychology*, 1958, *56*, 413–420.

Brophy, J. E., & Evertson, C. M. *Process-product correlations in the Texas teacher effectiveness study: Final report*. Austin: The University of Texas, 1974.

Camp, B. W., & Dahlem, N. Paired-associate and serial learning in retarded readers. *Journal of Educational Psychology*, 1975, *67*, 385–90.

Campbell, D. T., & Erlebacher, A. How regression artifacts in quasi-experimental evaluations in compensatory education tend to underestimate effects. In J. Hellmuth (Ed.), *Disadvantaged child. Compensatory education: A national debate (Vol. 3)*. New York: Brunner/Mazel, 1970.

Carlson, J. G., & Minke, K. A. Fixed and ascending criteria for unit mastery learning. *Journal of Educational Psychology*, 1975, *67*, 96–101.

Carnine, D. Effects of two teacher presentation rates on off-task behavior, answering correctly, and participation. *Journal of Applied Behavioral Analysis*, 1976, *9*, 199–206. (a)

Carnine, D. *Conditions under which children learn the relevant attribute of negative instances rather than the essential characteristic of positive instances*. Unpublished manuscript, Follow Through Project, University of Oregon, 1976. (b)

Carnine, D. *Establishing a discriminative stimulus by distributing attributes of a compound stimuli between positive and negative instances*. Unpublished manuscript, Follow Through Project, University of Oregon, 1976. (c)

Carnine, D. Similar sound separation and cumulative introduction in learning letter-sound correspondences. *Journal of Educational Research*, 1976, *69*, 368–372. (d)

Carnine, D. *Emphasizer effects on children's and adults' acquisition rate and transfer scores on simple and complex tasks*. Unpublished manuscript, University of Oregon, Follow Through Project, 1976. (e)

Carnine, D. *Frequency of corrections in beginning instruction*. Unpublished manuscript, Follow Through Project, University of Oregon, 1977. (a)

Carnine, D. *Two procedures for sequencing instances in discrimination tasks*. Unpublished manuscript, Follow Through Project, University of Oregon, 1977. (b)

Carnine, D. A comparison of two beginning reading approaches with regard to training time, sounds learned, and transfer scores on regular and irregular words. *Reading Teacher*, 1977, *30*, 636–640. (c)

Carnine, D. *Four procedures for introducing similar discriminations.* Unpublished manuscript, Follow Through Project, University of Oregon, 1977. (d)

Carnine, D. *Two procedures for teaching relational concepts.* Unpublished manuscript. Follow Through Project, University of Oregon, 1977. (e)

Carnine, D. *A comparison of strategy and practice-only treatments in teaching three fraction skills.* Unpublished manuscript, Follow Through Project, University of Oregon, 1977. (f)

Carnine, D. *Application of cumulative introduction to teaching math facts.* Unpublished manuscript, Follow Through Project, University of Oregon, 1978.

Carnine, D. Relationship between teaching method and correction procedure for initial word recognition skills. *Education and Treatment of Children,* 1980. (a)

Carnine, D. Three procedures for presenting minimally different positive and negative instances. *Journal of Education and Psychology,* 1980, *72,* 452–456. (b)

Carnine, D. Two letter discrimination sequences: High confusion alternatives first versus low confusion alternatives first. *Journal of Reading Behavior,* 1980, *12,* 41–48. (c)

Carnine, D. Preteaching versus concurrent teaching of the component skills of a multiplication problem-solving strategy. *Journal for Research in Mathematics Education,* 1980, *11,* 375–378. (d)

Carnine, D. Degree of implementation of pacing, corrections, and praise and preschoolers on task and correct responding behavior. *Education and Treatment of Children,* in press. (a)

Carnine, D. Relationship between stimulus variation and the formation of misconceptions. *Journal of Educational Research,* in press. (b)

Carnine, D., & Fink, W. T. Increasing the rate of presentation and the use of signals in elementary classroom teachers. *Journal of Applied Behavioral Analysis,* 1978, *11,* 35–46.

Carnine, L., & Carnine D. Determining the relative decoding difficulty of three types of simple regular words. *Journal of Reading Behavior,* 1978, *X*(4), 40–41.

Carnine, D., Kameenui, E. J., & Ludlow, R. *Rule saying, concept application, and rule application training in relation to rule application transfer performance.* Unpublished manuscript, Follow Through Project, University of Oregon, 1978.

Carnine, D., Prill, N., & Armstrong, J. *Teaching slower performing students general case strategies for solving comprehension items.* Unpublished manuscript, University of Oregon, Follow Through Project, 1977 and 1978.

Carnine, D., & Stein, M. Organizational strategies and practice procedures for teaching basic facts. *Journal for Research in Mathematics Education,* in press.

Carroll, J. B. A model of school learning. *Teachers College Record,* 1963, *64,* 723–732.

Cheyne, W. M. Vanishing cues in paired-associate learning. *British Journal of Psychology,* 1966, *57,* 351–359.

Clark, C. M., Gage, N. L., Marx, R. W., Peterson, P. L., Stayrook, N. G., & Winnie, P. H. *A factorially designed experiment on teacher structuring, soliciting, and reacting. Final report.* Stanford, Calif.: Center for Research and Development in Teaching, 1976. (ERIC Document Reproduction Service No. ED 134 591.)

Coopersmith, S. *The antecedents of self-esteem.* San Francisco: W. H. Freeman, 1967.

Cossairt, A., Hall, V., & Hopkins, B. L. The effects of experimenter's instructions, feedback, and praise on teacher praise and student attending behavior. *Journal of Applied Behavior Analysis,* 1973, *6,* 89–100.

Cowart, J., Carnine, D. W., & Becker, W. C. *The effects of signals on attending, responding, and following in direct instruction.* Unpublished manuscript. Follow Through Project, University of Oregon, 1973.

Crandall, V. C., Katkowsky, W., & Crandall, V. J. Children's beliefs in their own control of reinforcements in intellectual-academic achievement situations. *Child Development,* 1965, *36,* 91–109.

Danner, F. W. Children's understanding of inter-sentence organization in the recall of short descriptive passages. *Journal of Educational Psychology,* 1976, *68,* 174–183.

Dixon, R., & Becker, W. C. *A proposal for the analysis of a basic vocabulary to facilitate instruction in the language arts.* Unpublished manuscript, University of Oregon, 1977.

Drotar, E. Discrimination learning in normal and retarded children as a function of instruction, cue locus and cue relevance. *Child Development, 1974, 45,* 1146–1150.

Durling, R., & Schick, C. Concept attainment by pairs and individuals as a function of vocalization. *Journal of Educational Psychology, 1976, 68,* 83–91.

Egbert, R. *Planned variation in Follow Through.* Paper presented to The Brookings Institution Panel on Social Experimentation, Washington, D.C., April 1973.

Egan, D. E., & Greeno, J. G. Acquiring cognitive structure by discovery and rule learning. *Journal of Educational Psychology, 1973, 64,* 85–97.

Emrick, J. A. *Evaluation of the national diffusion network.* Menlo Park, Calif.: Stanford Research Institute, 1977.

Engelmann, S. The effectiveness of direct instruction on IQ performance and achievement in reading and arithmetic. In J. Hellmuth (Ed.), *Disadvantaged child* (Vol. 3). New York: Brunner/Mazel, 1968.

Engelmann, S., & Becker, W. C. *Forward from basics—the case for direct instruction.* In preparation.

Engelmann, S., & Carnine, D. *Theory of instruction.* Book in preparation.

Feldman, K. V. *The effects of number of positive and negative instances, concept definition, and emphasis of relevant attributes on the attainment of mathematical concepts* (Tech. Rep. No. 243, 1972). Wisconsin Research and Development Center for Cognitive Learning, Madison, Wisconsin.

Feldman, S. M., & Underwood, B. J. Stimulus recall following paired-associate verbal learning. *Journal of Experimental Psychology, 1957, 53,* 11–15.

Ferster, C. B., & Hammer, C. E., Jr. Synthesizing the components of arithmetic behavior. In W. K. Honig (Ed.), *Operant behavior: Areas of research and application.* New York: Appleton-Century-Crofts, 1966.

Fink, W. T. *Effects of a pre-correction procedure on the decoding errors of two low-performing first grade girls.* Unpublished manuscript, Follow Through Project, University of Oregon, 1976.

Fink, W. T., & Brice, K. J. *Effects of two programming strategies on the acquisition and recall of an academic task by moderately and severely retarded preschool children. Mental Retardation, 1979, 17,* 8–12.

Fink, W. T., & Carnine, D. W. Control of arithmetic errors using informational feedback and graphing. *Journal of Applied Behavioral Analysis, 1975, 8,* 461.

Fink, W. T., & Carnine, D. W. *Comparisons of group and individual instruction and individual and unison responding.* Unpublished manuscript, Follow Through Project, University of Oregon, 1977.

Fink, W. T., & Sandall, S. R. One to one versus group academic instruction with handicapped and nonhandicapped preschool children. *Mental Retardation, 1979, 16,* 236–240.

Francis, E. W. Grade level and task difficulty in learning by discovery and verbal reception methods. *Journal of Educational Psychology, 1975, 67,* 146–150.

Frase, L. T., & Schwartz, B. J. Effect of question production and answering on prose recall. *Journal of Educational Psychology, 1975, 67,* 628–635.

Frederick, W. C., & Klausmeier, H. J. Instructions and labels in a concept attainment task. *Psychological Reports, 1968, 23,* 1339–1342.

Gagné, R., & Brown, T. Some factors in the programming of conceptual learning. *Journal of Experimental Psychology, 1961, 62,* 55–63.

Gagné, R. M., Mayor, J. R., Garstens, H. L., & Paradise, N. E. Factors in acquiring knowledge of a mathematical task. *Psychological Monographs: General and Applied, 1962, 76(7).*

Gall, M. D., Ward, B. A., Berliner, D. C., Cahen, L. S., Crown, K. A., Elashoff, J. D., Stanton, G. C., & Winne, P. H. *The effects of teacher use of questioning techniques on student achieve-*

ment and attitude. San Francisco: Far West Laboratory for Educational Research and Development, 1975.

Gibson, E. J. *Principals of perceptual learning and development*. New York: Appleton-Century Crofts, 1969.

Gollin, E., Moody, M., & Schadler, M. Relational learning of a size concept. *Developmental Psychology*, 1974, *10*, 101–107.

Good, T. L., & Beckerman, T. M. Time on task: A naturalistic study in sixth grade classrooms. *Elementary School Journal*, 1978, *78*, 192–201.

Good, T. L., & Grouws, D. A. *Process-product relationships in 4th grade mathematics classes*. Columbia: College of Education, University of Missouri, 1975.

Good, T. L., Grouws, D. A., & Beckerman, T. M. Curriculum pacing: Some empirical data in mathematics. *Journal of Curriculum Studies*, in press.

Gordon, I. *Early child stimulation through parent education: A final report to the Children's Bureau*. Gainesville: University of Florida Press, 1969.

Granzin, A. C., & Carnine, D. W. Child performance on discrimination tasks: Effects of amount of stimulus variation. *Journal of Experimental Child Psychology*, 1977, *24*, 332–342.

Gruenenfelder, T. M., & Borokowski, J. G. Transfer of cumulative-rehearsal strategies in children's short-term memory. *Child Development*, 1975, *46*, 1019–1024.

Hall, R. V., Lund, D., & Jackson, D. Effects of teacher attention on study behavior. *Journal of Applied Behavior Analysis*, 1968, *1*, 1–12.

Higa, M. Interference effects of intralist word relatedness in verbal learning. *Journal of Verbal Learning and Verbal Behavior*, 1963, *2*, 170–175.

Horner, R. Establishing use of crutches by a mentally retarded child, *Journal of Applied Behavior Analysis*, 1971, *4*, 183–189.

Horton, G. O. Generalization of teacher behavior as a function of subject matter specific discrimination training. *Journal of Applied Behavior Analysis*, 1975, *8*, 311–319.

House, E. R., Glass, G. V., McLean, L. D., & Walker, D. E. *No somple answer: Critique of the "Follow Through" evaluation: Mimeo report*. University of Illinois, 1977.

Houser, L. L., & Trublood, C. R. Transfer of learning on similar metric conversion tasks. *Journal of Educational Research*, 1975, *68*, 235–237.

Hughes, M. *In the Tucson Early Education Model (Revised Ed.)*. Follow Through Project, College of Education, University of Arizona, November, 1971.

Imai, S., & Garner, W. R., Discriminability and preference for attributes in free and constrained classification. *Journal of Experimental Psychology*, 1965, *69*, 596–608.

Jeffrey, W. E., & Samuels, S. J. Effect of method of reading training on initial learning and transfer. *Journal of Verbal Learning and Verbal Behavior*, 1967, *6*, 354–358.

Jenkins, J. R., Mayhall, W. F., Peschka, C. M., & Jenkins, L. M. Comparing small group and tutorial instruction in resource rooms. *Exceptional Children*, 1974, *40*(4), 245–250.

Kameenui, E. J., Carnine, D., & Maggs, A. Instructional procedures for teaching reversible passive voice and clause constructions to three mildly handicapped children. *The Exceptional Child*, 1980, *27*, 29–40.

Kamin, L. J. "Attention-like" processes in classical conditioning. In M. R. Jones (Ed.), *Miami Symposium on the Prediction of Behavior: Aversive Stimulation*. Miami: University of Miami Press, 1968.

Kane, R. *Analyzing learning hierarchies relative to transfer relationships within arithmetic. Final report*. Grant OEG-5-70-0020 (509), Purdue University, 1971, ERIC ED 053 965.

Klausmeier, H. J., & Feldman, K. J. Effects of a definition and varying numbers of examples and nonexamples on concept attainment. *Journal of Educational Psychology*, 1975, *67*, 174–178.

Klausmeier, H. J., & Meinke, D. L. Concept attainment as a function of instruction concerning stimulus material, a strategy, and a principle for securing information. *Journal of Educational Psychology*, 1968, *59*, 215–222.

Kryzanowski, J. A. *Praise effects on inappropriate behavior during small group instruction*. Unpublished manuscript, Follow Through Project, University of Oregon, 1976.

Landau, B. L., & Hagen, J. L. The effect of verbal cues on concept acquisition and retention in normal and educable mentally retarded children. *Child Development,* 1974, *45,* 643–650.

Lessinger, L. L. *Quality control. The missing link in educational management* (Mimeo). Washington, D.C., Council of Chief State School Officers, 1976.

Lumsdain, A. A., Sulzer, R. L., & Kopstein, F. F. The effect of animation cues and repetition of examples on learning from an instruction film. In R. C. Anderson (Ed.), *Current research on instruction*. Englewood Cliffs, N.J.: Prentice-Hall, 1969.

Lyczak, R. A. Learning to read: The redundant cues approach. *The Journal of Educational Psychology,* 1976, *68,* 157–166.

Maccoby, E. E., & Zellner, M. *Experiments in primary education*. New York: Harcourt Brace Jovanovich, Inc., 1970.

Mackintosh, N. J. Stimulus control: Attentional factors. In W. K. Honig and J. E. R. Staddon (Eds.), *Handbook of operant behavior,* Englewood Cliffs, N.J.: Prentice-Hall, 1977.

Madsen, C., Becker, W. C., & Thomas, D. R. Rules, praise and ignoring: Elements of elementary classroom control. *Journal of Applied Behavior Analysis,* 1968, *1,* 139–150.

Mahoney, K., Van Wagenen, R., & Meyerson, L. Toilet training of normal and retarded children. *Journal of Applied Behavior Analysis,* 1971, *4,* 173–181.

Markle, S. M., & Tiemann, P. W. Some principles of instructional design at higher cognitive levels. In R. Ulrich, T. Stachnik, & J. Mabry (Eds.), *Control of human behavior* (Vol. 3). Glenview Ill: Scott, Forsman, 1974.

Marliave, R., Fisher, C., Filby, N., & Dishaw, M. *The development of instrumentation for a field study of teaching* (Tech. Rep. I-5). San Francisco: Far West Laboratory, 1977.

Massad, V. I., & Etzel, B. C. Acquisition of phonetic sounds by preschool children. In G. Semb (Ed.), *Behavior analysis and education*. Lawrence: The University of Kansas, 1972.

McDonald, F. J. *Research on teaching and its implications for policy making: Report on phase II of the beginning teacher evaluation study*. Paper presented at the Conference on Research on Teacher Effects: An examination by policy-makers and researchers, sponsored by the National Institute of Education, at the School of Education, University of Texas, Austin, November 1975.

McLaughlin, M. W. *Evaluation and reform*. Cambridge, Mass.: Ballinger, 1975.

Merrill, M. D., & Tennyson, R. D. *Attribute prompting variables in learning classroom concepts* (Working Paper No. 28). Division of Communication Services, Brigham Young University, 1971. Provo, Utah.

Metropolitan Achievement Tests. New York: Harcourt Brace Jovanovich, 1970.

Miles, C. G., Mackintosh, N. J., & Westbrook, R. G. Redistributing control between the elements of a compound stimulus. *Quarterly Journal of Experimental Psychology,* 1970, *22,* 478–483.

Nero and Associates. *The follow through resource guide*. Portland, Ore.: Nero and Associates, 1976.

Niedermeyer, F., Brown, J., & Sulzen, B. Learning and varying sequences of ninth-grade mathematical material. *Journal of Experimental Education,* 1969, *37,* 61–66.

Nimnicht, Glenn P. Overview of the Responsive Program for Early Childhood Education. Far West Laboratory of Educational Research and Development, 1972.

Oregon Follow Through Project. *Direct Instruction Model Implementation Manual*. 1. *Guidebook for Teachers*. 2. *Guidebook for Supervisors*. 3. *Guidebook for Administrators*. 4. *Guidebook for Directors, Parent Workers, and PACs*. Follow Through Project, University of Oregon, 1977.

Raven, J. C. *Coloured progressive matrices*. Sets A, A_B, and B. Dumfries, England: The Crichton Royal, 1956.

Restle, F. Additivity of cues and transfer in discrimination of consonant clusters. *Journal of Experimental Psychology,* 1959, *57,* 9–14.

Reynolds, G. S. Attention in the pigeon. *Journal of Experimental Analysis of Behavior,* 1961, *4,* 203–208.

Rosenshine, B. Classroom instruction. In N. L. Gage (Ed.), *The psychology of teaching methods*. Seventy-fifth yearbook of the National Society for the Study of Education. Chicago: University of Chicago Press, 1976.

Rosenshine, B. V. *Academic engaged time, content covered, and direct instruction*. Paper presented to the American Educational Research Association, New York, 1977.

Rosenshine, B. V., & Berliner, D. C. Academic engaged time. *British Journal of Teacher Education*, 1978, *4*, 3–16.

Rosenthal, T. L., & Carroll, W. R. Factors in vicarious modification of complex grammatical parameters. *Journal of Educational Psychology*, 1972, *63*, 174–178.

Rosenthal, T. L., & Zimmerman, B. J. Instructional specificity and outcome expectation in observationally-induced question formation. *Journal of Educational Psychology*, 1972, *63*, 500–504.

Royer, J. M., & Cable, G. W. Facilitated learning in connected discourse. *Journal of Educational Psychology*, 1975, *67*, 116–123.

Rule, S. A comparison of three different types of feedback on teacher's performance. In G. Semb (Ed.), *Behavior analysis and education*. Lawrence: The University of Kansas, 1972.

Saudargas, R. A. Setting criterion rates of teacher praise: The effects of video tape feedback in a behavior analysis Follow-Through classroom. In G. Semb (Ed.), *Behavior analysis and education*. Lawrence: The University of Kansas, 1972.

Shore, E., & Sechrest, L. Concept attainment as a function of the number of positive instances presented. *Journal of Educational Psychology*, 1961, *59*, 303–307.

Sidman, M., & Stoddard, L. T. The effectiveness of fading in programming a simultaneous form discrimination for retarded children. *Journal of Experimental Analysis of Behavior*, 1967, *10*, 3–15.

Siegel, M. A. Teacher behavior and curriculum packages: Implications for research and teacher education. In L. J. Rubin (Ed.), *Handbook of curriculum*. New York: Allyn & Bacon, 1977.

Siegel, M. A., & Rosenshine, B. *Teacher behavior in the Bereiter–Engelmann Follow Through Program*. Paper presented at the annual meeting of the American Educational Research Association. New Orleans: February 1973.

Siegler, R. S., & Liebert, R. M. Effects of presenting relevant rules and complete feedback on the conservation of liquid quantity task. *Developmental Psychology*. 1973, *7*, 133–138.

Silver, J. R., & Rollins, H. A. The effects of visual and verbal feature emphasis on firm discrimination in preschool children. *Journal of Exceptional Child Psychology*, 1973, *16*, 205–216.

Soar, R. S. *Follow-through classroom process measurement and pupil growth (1970–71): Final report*. Gainesville: College of Education, University of Florida, 1973.

Stallings, J. A. Implementation and child effects of teaching practices in follow through classrooms. *Monographs of the Society for Research in Child Development*, 1975, *40*(7–8, Serial No. 163).

Stallings, J. A., & Kaskowitz, D. *Follow-through classroom observation evaluation, 1972–73*. Menlo Park, Calif.: Stanford Research Institute, 1974.

Stolurow, K. A. C. Objective rules of sequencing applied to instructional material. *Journal of Educational Psychology*, 1975, *67*, 909–912.

Stromer, R. Modifying letter and number reversals in elementary school children. *Journal of Applied Behavioral Analysis*, 1975, *8*, 211.

Suchman, R. G., & Trabasso, T. Stimulus preference and cue functions in young children's concept attainment. *Journal of Experimental Child Psychology*, 1966, *63*, 188–197.

Suppes, P., & Ginsberg, R. Application of a stimulus sampling model to children's concept formation with and without an overt correction response. *Journal of Experimental Psychology*, 1962, *63*, 330–336.

Tennyson, R. D. Effect on negative instances in concept acquisition using a verbal learning task. *Journal of Educational Psychology*, 1973, *64*, 247–260.

Tennyson, R. D., Steve, M. W., & Boutwell, R. C. Instance sequence and analysis of instance attribute representation in concept attainment. *Journal of Educational Psychology*, 1975, *67*, 821–827.

Tennyson, R. D., & Tennyson, C. L. Rule acquisition design strategy variables: Degree of instance. *Journal of Educational Psychology*, 1975, *67*, 852–859.

Terrace, H. S. Stimulus control. In W. K. Honig (Ed.), *Operant behavior: Areas of research and application*. New York: Appleton-Century-Crofts, 1966.

Thomas, D. R. Preliminary findings on self-monitoring for modifying teaching behaviors. In E. A. Ramp & B. L. Hopkins (Eds.), *A new direction for education: Behavior analysis 1971*. Lawrence: The University of Kansas, 1971.

Thomas, D. R., Becker, W. C., & Armstrong, M. Production and elimination of disruptive classroom behavior by systematically varying teacher's behavior. *Journal of Applied Behavior Analysis*, 1968, *1*, 35–45.

Tikunoff, W., Berliner, D. C., & Rist, R. C. *An ethnographic study of the forty classrooms of the beginning teacher evaluation study known sampel* (Tech. Rep. No. 75-10-5). San Francisco: Far West Laboratory for Educational Research and Development, October 1975.

Tobias, S., & Ingber, T. Achievement-treatment interactions in programmed instructions. *Journal of Educational Psychology*, 1976, *68*, 43–47.

Touchette, P. Tilted lines as complex stimuli. *Journal of the Experimental Analysis of Behavior*, 1969, *12*, 211–214.

Touchette, P. E. Transfer of stimulus control measuring the moment of transfer. *Journal of the Experimental Analysis of Behavior*, 1971, *15*, 347–354.

Trabasso, T. Stimulus emphasis and all or none learning of concept identification. *Journal of Experimental Psychology*, 1963, *65*, 398–406.

Trabasso, T., & Bower, G. H. *Attention in learning: Theory and research*. New York: John Wiley & Sons, 1968.

Underwood, B. J., Runquist, W. N., & Schlutz, R. W. Response learning in paired-associate lists as a function of intralist similarity. *Journal of Experimental Psychology*, 1959, *58*, 70–78.

United States Office of Education. *Annual evaluation report on programs administered by the U.S. Office of Education, FY 1975*. Washington, D.C.: Capital Publications, Educational Resources Division, 1976.

Venezky, R., & Shiloah, Y. *The learning of picture-sound associations by Israeli kindergarteners* (Tech. Rep. No. 227). Madison, Wis.: Research and Development Center for Cognitive Learning, June 1972.

Warner, S. A. *Teacher*. New York: Simon & Schuster 1963.

Warren, J. M. Additivity of cues in a visual pattern discrimination by monkeys. *Journal of Comparative & Physiological Psychology*, 1953, *46*, 484–486.

Williams, P., & Carnine, D. Relationship between range of examples and of instinctions and attention in concept attainment. *Journal of Educational Research*, in press.

Wittrock, M. C. Verbal stimuli in concept formation: Learning by discovery. *Journal of Experimental Psychology*, 1963, *54*, 183–190.

Wolf, M. M., Giles, D. K., & Hall, R. V. Experiments with token reinforcement in a remedial classroom. *Behavior Research & Therapy*, 1968, *6*, 51–64.

Worthen, B. R. A study of discovery and expository presentation: Implications for teaching. *Journal of Teacher Education*, 1968, *19*, 223–242.

7

Behavioral Treatment of Juvenile Delinquency

Curtis J. Braukmann
Kathryn Kirigin Ramp
Montrose M. Wolf
University of Kansas

INTRODUCTION

This chapter attempts a broadly drawn overview and critique of behavioral approaches to delinquency treatment and prevention. Behavioral approaches of both institutional and community-based varieties are viewed against the descriptive backdrop of the nature, extent, and treatment of delinquency in the United States. Although each of the approaches to be discussed represents an application of procedures that are based on behavioral principles and research, the various approaches differ in comprehensiveness, sophistication, intrusiveness, and apparent effectiveness. In regard to this last dimension, summaries of pertinent programmatic and procedural research data are provided.

The second half of the chapter focuses on the approach with which the present authors are most familiar, the Achievement Place group–home model. Several procedural research studies concerning Achievement Place are described: some on skill training with delinquents and some on the education of group–home parents. This is followed by a discussion of the outcome results of the original Achievement Place group home and of several replication homes based on the Achievement Place, or Teaching-Family, model. In concluding, we indicate some of our current research directions and describe what we and others see as areas in need of further research and development.

AMERICAN DELINQUENCY AND TRADITIONAL RESPONSES

Throughout this chapter we are concerned with the treatment of adolescents who are adjudicated by the juvenile justice system in the United States. These are

211

persons under 18 who have engaged in unlawful behavior, usually against persons or property, and who have been apprehended and declared delinquent or unmanageable. This is a less than precisely defined group. Even with recent due-process legal protections, broad juvenile law statutes still permit police, court intake officers, and juvenile judges considerable discretion in defining and consequating detected "delinquent" activity. In addition, only a small portion of illegal adolescent activities are detected (Gold, 1970) and only a portion of these result in official court action. However, as might be expected, adolescents' self-report data indicate that probability of apprehension and official action increases with frequency of chargeable offenses (Elliott, Dunford, & Knowles, 1978; Gibbons, 1976).

Delinquent activity and involvement in the juvenile justice system in the United States is considerable. Although youngsters from ages 10 through 17 constitute only 16% of the population, they account for 45% of the arrests for serious offenses (Bayh, 1977). Approximately 1 million juveniles entered the juvenile justice system last year, and this number has been increasing since 1948 and at a rate faster than the youthful population growth (Conger, 1977). Although the probability of official contact is higher for boys than for girls, the gap is narrowing. Typical behaviors resulting in adjudication for boys include burglary, drug use, vandalism, truancy, and assault. For girls, typical behaviors are more likely to be status offenses that would not be crimes if engaged in by adults: for example unmanageability, running away from home, and illicit sexual behavior. However, the rate of female arrests for serious crime is increasing more rapidly than the rate for males (Conger, 1977).

Official delinquents are usually found to be doing poorly in school, both socially and academically, and to have "disturbed" home environments. They are more likely to be from lower socioeconomic families. Although this last relationship is supported by self-report data, such data suggests that delinquency is more evenly spread across socioeconomic strata than official data would suggest (Gold, 1970; Toby, 1974).

The social importance of developing effective means of preventing or treating delinquency has been emphasized by studies reporting a relationship between serious illegal and antisocial behavior among juveniles and subsequent adult criminality (Robins, 1966; Wolfgang, 1977). Further, Robins (1966) found that the antisocial adults she was studying were likely to have antisocial children. There would seem to be value in preventing or disrupting this sequence.

A traditional social response to delinquency in the United States, dating from 1825, has been institutionalization. However, increasingly in the past several decades, community-based alternatives have been emphasized (President's Commission, 1967). One of these alternatives has been family-style group homes that provide more family-like and cheaper services than institutional programs (Vinter, Downs, & Hall, 1975; Vinter, Newcomb, & Kish, 1976).

Most approaches to delinquency treatment have been marked by poor results and high rates of recidivism. Delinquency treatment has been notoriously unsuccessful with occasional short-term, but not often long-term, success (Bailey, 1961; Berleman & Steinburn, 1969; Dixson & Wright, 1975; Martinson, 1971; Robison & Smith, 1971). As summarized by University of Colorado psychologist, John Conger (1977): "Psychiatric treatment, work-study programs, family casework, the use of street-corner youth workers, foster-home placement, recreational programs, educational and vocational programs, youth service bureaus, or combinations of these or other approaches have not had widespread success [p. 586]." Clearly, delinquency treatment is one of the greatest challenges facing the social sciences.

INTERVENTIONS EMPLOYING
BEHAVIORAL PROCEDURES

The often disappointing results of delinquency treatment and prevention approaches have prompted an increasing interest during the past 15 or so years on implementation of procedures based on operant learning principles. Learning principles are derived from extensive and systematic laboratory research on the relationship between environmental events and behavior. Underlying the application in delinquency treatment of principles and procedures derived from operant learning studies is the social-learning view that behavior, including deviant behavior, is learned (Bandura, 1969). Behavior is viewed and defined as involving the interaction of the individual with a particular environment. Thus, the particular aspects of an individual's behavior are seen not only as a function of the individual and his or her tendencies but also as a function of the physical and social environment that may serve to shape, elicit, facilitate, and even provoke certain types of behaviors. This behavioral view is in harmony with the sociological view that delinquent development results from inadequate and inappropriate socialization and social control primarily in the family but also in the youth's neighborhood, peer group, and school (Gibbons, 1976; Toby, 1974).

In accordance with this view, behaviorally based treatment and prevention approaches have involved the rearrangement of social and environmental events and the introduction of instruction in a manner designed to affect the behavior of participating youths in specific ways presumed to help them become more successful members of their family, school, job, and community. Behavioral treatment approaches have typically involved at least three components: (1) the establishment of an incentive or contingency system in which reinforcing events occur contingent upon selected behaviors; (2) the use of methods designed to teach or elicit appropriate levels of target behaviors; and (3) the use of methods to increase the likelihood of maintenance of positive behavior changes after treatment. In this approach, then, the best intervention with an individual would likely precede from a careful diagnosis: a precise specification of the presenting behavior problems and of the social and nonsocial environmental conditions that maintain it (Milan & McKee, 1974).

Interventions designed to incorporate behavioral procedures have often been overlaid on traditional juvenile justice responses and thus have occurred in institutions, group homes, and probation situations. Other behavioral strategies, often with the mild or potential offender, have focused on family training. The beginnings of behavioral approaches with delinquents in the early 1960s were in case studies (Tyler, 1967; Wetzel, 1966) and in demonstration projects both at the institutional level (Burchard, 1967; Cohen, Filipczak, Bis, & Cohen, 1966) and in the natural community (Schwitzgebel, 1964).

OVERVIEW OF INSTITUTIONAL INTERVENTIONS: PROCEDURES AND RESULTS

At the institutional level, Cohen and Filipczak's (1971) well-known work in the CASE program at the National Training School for Boys represents one of the best and most systematic behavioral efforts. A key dimension of their approach was the use of a token economy in which seriously delinquent youths earned points for successful participation in a learning environment that focused on programmed, self-paced instructional material. Accumulated points could be used to purchase personal items, a private room, and access to a recreational lounge. Youths spent an average of 8 months in the program. Significant achievement test score increases were found during treatment. A long-term follow-up of released youths revealed that their rate of reinstitutionalization was initially considerably lower than might be expected on the basis of the national rate for youths in similar programs. By the third year, however, this difference had disappeared. The findings of this study present a theme to be reechoed in subsequent studies, including our work at Achievement Place: maintenance programs seem to be necessary to maintain behavior changes achieved during treatment.

Since the CASE project, token programs have been employed in numerous institutions (Braukmann & Fixsen, 1975). There has also been use of contingency contracting (Stuart, 1971) and of group social skill training sessions at the institutional level (Rose, Flanagan, & Brierton, 1971; Sarason, 1968).

Although the application of behavioral procedures has no doubt improved conditions in some institutional programs, there are problems inherent in many institutional settings that make optimal implementation of behavioral procedures difficult at best. These problems include situational pressures to emphasize control and institution-specific behavior and staff inconsistency in applying interventions. Staff inconsistency has been attributed to such factors as shift work, high staff/youth ratios, frequent staff turnover, and difficulty in attracting or training quality staff (Costello, 1972). Given these problems, the large-scale implementation of quality behavioral programs within institutions necessitates careful, ongoing monitoring and training. In the absence of tight quality-control procedures, such programs have a tendency to deteriorate rapidly (Bassett & Blanchard, 1977; Hobbs & Holt, 1976).

In contrast to these all-too-typical problems, the work of Phillips and Fixsen and their colleagues (Evans, Dowd, Schneider, Wallace, Fixsen, & Phillips, 1976) at Boys Town in Omaha, Nebraska, indicates that institutional programs given sufficient resources and expertise and a genuine concern for the individual can provide consistent, professional treatment. Here, pairs of "family-living teachers" (usually married couples) are involved in ongoing training to work with small groups of youths in relatively autonomous, family-style campus homes. The performance of these professional parents is monitored through systematic quality control procedures in which professional and personal rewards are contingent on multiple measures of performance.

Research in institutionally based programs has examined specific procedures as well as overall programs. Research on procedures has demonstrated the effectiveness of token economy fines and rewards in modifying some aggressive behavior (Burchard & Barrera, 1972), classroom and academic behaviors (Bednar, Zelhart, Greathouse, & Weinberg, 1970; Holt, Hobbs, & Hankins, 1976; Meichenbaum, Bowers, & Ross, 1969), and (what may be termed) *convenience* behaviors that allow for the smoother functioning of the institution. Research has also shown the effectiveness of other procedures in institutional contexts, including timeout (Tyler & Brown, 1967), self-recording of behavior along with youth-presented cues for staff praise (Seymour & Stokes, 1976), and positive teacher attention (Seymour & Sanson-Fischer, 1975; Young, Birnbrauer, & Sanson-Fischer, 1977).

The procedural research occurring in institutions has generally not looked at the issue of generalization (Davidson & Seidman, 1974; Emery & Marholin, 1977) and, if so, only for relatively short time periods. Indeed, the readiness with which behaviors have reversed to preprocedure level with contingency withdrawal strongly argues against assuming generalization (Burchard & Harig, 1976). Furthermore, there remain questions of whether or not behaviors selected for change really relate to, much less represent an analysis of, delinquency (Emery & Marholin, 1977; Ross & Price, 1976). Also of concern is the fact that the target behaviors were generally not individualized. Obviously, behaviors related to individual delinquency are likely to be different for different youths.

Of course, demonstration of behavior change *within* an institutional program is clearly of secondary importance. More important is demonstration of an impact on behavior following treatment. There are few examples of evaluation of follow-up effects. In one outcome study, youths were randomly assigned to one of two adjacent California institutions for boys. In one institution, behaviorally designed treatment was offered; in the other, treatment was based on transactional analysis. A 1-year follow-up indicated there were no differences in official reoffense data (a measure presumably somewhat reflective of actual youth behavior) between the programs (Jesness, DeRisi, McCormick, & Wedge, 1972).

In an outcome evaluation of a brief behavioral program conducted by Sarason (1976) and reported at the third of these international Symposia on Behavior Modification, 192 first offenders at a reception and diagnostic center were followed up. They had participated in one of three groups: a behavioral treatment group involving group modeling and practice of prosocial skills; a group that only discussed prosocial skills; and a no-treatment group. Immediate differences in staff ratings favored the modeling group. Although there were no differences in a 2-year follow-up between the modeling and discussion groups on official recidivism (subsequent institutionalization or adult parole), both groups did better than the controls. In another meausre, 53 of the 192 youths were located in the follow-up and asked to self-report if they had engaged in any law violations while on parole. The results favored the modeling (28%) and control (38%) groups over the discussion group (60%). The mixed results and lack of random assignment make a conclusive interpretation difficult.

Although there has been an increase in community-based efforts in the past decade, it is likely that institutional programs will continue to be a frequent dispositional alternative, especially for the more serious youthful offenders (Wilson, 1975). It also seems likely that behavioral-type programs will continue to be employed in many institutions in the foreseeable future. If these programs are to evolve, there is need for more emphasis and research on quality-control procedures and for more careful outcome studies. These outcome studies should employ multiple measures, including measures of positive adjustment in addition to traditional ''failure'' measures such as subsequent offending or reinstitutionalization.

OVERVIEW OF COMMUNITY INTERVENTIONS: PROCEDURES AND RESULTS

We now consider behavioral interventions at the community level. It is widely acknowledged that interventions should be carried out in the ''natural environment'' whenever possible. One of the earliest behavioral interventions with delinquents occurred in the open community. A behavioral street-corner research project in the Boston area (Schwitzgebel, 1964) recruited 20 delinquents with multiple arrests to participate in taped interviews several times per week for an average of 9 months. Wages and social consequences were used to reward cooperation, promptness, and talking about feelings. A 3-year follow-up indicated that participating youths had significantly fewer arrests and months incarcerated than a post hoc matched control group. In addition, although not statistically significant, the experimental group had a lower recidivism rate than the controls.

Subsequent behavioral community treatment and prevention programs have included nonresidential token economy programs (Cohen, 1972), contingency contracting involving parents (Tharp & Wetzel, 1969), teachers (Stuart, Tripodi,

Jayaratne, & Camburn, 1976), and probation officers (Fitzgerald, 1974), social skills training of aggressive adolescents in regular classrooms (Goldstein, Sherman, Gershaw, Sprafkin, & Glick, 1978), and parent training in behavioral techniques (Patterson & Reid, 1973). Typically, evaluations of these approaches have involved group comparison designs.

The Programming Interpersonal Curricula for Adolescents (PICA) program (Cohen, 1972; 1973) was a half-day out-of-school program for predelinquent youths who were on the verge of being expelled from school. Twelve predelinquent youths participated during each of 2 years. Points were earned for completing self-instructional material designed to teach academic, vocational, and interpersonal skills and were spent in a special lounge. Results indicated increased achievement scores, attendance, and grades and decreased court contacts. No control group data were available. A recent 5-year follow-up with a small sample (15) presents self-report data suggestive of a decrease in official contacts during program participation, a decrease that did not endure (McCombs, Filipczak, Friedman, & Wodarski, 1978). An extension of the PICA program into community schools was called Preparation through Responsive Educational Programs or PREP. Evaluations of the PREP program have revealed that PREP youths were performing significantly better than matched controls on measures of achievement test performance, attendance, grades, and discipline referrals (Filipczak, 1973). Long-term follow-up on youths in the PREP program is currently underway (McCombs et al., 1978).

Research on negotiated contingency contracts between delinquent or predelinquent adolescents and adults in their lives have had mixed results. In one study, Alexander and Parsons (1973) reported follow-up information on the youths of 99 families referred by the juvenile court for minor offenses. Youths were matched on the delinquency records and randomly assigned to a behavioral intervention group, a client-centered group, a psychodynamic group, or a no-treatment control. In a 6- to 18-month follow-up, the youths in the behavioral group, whose families were involved in negotiation and contingency contracting training, had significantly fewer court contacts. A subsequent study of the court records of siblings of the referred youths revealed similar between-group differences in favor of the contracting and negotiation group (Klein, Alexander, & Parsons, 1977).

In a study by Fo and O'Donnell (1974), contingency contracting was effective in reducing school truancy and the frequency of various other problems for youths with previous offenses. Although delinquent acts were not directly targeted, the treated group of previous offenders had considerably fewer criminal offenses during the treatment year than a corresponding random comparison group (Fo & O'Donnell, 1975). No follow-up data were presented; thus a during-effect but not a follow-up effect was demonstrated.

There are less positive findings concerning contracting. In the Fo and O'Donnell (1975) study described previously, it was found that school-referred youths without previous official offense records had more offenses during treatment than corresponding controls. In a small-scale study, Weathers and Liberman (1975) found that contracting had no effect on curfew violations and school attendance.

A large-scale implementation of behavioral contracting techniques with school-referred junior-high-school students has been reported by Richard Stuart and his colleagues. In this project, program therapists worked with families of 13- to 14-year-old males referred for severe social disruption in school. In one follow-up of 102 youths randomly assigned to either a treatment or control group (Stuart et al., 1976), the treated youths did significantly better than the controls. Ratings by parents and school personnel significantly improved. However, the more objective measures of academic performance and school attendance were unaffected.

Seidman, Rappaport, and Davidson (1976) described a promising advocacy program operated in conjunction with the local police department in Champaign, Illinois. Thirty-seven youths with police contacts were referred to the program by police. Youths were randomly assigned to treatment and no-treatment groups. In the treatment program, youths worked with an undergraduate student who served as a counselor/advocate for from 3 to 5 months. The undergraduate student was in turn supervised by a graduate student in clinical psychology. Intervention involved relationship development, contingency contracting, and child advocacy. Youths were taught negotiation skills and how to deal with various service systems and authority figures. The results indicated that treatment youths had lower levels of police contacts and court petitions during, and one and two years post treatment. In a replication, 36 youths were randomly assigned to contracting, advocacy, and control groups. Both the contracting and advocacy groups had significantly fewer and less serious contacts with police one year post. Analysis of school attendance rates indicated a maintenance of school attendance among both experimental groups across time and a highly significant decrement at a 2-month follow-up point in the control group. These are indeed promising results.

A behavioral program at Oregon Research Institute provided training for the parents of 4- to 13-year-old boys with aggressive behavior problems. The training involved parents a) reading a programmed textbook describing operant child management procedures (Patterson and Gullion, 1968) such as token systems and timeout and b) attending sessions on carefully defining, pinpointing, tracking, and recording rates of deviant and prosocial behaviors. The therapists then helped parents construct and implement modification programs in their homes (Patterson and Reid, 1973). In a study of 27 boys whose parents were trained in these behavioral techniques, direct in-home observation measures taken with a 29-category observation code found significant during-treatment decreases in deviant behaviors (e.g., physical aggression against siblings) over preintervention levels for two-thirds of the youths. These changes were generally maintained over a 1-year follow-up period for those who remained in the study (Patterson, 1974). While some of the evidence supporting the maintenance of the treatment effects during follow-up (Patterson, 1974) has been questioned (Kent, 1976; O'Donnell, 1979), Reid and Patterson (1976a) have conducted further reanalyses providing additional evidence in this regard.

The Oregon intervention program has been shown to a) produce greater decreases in target behaviors than those seen in control groups (Walter and Gilmore, 1973; Wiltz and Patterson, 1974), and to b) decrease observed deviant behavior in siblings of referred children (Arnold, Levine, and Patterson, 1975). Classroom intervention was needed for 14 of the 27 youths in the Patterson (1974) study. As a group, their postintervention appropriate behaviors, as measured by direct in-class measures in a three month follow-up, had significantly improved.

As reported by Reid and Patterson (1976b) at the 1973 International Symposium, the previously described direct home intervention did not work so well with children with considerable stealing behavior. These were children whose deviant behavior occurred primarily out of the home situation. The families of such children were characterized as having loose ties, disorganization, and low supervision. The parents were relatively unmotivated to change or control their children or to participate with the project. The description of these families suggests that they are more like families often characteristic of older predelinquent and delinquent youths. With modifications in their intervention procedures, training was conducted with the 10 families (out of 34 referred) who subsequently began treatment. Reductions in stealing behavior (as assessed by parental report) occurred.

In general, the outcomes of behavioral programs at the community-based level suggest that a number of these programs provide promising alternatives to traditional treatment and prevention approaches. There is a definite need for more and continued evaluations of such approaches.

In this regard, a recently completed study by James Alexander and his colleagues (Alexander, Barton, Schiaro, & Parsons, 1976) at the University of Utah points to an interesting direction in research on behavioral intervention with families of predelinquents. The data, although not allowing direct causal interpretations, suggests that therapist relationship skills, heretofore largely overlooked in the behavior modification literature, may be crucial determinants of therapy success. A priori, reliable behavioral assessments of 21 trained therapists' skills in structuring (e.g., skill behaviors classified as being directive and demonstrating self-confidence) and in relationship building (e.g., skill behaviors classified as warmth and humor) accounted for 60% of the variance in the therapy outcome measures with 21 families. The results, though preliminary, would seem to have implications for either the selection of therapists with such treatment facilitating skills or for the specification and shaping of such skills.

ACHIEVEMENT PLACE GROUP HOMES:
PROCEDURES AND RESULTS

We now consider behavioral treatment and research conducted at small residential centers and group homes. These have often, but not always, been based on Achievement Place (Phillips, Phillips, Fixsen, & Wolf, 1974). These group homes are often in the local communities of the participating youths, so the youths continue in public schools, often the same ones they attended before placement. Often in these programs youths are able to go home on weekends. These factors provide an opportunity for treatment staff to work on natural environment problems and thus might facilitate generalization and maintenance of treatment effects.

The treatment program developed at Achievement Place was described by Wolf, Phillips, and Fixsen (1972). It is centered around teaching parents, a couple responsible both for directing and carrying out the treatment program. The program is conducted in a small (6 to 8 youths), family-style setting which is usually an older renovated home in the community. This setting allows the teaching parents to provide individualized attention and treatment for each of the youths in their program. It also permits the youths to participate in the direction and operation of the program through the self-government procedures of the manager system (Phillips, Phillips, Wolf, & Fixsen, 1973) and the family conference (Fixsen, Phillips, & Wolf, 1973).

A component of the Teaching-Family model is the attempt to develop reciprocally rewarding relationships between the youths and the teaching parents. This facilitates the teaching of social, academic, vocational, and self-help skills to equip the youths with alternative and more adaptive behaviors. The goal is to increase youths' chances of survival and success in the community. The youths' daily interaction in the natural environment facilitates the identification of each youth's individual strengths and weaknesses.

The teaching parents utilize a series of token-economy motivational steps to enhance their effectiveness as educators. Success in the program advances the youth to the homeward-bound system, during which time he interacts progressively longer in his natural or foster family setting before being released from the program. The average length of stay is 1 year. Program participation occurs only with parental and youth voluntary informed consent.

Because the program is community based, the teaching parents can work with the youths' parents and teachers. The teaching parents can indirectly supervise the youths in their regular schools (which the youths continue to attend) and natural homes (to which they return on the weekends). Teaching parents also can advocate for the youth with community agencies. By working with youths in the natural community, then, teaching parents can better provide individualized teaching, guidance, and relationships.

Some procedural research in teaching-family programs, other group homes, and other small residential centers has focused on the effects of contingency management on the duration, frequency, and other measurable dimensions of various behaviors. This research has demonstrated the effects of contingent consequences on aggressive statements (Phillips, 1968), curfew violations (Alexander, Corbett, & Smigel, 1976), instruction following, (Phillips, Phillips, Fixsen, and Wolf, 1971), room cleaning (Phillips, Phillips, Fixsen, & Wolf, 1971), doing homework (Phillips, 1968), school attendance (Alexander et al., 1976), and classroom study behaviors (Bailey et al., 1970).

Other procedural research in group-home treatment, particularly in Teaching-Family homes, has evaluated the use of procedures in teaching skills to delinquent and predelinquent youths. The comprehensive teaching procedures used in these studies have included a number of components that have been found effective in teaching a variety of skills to various populations (Bandura, 1969). These components were (1) descriptions with demonstrations or modeling; (2) behavior rehearsal or other practicing; and (3) differential feedback on performance. Another teaching component used in these studies was the providing of "rationales": explanations and discussions concerning the long-term consequences of the behaviors being taught and the conditions under which the behaviors would be important. A number of questionnaire studies have suggested that the use of such parental explanations and discussions are preferred by the youths and that youths are more likely to model parents who use them (Baumrind, 1967; Elder, 1963; Pikas, 1961). It has been argued that rationale procedures may facilitate generalization of treatment effects (Goldstein et al., 1978).

These teaching procedures have been used to teach a number of skills in group-home settings including homework skills (Kirigin, Phillips, Timbers, Fixsen, & Wolf, 1977), the skills involved in the acceptance of negative feedback (Timbers, Timbers, Fixsen, Phillips, & Wolf, 1973), employment-interview skills (Braukmann, Maloney, Fixsen, Phillips, & Wolf, 1974), interaction skills with adults (Minkin, Braukmann, Minkin, Timbers, Timbers, Fixsen, Phillips, & Wolf, 1976), and parent negotiation skills (Kifer, Lewis, Green, & Phillips, 1974). Although these studies were often predicated at least partially on the notion that the lack of these skills was an important factor in maintaining the youths' delinquent activity, there have been no completely adequate demonstrations of this relationship.

Much of the procedural research efforts related to group–home treatment are subject to many of the same criticisms described earlier in regard to institutional procedural research: Namely, there have been failures to demonstrate empirically the relevance of target behaviors to ultimate adjustment and failures to collect data on generalization of specific behavior changes to situations outside of and following treatment in the group home (Burchard & Harig, 1976). When attention has focused on generalization, it has usually been generalization within the group home itself. Further, on several occasions such research has failed to control for the possibility of effects due to the presence of observers.

In regard to selecting relevant target behaviors, one way to determine the potential social impact of certain behaviors is to solicit opinions of individuals who have not been involved in a treatment, such as laymen, juvenile judges, parents, potential employers, and other youths, as to whether the behaviors studied or changes achieved were important. As described by Wolf (1978), an increase in the evaluations by the relevant judges along with an increase in objective behavioral measures can provide a "social validity" measure of the changes in behavior. Such procedures can and should be used along with the collection of normative data on peers in order to determine whether treatment brings the youth into the normative range.

As one example of this procedure, I would now like to briefly present a study we conducted several years ago (Minkin et al., 1976). In order to determine better what social interaction skills to teach girls in a group home so as to improve their general adult interaction skills, five female college students and five female junior-high-school students were video-taped while they conversed with previously unknown adults. The *conversation ability* of each girl was then evaluated by a group of adult judges who viewed each tape and rated each conversant from *poor* to *excellent* on a seven-point rating scale. The average rating of each girl by the judges correlated highly ($r = .85$) with the behavioral measures of *conversational questions* and *positive feedback*. This procedure was replicated with a new group of female college and junior-high-school students, and an equally high correlation between judges' ratings and behavioral measures was obtained. These data suggested that the behavioral measures were essentially tapping the same skills that people judge as important in maintaining good conversation. Following the introduction of training and positive consequences, the girls' conversation behaviors increased. Judges then rated pretraining and posttraining conversational skills of the delinquent girls. The results indicated that posttreatment ratings (mean 4.2) were higher than pretreatment ratings (mean = 2.9). The posttreatment mean rating of the delinquent girls (4.2) was between the average rating of the junior-high girls (3.4) and the college girls (5.2).

In another study more obviously related to official delinquency measures (Werner, Minkin, Minkin, Fixsen, Phillips, & Wolf, 1975) youths were coached on what to say and how to act with policemen. Police have broad discretion in decisions to detain or arrest, and considerable observational data suggests they are more likely to attend to youths with previous delinquent histories. Youths and police were interviewed about important behaviors for youths to engage in during police and juvenile encounters. Three youths were then taught to engage in these behaviors, which included statements of cooperation and reform. Policemen then evaluated preperformances and postperformances of the youths in simulated interactions with a policeman. After training, the youths were rated as less likely to be taken into custody or considered a troublemaker than three untrained youths. Of course, the ultimate criterion of the value of such training lies in whether the acquisition of the skills reduces delinquency, whether official or unofficial.

Procedural research has also been conducted on the training procedures involved in the year-long education program for teaching parents (Braukmann, Fixsen, Kirigin, Phillips, Phillips, & Wolf, 1975, for a description of that program). This research has been concerned with the training and validation of such skills as teaching (Kirigin, Ayala, Brown, Braukmann, Minkin,Phillips, Fixsen, & Wolf, 1975), rationale-giving (Braukmann, Kirigin, Braukmann, Willner, & Wolf, 1977), and behavior observation and description (Dancer, Braukmann, Schumaker, Kirigin, Willner,& Wolf, 1978). In one study (Willner, Braukmann, Kirigin, Fixsen, Phillips, & Wolf, 1977), six prospective teaching parents were trained to engage in a variety of social behaviors described as "liked" by the youths living in family-style, residential-treatment group homes for delinquent youths. With training, consistent increases in seven preferred social behaviors were observed in simulations (i.e., offering to help, getting to the point, giving positive feedback, point giving, smiling, giving rationales, and providing explanations for task mastery). These changes in behavior corresponded to subsequent increases in the youths' ratings of the trainees' videotaped social interactions. Posttraining levels of preferred social behavior and youth ratings compared favorably with normative measures of professional teaching parents.

In addition to conducting procedural research, we have been collecting follow-up data on the effectiveness of Achievement Place homes in Kansas. In this follow-up, we have collected offense data for four different groups: (1) youths in the original Achievement Place; (2) youths in the first two Achievement Place replication homes; (3) youths who participated in nine later replication homes; and (4) youths in seven non-Achievement Place comparison homes in Kansas. All the homes were community based, served court-adjudicated youths 12–16 years of age, and had similar criteria for admitting youth into the program. All the programs were staffed by married couples, except for one of the comparison programs where staff operated on a shift-work basis.

At the time of this writing, we have data on 28 youths who participated in the original Achievement Place home. They averaged about 3.4 officially recorded offenses the year before treatment, the same level as the comparison group–home youths. During treatment, the offense rate for youths in the Achievement Place program dropped about 1.6 per youth per year while the rate for youths in the seven comparison homes increased to about 7.3 offenses, a statistically significant difference. Five of the seven comparison programs showed more offenses per year during treatment than during the baseline pretreatment year.

The 11 youths who were in the first two Achievement Place replication homes had offense patterns similar to the comparison group homes, with increases in recorded offenses during the treatment period. However, the pre-to-during pattern of offenses for the 92 youths in the nine later Achievement Place replications was similar to that produced by the original Achievement Place program; that is, there was a clear reduction in the rate of offenses during the treatment year. This pattern was displayed by eight of the nine replication programs. These later replications differed from the first two replications in that several critical elements had been added to the training program for teaching parents as a result of the negative feedback received from the first two failures. These elements included the self-government, relationship development, and teaching components of the program.

Thus, the original Achievement Place home and the nine later replications have done significantly better than the comparison homes in terms of offenses during treatment. Nevertheless, during the first year posttreatment, the offense rates of all programs are much higher than desirable, in some cases approaching the offense rates occurring in the year preceding treatment. At this time, the programs that appear to be doing the best are the later replications.

We have also collected consumer satisfaction data for each of the four groups in the follow-up research. Ratings concerning each program were obtained from that program's consumer groups. These groups consist of the program's board of directors, juvenile court and social welfare personnel, teachers, parents, and the youths themselves. The consumers provide their evaluations of the program's effectiveness and pleasantness using seven-point rating scales, where a 7 corresponds to *completely satisfied* and 1 to *completely dissatisfied* (Phillips et al., 1974). Consumers' ratings of the first Achievement Place program indicated that they were satisfied with the effectiveness of the program (mean rating of 6.7), whereas comparison program consumers rated their programs at 5.6 (somewhat less than satisfied). The initial replications were rated at 4.9 and later replication homes at 6.4.

Having collected both subjective and objective data on these group-home programs, we have compared the two measures. When we compared the overall consumer ratings for each of the programs with the youths' offense rates during treatment, we found the correlation to be $-.66$ ($p < .01$). The higher the average ratings, the lower the offenses during treatment. Correlating the ratings provided by each consumer group we found the *youth* ratings of their group-home staff to be the most highly correlated (again inversely) with the level of offenses reported during treatment; that is, the higher the youths' ratings of the fairness, concern, effectiveness, and pleasantness of the group home staff, the fewer offenses occurred during treatment. The correlation was $-.74$ ($p < .001$). Next to the youth ratings, teacher ratings of the cooperation, effectiveness, and communication of the group-home staff in solving the youths' school-related problems were most highly correlated with offense rate during treatment. That correlation was $-.63$ ($p < .05$).

In looking at the correlations for each of the consumer groups we find what appears to be a fairly direct relationship between the predictiveness of a consumer group's ratings and the level of direct contact the group has with the program and the youths. The youths themselves and the teachers, who are in almost daily contact with the youths in the program, appear to provide the best indicators of effectiveness, followed by juvenile court, social welfare personnel, and parents. The ratings provided by the board of directors—who have little contact with the program and the youths—showed a near-zero correlation with effectiveness. These preliminary results suggest that the overall consumer ratings are sensitive predictors of program effectiveness; particularly sensitive are those consumer groups who have the most direct contact with the program and its participants, the exception being the parents. Lack of agreement between parent ratings and more objective measures of child behavior change have been found by other researchers (Schnelle, 1974).

In looking at the relationship between consumer ratings and *post*treatment offenses, we find the consumer evaluations to be less predictive of outcome. Here there were no significant correlations. This is perhaps not totally surprising because the consumers typically evaluate the program whereas the treatment is ongoing for the youths.

The fact that subjective consumer ratings, particularly the ratings of the youths and their teachers, apparently provide a somewhat valid and sensitive measure of the effectiveness of the staff in reducing offense rates during treatment suggests that the opinions of consumers, which can be obtained rather inexpensively, provide an important source of almost immediate feedback that should be taken seriously by those who administer and operate group home programs for children.

Currently, in addition to the continued collection of outcome data, we are also engaged in process studies. For example, in order to understand better what parenting and treatment behaviors on the part of teaching parents are related to better outcomes, and thus to select better for, teach, and monitor such behaviors, we are doing a number of across-home correlations between behavioral measures of teaching-parent/youth interactions and various outcome measures. Preliminary data suggests that measures of ongoing, integrated teaching activities and of the frequency of interactions between teaching parents and youths are highly correlated with positive treatment outcomes. We intend to continue to gather data in this area.

CONCLUSION

Behavioral applications in delinquency remediation and prevention have resulted in rather clear evidence that environmental rearrangements and instruction can modify a wide range of personal and interpersonal behaviors. Evidence of increased academic performance, higher levels of social skill performance, decreased aggressive behaviors, and other examples of control and education with delinquents have been displayed.

In addition to demonstration of such effectiveness, behaviorally oriented approaches have been as humane, if not more so, as other approaches. Behavioral programs have often been more likely to involve ongoing data collection and procedure specification. They are correspondingly more likely to be replicable.

In some cases data has been gathered on consumer satisfaction for behavioral procedures and programs. The importance of shaping programs to maximize client satisfaction and correspond to client preference is hard to overemphasize. There is a need for more widespread use of consumer satisfaction evaluation procedures to ensure that these approaches are conforming to the goals and needs of their consumers.

Together, evaluations of the behavioral approaches underscore the fact that there are no magic solutions. Although during-treatment effects have been demonstrated for a number of interventions, when evidence for long-term maintenance is examined, the overall effects of a program have often been found to have dissipated or diminished. Clearly, efficient and effective maintenance systems need to be developed (Goldstein et al., 1978; Kazdin, 1975; Stokes & Baer, 1977). It may be that such systems will best result from careful assessments of relevant postintervention settings.

Correspondingly, there needs to be an increased emphasis on program evaluation, especially on sound evaluation that utilizes sensitive, multiple, and varied measures; random selection or random assignment; larger groups; and longer follow-up periods. Such outcome evaluations will allow more definitive statements concerning the effectiveness of various programs.

There is also a need for more naturalistic study of treatment variables. Alexander's (Alexander et al., 1976) work in looking at the relationship of therapist skills and outcome and our own work that relates treatment interaction measures and outcome provide good examples here. Such correlation studies should be used collaboratively with experimental studies as a basis for continued improvement of program effectiveness.

The importance of generalization of treated behaviors to the natural environment, the need to deal with early prevention, the rights of participants to the least restrictive treatment environment necessary, and the need to focus on social systems directly affecting youths in treatment as well as cost-efficiency considerations all point to the need for increased emphasis on *community-based* behavioral approaches. Increased and continued emphasis at both community-based and institutional levels needs to be given to: (1) teaching adaptive community skills; (2) the selection of target behaviors designed to facilitate individual delinquent's ability to modify his social environment so that it responds to him in different, more satisfactory ways (Emery and Marholin, 1977; Seymour and Stokes, 1976); (3) the participation of youths in program decision-making processes; and (4) voluntary and informed program participation (Braukmann, Fixsen, Phillips & Wolf, 1975).

ACKNOWLEDGMENTS

The preparation of the manuscript and the Achievement Place research described in this chapter have been supported by grants MH13364 and MH20030 from the National Institute of Mental Health (Center for Studies of Crime and Delinquency) to the Bureau of Child Research and Department of Human Development at the University of Kansas. Reprints may be obtained by writing the authors at the Achievement Place Research Project, 111 Haworth, University of Kansas, Lawrence, Kansas 66045.

REFERENCES

Alexander, J. F., Barton, C., Schiaro, R. S., & Parsons, B. V. Systems-behavioral intervention with families of delinquents: Therapist characteristics, family behavior, and outcome. *Journal of Consulting & Clinical Psychology,* 1976, *44,* 656–664.

Alexander, J. F., & Parson, B. V. Short term behavioral intervention with delinquent families: Impact on family and recidivism. *Journal of Abnormal Psychology,* 1973, *81,* 219–225.

Alexander, R. N., Corbett, T. F., and Smigel, J. The effects of individual and group consequences on school attendance and curfew violations with predelinquent adolescents. *Journal of Applied Behavior Analysis,* 1976, *9,* 221–226.

Arnold, J. E., Levine, A. G., & Patterson, G. R. Changes in sibling behavior following family intervention. *Journal of Consulting & Clinical Psychology,* 1975, *43,* 683–688.

Bailey, J. S., Wolf, M. M., & Phillips, E. L. Home-based reinforcement and the modification of predelinquents' classroom behavior. *Journal of Applied Behavior Analysis,* 1970, *3,* 223–233.

Bailey, W. G. Correctional outcome: An evaluation of 100 reports. *Journal of Criminal Law, Criminology, and Police Science,* 1961, *57,* 153–160.

Bandura, A. *Principles of behavior modification.* New York: Holt, Rinehart & Winston, 1969.

Bassett, J. E., & Blanchard, E. B. The effect of the absence of close supervision on the use of response cost in a prison token economy. *Journal of Applied Behavior Analysis,* 1977, *10,* 375–380.

Baumrind, D. Child care practices anteceding three patterns of pre-school behavior. *Genetic Psychology Monographs,* 1967, *75,* 43–83.

Bayh, B. New directions for juvenile justice. *Trial,* February 1977, 19–23.

Bednar, R. L., Zelhart, P. F., Greathouse, L., & Weinberg, S. Operant conditioning principles in the treatment of learning and behavior problems with delinquent boys. *Journal of Counseling Psychology,* 1970, *17,* 492–497.

Berleman, W. C., & Steinburn, T. W. The value and validity of delinquency prevention experiments. *Crime & Delinquency,* 1969, *15,* 471–478.

Braukmann, C. J., Fixsen, D. L., Kirigin, K. A., Phillips, E. A., Phillips, E. L., & Wolf, M. M. Achievement Place: The training and certification of teaching-parents. In W. S. Wood (Ed.), *Issues in evaluating behavior modification.* Champaign, Ill.: Research Press, 1975.

Braukmann, C. J., & Fixsen, D. L. Behavior modification with delinquents. In M. Hersen, R. M. Eisler, & P. M. Miller (Eds.), *Progress in behavior modification* (Vol. 1). New York: Academic Press, 1975.

Braukmann, C. J., Fixsen, D. L., Phillips, E. L., & Wolf, M. M. Behavioral approaches to treatment in the crime and delinquency field. *Criminology,* 1975, *13,* 299–331.

Braukmann, C. J., Maloney, D. M., Fixsen, D. L., Phillips, E. L., & Wolf, M. M. Analysis of a selection interview training package for pre-delinquents at achievement place. *Criminal Justice & Behavior,* 1974, *1,* 30–42

Braukmann, P. D., Kirigin, K. A., Braukmann, C. J. Willner, A. G., & Wolf, M. M. *Analysis and training of rationales with child-care personnel.* Paper presented at the annual meeting of the American Psychological Association, San Francisco, August 1977.

Burchard, J. D. Systematic socialization: A programmed environment for the habilitation of antisocial retardates. *Psychological Record,* 1967, *11,* 461–476.

Burchard, J. D., & Barrera, F. An analysis of timeout and response cost in a programmed environment. *Journal of Applied Behavior Analysis,* 1972, *5,* 271–282.

Burchard, J. D., & Harig, P. T. Behavior modification and juvenile delinquency. In H. Leitenberg (Ed.), *Handbook of behavior modification and behavior therapy.* Englewood Cliffs, N.J.: Prentice-Hall, 1976.

Cohen, H. L. Programming alternatives to punishment: The design of competence through consequences. In S. W. Bijou & E. L. Ribes-Inesta (Eds.), *Behavior modification.* New York: Academic Press, 1972.

Cohen, H. L. Behavior modification in education. In C. E. Thoreson (Ed.), *The seventy-second yearbook of the national society for the study of education.* Chicago: University of Chicago Press, 1973.

Cohen, H. L., & Filipczak, J. A. *A new learning environment.* San Francisco: Jossey-Bass, 1971.

Cohen, H. L., Filipczak, J. A., Bis, J. S., & Cohen, J. E. *Contingencies applicable to special education of delinquents.* U.S. Dept. HEW, 1966.

Conger, J. J. *Adolescence and youth.* New York: Harper & Row, 1977.

Costello, J. *Behavior modification and corrections* (National Technical Information Service #PB-223-629/AS). Washington, D.C.: The Law Enforcement Assistance Administration, 1972.

Dancer, D., Braukmann, C. J., Schumaker, J. B., Kirigin, K. A., Willner, A. G., & Wolf, M. M. The training and validation of behavior observation and specification skills. *Behavior Modification,* 1978, *2,* 113–134.

Davidson, W. S., & Seidman, E. Studies of behavior modification and juvenile delinquency: A review, methodological critique, and social perspective. *Psychological Bulletin,* 1974, *81,* 998–1011.

Dixson, M. C., & Wright, W. E. *Juvenile delinquency prevention programs: An evaluation of policy related research on the effectiveness of prevention programs.* Nashville, Tenn.: Office of Educational Services, Peabody College for Teachers, 1975.

Elder, G. H. Parental power legitimation and its effect on the adolescent. *Sociometry,* 1963, *26,* 50–65.

Elliott, D. S., Dunford, F. W., & Knowles, B. A. *Diversion—A study of alternative processing practices: An overview of initial study findings.* Boulder Colo.: Behavioral Research Institute, 1978.

Emery, R. E., & Marholin II, D. An applied behavior analysis of delinquency: The irrelevancy of relevant behavior. *American Psychologist,* October 1977, 860–873.

Evans, J. H., Dowd, T. P., Schneider, K., Wallace, E. M., Fixsen, D. L., & Phillips, E. L. *Evaluation of the Boys Town youth care program.* Nebraska: Department of Youth Care, 1976.

Filipczak, J. *Press and community response to behavior modification in public schools.* Paper presented at the American Psychological Convention, Montreal, Canada, 1973.

Fitzgerald, T. J. Contingency contracting with juvenile offenders. *Criminology,* 1974, *12,* 241–248.

Fixsen, D. L., Phillips, E. L., & Wolf, M. M. Experiments in self government with predelinquents. *Journal of Applied Behavior Analysis,* 1973, *6,* 31–47.

Fo, W. S. O., & O'Donnell, C. R. The Buddy System: Relationship and contingency conditions in a community intervention program for youth with paraprofessionals as behavior change agents. *Journal of Consulting & Clinical Psychology,* 1974, *42,* 163–169.

Fo, W. S. O., & O'Donnell, C. R. The Buddy System: Effect of Community intervention on delinquent offenses. *Behavior Therapy,* 1975, *6,* 522–524.

Gibbons, D. C. *Delinquent behavior.* Englewood Cliffs, N.J.: Prentice-Hall, 1976.

Gold, M. *Delinquent behavior in an American city.* Belmont, Calif.: Brooks-Cole, 1970.

Goldstein, A. P., Sherman, M., Gershaw, N. J., Sprafkin, R. P., & Glick, B. Training aggressive adolescents in prosocial behavior. *Journal of Youth & Adolescence,* 1978, *7,* 73–92.

Hobbs, T. R., & Holt, M. M. The effects of token reinforcement on the behavior of delinquents in cottage settings. *Journal of Applied Behavior Analysis,* 1976, *9,* 189–198.

Holt, M. M., Hobbs, T. R., & Hankins, R. The effects of token reinforcement on delinquents' classroom behavior. *Psychology in the Schools,* 1976, *13,* 341–347.

Jesness, C. F., DeRisi, W. J., McCormick, P. M., & Wedge, R. F. *The youth center research project.* Sacramento: California Youth Authority, 1972.

Kazdin, A. E. *Behavior modification in applied settings.* Homewood, Ill.: Dorsey Press, 1975.

Kent, R. N. A methodological critique of interventions for boys with conduct problems. *Journal of Consulting and Clinical Psychology,* 1976, *44,* 297–299.

Kifer, R. E., Lewis, M. A., Green, D. R., & Phillips, E. L. Training predelinquent youths and their parents to negotiate conflict situations. *Journal of Applied Behavior Analysis,* 1974, *7,* 357–364.

Kirigin, K. A., Ayala, H. E., Braukmann, C. J., Brown, W. G., Ninkin, N., Phillips, D. L., Fixsen, D. L., & Wolf, M. M. Training teaching-parents: An evaluation and analysis of workshop training procedures. In E. A. Ramp & G. Semb (Eds.), *Behavior analysis: Areas of research and application.* Englewood Cliffs, N.J.: Prentice-Hall, 1975, pp. 161–174.

Kirigin, K. A., Phillips, E. L., Timbers, G. A., Fixsen, D. L., & Wolf, M. M. Achievement place: The modification of academic behavior problems of youths in a group home setting. In B. Etzel, J. M. LeBlanc, & D. M. Baer (Eds.), *New developments in behavioral research: Theory, method, and application.* Hillsdale, N.J.: Lawrence Erlbaum Associates, 1977.

Klein, N. C., Alexander, J. F., & Parsons, B. V. Impact of family systems intervention on recidivism and sibling delinquency: A model of primary prevention and program evaluation. *Journal of Consulting & Clinical Psychology,* 1977, *45,* 469–474.

Martinson, R. *The treatment evaluation survey.* New York: Office of Crime Control Planning of the State of New York, 1971.

McCombs, D., Filipczak, J., Friedman, R. M., & Wodarski, J. S. Long-term follow-up of behavior modification with high-risk adolescents. *Criminal Justice & Behavior,* 1978, *5,* 21–34.

Meichenbaum, D. H., Bowers, K. S., & Ross, R. R. A behavioral analysis of teacher expectancy effect. *Journal of Personality and Social Psychology,* 1969, *13,* 306–316.

Milan, M. A., & McKee, J. M. Behavior modification: Principles and applications in corrections. In D. Glaser (Ed.), *Handbook of criminology.* Chicago, Ill.: Rand McNally, 1974.

Minkin, N., Braukmann, C. J., Minkin, B. L., Timbers, G. D., Timbers, B. J., Fixsen, D. L., Phillips, E. L., & Wolf, M. M. The social validation and training of conversational skills. *Journal of Applied Behavior Analysis,* 1976, *9,* 127–139.

O'Donnell, C. R. Behavior modification in community settings. In M. Hersen, R. M. Eisler, & P. M. Miller (Eds.), *Progress in behavior modification.* New York: Academic Press, 1977.

Patterson, G. R. Intervention for boys with conduct problems: Multiple settings, treatments, and criteria. *Journal of Consulting & Clinical Psychology,* 1974, *42,* 471–482.

Patterson, G. R., & Gullion, M. E. *Living with children: New methods for parents and teachers.* Champaign, Ill.: Research Press, 1968.

Patterson, G. R., & Reid, J. B. Intervention for families of aggressive boys: A replication study. *Behavior Research & Therapy,* 1973, *11,* 1–12.

Phillips, E. L. Achievement place: Token reinforcement procedures in a home-style rehabilitation setting for pre-delinquent boys. *Journal of Applied Behavior Analysis,* 1968, *1,* 213–223.

Phillips, E. L., Phillips, E. A., Fixsen, D. L., & Wolf, M. M. Achievement place: The modification of the behaviors of pre-delinquent boys within a token economy. *Journal of Applied Behavior Analysis,* 1971, *4,* 45–59.

Phillips, E. L., Phillips, E. A., Fixsen, D. L., and Wolf, M. M. *The teaching-family handbook.* Lawrence: University of Kansas Printing Service, 1974.

Phillips, E. L., Phillips, E. A., Wolf, M. M., & Fixsen, D. L. Achievement Place: Development of the elected manager system. *Journal of Applied Behavior Analysis*, 1973, *6*, 541–561.

Pikas, A. Children's attitudes toward rational versus inhibiting parental authority. *Journal of Abnormal & Social Psychology*, 1961, *62*, 315–321.

President's Commission on Law Enforcement and Administrative Justice. *Task force report: Juvenile delinquency and youth crime*. Washington, D.C.: U.S. Government Printing Office, 1967.

Reid, J. B., & Patterson, G. R. Follow-up analyses of a behavioral treatment program for boys with conduct problems: A reply to Kent. *Journal of Consulting & Clinical Psychology*, 1976, *44*, 297–302. (a)

Reid, J. B., & Patterson, G. R. The modification of aggression and stealing behavior of boys in the home setting. In E. Ribes-Inesta & A. Bandura (Eds.), *Analysis of delinquency and aggression*. Hillsdale, N.J.: Lawrence Erlbaum Associates, 1976. (b)

Robins, L. N. *Deviant children grown up*. Baltimore: Williams & Wilkins, 1966.

Robison, J., & Smith, G. The effectiveness of correctional programs. *Crime & Delinquency*, 1971, *17*, 67–80.

Rose, S. D., Flanagan, J., & Brierton, D. *Counseling in a correctional institution: A social learning approach*. Authors' Forum National Conference on Social Welfare, Dallas, Tex., 1971.

Ross, R. R., & Price, M. J. Behavior modification in corrections: Autopsy before mortification. *International Journal of Criminology & Penology*, 1976, *4*, 305–315.

Sarason, I. G. Verbal learning, modeling, and juvenile delinquency. *American Psychologist*, 1968, *23*, 254–266.

Sarason, I. G. A modeling and informational approach to delinquency. In E. Ribes-Inesta & A. Bandura (Eds.), *Analysis of delinquency and aggression*. Hillsdale, N.J.: Lawrence Erlbaum Associates, 1976.

Schnelle, J. F. A brief report on invalidity of parent evaluations of behavior change. *Journal of Applied Behavior Analysis*, 1974, *7*, 341–343.

Schwitzgebel, R. K. *Street corner research: An experimental approach to the juvenile delinquent*. Cambridge,: Harvard University Press, 1964.

Seidman, E., Rappaport, J., & Davidson, W. S. *Adolescents in legal jeopardy: Initial success and replication of an alternative to the criminal justice system*. Paper presented at American Psychological Association Convention, Washington, D.C., 1976.

Seymour, F. W., & Sanson-Fisher, R. W. Effects of teacher attention on the classroom behavior of two delinquent girls within a token programme. *New Zealand Journal of Educational Studies*, 1975, *10*, 111–119.

Seymour, F. W., & Stokes, T. F. Self-recording in training girls to increase work and evoke staff praise in an institution for offenders. *Journal of Applied Behavior Analysis*, 1976, *9*, 41–54.

Stokes, T. F., & Baer, D. M. An implicit technology of generalization. *Journal of Applied Behavior Analysis*, 1977, *10*, 344–367.

Stuart, R. B. Behavioral contracting within the families of delinquents. *Journal of Behavior Therapy and Experimental Psychiatry*, 1971, *2*, 1–11.

Stuart, R. B., Tripodi, I., Jayaratne, S., & Camburn, D. An experiment in social engineering in serving the families of predelinquents. *Journal of Abnormal Child Psychology*, 1976, *4*, 243–261.

Tharp, R. G., & Wetzel, R. J. *Behavior modification in the natural environment*. New York: Academic Press, 1969.

Timbers, G. D., Timbers, B. J., Fixsen, D. L., Phillips, E. L., & Wolf, M. M. *Achievement place for pre-delinquent girls: Modification of inappropriate emotional behaviors with token reinforcement and instructional procedures*. Paper read at the American Psychological Association, Montreal, Canada, 1973.

Toby, J. The socialization and control of deviant motivation. In D. Glaser (Ed.), *Handbook of criminology*. Chicago, Ill.: Rand McNally, 1974.

Tyler, V. O. Application of operant token reinforcement to the academic performance of institutionalized delinquents. *Psychological Reports,* 1967, *21,* 249–260.

Tyler, V. O., & Brown, G. D. The use of swift, brief isolation as a group control device for institutionalized delinquents. *Behavior Research & Therapy,* 1967, *5,* 1–9.

Vinter, R. D., Downs, G., & Hall, J. *Juvenile corrections in the states: Residential programs and deinstitutionalization.* Ann Arbor: Institute of Continuing Legal Education, University of Michigan, 1975.

Vinter, R. D., Newcomb, T. M., & Kish, R. (Eds.). *Timeout: A national study of juvenile correctional programs.* Ann Arbor: National Assessment of Juvenile Corrections, University of Michigan, 1976.

Walter, H., & Gilmore, S. K. Placebo versus social learning effects in parent training procedures designed to alter the behaviors of aggressive boys. *Behavior Research & Therapy,* 1973, *4,* 361–377.

Weathers, L., & Liberman, R. P. Contingency contracting with families of delinquent adolescents. *Behavior Therapy,* 1975, *6,* 356–366.

Werner, J. S., Minkin, N., Minkin, B. L., Fixsen, D. L., Phillips, E. L., & Wolf, M. M. Intervention package: An analysis to prepare juvenile delinquents for encounters with police officers. *Criminal Justice & Behavior,* 1975, *2,* 55–83.

Wetzel, R. The use of behavioral techniques in a case of compulsive stealing. *Journal of Counseling Psychology,* 1966, *30,* 367–374.

Willner, A. G., Braukmann, C. J., Kirigin, K. A., Fixsen, D. L., Phillips, E. L., & Wolf, M. M. The training and validation of youth-preferred social behaviors of child-care personnel. *Journal of Applied Behavior Analysis,* 1977, *10,* 219–230.

Wilson, J. Q. *Thinking about crime.* New York: Basic Books, 1975.

Wiltz, N. A., & Patterson, G. R. An evaluation of parent training procedures designed to alter inappropriate aggressive behavior of boys. *Behavior Therapy,* 1974, *5,* 215–221.

Wolf, M. M. Social validity: The case for subjective measurement or how applied behavior analysis is finding its heart. *Journal of Applied Behavior Analysis,* 1978, *11,* 203–214.

Wolf, M. M., Phillips, E. L., & Fixsen, D. L. The teaching family: A new model for the treatment of deviant child behavior in the community. In S. W. Bijou & E. Ribes-Inesta (Eds.), *Behavior modification.* New York: Academic Press, 1972.

Wolfgang, M. E. *From boy to man—From delinquency to crime.* Paper presented at the National Symposium of the Serious Juvenile Offender, Minnesota Department of Corrections, Minneapolis, 1977, 51–62.

Young, P., Birnbrauer, J. S., & Sanson-Fischer, R. W. The effects of self-recording on the study behavior of female juvenile delinquents. In B. C. Etzel, J. M. LeBlanc, & D. M. Baer (Eds.), *New developments in behavioral research: Theory, method, and application* (In honor of S. W. Bijou). Hillsdale, N.J.: Lawrence Erlbaum Associates, 1977.

8 Illiteracy: Methodological Bases For a Behavioral Approach

Henry Casalta C.
Universidad Central de Venezuela

INTRODUCTION

In the report entitled "Method for Literacy Campaigns L.A.-I Methodological Project, Organizational Design and Research Plan" (Ibedaca, Aleman, Garcia, Sojo, & Casalta, 1976), it was suggested that a rural literacy campaign should include programmed research and operational development based upon the following considerations:

1. Illiteracy is an obstacle in any training program, because it typically demands that all training must be done through the use of demonstrative and repetitive techniques by highly skilled instructors. This involves extremely high costs due to the scarcity of such experts and to the slow learning process of training skills in absence of appropriate written materials.

2. Contrarily, when the rural population does know how to read and write, it has direct access to all kinds of written information concerning general technical, scientific, and cultural knowledge. This acquisition of knowledge helps to extend the range and effects of farming activities directed by technical agencies and personnel. Moreover, literacy facilitates communication among members of different social classes living in the same area and is essential for the preservation of historic testimony of individuals (scripts) and makes learning through correspondence courses possible. However, too often the follow-up training in literacy campaigns tends selectively to promote in civic, economic, and social aspects those in the population who are already literate.[1] We insist that literacy cam-

---

[1] Article 147 of the National Constitution of Brazil prohibits illiterates from voting or being elected to office. There are other similar instances of limitations related to union and economic aspects (UNESCO, 1974).

paigns must avoid committing further historic injustices, such as those already evident in low-income groups. At this point, only massive literacy campaigns throughout the country will totally eradicate illiteracy.

Macrosocial View

Several international organizations (UNESCO, 1972 and 1973) have stressed the need for functional literacy campaigns that consider teaching reading and writing as a part of a comprehensive educational program directed toward social, cultural, economic, and political change for the improvement of mankind. However, functional literacy campaigns must also include instrumental literacy skills (i.e., development of specific skills for adult reading and writing) so that one can go beyond learning enough so that he or she can earn a living.

We have proposed a wide range of guidelines (Ibedaca et al., 1976) that permit continuity between instrumental and functional literacy campaigns, as previously described. These guidelines are based on a macrosocial analysis and eventually guarantee the feasibility of implementing a massive literacy campaign for rural education in Venezuela. They include:

1. Establishment of an infrastructure for the development of agriculture and/or handicraft activities.

2. Establishment of programs by economic, social, and educational institutions and by agencies that train and develop community and social populations at a regional or sectional level.

3. Carrying out preliminary empirical evaluations and diagnoses by zones through pilot tests.

4. Evaluation of illiteracy costs and other costs.

5. Consideration of the functional aspects of literacy campaigns based upon follow-up programs for individual and community development, elementary education, and curricular design for new readers.

In Table 8.1 we see that for each aspect considered its inclusion guarantees the adequate implementation of the program itself, reduces migration, generates transforming needs, ensures the stable assistance of this and other low-cost programs dealing with newly acquired behaviors, and determines new goals with community participation. Should these aspects be deleted from the program, serious repercussions would result.

An approach of this nature should be supported by empirical data and by effective decisions and programs that implement the project and by its gradual expansion into other zones or communities.

Table 8.2 illustrates the previously mentioned aspects, that is, the means and decisions proposed by Ibedaca et al. (1976). Certain of these investigations have been carried out. (Their methodology will be described later.) Some of the others

TABLE 8.1

Macrosocial Approach

Criteria Proposed for Implantation of the Rural Literacy Program

(General Consequences of the Program)

	Its Adoption Facilitates or Permits:	*Its Absence Produces:*
A. Infrastructure	1. Population stability	1. Migratory waves to urban centers
	2. Generation of transforming needs, associated with the economic and social nucleus where it is implanted	2. Contribution to urban marginality
		3. Artificial, nontransforming needs
B. Existence of institutional development programs	1. Follow-up programs—both complementary and leveling	1. Weakening of the organization of subsequent programs
	2. Guarantees of continuous institutional assistance in training, education, and employment	2. Circumstantial bureaucratic systems
	3. Lowered costs and improved program control	3. Deviation of attention and nonevaluation of the educational problem
C. Previous evaluation	1. Use of self-corrective tactics in goals and procedures in behavior modification programs	1. Tendency to consider materials and "prescriptions" as a technology
	2. Evaluation of the relationship between materials and behavior	2. Ignorance of the social context where the technology is used
		3. Propagandistic use
D. Estimation of illiteracy rates and costs	1. Selection of priority area	1. Prohibitive costs
	2. Because material is easy to apply, use of less educated persons as "monitors" (teachers)	2. Change of priorities
	3. Multiplication of the number of possible monitors, reducing costs	
E. Instrumentality, functionality	1. Emphasize need for postliteracy programs for training, personal and community development	1. Use of verbal rules to change behaviors; attitudes and values not associated with nor articulated to the program
	2. Include other development agencies in articulated programs	2. Propaganda and persuasion for social change
	3. Follow-up. Promotes the census of regressive literacy, other objectives, and educational goals	

TABLE 8.2
Macrosocial Approach
Means and Decisions Associated With Criteria

Criterion	Means and Decisions
A. Infrastructure	1. Evaluation of economic, social, and educational characteristics in a diagnosis by zones (questionnaires)
B. Empirical evaluation	1. Articulation of literacy program with other agencies of community; promotion, agricultural development, training, etc.
C. Empirical evaluation	1. Compare methods
	2. Estimate degree of supervision to prevent deterioration
	3. Evaluate difficulty of training monitors, materials, and techniques
	4. Evaluate related effects of sociopsychological variables
	5. Weigh necessary behaviors for learning, in general terms, and redesign training when it weakens
	6. Evaluate administrative decisions and their functionality
	7. Evaluate organizational schemes (sociopolitical structures), and propose adjustments or corrections
	8. Criteria for other basic research
D. Literacy rates and costs	1. Initial emphasis on the acquisition of reading and writing skills
	2. Programs for new readers with special and remedial materials
	3. Use of periodical publications (newspapers, magazines, texts); evaluation of reading interests
	4. Improvement in postal services or creation of these in the zone, as group contingencies
	5. Participation of basic community organizations (farm workers' groups, borrowers' associations) in making and carrying out decisions
	6. Use of part of initial staff as paraprofessionals in later education and training programs (home demonstrators; assistant mothers; tractor-driving instructors; teaching use of plows, cultivation, etc.). Use of the monitors' handcraft ability for courses meant to diversify production (i.e., preparation of canned foods, weaving)

refer to a varied range of decisions and some to priority programs and objectives concerning ultimate cultural and educational goals.

We suggest, after careful evaluation of the previous, that the following recommendations be considered as the general technical bases for a rural literacy campaign:

1. Systematic evaluation of methods, procedures, organizational structure, and feasibility for the self-correction of the plan and the improvement of its essential elements.

2. Provisions for adult rural education that would limit or restrain regressive literacy.

3. Adoption of recommendations related to the previously mentioned guidelines: the existence of infrastructures for production, training programs and/or changes in material in use, assessment of the program itself, census of

illiteracy, and maintenance and generalization of the changes achieved by the follow-up programs.

Microsocial View (Individual)

A functional analysis of reading and writing required for the development of the behavioral technology in teaching adult illiterates (Casalta, 1976) underlines the beliefs that:

1. The processes of acquisition, maintenance, and/or extinction of reading and writing behaviors do not differ much regardless of the different behavioral repertoires in school-age children and adult illiterates.

2. Illiterates do not have lower capacities or abilities than other human beings, but they do have behavioral deficits in academic repertoires, particularly a lack of "textual control" (Casalta, 1976; Skinner, 1957; & Staats, 1964). For example, discrimination of similar printed texts and the discriminative control of these for making overt verbal or subvocal responses does not exist because of the absence of a specific history of reinforcement associated with such stimuli. This inability is the product of cultural and school deprivation or early deprivation of primary education. However, an adult illiterate can clearly distinguish with precision the different types of leaves from the same fruit family.

3. The rural zones that are the natural environment of illiterates do not demand reading or writing skills, because the oral pattern is the most common channel of communication. In zones near cities, there are "translators" who transmit information seen on TV or heard on the radio that have an equivalent or even greater coverage than the printed press. Consequently, the natural environment does not provide the stimuli to develop reading and writing skills. A clear illustration of this is that in some rural areas there is a scarcity and even a total lack of post offices.

4. It is relatively easy through the use of an inventory to identify an adult's present level of reading and writing skills and to assess the necessary behaviors precurrent to learning. As soon as the level is ascertained, appropriate reading and writing programs are promptly introduced.

THE PROGRAM

As viewed from the approach developed by Skinner (1957) for textual control and from the writings of Staats (1974), Staats and Butterfield (1965), and Ribes (1972, 1974a, 1974b), Casalta (1974) developed a set of materials that demonstrated its efficiency on three adult illiterates and a 7-year-old girl. The material was grouped in fascicles that initially used a prompting figure under the words: "SAY WHAT YOU SEE." After the reinforced emission of a denomination or "tact" (Skinner, 1957), the subject was shown the corresponding written word and was told to: "LOOK AT WHAT YOU SAY." He was then asked to copy the same word, following the instruction: "WRITE WHAT YOU SAY" and was later given a match-to-sample test and a test of direct reading of words, where he was asked: "WHICH ONE IS THE SAME?" "WHAT DOES IT SAY HERE?"

This incipient development will be improved with the use of appropriate writing supports and through research of the optimum conditions necessary for learning, bearing in mind the key objective: positive student–teacher behaviors throughout the entire educational process.

In view of the fact that many procedures and techniques may stem from a functional analysis of reading and writing, we wish to stress the general characteristics concerning (1) materials, (2) training of paraprofessionals, (3) programming of generalization. These are aspects of the L.A.-I Method, developed by the author in collaboration with the professional and technical personnel of INCE during 1975–1976 and which this institution uses at present in rural zones.

Materials

The following are the basic tenets regarding the materials.

1. If the materials are adequately programmed, participants will be able to learn with a minimum of training how to teach according to the method advocated here. Furthermore, if the essential supervision is guaranteed, two major effects will undoubtedly result: (a) the opportunity to exchange shared ideologies, individual experiences, beliefs, and common values between the participant and the monitor, both of whom have the same social background; this arrangement also enhances the possibility of using some of the monitors who reside in the same zone as paraprofessionals in later programs designed to strengthen and develop community education. (b) production of a multiplying effect. A community capable of reading and writing without special educational training can be more readily incorporated into tasks of general educational improvement, which because of its massive character will be inexpensive.

2. A functional conception of teaching reading and writing arranges the contingencies, particularly the social reinforcers (contingent social attention, redirection, support, verbal reinforcement) that are related to the acquisition of increasingly difficult behaviors.

3. The materials should use facilitating vocal stimuli, provide exposure to tests, allow space for writing samples, and utilize other support stimuli that are gradually faded out.

The materials in the fascicles stress the syllabic components that may be separated or reassembled to make new words. They include meaningful and relevant messages for the adults, discrimination exercises, dictation, tests of mixed words, different letter models, punctuation marks, and numbers. In writing, the letters are first made large and gradually reduced in size until they reach book-size type. The slant of the letters is tilted and looped continuously in order to facilitate the step from printing to cursive writing.

4. A total of 40 individual fascicles was used, grouped in four units or modules: Food/Health;   Community/Family;   Work/Economy;   Culture/ Environment. Each unit consisted of 10 fascicles and each fascicle contained two generating words and five new words made composed of new syllabic combinations. At the conclusion of the practice of each set of 10 fascicles, a general test of mixed words was given. A progressive reading test was also developed and used.

This type of unit materials was chosen because it facilitated making corrections during or after the trials and kept editorial costs at a minimum.

5. Finally, supportive programs were developed for new readers using fotograms, post cards, and remedial tests. These were designed to maintain the recently acquired behaviors.

Training for Paraprofessionals

Paraprofessionals are helping persons working in any particular field of work who do not have the educational or professional training generally required of the professionals in that field, for example, practical nurses versus registered nurses. Reports by Ayllon and Azrin (1968); Ayllon and Michael (1959); Patterson (1973); Surrat, Ulrich, and Hawkins (1970); Cohen (1975); Dominguez, Acosta and Carmona (1972), among others, state that desirable effects may be achieved by individuals or communities using patients, relatives, schoolmates, and members of social agencies (Ayllon & Michael, 1959).

For paraprofessionals to be effective in this program, they must be trained in the skills needed for the observation of predefined behaviors; for adequate intervention in the selected behavior; and for objective recording of behavior before, during, and after the intervention. Additional skills are also often required for the proper use of the materials and it is necessary to provide clear examples and demonstrations of the correct performance. For example, a work recently developed by undergraduate students (Pujol & Arnal, 1978) under our supervision demonstrated that when the teacher's speech exemplified correct intonation, pronunciation, and phonetic emphasis, the school children made significantly fewer spelling errors in dictation exercises.

The recommended method for training monitors for literacy teaching is contained in a series of direct or videotaped demonstrations created by the designers of the method. They are transferred to the supervisors or promotors, who turn them over to the voluntary monitors. The scheme used in the case of Method L.A.-I proceeds as follows:

1. Initial contact and explanation of the purpose of the program.
2. Demonstration by the trainer of the procedures used in the literacy teaching program.

3. Simulation of the demonstrations by the monitor candidates with an evaluation of their performance by the supervisor. The evaluation included critical and noncritical categories in each step of the lesson (strengthening, command, redirection, direct demonstration to the participant, explanation, etc.). The criteria for a passing performance may vary and opportunities for retraining are provided.

If the monitor uses instructions and models to correct errors and if the monitor promptly reinforces through contingent attention and social approval the behavior of the participant in the presence of the materials, it is highly probable that the participant will show progress toward the objectives of the educational programs. Because all training is done by monitors who model the correct behaviors and because of the effective arrangement of the contingencies the relationship between the supervisor and monitors tends to acquire a positive value.

Programing for Generalization

After the completion of training, measures must be taken to ensure maintenance of the behaviors acquired. The basic strategy for maintenance is to supply an adequate amount of material to new readers, to other members of the community, and to various agencies for community development in each area. One effective way to achieve this might be to distribute the material through newspapers.

It is recommended that the monitor should reside in the zone where the program is being undertaken. This is of particular importance in rural training projects. Whatever the nature of the specifically programmed materials (leaflets, posters, foldups, postcards, fotograms, brief texts, advertisements), the same or similar contingencies as those used in the literacy program initially should be

TABLE 8.3
Adaptation of the Triple Contingency Model for
Behavior Maintenance in Postliteracy Programs

Situations and Materials	New Reader	Monitor
Discriminative stimuli for:	Behaviors (Criteria)	Consequences
Printed materials	Read Correctly	Social approval (Reinforcement)
	Write Incorrectly	Redirection
	Comment absent	Instigation and Demonstration
	Answer questions	

used (see Table 8.3). During this stage of the program it is necessary to observe whether individual or group problems and needs appear during the group discussions. If the problem is general, solutions may be suggested by group members. However, other members of the community should also participate during this period of the program. Apart from the monitor, other members of the community are a source of social reinforcement for both the monitor and the participants (Tharp & Wetzel, 1969).

Establishment of community workshops, handicrafts centers, study areas, libraries, radiophonic facilities, etc., permits the participation of all the community in maintenance programs. The number of such organizations established indicates to what extent the initial program is being carried out. Techniques for the observation of participation, such as PLACHECK, may be easily developed to evaluate such programs and the degree of expansion they have covered over a specific area.

Skinner (1957) stated that reading and writing are not "capacities" but tendencies that require particular procedures for their development. If the supporting conditions totally disappear, reading and writing behavior will be extinguished and regressive literacy will appear.

DESIGN OF INVESTIGATIONS

We have stressed (Casalta, 1976) that a behavioral teaching technology should be understood not as the mere preparation of material but as the application of research findings in learning. This application should specify desirable behavioral objectives, develop techniques that effectively promote the acquisition and maintenance of the acquired repertoires, and develop materials specifically designed and tactics to evaluate progress and to correct procedures.

Two research groups were created for this purpose based upon the Method L.A.-I. However, the author does not yet have the final results from these groups because he did not participate in the evaluation of the results.

Methodologic Project

Design 1. A statistical investigation of two groups of variables was conceived that involved: (1) supervision: the frequency of contacts between supervisors and paraprofessional monitors to determine the performance levels according to the number of such contacts [i.e., one, two, three, or five per week (see Table 8.4]); and (2) teaching materials: ascertaining the correlation between the variables of difficulty contained in the material (the number of vowels, conso-

TABLE 8.4
Design for Research Project 1
(Methodological Project)

	Supervision						
	Days of the Week					Number of	Number of
Groups	M	T	W	Th	F	Participants	Contacts/Week
A	X					25	1
B		X		X		25	1
C	X		X		X	25	3
D	X	X	X	X	X	25	5
						125	

Key: X = day of supervision.
Total supervisors = 10.

nants, dipthongs, tripthongs, direct simple syllables, inverse syllables, etc.) and incidental variables with performance variables (see Table 8.5).

Design 2.   Observation of critical behaviors under natural conditions. Training was provided by videotapes with a group of 15 observers and reliability recorders on a set of categories of objectively defined behaviors of: (1) the participant: spontaneous reading, directed reading and writing, solutions of tests, assistance, expression of needs, resistance or rejection, collaboration, and suspension of sessions; and (2) the monitor: strengthening, redirection, support, demonstration, and use of commands.

The technique of interval recording every 60 seconds was used, alternating the period of observation of each participant with that of the monitor.

This project involved 100 participants in Carmen de Cura, State of Aragua. The number in each group ranged from seven to one. No intervention was planned because methodology was the focus of the study.

Design 3.   This design was carried out with a group of enlisted soldiers, the majority of them from rural areas. A specially trained instructor applied the method to a group of about 25 participants. An attempt was made to observe the changes concomitant with the introduction and/or elimination of two critical variables: (1) self-recording: providing the participants with forms to jot down their daily progress on the several tests included in the fascicles; and (2) reinforcement: response of the monitor with comments such as "very good," "that's all right," "correct," "sure," "very well done," "great," and "you are doing fine." In Designs 2 and 3, recorders were used for evaluating reliability of the observations. These were applied at random to 20% of the sessions of each observer.

TABLE 8.5
Variables Indicative of the Degree of Difficulty of the Materials
(Methodological Project)

1. Number of letters/number of words for each fascicle (F) and module (M)
2. Ratio R consonants/vowels for each fascicle (F) and module (M)
3. Number of direct simple syllables for fascicles (DS) and average for each module (SC)
4. Number of compound syllables for fascicles (C) and average for module (XM)
5. Number of dipthongs for each module (DM)
6. Number of possible syllabic combinations for fascicles and modules (SF) (SM)
7. Number of syllables for words (SP)
8. Number of new syllables less previous syllables (N)
9. Distance between the fascicle that repeats the syllables and previous fascicles containing them (average distance will be calculated in case of repetition)
10. Pretest score (progressive test)

Incidental Social Variables

1. Sex of participant
2. Age of participant
3. Individual training, two participants, more than two (maximum of five)
4. Time of residence in area
5. Number of persons in family group
6. Number of adults who attend school
7. Gross annual income
8. Hours of work daily, average per harvest
9. Average daily free time per harvest (8-HT)
10. Average of persons in the home who do not know how to read and write, by ages
    Average of persons in home who can read and write, by ages
    Average degree of education (schooling) of persons in home
11. Communal associations actively participated in
12. Frequency of trips to populated areas
13. Manifest reasons for school absenteeism
14. Number of training courses taken
15. Extent of information according to survey
16. Score on attitude questionnaire (cooperation, individualism, dependence/independence)

Dependent Behavioral Variables

1. Number of writing exercises completed for fascicle and mocule
2. Number of correct match to samples for F and M
3. Number of dictation exercises completed for F and M
4. Number of correct identifications in mixed word test for F and M
5. Number of words produced in free exercise
6. Score on mixed word tests for each module (M)

ORGANIZATIONAL PROJECT

The organizational project for the generalization of the initial findings was undertaken for the purpose of supervising and evaluating the performance of a thousand families in a massive project in the State of Lara. The project stressed the need to decentralize the activities through the establishment of regional and municipal coordinating units and supervisory programs as well. The need to use a variety of rural experts, promoters, and others who were high-school graduates to train and supervise monitors who were mainly peasants was also emphasized.

Upon completion, this large-scale application of material was evaluated by means of special techniques to record the events, and PLACHECK was used for the behavior of the monitors and participants. The criteria used to determine the selection of the testing zones are shown in Table 8.6. Tables 8.7 and 8.8 are self-explanatory. The organizational scheme proposed for regional implementa-

TABLE 8.6
Criteria for Selection of Trial Area
(Organizational Project)

1. Illiteracy index per district and municipality
2. Indexes of farming and/or handcraft development
3. Interinstitutional resources
4. INCE training programs
5. Infrastructure works
6. Feasibility of dissemination of program

TABLE 8.7
Necessary Base Research
(Organizational Project)

1. Geographical and economic study of the area
    1.1 Location of points of action
    1.2 Climatology
    1.3 Distance from consumer centers
    1.4 Production in the area
    1.5 Infrastructure works

TABLE 8.8
Required Demographic and Social Studies
(Organizational Project)

1. General population traits
    1.1 Family structure (composition)
    1.2 Illiteracy (by ages)
    1.3 Schooling (by ages)
    1.4 Geographic mobility
2. Social and/or trade union organizations
3. Official institutions and others

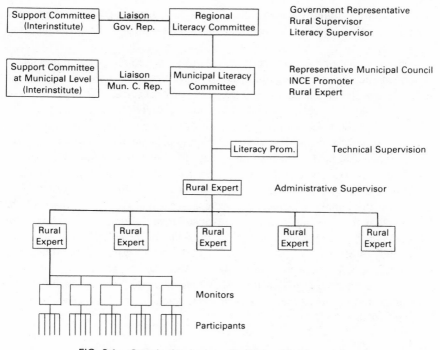

FIG. 8.1.   Organizational scheme for Regional Implementation.

tion is shown in Fig. 8.1. An attempt was made to promote the test at government, municipal, ministerial, and other institutional levels to determine policies concerning the project.

It should be pointed out that the previous projects were based on the "social education" of adults in accordance with the recommendations proposed at the UNESCO conference III on adult education (UNESCO, 1972).

If it is necessary to offer adults an alternative to school education, the adults should voluntarily express their wish to participate and preferably should live within the zone in which the project is to be developed. This would help greatly to solve the operational problems of the initial literacy campaigns and would considerably diminish the efforts and costs, because motivation and regular attendance would be maximized. The community that reads and writes correctly assists in the task of teaching others to read and write. If the material is adequate and easy to administer and the time required to train a peasant monitor ranges from only 5 to 15 hours, with an efficient supervisory structure, adequate conditions for learning can be created at a national or massive level. It requires, however, all the cooperation of the illiterate community to help overcome the initial obstacles to any literacy program and a willingness to participate fully in the short-term training (Qtata[2]).[2] Needless to say, the effective training of the adult monitor/supervisor, and their relationships, is critical to the development of the program.

Certain limitations and obstacles will always apply to the program previously described and any other program of equal scope. An adequate assessment of its effectiveness should supersede the mere claim of its success, and charts illustrating specific data should be presented by the responsible institutions.

Aside from an effective methodological evaluation of the research programs that produces the raw data, an analysis of these data should be presented by the professional personnel of the institution that sponsored the program. The patterns for such an analysis were explicitly determined although the nature and type of conclusions that might be derived from the analysis were not suggested. Furthermore, the behavioral objectives were described for the acceptance of the project as a feasible one and for an evaluation in administrative terms. This action has not yet been concluded. If the methods for the collection of data were adequately implemented and developed, and if the data are available, obviously it should not be difficult to evaluate the results of the program.

A simple chart to highlight the advantages of the technology developed for this program as well as the dangers and limitations of continuing without it is shown in Table 8.9.

Alternatives

A general program of behavioral change, particularly in Latin America, which might be of national scope, should have a strict methodological basis at the individual (microsocial) level as well as at the massive (macrosocial) level.

It is generally desirable to carry out research, and particularly so when the research can be done at low cost and because well-trained, experienced researchers will be in charge, guarantees that no unnecessary risks will be taken in decisions affecting the entire community. However, ignorance on the part of a researcher of the basic research methodology may produce marked errors and ultimate failure by not identifying the essential factors involved in an undertaking of such a great scope. A skilled researcher, on the other hand, is able to utilize even negative results to improve future programs. Thoughtful careful research and its objective evaluation and dissemination serves, in addition to its primary purpose, as an example and an experience shared by others working in similar situations through publications in professional journals. In this manner, science tends to become self-corrective and the institutions involved that use scientific knowledge may thereby fulfill adequately, efficiently, and honestly the objec-

[2]Qtata[2]—Idiomatic expression used in Cuba during the literacy campaign referring to the objectives of the second stage. It implies that each illiterate should have an instructor and vice versa, that there should not be any illiterate without an instructor in Cuba. Published by the Ministry of Education, Cuba, 1964.

TABLE 8.9
Consequences of Evaluation of the Proposed Literacy Program
Versus Its Nonevaluation

		Advantages	*Limitations or Dangers*
A.	Levels of supervision	1. Selection of optimum contacts to prevent deterioration	1. Quality levels unknown
		2. Cost estimates for other areas	2. Self-serving decisions regarding number of supervisors with increase of bureaucratic cost
B.	Materials	1. Reprogramming and improvement of materials; self-correction and improvement for more efficient training	1. Repetition of cumulative errors of multiplying effects on the national level
		2. Increase or decrease in training time	2. Training time increase due to spurious factors
C.	Behavior observation	1. Development of alternative procedures	1. Use of procedure as "prescriptions"
		2. Generalization of key and effective behaviors	2. Ignorance of key behaviors and repetition of stereo-typed behaviors
D.	Self-recording and reinforcement	1. Possibilities for sources of self-reinforcement in adults	1. Use of school treatment with adults
E.	Selection criteria	1. Appreciation of effective indicators for mass training	1. Zone ignorance
		2. Decisions in accord with indices and feasibility	2. Decisions of a political nature without pre-decisional information
			3. Opportunistic use of the plan
F.	Necessary basic research	1. Adequate logistics and operational knowledge	1. Risk of failure because of uncontrolled conditions
			2. Possible abandonment of plan
G.	Demographic and social studies	1. Foresight regarding plan's penetration	1. Use by self-serving political groups
		2. Articulation for adequate executive decisions	2. Nonparticipation by development organizations

tives set for them by the laws of the land and may consequently have a clearer view of their national responsibility.

However, the risks just mentioned of proceeding in an unwarranted way may not seem important to those who see limitations in programs of behavioral modification in education. Therefore, two alternatives are presented to the designer of the program:

1. Development of newly improved methods covering aspects not included in initial programs. This should lead to tax agreements with institutions who support or are interested in the project to prevent the inadequate application of the technology developed.

2. The development of tactics to evaluate independently and/or comparatively the different technological projects or methods for dealing with the problem. This evaluation should be launched through a system of behavioral observation records when possible and a system of analyzing organizations within the institutions that currently deal with this problem.

Both alternatives have their advantages and limitations. However, if these are analyzed, contrasting effects may become apparent and may, as a result, generate a correct understanding of the illiteracy problem and its feasible solutions. We are presently involved in developing both of these alternatives.

SUMMARY

This work describes two levels of analysis through the strategies and methodolgical bases involved in teaching illiterates to read and write: macrosocial (communities) and microsocial (individuals).

The characteristics of a behavioral technology are highlighted within a functional approach concerning: (1) teaching material; (2) training of paraprofessional individuals; and (3) programming of the generalization of the changes achieved, stressing the need for adequate evaluations.

Through a method for rural literacy (Method L.A.-Literacy Campaign INCE), prepared by the author and jointly developed with the technical and professional personnel of the National Institute of Educational Cooperation (INCE), research programs were analyzed for their improvement and evaluated according to their adequate implementation.

REFERENCES

Alfabetizacion Nacional de la Ensenanza. Año de la Educacion. Publicación del Ministerio de Educación. La Habana. Cuba, 1961.

Ayllon, T., & Azrin, N. *The token economy: A motivational for therapy and rehabilitation.* Englewood Cliffs, N.J.: Prentice-Hall, 1968.

Ayllon, T., & Michael, J. The psychiatric nurse as a behavioral engineer. *Journal of Experimental Analysis of Behavior,* 1959, *2,* 323-334.

Casalta, H. Efectos de la Igualación a la Muestra en un Programa Elemental de Alfabetización. Materiales de Trabajo. *Cátedra de Psicología Experimental,* Universidad Central de Venezuela, Caracas, 1974.

Casalta, H. Tecnología de la Ensenanza de Adultos Analfabetos. *Psicología.* Universidad Central de Venezuela, Caracas, 1976, *3,* Nos. 3 and 4.

Casalta, H. Los paraprofessionales y los programas de formación básica de adultos. Enviado para su aceptación a la revista. *Psicología,* Escuela de Psicología, Universidad Central de Venezuela, Caracas, 1977.

Cohen, H. L. Bplay-support system in the community. In A. Bandura & E. Ribes (Eds.), *Behavior modification: Analysis of aggression and delinquency.* New York: Academic Press, 1975.

Dominguez, T. B., Acosta, N. F., & Carmona, D. Discussion: A new perspective—chronic patients as assistants in a behavior rehabilitation program in a psychiatric institution. In S. W. Bijou & E. Ribes-Iriesta (Eds.), *Behavior modification: Issues and extentions.* New York: Academic Press, 1972, 127-132.

Ibedaca, R., Aleman, R., Garcia, R., Sojo, V., & Casalta, H. *Método de Alfabetización L.A.-I* (Mimeografiado). INCE, Caracas, Mayo 1976.

Patterson, G. R. Changes in status of family and members as controlling stimuli. In L.A. Hamerlynck, L. C. Hancy, & E. J. Mash (Eds.), *Behavior change: Methodology, concepts and practice.* Champaign, Ill.: Research Press, 1973.

Pujol, L., & Arnal, B. Y. *Efectos del modelo y la repetición vocal del dictado en los errores de ortografía.* Trabajo desarrollado en el curso de Psicologia Experimental, Universidad Central de Venezuela, Informe de Investigación, 1978.

Ribes, E. *Técnicas de Modificación de Conducta. Su aplicación al Retardo en el Desarrollo.* México: Trillas, 1974. (a)

Ribes, E. *Limitaciones y Perspectivas de una Tecnología Conductual,* XIV Congreso Interamericano de Psicología, Colombia, 1974. (b)

Skinner, B. F. *Verbal behavior.* Englewood Cliffs, N.J.: Prentice-Hall, 1957.

Staats, A. W. *Human learning.* New York: Holt, Rinehart & Winston, 1964.

Staats, A. W., & Butterfield, W. H. Treatment of non-reading in a culturally deprived juvenile delinquent: An application of reinforcement principles. *Child Development,* 1965, *35,* 925-942.

Surrat, P. R., Ulrich, R., & Hawkins, R. P. An elementary student as a behavioral engineer. In R. Ulrich, T. Stachnik, & J. Mabry (Eds.), *Control of human behavior,* Vol. II, Glendale, Ill.: Scott, Foresman & Co., 1970, 263-283.

Tharp, R. G., & Wetzel, R. J. *Behavior modification in the natural environment.* New York: Academic Press, 1969.

UNESCO. *Tercera Conferencia Internacional sobre Educación de Adultros.* Tokyo, 1972, Documento de Referencia.

UNESCO. *La Experiencia Brasileña de alfabetización de adultos-Mobral.* Estudios y documentos de educación No. 15, 1974.

III APPLICATION OF BEHAVIOR ANALYSIS TO HIGHER EDUCATION

9 Curriculum Design in Higher Education from a Behavioral Perspective: A Case Study

Emilio Ribes
Universidad Nacional Autonoma de Mexico (Iztacala)

INTRODUCTION

The First Latin-American Meeting on Professional Training for Psychologists was held in Bogota, Colombia, December, 1974, sponsored by UNESCO. In this meeting, the author presented a paper that stressed the need to depart from the present emphasis placed on curricular content and to insist on behavioral objectives consistent with psychologists' professional activity (Ribes, 1975). At that time, the possibility of venturing into a project of this nature seemed remote. However, the author was appointed coordinator of a new School of Psychology at the Universidad Nacional Autonoma de Mexico, which opened up the possibility of designing new curricular systems and teaching procedures. This took place 2 months later in February, 1975, and a set of methodological and theoretical considerations had to be transformed into a concrete program to be implemented in a short term: the psychology program at the National School of Professional Studies - Iztacala, Mexico (Ribes & Fernandez Gaos, 1979).

First, we shall comment on the characteristics of a behavioral approach to curricular design in higher education. Although behavioral techniques have been developed in the field of higher education, their applications have been restricted to changes in teaching procedures, overlooking the content of what is being taught or the very nature of curriculum based on courses.

In order to design a complete curriculum from a behavioral perspective, the following elements should be taken into account:

1. The curriculum should specify professional functions, such as general repertoires to be developed in the community.

2. These professional functions should be evaluated as precise terminal behaviors.

3. Instructional objectives that define verbal or informative contents should be secondary and depend on their functional relevance to the previously specified terminal behaviors.

4. Target behaviors should be prescribed in relation to general teaching situations (laboratories, natural settings, libraries, etc.) and to specific tasks to be developed in particular environments (direct observation, administration of consequences, program design, etc.). Thus, the prescription of situations where learning takes place fosters stimulus control and natural consequences similar to those involved in professional activity.

5. Being terminal teaching objectives behaviorally defined, training situations should stimulate the behaviors to be learned.

6. Although higher education is planned for groups and not for the individual, the curriculum should provide conditions to ensure individualized supervision and assessment as well as the possibility of students self-pacing their learning.

7. Learning tasks should be sequenced according to their complexity.

8. Evaluation should be a continuous and permanent component of the teaching program.

To some extent, these curricular elements emphasize two essential aspects: (1) Formulation of the specific professional activities to be performed by a psychologist, considering the practical problems to be solved and (2) particular training programs to develop skills and behaviors exemplifying professional terminal activities. These considerations lead to certain decisions prior to curriculum development:

1. Elimination of certain courses.
2. Contents conceptually and methodologically homogeneous.
3. Instructional objectives secondary to behavioral objectives.
4. Curriculum core designed in terms of specific activities and situations.
5. The curriculum formulated "backwards," starting from the ultimate goals until gradually reaching elementary professional behaviors to begin the teaching program.

Iztacala, the selected curricular model, was to integrate teaching conditions not merely in terms of information or contents but as situations defining homogeneous sets of teaching/learning activities and tasks. Contrary to traditional curricula, in which the educational process consists of separate units defined in courses, a modular system was selected to provide a wider organizational framework. The most customary modular systems are those defined by a familiar subject or those dealing with specific problems. In our case, the modular system was formed by teaching *situations* specifying generic *activities* characteristic of each module. Therefore, prior to determining the teaching contents and tasks to be included in the curriculum, it was decided that these should be separated into three major teaching/learning situations or modules defining *where* and *how* the student is capable of learning general repertoires conducive to professional activity.

These modules were: the theoretical module (in which the student acquires verbal repertoires); the experimental module (in which the student acquires methodological repertoires), and the applied module (in which the student acquires technical and problem-solving repertoires). Such a modular system allows for integration of teaching contents and tasks based upon the learning situations, liberating the curricular design process from commitments and assumptions that are demanded by the subject-labeling system. Furthermore, the tradition of considering lectures as the prototype of teaching and laboratory, seminars, and practical activities as complements was abandoned.

THE SEARCH FOR CONGRUENCE BETWEEN
THE SYSTEM AND ITS CONTENTS:
THE CASE OF PSYCHOLOGY

It is characteristic among psychology schools to adopt an eclectic system comprising conflicting theoretical and methodological elements, under the assumption that they are equally valid and that the student will eventually select the most appropriate to his professional needs and interest.

The author does not consider it necessary to clarify his personal views on this matter. However, it is evident that, irrespective of the particular philosophy of science adopted, psychology curricula must depart from eclectic orientation and achieve an integrated conceptual and methodological framework.

In the case of Iztacala, the new psychology curriculum was based upon a clearly defined philosophy of science: *behaviorism* and a precise theoretical and methodological framework: *the analysis of behavior*. Although other viewpoints were critically considered on the basis of a parametric and historical analysis of problems and phenomena, it was decided to go beyond the restricted and linear model of the three-term contingency paradigm of operant conditioning.

The adoption of a behavioral framework has varied epistemological justifications and because its discussion here is irrelevant, we shall not go into further detail about it. Nonetheless, it should be noted that, from a strictly curricular viewpoint, the determination of a behavioral methodology offers several advantages. The first is that in contemporary psychology analysis of behavior is the only experimental methodology of investigation in basic science that has developed an *applicable technology* to all the problems involved in professional practice. This, in a curricular context, allows for a coherent integration of theoretical and methodological training in basic science and technical training in the different areas of applied psychology. Second, the analysis of behavior is the only theoretical and methodological system that allows for an orderly collection of data and observations of human and animal behavior as well as of social behavior, regardless of the theoretical or conceptual "origin" of those facts. In relation to the curriculum, this represents a possibility of conceptually overcoming the apparently insurmountable differences among "approaches" and "areas" that give chaos and fragmentation to psychological theory.

In order to organize the theoretical and practical contents of the curriculum, two criteria were adopted. The first was a parametric criterion, according to which the phenomena, data, and techniques were dealt with as a function of the growing complexity of number and types of determinant variables. Thus, a systematic sequence was structured, stemming from the consideration of behavior as a continuous stream and its "alterations" by a sole variable of stimulus (e.g., the paradigm of stimulus intrusion) up to phenomena of complex human, social, and abnormal behavior, all linked to theoretical problems of applied psychology. The second criterion consisted of analyzing the phenomena and problems from a historical perspective, avoiding the fallacy that different interpretations in the history of psychology are to be seen as equally valid or optional "approaches" bearing equivalent scientific values. This historical analysis allows for a critical assessment of extremely varied data and problems that have arisen continuously throughout the development of psychology as a science; furthermore, it clarifies the sociocultural factors that affected a particular theoretical or methodological approach.

Description of Iztacala Project

Initially, we shall describe the development of curriculum design in order to comment about the organization and characteristics of the contents.

The following strategy was applied to formulate the curricular system:

1. Determination of Social Needs and Relevant Professional Problems. In order to define the professional profile of the psychologist, a survey of the country's social problem was made. An analysis of government figures on health, production, education, and income of the Mexican population was undertaken to detect these basic problems: high death rate from gastrointestinal and respiratory disease, low income, and insufficient production in the primary sectors of the economy. It was considered essential to define the supportive role of the psychologist through the available technology for informal education in the aforementioned areas of public health and production.

2. Definition of Professional Objectives. A chart (see Fig. 9.1) was developed to map out professional functions and problem social areas in order to establish a logical framework for their classification. Four major problem areas

AREAS

PROFESSIONAL FUNCTIONS	PUBLIC HEALTH				ECOLOGY AND HOUSING	PRODUCTIVITY AND CONSUMPTION	INSTRUCTION
	DU	MU	DR	MR			
DETECTION				I			
				IG			
				NIG			
RESEARCH							
PREVENTION AND PLANNING							
DEVELOPMENT							
REHABILITATION							

Social sectors
  DU—Developed urban
  MU—Marginal urban
  DR—Developed rural
  MR—Marginal rural

Populations
  I—Individuals
  IG—Institutional groups
  NIG—Noninstitutional groups

FIG. 9.1.   Framework for classifying professional functions and problem sound areas.

were identified: instruction, ecology and housing, public health, and productivity and consumption. Five professional objectives were defined: detection, development, rehabilitation, planning, and research. As may be seen, most of these functions take into account the character of the problem to be solved (such as development versus rehabilitation) or the activity outcome (prevention versus development).

3. Curricular Objectives.   These are represented by the terminal behaviors that result from the 4-year training program. Behaviors are prescribed as generic repertoires including the analysis of empirical variables affecting behavior; definition of problems and designing programs; selection of adequate techniques and formulation of new techniques based on experimental research; evaluation of procedures outcomes and their follow-up in natural settings; training of para-professionals and nonprofessionals within the community; and knowledge about legal and social aspects of professional activity. The curriculum makers should foresee teaching situations adequately to train students in these repertoires that simultaneously cover part of the basic problem areas defined in the professional chart.

4. Modular Objectives.   Modules are defined as the basic curricular structures that replace traditional courses. They are specified as generic teaching situations. There were three situations: (1) the theoretical module; (2) the experimental module related to laboratory research on animal or human behavior; and (3) the applied module concerning practical natural situations. Figure 9.2 describes the organization of these modules.

The theoretical module remains virtually constant during the 4-year program, limited in time compared to other modules. The experimental module encompasses the major part of the first 2 years, and the applied module extends over the latter 2 years. The student puts in 1310 house on theory, 1284 on laboratory work, and 1088 on applied training, bringing the total hours of practical training up to 2372 compared to 1310 hours of verbal teaching. In this way, the applied module concentrates on the terminal objectives of the curriculum, the other two being conceived as basically supportive curricular systems.

5. Specific Objectives, Teaching Situations, and Assessment Procedures. The curriculum is presented in the form of courses and semesters; each module is

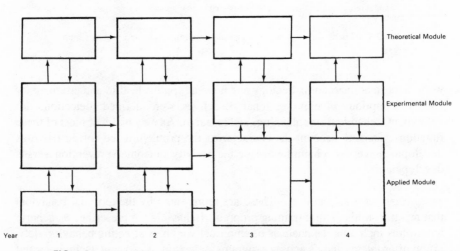

FIG. 9.2.   Theoretical, experimental, and applied models in relation to year in the program.

derived "backward," prescribing component units that allow the accomplishment of intermediate objectives.

Each unit covers one topic, or a set of skills, that are sequentially related to other units in the same or different modules. Each unit develops relevant specific behaviors to increasingly complex objectives. For example, in the advanced semesters, students are required to design reading programs in special education centers as well as in public schools. Specific skills are related to: (1) theoretical analysis and laboratory work about matching-to-sample and conditional discrimination; (2) analysis of textual and tacting responses as verbal behavior under the control of verbal and nonverbal stimuli; and (3) design of programs as well as the analysis and evaluations of tasks.

Instead of being selected on the basis of some established instrinsic behavior or by an analysis of the contents, teaching situations are planned as ad hoc situations to foster the development of generic behaviors common to some cells or areas of the professional objectives chart. Lectures, seminars, and tutoring promote the acquisition of complex verbal behaviors related to library research, analysis and understanding of texts, integrating information, critical evaluation of data and scientific reports, elaboration of essays, learning new theoretical options, etc. Because the curriculum does not have a merely informative objective, verbal behavior thus established becomes functional through its relation to observational, quantitative, and manipulative skills acquired in the laboratory as well as through the complex interaction repertoires created in institutions and the community. Assessment procedures are congruent with a behavioral orientation. Examinations are eliminated and evaluation is based on performance criteria. In the laboratory and in natural settings, direct evaluation is made from the behaviors of students, taking into account behavior during practice; behavior of the population being worked with (animal or human); and verbal behavior that reports, analyzes, and interprets their behavior in those situations. For instance, evaluation in the experimental module consists of the following:

1. Accomplishment of the practical requirements (terminal behaviors in animals; number of hours and experimental sessions; recording relevant data; and, once every semester, designing one experiment).

2. Writing a report on the experiment including the experimental problem, dimensions and parameters analyzed, values selected concerning independent and dependent variables, and a description of the procedures applied, as well as processing and plotting the experimental data.

3. Discussion regarding how the specific problem is parametrically related to some previous experiment (for example, the relation between "avoidance behavior" and "delayed reinforcement").

4. A brief theoretical rationale for the experiment and relevant references.

5. Suggestions for designing new experiments based upon the data obtained and their relation to applied procedures.

The evaluation of the verbal behavior acquired through reading, listening, or discussing is made on the basis of student participation in seminars as well as in the preparation of term papers varying in difficulty and complexity, that is, review, integration, methodological criticism, and theoretical formulation papers. This kind of assessment discourages studying solely for the sake of being promoted, as well as memorizing and superficial understanding. Furthermore, assessment based on reports and essays self-sustained and self-motivated study and encourages individualized and self-regulated instruction.

This occurs because evaluation is based on criteria of terminal performance and not on sampled behavior (such as in exams). A promoted student concludes his essay with the same quality standards as others. The essay begins when the student is assigned a tutor who supervises his behavior throughout the semester until meeting the standards of terminal performance established. The student is encouraged and taught to define the essay topic, how to select and seek references, and to prepare resumes and related articles, as well as to organize the entire essay. Such behavior is markedly different from the typical behavior of study in a fixed interval, such as the examination behavior and learning by memorization to repeat the texts and opinions of professors. Moreover, aside from lectures and seminars, the student may progress at his own pace in writing the essay.

6. Modular Organization of Curricular Contents. The Iztacala program devotes the first four semesters to learning basic principles, theoretical concepts, quantitative methods, and laboratory skills and to applying of this knowledge to natural settings.

The theoretical module covers four courses in theoretical experimental psychology, which includes animal and human behavior, being in its sequence parallel to Experimental Laboratory (eight semesters). The experimental area (both theoretical and laboratory) is based on a parametric analysis of the paradigms that define the field functions between behavior and the environment. Thus, instead of grouping topics and procedures in the traditional areas of motivation, learning, perception, etc., the student is taught to segment behavior and environment and is introduced to the analysis of the more simple and general paradigms of interaction (paradigm of stimulus intrusion and paradigm of the noncontingent stimulus). In this way, as new dimensions and parameters are gradually added to the situation, the events proceed smoothly from simple animal conditioning to complex human social behavior including the analysis of atypical interactions, that is, abnormal behavior.

The concepts of stimulus function, response function, setting factors, medium interaction, history, field boundary, etc., are basic analytic tools which replace the linear model derived from the reflex and presents psychological phenomena as complex field functions (Kantor, 1959).

This provides an unorthodox view of behavior from a classic behavior approach, because it eliminates discontinuous aspects in favor of parametric continuity. In experimental psychology, biological information is included in sections according to its relevance to the topic or phenomenon, and each problem is analyzed according to its historical development. This allows for a theoretical and methodological analysis of problems from a longitudinal perspective, avoiding the traditional "cross section" that fosters the formulation of theories or approaches to behavior that professes the same validity. For example, conditioned suppression is analyzed as a compound stimulus function paradigm and not as "emotional" behavior or as an instance of "aversive control." Thus, it is reviewed after the "discriminated operant paradigm" and related to its origins as an experimental model of "anxiety" in the clinical context of Freud's theory. The parameters that define the field function of the paradigm are described, and it demonstrates how supression with positive stimuli and acceleration with negative stimuli are produced when the duration of the conditioned stimulus is increased, etc.

Quantitative methods are taught during the first five semesters, ranging from descriptive statistics up to the construction of surveys. Each unit in this area has to be evaluated in reports of experimental and applied laboratories, through the design of the instruments for the data collection as well as through procedures of data analysis and representation. At the same time, the students have field work in order to identify in natural settings the variables and procedures used in the animal laboratory. This helps to transfer methodological skills to relevant social environments. During the last four semesters, emphasis is placed on laboratory work in applied psychology. The theoretical module covers information about the four areas of applied training: development and education, special education and rehabilitation, clinical psychology, and social psychology. The last area provides the student with the information and conceptualization concerning the conditions in which he will eventually carry out his profession, concentrating on the history of the political, social, and economic problems of Mexico and Latin America. Theoretical contents about social behavior are included in Theoretical Experimental Psychology. As in the first four semesters, there is not a close relation in time between the contents of the theoretical module and the teaching tasks of the applied module. Applied training is carried out in four types of centers: (1) centers for special education and rehabilitation; (2) centers for education and development (public schools and care centers); (3) clinical assistance centers (University Clinic for Integral Health); and (4) the community. Although specific training in these areas is a representative sample of the professional space described in the matrix, these were planned as training conditions in which the student learns to solve practical problems. The sequence, as described, leads the student from a highly controlled and supervised institutional environment (e.g., Center of Special Education and Rehabilitation) to a terminal condition, the community, in which control has waned through the school environment and the clinical situation. The student therefore learns to deal with contingencies less susceptible to being directly arranged and has to transfer part of his professional skills to a client or a group. This is the terminal objective of the entire training system: to teach the student to "deprofessionalize" his exercise, providing his basic technical skills to the traditionally passive recipients of psychological services.

Problems in the Implementation of the Project

We shall now comment on the fundamental problems arising from the implementation of such a curriculum, in terms of the following four areas:

1. The behavior of the professor.
2. The behavior of the student.
3. Administrative limitations.
4. Curricular adjustment and coordination.

1. The Behavior of the Professor.   It is evident that a program in which it is fundamental to specify the behaviors required of the student requires a different conception of the teacher's role and his characteristics as an element in the teaching/learning relationship. We may therefore conclude that the teacher undoubtedly is the backbone of a program of this nature.

Because we have previously described teacher training in the ENEP Iztacala project (Ribes, 1977), we shall concentrate on three basic problems involved in the teaching practice. These problems, although currently unsolved, have received attention aiming toward their solution.

The first consists of the theoretical and practical capacity of teachers. Because the new program of psychology at Iztacala establishes professional roles and conceptual frameworks that, aside from being innovative, deeply affect Mexican and Latin-American psychology, there is no further need to emphasize that recruiting of professors is a major problem. University graduates in the country have insufficient repertoires, in information as well as in practice in relation to objectives defined by the Iztacala curriculum. We are therefore aware of the fact that during the initial phase the teaching staff will consist of promising first generation of graduates. This realistic attitude has enabled us to adopt some facilitating steps in the process of teacher training.

The second problem is directly related to the operative aspects of the program. The teacher must show those specific repertoires that the student must acquire: Teachers should preach setting the example. This has compelled us to improve and determine in a more detailed manner the specific objectives involved in the different teaching/learning tasks, because their specification in concrete terms is the only way in which a teacher may abandon outdated practices and participate in the learning/teaching situation in which he must meet requirements similar to those demanded of the students.

Finally, the third problem is concerned with teaching itself. The artificial separation of teaching, research, and services has fragmented the integral formation of the university professor who, with few exceptions, devotes himself exclusively to one of those activities, overlooking the others. The conception that follows from the curricular philosophy of psychology at Iztacala requires a professor to teach what he practices himself, and therefore this requires him to be more than transmitter of other experiences, to also be a promoter of the learning activities that he masters and practices daily. Thus, a fundamental aspect of teacher training is projected through the establishment of institutional research programs that allow the incorporation of the teaching staff and permanent training and development. This would undoubtedly be the cornerstone of an integral teaching program.

2. The Behavior of the Student.   Just as the teacher arrives at a new curricular structure with the routine of the traditional system and with the ideological suppositions that governed his past professional and nonprofessional practice, the student is also influenced by the social practices that interfere with what is expected from him and which he demands for his education. The Iztacala curriculum requires students whose characteristics differ from those preestablished and promoted in the traditional system.

Some characteristics required are listed as follows:

1. He should self-initiate a considerable portion of the teaching/learning tasks.
2. He should be self-sufficient in the directed search for information.
3. He should be critical.
4. He should relate practice to theory.
5. He should classify and program his learning activity continuously.

When the new curriculum was designed, it was foreseen that the average new students would not meet the qualifications and that undoubtedly this would cause conflicts. Such conflicts are expressed in different ways, but at an initial stage of transition they are unavoidable. The student arrives at the university to pass courses and obtain a degree and expects that the professor will "teach" him; therefore he makes the teacher responsible for his learning. The student is used to "the text of the subject" or his class notes, and practice becomes a simple demonstration of theory entirely apart from what is learned in the classroom and is an occasion for smaller groups to break away from the monotony of class recitation. He learns to accept many incompatible "truths"—as many as numbers of professors he is studying under—and to protect the conceptual anarchy under a pretended pluralism of ideas. He is not used to investigating the basic concepts of knowledge and accepts these without further critical analysis; he does not know how to analyze rigorously. Furthermore he has no scruples about resorting to slight cheating to pass his courses. He is not trained to integrate the several areas of theory and practical knowledge, and he lacks the linguistic abilities to comprehend and communicate, etc.

However, even though these shortcomings exist due to the faulty inherited practices that resist change, nevertheless the system must promote and produce a change. In order to do so each and every one of the contingencies that operate in the learning/teaching situations must be closely analyzed and monitored. Once this is done with sufficient care and attention, changes will gradually take place (they are already evident). The effects will show the natural results that accelerate the transformation of the student into responsible participation in his learning and his commitment to society. This evolution in the professional and social activity of students within and outside the university will ultimately prove the effectiveness of the implemented curricular structure.

3. Administrative Limitations.   Although at first there were questions about the cost per student in the modular system selected and the high level of individualization programmed for the teaching/learning relation, the resulting figures have shown that the cost was approximately 40% of the expense incurred per average student in the Universidad Nacional Automa de Mexico, and even lower in relation to the cost per student in other departments. Administrative problems became apparent in other areas. On one hand, certain regulatory restrictions demand teaching by courses and semesters under strict administrative procedures that require traditional grading for passing and failing marks. This problem has been successfully overcome, despite the fact that certain dispensable measures are still imposed that hinder the development of some curricular characteristics such as individualized progress through the program. In the long run, the university will have to revise its regulations in adjustment to the changing needs of the new teaching practices.

On the other hand, the difficulty in administratively professionalizing the teaching practice (and research) is a serious obstacle in ensuring new qualified personnel, guaranteeing continuous training of the previously contracted teachers, and permanence of the staff who prove themselves with time. Cumbered with administrative guidelines, educational institutions have opposed functions that should be complementary. The lack of *precise objectives* in institutions of higher education within the socioeconomic context of the country inevitably makes academic criteria dependent on administrative and political considerations. Nonetheless, there is growing evidence of the need for professionalizing teaching and research, and we are confident that it will result in the progressive formation of a full-time professional teaching staff.

4. Curricular Adjustment and Coordination.   A final basic aspect in the implementation of the new program is its permanent adjustment and coordination.

This process requires several joint tasks:

1. Integration and interrelation among the activities of the different modules.
2. Revision and up-dating of bibliography, equipment, and facilities.
3. Evaluation of task sequencing.
4. Adjustment of teaching/learning tasks to the modular and professional objectives.
5. Adjustment of evaluation criteria to unit and modular objectives.
6. Improvement, diversification, and integration of teaching practices and teaching situations.
7. Evaluation of the teaching staff.
8. Evaluation of curricular and extracurricular factors that affect student learning.

With this aim, joint participation of teachers grouped in subject areas has been encouraged to detect problems and recommend and implement solutions. The only elements that guarantee academic effectiveness are the involvement of the entire teaching staff and a gradual incorporation of the student body into the evaluation, analysis, and proposal of concrete measures to solve the problems involved in the varied and rich experience of higher education.

Evaluation of the Project

An important aspect of the curricular project is its evaluation compared with other programs in three specific areas: (1) cost; (2) efficiency; and (3) effectiveness.

1. Cost of the Project. A wide range of criteria to evaluate the cost of an educational program exists. Among others, we may mention the overall budget, the budget for teachers' salaries, the total amount of budget divided by the number of students registered minus those who have dropped out, and the total amount of budget divided by the number of students being graduated.

In the particular case of Iztacala, because psychology is contained in the health sciences unit, the administrative expenses are shared by the various departments, and it is difficult to determine the percentage of the annual cost allocated to each. We have therefore calculated the annual cost per student by dividing the total expense of teaching by the total number of students registered, which includes adjustment for dropouts.

Based on this calculation, the student of Iztacala represents an annual average cost of 7130.60 Mexican pesos (United States currency, $310), which is only 41% of the average annual cost per student of the Universidad Nacional Autonoma de Mexico, whose figures amount to 17,304 Mexican pesos (715 U.S. dollars). Planned budgetary increases to ensure that research becomes a permanent part of teaching represent an annual increase of between $30 and $40 per student. This figure hardly affects the previously mentioned average cost. The cost of facilities does not exceed $150,000 over a span of 4 years (eight laboratories for experimental psychology with 10 working units in each). This amount spread out over an annual budget represents an average increase in the cost per student of $19 per year based on a total student population of 2200).

A frequently asked question is, how is it possible to maintain a program of this nature at such a low cost? There are two answers. On one hand, it is proof that teaching in groups of 30, 15, or even 5 students (as in the case of Iztacala) does not necessarily require a high budget because the typical unnecessary courses of a "content" curriculum are reduced. On the other hand, by specifying concrete teaching/learning situations and tasks in the curriculum, maximum advantage is taken of the teacher's time, which in our institutions is normally a drain of human and economic resources. In Iztacala, each professor covers a range of diverse activities that are proportionally assigned in accordance with the time specified (40, 30, or 20 hours in the case of teachers and 12 hours for teachers' assistants). The teaching loads are distributed as follows: 5% for continuous teacher training; 20% for lecturing or seminar teaching situations; 24% for research, 30% for the supervisory services of tutors and the preparation of teaching material, and 21% for miscellaneous activities.

2. Efficiency of the Program.   We refer here to the operation of the program and not the quality of graduate training. Consequently we may state that a system is efficient when it meets two requirements: (1) low depletion of resources, and (2) detection of flaws in its operation.

As for the depletion of resources, we have already considered the financial and teaching resources under the section on cost evaluation. We must therefore analyze the registration–graduation and dropout retention ratios.

Because the first graduating class has not yet concluded its studies, the information available only indicates certain trends. The first and second incoming generations (March 1975 and January 1976, respectively) entered under the program in operation at that time, that is, the traditional curriculum planned by subjects. These two generations were incorporated into a provisional modular program that in no manner can be considered adequate when viewed from the perspective proposed in this work. The incoming generation of March 1975 had 632 students, and the January 1976 incoming generation numbered 592. At present, these figures have been reduced to 340 students for 1975 (including 93 students held back in previous semesters) and 464 for 1976 (54 students held back in previous semesters). This represents a nominal average dropout of approximately 46% for March 1975 and 28% for 1976. These figures are nominal because many students in their first year requested a transfer to the Psychology School, the mother school at the South campus of the University. During November 1976 and October 1977, 712 and 651 students enrolled, respectively. We do not have dropout rates for the latter because the first semester has not ended; however, in relation to the November 1976 incoming generation, there are to date 487 students, representing a 32% rate of dropouts with 60 students held back in previous semesters.

This information apparently indicates that taking into account the normal population variability, which is tied in many ways to the educational system, we may operate with a loss no greater than 10% of the student body. In this case, the efficiency of the program would be considered high, and we expect to reach this operating level in two academic years.

A second aspect in the evaluation of the efficiency of the system is the detection of the flaws in its functioning. The precise specification of the tasks to be carried out by the teacher, the uniformity of teaching situations and materials, and the objectivity and homogeneity of evaluation criteria and procedures make Iztacala an efficient system. This system of education is efficient inasmuch as it has a built-in, self-corrective mechanism.

Through regular meetings between representatives of the student body and the professors and heads of the curricular areas, the system is continuously evaluated. Furthermore, each year a curricular evaluation of students and teachers is made to systematize the information obtained and to carry out a continuous follow-up of the program efficacy.

Combined commissions are currently being organized by teachers and students for each subject or curricular area to ensure an effective participation of the academic community in the evaluation and improvement of the curriculum.

3. Effectiveness of the Program.   Finally, we wish to mention briefly the effectiveness of the curriculum. By this we mean that the program should accomplish the previously stated objectives and therefore the students and teachers should acquire the specified repertoires and skills. Despite the fact that we do not have a final assessment of results from the first graduating generation, we can trust in the effectiveness of the program for two reasons: (1) the progressive incorporation of students into teaching situations, with considerable decrease in the "complaints" concerning the nature and procedures of teaching, which is reflected in a lower failure rate; (2) the adequate and creative development of teamwork in which the student himself structures the teaching situation.

The direct evaluation of behavior as a general curricular criterion ensures that these observations are based upon the strict fulfillment of the particular tasks precisely specified.

The procedures for behavior evaluation required by the curriculum break away from the traditional programs, which structure and evaluate contents and information and raise the need to evaluate the efficiency in previous activities that are not considered in the program. The efficiency of Iztacala's curriculum is evaluated continuously, in each and every teaching/learning task, because learning, teaching, and evaluating are an integral part of the process itself.

4. Final Considerations.   The program outlined has several important characteristics:

268   RIBES

1. It links professional teaching to high-priority social problems.

2. It breaks with the scholarly and elite conception of professional activity by proposing as its fundamental objective the training of paraprofessional and non-professional individuals.

3. It behaviorally defines teaching situations, ensuring the relevance of the learning tasks and the curricular contents.

4. It treats evaluation as an integral part of the teaching/learning process.

5. It stresses objectively the necessary reciprocity between the behaviors of the teacher and the student.

6. It reorganizes in an innovative manner the traditional problems of psychology and provides a parametric conception of behavior.

7. It demands the effective participation of teachers and students.

The project and its implementation are not a perfect, well-worked-out system; however, it represents an attempt to transform radically our conceptions of teaching in higher education and of the science and profession of psychology. It is particularly meaningful that such a model could arise in a Latin-American country, and we earnestly urge that its implementation, with the necessary modifications applicable to each area of psychology, be considered.

REFERENCES

Kantor, J. R. *Interbehavioral psychology*. Bloomington, Ind.: Principia Press, 1959.

Ribes, E. Formación de profesionales e investigadores en psicología con base en objetivos definidos conductualmente. *Enseñanza e Investigación en Psicología,* 1975, *1,* 18–23.

Ribes, E. *Un programa de formación de profesores: objetivos normativos y esfuerzos iniciales.* Presented at the Third National Meeting for Teaching and Research in Psychology, Monterrey, México, May 1977.

Ribes, E., & Fernández-Gaos, C. Diseño curricular y un programa de formación de profesores: un proyecto de la ENEP-Iztacala. In V. Arredondo, E. Ribes, & E. Robles (Eds.), *Técnicas Instruccionales Aplicadas a la Educación Superior.* México: Trillas, 1979.

10 PSI: Variations on a Theme

Daniel M. Sussman
*Queens College of
the City University of New York*

INTRODUCTION

In his paper entitled "Goodbye Teacher," Keller (1968) described the foundations upon which the personalized system of instruction (PSI) was built. This paper presents five characteristic features of PSI:

(1) The go-at-your-own pace feature, *which permits a student to move through the course at a speed commensurate with his ability and other demands on his time*
(2) The unit perfection requirement for advance, *which lets the student go ahead to new material only after demonstrating mastery of that which preceded*
(3) The use of lectures and demonstrations as vehicles of motivation, *rather than sources of critical information*
(4) The *related* stress upon the written word *in teacher–student communication, and, finally:*
(5) The use of proctors, *which permits repeated testing, immediate scoring, almost unavoidable tutoring, and a marked enhancement of the personal–social aspect of the educational process* [p. 83].

The go-at-your-own pace feature in conjunction with the unit perfection requirement may be expected to produce several highly desirable outcomes. In a multiple-exit system (Greenspoon & Jenson, 1971), in which students' behavior is not constrained by the calendar, they may take full advantage of the freedom given them by self-pacing and complete the course materials at whatever pace best suits them. The variability in the strengths of students entering the system should manifest itself as differences in rate of progress rather than as differences in amount learned; that is, because all students would at some time or other have demonstrated mastery of *all* course materials, there would ultimately be no variability in unit test scores. Because the course materials need not be completed by some fixed date, failure to meet the unit perfection requirement on any given test produces no aversive consequences, and the unit tests serve not only as instruments of measurement but also as valuable teaching vehicles. In a truly open-ended system, the course grade distribution takes on unusual characteristics. All students who complete the course have done so with perfect scores on all tests, and, some variability of scores on final or other uniform examinations notwithstanding, completion of the course assures very high grades. The grade distribution is, in fact, not at all influenced by unit test scores if the unit perfection requirement is employed.

A very different state of affairs prevails when a PSI course is developed with fixed beginning and ending points. If students are required to complete course work in some prespecified period of time, the self-pacing feature is most certainly compromised. More important, the influences of the unit perfection requirement are altered. Failure to achieve a perfect score impedes a student's progress and may, in fact, prevent completion of the course by the deadline. When the end of the allotted time arrives, students will have completed a varying number of units and the grade distribution now is reflective of differential amounts achieved. Some students will have mastered all the course materials, whereas others will have mastered only a portion of them. Under these conditions, a grade distribution is to be expected. Keller has described this as an "upside down" distribution of grades; there is a marked shift in the measures of central tendency toward the higher grades. That there is a grade *distribution,* in the real sense of the word, reflects a shortcoming of a PSI system with semester constraints added.

The most common difficulties associated with PSI systems of this kind are the problems of procrastination and high withdrawal rates. The former is evidenced by uneven rates of progress, with an "end spurt" feature that is most troublesome from both the pedagogical and administrative points of view. If students take many unit quizzes closely spaced in time as the end of the allotted time approaches, the efficacy of their studies must suffer and the "almost unavoidable tutoring" declines in both quality and quantity as proctors are pressured to grade ever-increasing numbers of tests.

The high withdrawal rates associated with PSI courses have been subjected to close scrutiny (Born & Whelan, 1973; Ferster, 1968). These relatively high failure-to-complete ratios are especially irksome in that the students who withdraw with the greatest frequency are those of lesser academic achievement—the very students who might well derive the greatest benefit from the personalized aspect of such courses. That high withdrawal rates have been reported in courses of graduate study (Purohit, Kulieke, Manasse, & Joseph 1977) is further cause for concern.

The aforementioned difficulties were of great concern to us when we considered a design for our ''Introductory Psychology'' course at Queens College. The students who enroll in our course are, for the most part, freshmen and sophomores. There has been a remarkable change in the level of preparation that can be expected of incoming students over the past years. The reading abilities that we have observed have been declining steadily, and in a PSI course in which the greatest stress is placed upon the written word reading ability is of paramount importance. The option to proceed as though nothing had changed was open to us, but there was every reason to suspect that the standard PSI procedure would prove unsatisfactory in dealing with the issues of withdrawal and procrastination for our population of students. Although we did not wish to penalize the stronger students by diluting the quality of the course itself, we did wish to arrange the circumstances such that the weaker students would be able to cope with the demands made of them. The self-pacing feature of PSI obviates the need for a selection of a rate at which materials are to be presented; a judicious choice is crucial in non-PSI curricula if the stronger students are to be challenged and the weaker are not to be overwhelmed. The selection of a text is, however, a more difficult problem for PSI courses. The student is entirely dependent on the text as the primary source of information. Our choice of text was somewhat constrained by our apprehensions concerning reading ability, and the book that was eventually chosen was (by the authors' estimate) written at an eleventh-grade reading level. The informational content is extensive enough so that no students have complained that the course is trivial, and very few students have expressed difficulty with merely reading the text. It was against this background that our reconsideration of certain aspects of the classical PSI format was undertaken.

First, the unit perfection requirement was examined. It should be noted that in many PSI implementations unit perfection has been abandoned in favor of a ''unit mastery'' criterion and that this criterion varies from case to case. It should also be noted that Keller's unit perfection feature emerged directly from the model upon which the system's original design was based and, indeed, that this requirement is dual in nature. The student is required to demonstrate complete facility with the material of the unit and is not permitted to proceed before doing so. The assumption that there exist sequential dependencies among units is most compelling for certain kinds of courses, but this does not seem necessarily to apply to the first course in psychology. It is rather the case that the authors of many introductory psychology texts inform their readers that the sequence in which the chapters in the text are read is immaterial and that chapters may be deleted as the instructor's needs dictate without detrimental effect upon the students' comprehension of the material in other parts of the text. In such cases, the requirement of unit perfection may be separated from rules concerning progress through the course materials without ill effects; that is, even if students are required to meet a perfection criterion, there is no obvious rationale for making advancement contingent upon perfection; the point at which mastery is demonstrated need not be determined by the ordinal position of the unit in question.

Given these considerations, the course that we designed took two important departures from the usual PSI format. First, the unit perfection requirement was altogether eliminated, and students were allowed to proceed to the subsequent material at their own discretion. Second, they were allowed to return to earlier units at any time in order to improve their performances.

The elimination of the unit perfection requirement was not undertaken lightly. The prospect of all or at least most students leaving a course with complete mastery of the material presented is certainly a most attractive feature of personalized instruction. The mastery concept is so much an integral part of PSI that the first of the "fifteen reasons not to use PSI" enumerated by Green (1974) is: "mastery is not the object of your course." It should be made clear at this point that mastery *was* the object of our course but that the demand for mastery by all students carries with it consequences that we deemed highly undesirable. The decision to allow each student to determine his/her own criterion was vindicated by the fact that the majority of our students chose to impose upon themselves criteria stringent enough to meet the standards externally imposed in many PSI courses. It is of course true that this was not the case for all students, but it is never the case that all students master all units even when mastery requirements are in effect.

What follows is a description of the PSI course in introductory psychology that was offered in the Spring 1977 semester and the outcomes of this course.

THE QUEENS COLLEGE PSI COURSE

The text that was the core of our curriculum was *Foundations of Psychology* by Lamberth, McCullers, and Mellgren (New York: Harper and Row, 1976). There are 14 chapters in this book and each of these constituted one unit. Beginning with a 75-item question pool for each unit, 50 alternate forms of each unit quiz were generated by a computer program that guaranteed that each form would test all the 15 behavioral objectives written for each unit. Students were given access to unit quizzes for 2 hours per week with the restriction that no more than two quizzes could be attempted during 1 hour and that no more than one test on a particular unit could be attempted in 1 hour. Advancement to unit $n + 1$ was contingent solely upon having attempted unit n at least once, and students were free to retrace their paths through the units. A maximum of four attempts per unit was allowed, and only the highest score obtained was counted toward the course grade. The quizzes were graded immediately by undergraduate proctors, who discussed with the students any difficulties revealed by the test. Each proctor was responsible for approximately seven students; the personal–social aspect of tutoring was enhanced by the permanent assignment of students to particular proctors.

The proctors were selected via written applications and interviews, and they were given course credit as compensation for their efforts. There was a graduate student present in a supervisory role at all times.

In addition to the 2 hours of testing, students were scheduled for 2 hours per week that were devoted to lectures and group discussions. None of the material presented at these meetings appeared on any test. These lecture–discussion meetings were supervised by a graduate student, and the size of each group was initially 50. As attendance at these meetings was not mandatory, the number of students who took advantage of them declined rapidly.

A comprehensive final examination was administered to all students at the end of the semester; it consisted of 10 items from each unit, or a total of 140 items. The final examination contributed 19% of a student's course grade; the remainder was determined by unit test scores.

Analysis of Data

Figure 10.1 is the grade distribution that resulted from the procedure just outlined; this is the "upside down" distribution discussed by Keller (1968) and widely reported in the PSI literature. The modal grade was A, the median A−, and the mean B+.

Figure 10.2 presents mean high score for all students for each of the units (broken line, right ordinate) and the mean date on which each of these was obtained (solid line, left ordinate). A total of 28 testing sessions was available during the semester and, for ease of presentation, session numbers rather than calendar dates are used as the metric of progress rates.

Mean high score across units is 90%, and this in the absence of any mastery criterion. The mean date function is very well fitted by a line ($y = 1.66\ x\ +$

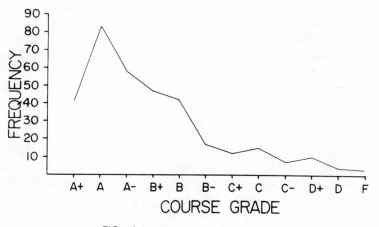

FIG. 10.1.   Course grade distribution.

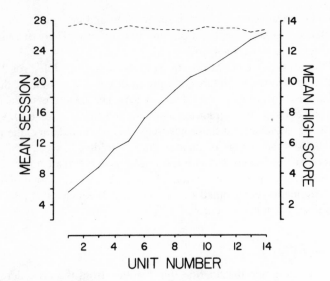

FIG. 10.2.   Mean high score (broken line) and mean date (solid line) as a function of unit number. Scores are read on the right ordinate; dates, on the left.

4.50, r^2 = .99). These data indicated very high overall achievement level with
no evidence of procrastination.

A further examination of progress rates was performed by partitioning the
population according to course grade obtained at the end of the course. The
resulting functions are presented in Fig. 10.3. Regardless of course grade, progress rates are linear.

As mentioned earlier, a course such as the one presently described cannot be
expected to eliminate differential quiz performance as would be the case in a
perfection-oriented open-ended course. Differences among students are presented in two ways in Fig. 10.4. The mean scores of first attempts on Unit 1 as a
function of course grade obtained are depicted by the function labeled FIRST. As
this function reflects performances on the very first test that students take, it may
be viewed as an indication of incoming differences. The function labeled ALL
presents mean scores on first attempts pooled across all units as a function of
course grade. Although there are small changes in scores of the students who
obtained the lower scores, the ranking of students is consistent with the FIRST
function.

Repeated testing is a central feature of a PSI system and as we limited the
number of tests that could be taken on any single unit, analysis of the effects of
retesting was certainly necessary. It should be noted that few students exhausted
all available testing opportunities and there was a positive correlation between
course grade and total number of tests taken. More will be said about this
correlation when final examination results are discussed.

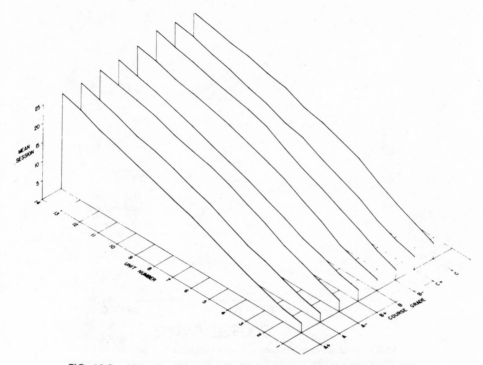

FIG. 10.3.   Mean date for each unit for the grades of A+ through C. Lower grades are not included due to the low frequency of grades below C.

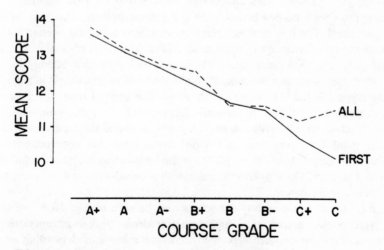

FIG. 10.4.   Mean scores of first attempts at Unit 1 (FIRST) and first attempts across all units (ALL) as a function of course grade.

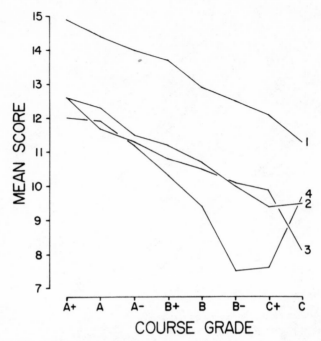

FIG. 10.5. Mean score on first attempt across all units as a function of course grade. Four functions are presented—one for units taken once (1), one for units taken twice (2), and so on. The reader should note that the data are all for *first* attempts regardless of the number of attempts made.

Figure 10.5 presents data concerning mean scores on first attempts at unit quizzes. Data were pooled across units and across students, and four functions were generated. The first of these relates mean score on the first attempt for those units attempted only once to course grade. This function is identified as "1" in Fig. 10.5. The second function depicts mean score on the first attempt for those units attempted twice as a function of course grade. This function is labeled "2." The function labeled "3" refers to those units attempted three times, and the units attempted four times are shown in function "4." What is noteworthy here is that the students who will not attempt a unit a second time are clearly discriminable from those who will take additional quizzes, but no prediction as to number of attempts that will be made can be based upon the score achieved on the initial attempt. Once again, the relationship between quiz scores and course grade remains consistent.

The effects of retesting on quiz scores may be seen in Fig. 10.6. Again, the data were pooled across units and across students, and four functions were generated. First, units were separated into four categories depending on how many attempts were made. A mean score was computed for all units taken only once. For units taken twice, means were calculated for the first and second

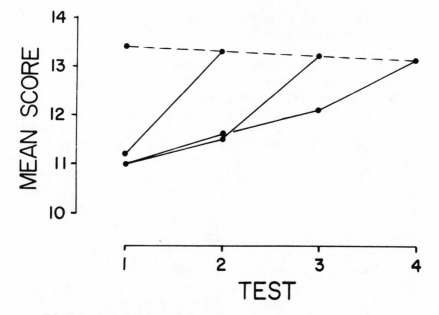

FIG. 10.6.   Mean score on unit quizzes as a function of successive attempts. Data are pooled across students and units; separate functions are shown for units attempted once, twice, three, and four times.

attempts separately. Analogous treatment was given to those units attempted three and four times. The functions in Fig. 10.6 depict progressive changes in test scores. The point in the uppermost left location is the mean score for those units attempted once. The function consisting of two points depicts mean first and second attempt scores for units taken twice, and so on. The broken line represents final performance level and reveals that the ultimate score obtained is independent of number of attempts made. Final performance level is 90% correct, the maximum attainable score being 15.

Performance on the cumulative final examination is also of interest. The examination consisted of 140 items, 10 from each of the 14 units. The mean score was 83% correct, a figure that is consistent with reports from mastery-based systems. There was no evidence of serial position effects.

Some attention was given to the correlation between course grade and number of units taken. As the items on the final examination were drawn from the same pool as those on the unit quizzes, differential numbers of tests taken results in differences in preexposure to items on the final examination. As there was a very high correlation between unit quiz performance ($r = .81$) and final examination score, the hypothesis that variance in final examination scores could be accounted for by differences in number of items preexposed was considered. Suffice it to say that the functions relating mean number of items preexposed and mean score on the final examination to course grade have slopes sufficiently different to discount this hypothesis.

The course as presently described has been in operation for three semesters and has, to date, served more than 1500 students. For all semesters, dropout rates have been less than 9%, a figure not different from that observed in standard courses at Queens College. This finding gains importance from the fact that the grade of "Incomplete" has never been used in the PSI courses and that students are permitted to withdraw without penalty at any time from the PSI course. Both of these features should inflate withdrawal rates, and the comparison of the PSI course to those in which "Incomplete" is an option open to students and the possibility of a "Withdrawn while failing" grade acts to suppress withdrawals is heavily weighted in favor of the standard courses. In spite of this, our dropout rates are no higher than those associated with the non-PSI courses and are considerably lower than those reported in the PSI literature.

Surveys of student opinion have produced data highly favorable to a PSI approach. Students enjoy the course, prefer self-pacing and repeated testing, and report that they invest a great deal of time and effort in study. We have also conducted a survey of those students who did withdraw, and the great majority of those responding indicated that problems not related to the course were the primary determiners of withdrawal. Most indicated that they would enroll in another PSI course and would recommend this format to others.

Discussion

It is our belief that two of the findings reported—no evidence of procrastination and low withdrawal rates—are due to the fact that students were permitted to proceed through the course materials whenever they saw fit. It is never the case that a student is forced into repeated testing on a single unit in order that some criterion score be achieved. They were allowed the freedom of returning to earlier units to improve a score or "settling" for any score. Although it is true that some students settle for performances that we would very much prefer to see improved, these students do not withdraw from the course. Not all our students master all the material in our curriculum. This is, of course, also true of any system from which a grade distribution results. In our case, nonmastery may occur within units, whereas in criterion-based systems in which the units must be taken in sequence nonmastery most often implies that some units were never attempted. One variety of nonmastery does not seem preferable to the other, but the concomitant effects recommend one approach in our view.

It is clearly the case in our course that most students set high standards for themselves; this argues that the elimination of the mastery requirement is not of primary importance with respect to our other findings. Unfortunately, our initial design was somewhat shortsighted with respect to the isolation of critical variables, and our myopia is only now being corrected. We are at present conducting a study aimed at determining the importance of requiring that the units be taken in only one order. We presently have 600 students in the PSI system; they are enrolled in 12 classes of 50. Four different methods are being employed with these students, and 150 are being exposed to each variation. One group is required to demonstrate mastery of a unit before being allowed to proceed to the next and will not be permitted to return to earlier units. A second group is also required to meet the mastery criterion, but they are allowed to do so in whatever order they elect; that is, failure to meet the mastery criterion (14 of 15 correct) on Unit n does not preclude advancement to Unit $n + 1$ with a return to Unit n at some future date. At the semester's end, however, these students will be given credit only for those units on which they have scored at least 14. For the two additional groups no mastery criterion is being employed. The students in one of these groups are not permitted to return to an earlier unit in order to improve a score obtained prior to advancement, although for the other students this option is available. It should be possible, on the basis of the data that we collect during the current semester, to assess the importance of a mastery criterion or lack thereof and the importance of an imposed sequence requirement. With the exception of some few necessary changes (e.g., the elimination of the four-tests-per-unit restriction), all other features of the course remain unaltered. This will allow for interesting comparisons of data from previous semesters with each of the four variations now being used. It is our hope that we will be in a position, at the close of this semester, to implement a system that will yield the greatest benefit to the student population we are called upon to serve.

ACKNOWLEDGMENTS

The author wishes to thank K. Pospisil and N. Detsis for their help in the preparation of unit quizzes. To Richard Valente and to Dorothy Mao-Cohen, whose assistance and advice have been indispensable, the author expresses deepest gratitude.

REFERENCES

Born, D. G., & Whelan, P. Some descriptive characteristics of student performance in PSI and lecture courses. *The Psychological Record, 23,* 1973, 145–152.

Ferster, C. B. Individualized instruction in an introductory psychology course. *The Psychological Record, 18,* 1968, 521–532.

Green, B. A. Fifteen reasons not to use PSI. In Sherman, J. G. (Ed.), *41 germinal papers.* Menlo Park, Calif.: W. A. Benjamin, 1974.

Greenspoon, J., & Jenson, P. G. New dimensions in higher education: The new college program of Temple Buell College. *Educational Technology,* 1971, *11,* 20–23.

Keller, F. S. Goodbye teacher . . . *Journal of Applied Behavior Analysis,* 1968, *1,* 79–89.

Purohit, A. A., Kulieke, M. J., Manasse, H. R., & Joseph, P. A. *Student withdrawal rates, their personality correlates and the self-directed/regular students.* Paper presented at the Fourth National Conference of the Center for Personalized Instruction, San Francisco, 1977.

11 Do the Data Count?

J. Gilmour Sherman
Georgetown University

INTRODUCTION

The title of this chapter "Do the Data Count?" perhaps unfairly places an extra burden on a message that must cross language barriers. The title is intended to have several meanings. Under less demanding circumstances I might proceed without clarification, letting those multiple meanings emerge as the discussion goes on. In this case let me be less subtle and enumerate the three interpretations of the title; the three aspects of PSI that I want to discuss.

The first meaning of "Do the Data Count?" is do the data add up? What are the data? What do we know? What do the data indicate at this point?

The second meaning of the title can be rephrased as "do the data matter?" What difference do the data make? Has anything changed in the classrooms? Has anything changed in the councils of educational administrators because of what the data tells us? Is anyone paying any attention to the data?

Finally as a third meaning, there is the question of whether or not we know how to count what is important. Do the quantitative measures we now have serve to measure what we know (in a qualitative way) are important results of PSI? Are we counting, measuring, and quantifying the right things?

To further forecast what I want to talk about, let me indicate that in the first sense of the title the data add up to a story that is almost embarrassingly success-ful. That only serves, by contrast, to make the rest of this chapter somewhat gloomy. Perhaps that tells us something about what we should do next.

BACKGROUND

Let me now retreat and, for the benefit of those not familiar with the Personalized System of Instruction, briefly describe PSI. Generally PSI is a procedure or method for implementing the philosophy of individualized instruction. It shifts the emphasis of education to a goal of teaching for accomplishment from that of merely selecting for achievement.

In practice, the normal lecture format is replaced by permanent forms of content presentation. Carefully prepared assignments consisting of sections from standard textbooks, articles, and specially prepared supplements are given to the student, along with study questions and other instructions as to what to read, in what order, and for what information. Other sources of important content may be derived from the laboratory, the media, and the community. When the student thinks he has mastered the material, he comes to the classroom to take a brief quiz. This is immediately corrected by a proctor. If there are errors, the proctor indicates what part of the assignment needs further study; the student goes off to work some more and then comes back to try again. The tests are not exams in the normal sense; students are not penalized by a lowered grade because of an error. The tests are not graded at all but, rather, are a device and an opportunity to demonstrate master or detect confusions, the latter to be corrected before they lead to serious trouble. Because there is no penalty for mistakes, the student is free to keep trying until mastery is achieved. Excellence can be demanded and grades are determined solely on how much of the material is finally mastered. As a student masters a unit, he then moves on to the next unit, proceeding through the course at his own pace, demonstrating his competence each step of the way.

I would mention only four more things by way of background. First, in spite of all that people have tried to do to it, PSI is a simple idea. That may be one of its main virtues. I am sometimes embarrassed to describe PSI to a group of teachers, feeling that the reaction may well be "Yes, but we all knew that; now tell us something new." It is only when I visit classrooms and find these same teachers violating everything we know about procedures that lead students to learn that I gain the courage to speak again about something so simple.

Second, let me emphasize that PSI resulted from a deliberate application of learning theory and is related to a data base and a theory that is by no means simple. Whim, fancy, and caprice played little part in the design of PSI. Teachers wishing to teach PSI courses need not delve deeply into this basic literature, but those wishing to modify the basic procedures of PSI might well do so.

That PSI is simple and yet related to a sophisticated theory of learning gives rise to my third background point, which is to stress that the Personalized System of Instruction *is* a system. It is a method designed to be used by chemists, language instructors, and grade-school teachers who have not the time, opportunity, or even inclination to learn the principles of instructional design. Now I am aware that many readers, with expertise in education and/or psychology, could add modifications with wisdom or devise complex, elegant, alternative procedures that would prove as successful, or perhaps even more so. But that is not quite the point. One advantage of PSI is that, with minimal preparation, it is available to a community college English teacher in Iowa, a teacher in the technological schools of Mexico, someone working to decrease the illiteracy problem in northeast Brazil, or a third-grade math teacher in the Netherlands, as well as to those of us who are specialists in educational psychology. I am pleased that several teachers in Venezuela are teaching PSI courses. Two who come immediately to mind are Professor J.A. Rodrequez of Instituto Pedagogico and Professor Dario Moreno of Simon Bolivar University. Their work, along with other Venezuelan colleagues, is important and it counts.

I mentioned Brazil a moment ago, and it is my fourth and final background note. The initial development of PSI was a collaborative effort of two North Americans and two Brazilians. Most of the early work was done at Brazilia and PSI research and application continues vigorously in Brazil today.

WHAT THE DATA INDICATE

Because the invitation for this chapter requested that I discuss the data, let me turn to that meaning of the title first. Without taking an actual count, the number of articles about PSI must exceed 1000. There are a number of reviews of this literature. So that the references are available, let me cite three excellent and comprehensive summaries—one by Hursh (1976); another by Robin (1976); and a third by Johnson and Ruskin (1977). With some duplication, these reviews cite many hundreds of studies.

This research falls into two main categories: (1) studies comparing PSI to more conventional styles of instruction; and (2) experiments attempting to analyze the essential characteristics or components of PSI. There have been hundreds of comparative studies. Thomas Taveggia (1976) examined some of these and wrote ''The major conclusion suggested by this summary of research is that, when evaluated by average student performance on course content examinations, the Personalized System of Instruction has proven superior to the conventional teaching methods with which it has been compared.'' One would only have to add that ''no other teaching method can make that claim'' to make the whole thing sound like a television commercial advertising toothpaste! Whatever the rhetoric, the conclusions were justifiable then. The multiplying number of research reports during the last 4 years would not change that conclusion.

James Kulik (1976) examined a greater number of studies, and in more detail. He considered five indicators: (1) end-of-course performance; (2) retention; (3) transfer; (4) facilitation; and (5) student attitudes and preference. He found PSI to have advantages in all five categories. But many of us working in education are familiar, even flooded, with statistics. Sadly, variables that require a ''t-test'' to find are of very little significance to students, teachers, and classroom procedure.

Addressing this question, Kulik (1976) wrote:

> Let us take an average student, who may take his introductory physics course, for example, by a conventional method or by PSI. If he takes a typical lecture course, his achievement in physics will place him in the 50th percentile on a standardized test. He is an average student in an average course. If he takes the same course in a PSI format, he will achieve at the 75th percentile on the same standardized test. This increment—the PSI effect—is what PSI has to offer the individual student. If you take the PSI effect and multiply it by 100—the number of students a typical teacher has in a term—you have some conception of what PSI has to offer the individual teacher. . . . For most students and most teachers, these effects will not seem small.

To me, the more interesting type of research is studies attempting to analyze the essential characteristics or components of PSI. Since Keller's (1968) original paper, the five defining characteristics of PSI have been taken to be (1) the mastery criterion; (2) self-pacing; (3) a stress on the written word; (4) lectures as a source of motivation rather than information; and (5) the use of proctors. All five characteristics have been the subject of extensive research, attempting to determine the importance of each, and further define the meaning and limits of each.

The Hursh (1976) paper I mentioned earlier examines the research of these components, some in great detail. For example in terms of the function of the written word he considers the construction of units, unit size, use of study questions, types of quiz questions, etc. In the category of proctors, Hursh examines the research on internal and external proctors, appropriate proctor behaviors, and proctor training. All this is too extensive and too complex to report here, and it is readily available in the literature. Let me simply quote Hursh's conclusions:

> Data presented in investigations of various aspects of components of PSI give reason to be confident of some, but impel further investigation of many more. Use of study questions and/or objectives, inclusion of a mastery criterion, provision of incentives for reasonable rates of progress through a course, and appointment of proctors all appear to be well supported by the experimental literature. The literature fails to provide clear-cut definitions for unit size and format, format of study questions and/or objectives, and quizzing routine and format. We still do not know the best way to shape student pacing, how to delineate the most effective proctor behaviors and train for them, or whether the lecture has a part to play in a personalized course.

The data then tells us that PSI is advantageous and that all components of the system have been experimentally validated as important (with the possible exception of the motivational lecture). We are approaching a more precise understanding of the limits and value of each component, and there is more to do and improvements to make.

IMPACT OF THE DATA

But has all this data made any difference? On the positive side PSI may well have generated the largest body of coherent, systematic research in the literature of education. The rest of the story is less happy. Researchers continue to expend scarce and valuable time and money to repeat the comparative experiment. Although healthy scepticism is probably a virtue, after hundreds of such experiments, yielding consistent results, to repeat it can only mean the data do *not* count.

From another viewpoint, what would a comparative study showing a lecture course to produce better results mean at this point? After several hundred such studies, if the data counts, we should be forced to conclude that this particular PSI course was poorly designed. But we learn more about how to design a poor PSI course and also how to design a still better one from component analysis studies. If data counts, it is time to stop repeating the comparative study.

Teachers do not appear to adopt PSI because of the data. In a recent dissertation Boylan (1977) asked respondents for their reasons for adopting PSI. Of the 102 responses to this question only seven teachers said their reason was that the system appears to have some validity. Although some other responses were related to research results, particularly student attitude and preference data, most teachers adopt PSI for "other" reasons—if Boylan's data are to be believed, if his data count.

The data do not appear to matter to most educational journals. They go on publishing studies of little relevance or usefulness in the classroom. As is the case in general, educational journals appear willing to look at almost anything—age; sex; racial, demographic, curriculum restructuring; forgetting curves; class size; team teaching; cost effectiveness; grading policies; and 12 factor theories of intelligence—everything except what is happening to an individual student at the moment he learns something.

If teachers, researchers, and educational journals are ignoring the data, perhaps we should not be too critical when administrators, foundations, and government agencies ignore them also. Vast sums have been spent on educational research and development, but the return on this investment has been slight because serious efforts at application of what has been learned are almost nonexistent. In schools and classrooms, not much happens of any significance, magnitude, and duration. A fascinating "demonstration" takes place for a year or two, on one or two campuses, and then is replaced by what funding agencies constantly seek—"somethine new." It is my opinion that fads in education, and the general lack of progress, is at least in part the result of a funding-support policy constantly in search of novelty. It is sad that the greater appeal of novelty, over the appeal of data, works to prevent the very changes supposedly sought. Those who support novelty for its own sake, perhaps unwittingly, contribute to gimmicks, opportunism, transitory real improvements, disillusion, and the low estate of education in practice, results, and as a discipline.

Governments appear to be particulary attracted to not only something new but specifically new machines, new hardware, and new pieces of instrumentation. The potential benefits of hardware are sufficient to use this as an example, digressing for a moment to comment on how the data might matter in considering the function of hardware. The appeal of hardware is *probably* not unrelated to the tangible properties of machines. It is the *form* of hardware rather than its *function* that generates enthusiasm. Decisions about the purchase of everything from a slide projector to a satellite come under the control of things that have nothing to do with the learning process. The consequences can only be that students won't learn, money will be wasted, valuable instruments will become gadgets, hardware and educational technology in general will be discredited, and the potential for systematically developing more effective instructional systems will be lost.

THE COMPONENTS OF THE LEARNING PROCESS

We must look at exactly what we almost always neglect—a student in the process of learning. A learner's progress is dependent on three things: (1) the information, materials, and situation presented; (2) the performance required; and (3) the immediate feedback or consequences provided. All three components are essential; no one is sufficient; not one can be neglected. Of paramount importance is the adjusting *relation* among presentation, performance, and results. Any delivery system, to be effective, must function so as to relate the three components. *Hardware must be designed, purchased, used, and judged in terms of its ability to serve this function.*

When not designed with the three components of the learning process in mind there is the danger of conceiving of delivery systems in terms of presentation alone. Although hardware (media) may at times present material more dramatically, more spectacularly, and more accurately, revealing greater complexity than is otherwise possible, presentation is only one-third of the problem. How the student makes contact with what is presented, what he is called upon to do, and what happens to him as a consequence are of equal importance. There are some kinds of information, some concepts, that cannot be presented without the use of hardware. But again we cannot take a better presentation as sufficient.

Effective teaching must maintain the appropriate relation among the three components essential for learning. This statement is neutral with respect to the use or nonuse of hardware, or lectures, or any other educational practice. But it does tell us how to judge, evaluate, and use appropriately the various tools of education. In its broadest sense the data tell us we must be concerned with the presentation of information, student response, and consequent feedback. When any kind of instruction provides for only presentation (or only response, or only feedback), it must be used in an educational environment that otherwise supplies the missing components. Seldom are educational decisions discussed in these terms. Again the data do not seem to matter.

If I have overstated the case and presented too gloomy a picture, it is because if anyone is to respect the data, they must first be respected by groups such as this. We can expect teachers, researchers, journals, administrators, foundations, and governments to listen only when we are willing to say the data count.

THE COMPREHENSIVENESS OF PSI RESEARCH

Let me touch upon very briefly, the third meaning of my title—are we measuring all that is important in a PSI course? I have said before (Sherman, 1977) that regardless of the array of facts learned and syllogisms solved, instruction is not adequate if the student remains dependent on others to prescribe what to learn and when to learn it, motivated only by the approval or criticism of an authoritarian figure or the artificial rewards currently used by our educational systems.

Such issues may include the problem of learning to learn, even more clearly, learning to make judgments about what is worth learning, and finally deciding when something has been learned. Terms like *self-assessment, self-sufficiency,* and *responsibility* come to mind. Whether the problems I am discussing are assigned to the cognitive or affective domain, related to creativity or self-actualization, *the question comes down to considering the locus of control.* No system of education is adequate if the teacher makes all the judgments until graduation day; the dependent student is set free to go it alone thereafter. Such instruction is defective in ways clearly important to later life.

What is needed is a procedure for the gradual transfer of control from the teacher to the student, *at a rate commensurate with the student's demonstrated ability to make appropriate judgments.* The balance between structure and choice will probably not be a straight-line function for any individual and certainly could not be prescribed for groups according to some formal property of time. The transfer of control calls for personalized instruction and fits neatly with the procedure of PSI.

The transfer of control should include transferring decisions about competency goals, teaching procedures, and assessment criteria and presentation, performance, and results. I see no way in which such an adjusting, individually adjusted transfer of control can be accomplished within education as normally practiced.

The Role of the Proctor

Here the proctor can be of special importance. The proctor as originally conceived was introduced as a solution to some logistical problems and/or as a cost-saving character. But the proctor has proved to be more than that. There has been an assumption of long-standing duration in education that students need to be taught by experts, and the more expert the better. This turns out not to be true, but the belief has led us into wasteful, gross misallocation of talent. The mistake is expensive. The proctor has proved in many instances to be a more effective instructor than the professional. The gap between those who know almost everything about a subject and those who know almost nothing about it is too large to bridge easily, comfortably, or effectively for long periods. I am constantly embarrassed to find my proctors doing a better job of explaining something than I can. On the one hand, professionals are inclined to provide answers considerably more complex than is warranted by the question asked. On the other hand, we teachers have often solved the problem for ourselves so long ago that we can no longer understand why there is a problem or why the answer isn't obvious. We do need experts. They have an important teaching function *when their talent is required* and an important role to monitor the system—but proctors can carry much of the instructional role, and do it better!

But that is only part of the story. The proctor is a new figure in education important for yet other pedagogical reasons. Studies have shown that the proctor learns more than anyone. The proctor role provides the student with the opportunity to *use* newly acquired knowledge—if only to teach others. The reward for learning becomes the usefulness of the information itself. Rather than collecting trinkets, the student, as proctor, will learn because he is reinforced for knowing. Proctoring becomes a way of making the acquisition of information immediately worthwhile. Because most information is not normally of immediate benefit, instruction that does not include the proctor function must continue to rely on more contrived rewards.

Both self-assessment and peer-assessment are integral parts of PSI, although not fully exploited in this sense to date. The proctor and other aspects of PSI provide ways for the *gradual* transfer of control from the teacher to the student. There is much we can do to teach students to manage their own learning systematically. There is every reason to do so. But this means we must learn to quantify more subtle aspects of PSI than what we have been counting so far.

CONCLUSION

I have tried to suggest that the data add up to a record of accomplishment that warrants the implementation of PSI courses. Education has not really changed on a large scale. It is time that it should. As it does, we should go on to learn how PSI can be used to teach more than the mastery of facts. Learning could become a major part of life, an experience full of fun and joy, resulting in self-control and consequent self-respect. Those who administer educational systems will only help us achieve this very possible goal when *we* are willing to make it clear that the data count.

REFERENCES

Boylan, H. R. *A survey of adoption and implementation practices among users of the Personalized System of Interaction*. Unpublished doctoral dissertation, Bowling Green State University, Ohio, 1977.

Hursh, D. E. Personalized system of instruction: What do the data indicate? *Journal of Personalized Instruction*, 1976, *1*, 91–105.

Johnson, K. R., & Ruskin, R. S. *Behavioral instruction: An evaluative review*. Washington, D.C.: American Psychological Association, 1977.

Keller, F. S. Goodbye teacher . . . . *Journal of Applied Behavior Analysis*, 1968, *1*, 79–89.

Kulik, J. A. PSI: A formative evaluation. In B. A. Green (Ed.), *Personalized Instruction in Higher Education—Proceedings of the Second National Conference*. Washington, D.C.: Georgetown University, 1976.

Robin, A. R. Behavioral instruction in the college classroom. *Review of Educational Research*, 1976, *46*, 313–354.

Sherman, J. G. Individualizing instruction is not enough. *Educational Technology*, 1977, *17*, (9), 56–60.

Taveggia, T. C. Personalized instruction: A summary of comparative research, 1967–1974. *American Journal of Physics*, November 1976, *44*, 1028–1033.

IV COMMENTS

12 Notes on Educational Reform

Fred S. Keller
University of North Carolina, Chapel Hill

INTRODUCTION

I shall direct my remarks to *students* and shall begin with a description of the teaching behavior of a man I knew at Columbia University many years ago. I shall not disclose his name, for reasons that will soon become apparent.

This man gave lectures to his pupils. In these lectures he often pretended that he knew things that he really didn't. Sometimes in his lectures he would make a beautiful statement but forget to put quotation marks around it. Sometimes, in the classroom, if he were asked a question that he could not answer, he would use tricks to avoid disclosure of his ignorance. When the hand went up, he might look the other way, or he would call the question esoteric or too complicated for a general discussion. He would sometimes tell the student to wait until after class to talk about it, when he knew that he or the student would have to be at some other place as soon as the class was ended.

Sometimes he lied to his students. For example, he would tell them: "All of you should pass this course successfully," when this was not at all what he expected. He would say, "I would like you all to receive to receive an *A* (the highest grade)," but he would have been upset if this had happened. He would say, "Anyone can understand the content of this course," when he knew that there were places in the textbook that he couldn't understand himself. He would say, "I shall treat you fairly." But then he would change the letters around at the end of the course in order to bring about a satisfactory distribution of the grades. He gave examinations to his pupils twice each term, with never an opportunity to defend their answers to the questions. He let the better students in his class determine the grade that we would call an *A*—the best performance of the group;

and the better students learned that if they were unable to understand some passage of the text, no one else could, and there would probably be no questions based upon it.

He ignored the personal problems of the student that might sometimes interfere with study, except for absence from the class through illness. He generally avoided students who had complaints. His office hours were rarely used for personal consultation.

He engaged in self-deception. He thought himself successful as a teacher when 10% of his class did as well as all of them should have done, when an even smaller percentage went on to higher studies, or when his class maintained a large enrollment. He felt especially successful when he was rated highly on a student popularity scale.

Worst of all, I think, this man helped to corrupt his pupils. He often led them to lie, to steal, to bribe, to beg, to plagiarize, and to practice other evils. He made some of his pupils hate the educational process and everything connected with it. He taught a few of them to be exhibitionistic and pedantic. He taught many of them to feel inferior for years to come. And he did all this in the name of service to society.

I saw this man frequently as the years went by, and I noticed certain changes taking place in his behavior. More and more his lectures were diluted in their content. He earned some reputation as a showman. He told more jokes and anecdotes. He used more visual aids than he had used in earlier years. He graded tests with somewhat less severity. He reduced his lecture load as much as he was able. Students came to speak of him as a "character." I think you get the general picture. And I guess you probably know by now that the teacher I am describing was myself.

THE PSI FORMAT

When the Brazilian dream was realized by Professor Sherman and myself at Arizona State University, we discovered that we had a system in which it was impossible to escape from students. It was unnecessary and we did not want to do so. We gave them tasks that were within their reach and we gave them guidance when it was needed. We required that they did their learning before they went ahead to other learning; and we gave them maximal reward when the tasks assigned had been completed. We gave them personal consideration such as they had never had before. The most important agent in providing this, as Professor Sherman noted in Chapter 11, was the student *monitor* (we called him *proctor*). It was this feature of our system, more than any other, that provided the "personal" touch to "personalized instruction."

As a result of our adoption of this system, student lying, cheating, stealing, whining, and complaining decreased in volume. We no longer had to be concerned, as teachers, with showmanship and classroom tricks. No longer was there need for self-deception, compromise of principle, or distortion of our records. We knew exactly what was studied by our students, and we knew the difficulties with it—theirs and ours. We knew what we expected of them and their monitors, and we got it. Moreover, when we walked among these young men and women at their work or met them on the campus, we received friendly smiles and respectful greetings—approach behavior rather than avoidance.

Since 1965, a great deal has happened. The system has been extended, as you know, to other courses, other disciplines, and other levels of education; to technological institutes, to military and industrial training, and in other quarters, not just in Brazil and the United States but in almost every major country of the world.

Almost always individual instructors are the ones who adopt the procedure; seldom do entire departments or institutions do so. And almost always modifications must be made in order that it may survive within an educational establishment that was built up to support a rival system—that of group instruction. Sometimes I think that PSI will be absorbed within the older system; at other times I feel that it will ultimately win the battle. There are several reasons why it should:

1. The entire field of education is in trouble, especially in the United States. It has failed to carry out its basic function of transmitting culture from one generation to the next. This weakness may have been disclosed by the war in Vietnam and by other factors, but it was there before, only waiting to be brought to light. We simply have not done the job of teaching that we should have or that the needs of modern times require. The decline of education is a matter of growing concern throughout our land.

2. The spread of PSI, or something like it, goes on at an increasing pace, as individual instructors continue to adopt the plan. In the end, sheer weight of numbers may prevail.

3. PSI is based upon the experimental analysis of behavior. It will grow in both efficiency and effectiveness as the science of behavior continues to develop and expand.

IMPLICATIONS OF WIDESPREAD ADOPTION OF PSI

Widespread adoption of our system, if it happens, should have some interesting effects. The power of the calendar and the clock may disappear in education. Students of all ages may be involved, not just in groups at special hours or on special days but as individuals going to and from their teachers and their monitors for personal consideration, guidance, and evaluation.

We can look for changes in the size of courses and corresponding changes in our textbooks, in accordance with the nature of the subject matter taught. The analysis of educational content will continue to be made and will provide more routes to different goals, in accordance with the student's desires, the community requirements, or the nation's needs.

All subject matters are, I think, intrinsically interesting when well taught, but we may find that emphasis on those subjects that lead to university degrees will be reduced. Universities will continue to provide support for scholars and researchers; libraries and laboratories will continue to have great importance; but other occupations and professions have intrinsic interest too and give equal satisfaction when continued failure is impossible in any sphere.

The physical structure of the universities and other educational institutions will be altered. Amphitheatres may be used on rare occasions; and crowds will not collect except at games and other entertainments. The inner structure of our buildings will be altered to suit the individual needs of those who use them.

Students will be evaluated not in relative terms but on the basis of their record of achievement—the catalog of their accomplishments. Universities and colleges should probably not pretend to grade them on some merit scale that goes beyond the boundaries of what was actually taught and learned within their courses. Let the user of the product do the grading.

All this is dreaming, I suppose. Since 1638, however, when Comenius set the stage for group instruction, changes have been made in almost every sphere of knowledge and of practice; why not in education?

13 Behavior Modification: Problems and Limitations

Roberto Ruíz
Edmundo Chirinos
Universidad Central de Venezuela

Behavior modification is basically a technological development derived from the findings of operant conditioning. These findings have the framework of B. F. Skinner's research with his well-known experimental procedure. However, reference to Skinner is not always exclusively related to his experimental discoveries; it is also associated with a set of assumptions about the development of a science of behavior and its relationship to a behavioral technology. Thus, in "Beyond Freedom and Dignity" (1971) and in "Science and Human Behavior" (1953), Skinner states with great optimism that it is possible to develop from the findings in operant conditioning a technology capable of solving problems as wide and different as pollution and urban planning, legal norms and ethics.

THE MEANING OF A TECHNOLOGY OF BEHAVIOR

A first question refers to what a technology of behavior is. For many it has a simple answer: The technology of behavior, better known as *behavior modification* or *applied behavior analysis,* is the application of the principles of reinforcement. The issue appears to be what these applications are: Do they consist of any response or system of responses being governed by the laws of reinforcement? And, in consequence, is it a fact that any unit of behavior can be changed according to these principles? The answer to the former question seems to be negative: The findings about reinforcement seem to apply only to some responses and it is not perfectly clear to which they do not. For instance, can we say that cardiac conditioning is governed by the laws of reinforcement? And if the answer is affirmative, how can we explain the difficulty in the extinction of a conditioned cardiac response? In short the first problem refers to the inherent limitations of the principles of reinforcement as we know them for the understanding and control of different types of behavior. In the origin of this problem there is a conception developed by Skinner that can be summed up as follows: The criterion to determine whether the dependent variable, the behavior, constitutes a class or a unit is a function of the controlling conditions. Then, a response is a legitimate class of behavior susceptible to scientific description as long as it becomes governed by the laws of reinforcement no matter what its kind, length, or topography. This is what has permitted the classification of behaviors such as pressing a lever, pecking a lighted key, writing a poem, or verbally manifesting self-devaluating behaviors. It is evident that the first two responses (lever pressing and key pecking) can be explained by the principles of reinforcement, but is it legitimate to extrapolate this to behaviors such as writing a book, attending class, or committing suicide? As far as we know, there is no definite answer to this question. Perhaps the most important issue in extrapolation is a methodological one. In this case, extrapolation would be fundamentally a hypothesis and as such must undergo the most rigorous empirical tests. To this effect, the bridge between the animal laboratory and human problems would consist of hypothesizing about a behavioral process considered important for explaining practical problems. But any of these hypotheses would demand a rigorous methodological verification in each particular problem.

On the other hand, extrapolation can be simply considered the admission of some general assumption of radical behaviorism (Skinner, 1974), in other words, the recognition of the importance of the environmental variables and the necessity of experimental rigor. These assumptions would guide the research of behavioral problems of all organisms. But in the case of more complex behaviors, the findings on simple behaviors are considered a requisite. Summarizing, at this stage of the development of behavior modification it seems adequate to ask what would be the procedure to apply the knowledge of the laboratory to the development of behavioral technologies: What is the logic behind extrapolation? Should there be an experimental analog for each behavioral process? If the answer is affirmative, which animal laboratory findings are fundamental to techniques like self-control or systematic desensitization?

THE QUESTION OF MULTIPLE RESPONSES

A second problem refers to the interaction of different behaviors to the same stimulus conditions. When a small portion of the total behavior is studied in the laboratory, it is considered representative of the total behavior. This representativeness is an assumption; consequently, it has not been sufficiently demonstrated. Nevertheless, the laws derived from that response or that class of specific responses are the one applied to general behavior. How does the stimulus influence behaviors that we are not observing or measuring, either because we are not concerned with them at the moment or because our measuring techniques cannot measure all the responses simultaneously? In every experiment of operant conditioning, and generally in every technique of behavior modification based on the contingency model, reinforcements are contingent with respect to one or more responses and noncontingent with respect to others. In Chapter 2, by Baer, Holman, Stokes, Fowler, and Rowbury, it is shown how the same system of responses affects several responses simultaneously. There seems to be a need for solving this type of problem. Some experimenters, among them W. N. Schoenfeld, have been able to condition the "nonresponse," defining it as the nonemission of the response measured during a certain interval of time. Does this suggest we should seek a wider and more totalizing view of the study of behavior?

THE QUESTION OF PERFORMANCE CRITERION

A third problem refers to success as a criterion in a basic situation or in the solution of problems in the applied field. In the laboratory, the experimenter defines the conditions of manipulation of the independent variable and establishes as the criterion of success the observed regularities of the organism's behavior. In the applied situations we are interested basically in the results, whether these be coherent or not with what we already know about the behavior of organisms. Perhaps, applied research emphasizes the results rather than conceptual analysis; practical importance rather than response simplicity; and situational rather than complexity situational simplicity. We might, then, define applied behavior analysis as a translation of the principles of the operant laboratory to the solution of real human situations.

REFERENCES

Skinner, B. F. *Science and human behavior.* New York: Macmillan, 1953.
Skinner, B. F. *Beyond freedom and dignity.* New York: Alfred A. Knopf, 1971.
Skinner, B. F. *About behaviorism.* New York: Alfred A. Knopf, 1974.

Author Index

Italics denote pages with bibliographic information.

Subject Index

A

Abt reports, 146-147, 153-157
Academic performance
  and social behavior, 51
Achievement Place model, 211, 220-225
  characteristics, 220
  research
    consumer satisfaction, 224-225, 226
    follow-up, 223-224, 226
    generalization, 226
    procedural, 221-223, 226
    process, 225
    selection of target behaviors, 222-223
Applied behavior analysis, 112-116, 297
  and behavior modification, 297
  characteristics, 114-116
    daily measurement, 114-115
    direct measurement, 114
    experimental control, 115-116
    individual analysis, 115
  definition, 299
  and experimental anolog, 298
  and extrapolation, 298
  history, 112-114
  replicable teaching procedures, 115
Attention, 8
Attitudes, teacher's
  and handicapped child, 98

B

Behavior modification, 60, 113
  in education, 63
  and behavior problems
    treatment, 87
  and operant conditioning, 287
Behavior principles, applications, 99-105
  antecedent events, 99-102
  instructions, 99-100
  prompting, 100-101
  sequencing subject matter, 101-102
Behavior therapy, 60
Behavioral consequences (*see also* consequences, responses and reinforcers)
  overemphasis in education, 74
Boys Town, 215

C

CASE programs, 214
  contingency contracting, 214, 216
  token economy, 214
Classroom management, 64-73
  causal conditions, 68-73
  goals selection, 64-73
  teacher's attention, 65
  variables, ecological, 68
Client
  in behavior modification, 73
  in education, 73
    specification, 73-74
  parents, 74
  peers, 74
  principals, 74
Consequences, response, 83-85, 102-103, 104-106 (*see* reinforcers)